FRANCE
for the
GOURMET
TRAVELER

Other books in this series:

FRANCE
for the
GOURMET
TRAVELER

Pamela Vandyke Price

PASSPORT BOOKS
a division of *NTC Publishing Group*
Lincolnwood, Illinois USA

Author's Note

In the regional sections an attempt has been made to put the places in alphabetical order, but the specialties and dishes are less tractable and therefore the order has been dictated by what may be required first in a meal. Sweet dishes and any general comments usually come at the end; peasant fare, unlikely to be featured in hotels and smart restaurants, is listed after the dishes frequently seen on menus.

P.V.P.

cover photo courtesy of the French Government Tourist Office of Chicago, © *copyright Choisnet.*

This edition first published in 1991 by Passport Books,
a division of NTC Publishing Group, 4255 West Touhy Avenue,
Lincolnwood (Chicago), Illinois 60646-1975 U.S.A.
Originally published by Harrap Ltd. Copyright © Pamela Vandyke Price 1988.
Manufactured in the United States of America.

0 1 2 3 4 5 6 7 8 9 VP 9 8 7 6 5 4 3 2 1

Contents

Acknowledgements

Over the years when I have been assembling the material for this book, a vast number of people have contributed to the information — friends, official bodies, trade associations, members of the wine trade both in the UK and in France, many colleagues who have not only shared their knowledge with me but have allowed me to make use of their own books and articles. To FOOD & WINE FROM FRANCE I owe an infinite debt of gratitude for their kindness and help throughout; the French Government Tourist Office have likewise been of enormous assistance to me. Many friends in France, together with their families, have enlightened me about many details of French life and gastronomy, among them Peter and Diana Sichel, John Davies, M.W., John Salvi, M.W., Peter and Susan Vinding-Diers, William and Trudy Bolter, Robert and Violette Cointreau, Jacques and Brigitte Saint-Martin — but there are many more. In London, I must particularly thank Helen Thomson for much useful advice and, especially in connection with the vocabularies, David and Elizabeth Rutherford. Pamela Ruff has once again edited my text impeccably and, always, my dear agent, Carole Blake, has been a source of encouragement and help. My thanks, too, to my illustrator, Carol Vincer, my indexer, Martin Noble, and my designer, Gwyn Lewis.

For every traveller who has any taste of his own, the only useful guide-book will be the one which he himself has written.

ALDOUS HUXLEY, *Along the Road*, 1925

Introduction

Over twenty years ago, I wrote a guide to eating and drinking in France. It aimed at helping the ordinary traveller, who might not have much command of French, but who wanted — without undue expense — to get some experience of regional gastronomy. I had begun to think about this when, while travelling with my late husband, some of us, who had met and shared a meal, wanted to know how to say 'Each of us wants a separate bill.' As one colleague comments, gastro-operatic phrases may not always cope with the occasion — I once astounded a Swiss waiter who had asked me if I were hungry, by replying, in a remembered phrase from Fafner, the dragon, in Wagner's *Ring* cycle, that 'I am hungry for thee!'

Then there were the shades of difference between a bar, a café, a *brasserie* — what could one expect to eat and drink in each? There were the mineral waters — some fizzy, some still. There was the infuriating difficulty in getting toasted bread for breakfast, before I discovered that 'toast' means a soggy pre-sliced white bread that has horribly invaded France; I required *'pain grillé'*. As for the local *'specialités'*, there are definite difficulties in sorting them out, as there are in the attempts by small restaurants everywhere to translate the names of certain British dishes into the local language — it is useless to attempt to explain to a Frenchman that 'le Chester' is not a well-known classic British cheese.

As I became seriously interested in wines and spirits, I attempted to compile a vocabulary of terms used about them that one is unlikely to find in any ordinary dictionary. If, in an enthusiastic conversation with a wine grower, one gets lost because of not understanding the significance of *'une pièce, 'un fût'*, *'hectos per hectare'*, *'la veraison'*, *'coulure'*, then the rest of the talk may go wholly astray. I tried to provide translations of the words and phrases that the traveller might hear used in a wine context.

Today, the scene is very different from a quarter of a century ago. I certainly did not include the term for 'mechanical harvester' in my original guide, nor did I know anything about 'diet biscuits' or how 'self-caterers' might ask for various pieces of kitchen equipment or sort out the varieties of vegetables when going to market from their *'gîte'*. Many travellers today will have more knowledge of French and know more about both food and wine than we did then. They will want to gain some experience of *cuisine bourgeoise* and *cuisine paysanne*, as well as *haute cuisine*, and they certainly ought to be knowledgeable about the small-scale wines in addition to the aristocrats of A.O.C. There are still travellers who do tour from three-star restaurant and luxury hotel to ditto nearby, but even they now like, I think, to venture a little from the well-beaten tracks in regions famous for their gastronomy and vineyards world-renowned for their wines. Some of the things I wrote about in the past are virtually archaic today, when 'le fast food' and the *'supermarché'* have transformed French life and even the most dedicated housewife may have a job and be unable to devote many hours to the preparation of some classic recipe. Even so, some things remain the same and are prized accordingly — bread is still the staff of French life, many of the classic wines and plenty of the *'petits vins'* are better than ever, and appreciation of some of the traditions of French country living are preserved; even if one has to view antique kitchens and tableware in museums these days, their use has not been forgotten.

This book, though, is quite different both in content and concept from my previous guide. It aims at helping the sympathetically inclined to deepen their knowledge of French foods, regional dishes, wines and even of French life. It is not a cookery book, nor does it attempt to be a wine manual — there are so many of both these days that anyone professing ignorance of either subject is admitting that they are too lazy to try to find out! It cannot deal with such problems as travelling with young children, touring on the cheap, camping, caravanning or getting holiday jobs in France — there are plenty of books that deal with these aspects too. This volume is intended to be the friend at one's elbow, the handy reference in the glove compartment of a car or suitcase, the guide to coping with a formal French luncheon party (which can be intimidating), how to sort out different varieties of beans or bread when shopping, what sort of gifts may please French friends, how to express appreciation when tasting wine — and how to tackle this tricky exercise — plus things of interest to the lover of food and wine that might otherwise be left out of the traveller's itinerary. The book hopes to open the door a little wider on a huge and wonderful subject and the food snob, as tedious a person as the wine snob, will find it of scant use — unless they are ill or grappling with some minor personal disaster, such as requiring a safety-pin, a dry cleaner, or dealing with a bunged-up washbasin. My criterion throughout has been — would I, will I, find a certain piece of information of use and interest? If so, then in it goes! Although many people have helped and advised me, the responsibility for the book and any mistakes therein must be mine alone. May everyone visiting France share some of the happiness that has been my good fortune to enjoy there. Wine and food may, indeed *should* be taken seriously — but never solemnly; they should make glad the heart. It is my hope that this book may encourage such enjoyment.

How much difference can be accounted for between the two countries by the fact that French children are expected to eat like adults and English people eat like their children?

Sunday Times, 1955

1

France — the World's Greatest Larder and Vineyard

One glance at the map will indicate why France is so special as regards food and wine. Simultaneously, it is a Mediterranean country, and one that reaches out to the north; a country with a lengthy western coastline, and one that abuts on Germany, Switzerland and Italy on its eastern frontiers. It is a land of mountains and of plains, bounded by several different seas and watered by many major rivers (hence the huge assortment of fish). Its neighbours range from the inhabitants of Belgium, itself a varied country, to the equally varied Swiss, and, along the Pyrenees, there are the peoples of the former kingdoms — Navarre and Catalonia being the two best-known today — in addition to the Spaniards proper. Many of the gastronomic traditions, recipes and foodstuffs have been absorbed over the centuries from all these sources, as well as from within the former main divisions of France itself, before communications became easy: Guyenne and Gascony, Alsace — even today a Frenchman may only hesitantly accept that Alsace is really French — the sunny provinces of the south and the fiercely independent regions of Brittany and Normandy. The way in which even quite poor regions have developed their resources makes a cornucopia of the country today, when 'regional specialities' enjoy commercial as well as aesthetic respect and 'cuisine bourgeoise' and even 'cuisine paysanne' have become as interesting to the gourmet as 'haute cuisine'.

In spite of the industrial cities, France is markedly still an agricultural economy. The regular open-air market is a monthly or weekly feature of all but the tiniest villages. Permanent marketplaces, sometimes interesting examples of modern architecture, are centrally placed in most towns, even though the 'grandes *surfaces'* or supermarkets tend to occupy places in the outskirts, where lorries and cars can park. The range of produce is huge: the most barren uplands yield honey and herbs, the reclaimed and desalinated coastal lands are becoming known for wine and rice. If the French Caribbean is included — and its produce also reaches *'la patrie'* — then there is very little that France lacks from its own lands and waters, whether the produce is fished, farmed, pastured, hunted or somehow made into what is edible or drinkable. True, certain tropical fruits and vegetables may only be on sale in large towns, nor do the French make 'fortified wines' in the sense that the British understand them — that is, wines like port, sherry, Madeira — though this is somewhat strange because the French drink more *'porto'* of an ordinary quality than we do in the UK. The French do, however, have their feet firmly in the soil. They cultivate their gardens and, where a Briton will lay out flowerbeds and lawns, they will plant vegetables and orchards. Only a possible 11 per cent of the population are actually engaged in agriculture, but this figure must be much larger if those concerned with administration and the regulations affecting food and drink are counted in too.

Food is not cheap in France yet a higher proportion of the French income is spent on food and drink than in the UK. The circumstance of so many women going out to work even when they are married and have children, has meant a quiet but radical change in the attitude to domestic catering and, especially at weekends and on public holidays, has enormously increased the frequency with which people eat out. Many of them shop daily, aiming to buy perishables while these are as fresh as possible, although no one despises modern kitchen equipment and, if there is no mains power, the refrigerator will be running on something equally efficient; the *'gîtes'*, or holiday homes, even the simplest, frequently include up-to-date devices and gadgets. When shopping for food one is expected to match one's experience with that of the shop or stallkeeper — for what purpose does madame want a litre of milk and should it be that of the morning's or previous evening's milking? Is the bread to be well-cooked or not? No one will object to the nose that sniffs, the finger that prods for tenderness or the hand that sorts out fruits or vegetables of equal size — or feel reluctance to give advice on cooking, carving or presenting; nor will the waiting customers become impatient while value is being sought.

The average French living-room may not have a three-piece suite. The dining-room will have an adequately sized table and substantial chairs. Even in these days of television, people still practise the art of conversation while dining, though children are expected to remain quiet and tractable during the several hours that the family will spend at table. A small country hotel may not have 'somewhere to sit', as some tourists comment plaintively, but there will usually be a café or bar where one can sit until time for the meal — and, later, especially in the country, one goes early to bed, after an agreeably lengthy dinner.

The sadder and harder aspects of French history explain why land is so tenaciously held and why the everyday occurrences — eating and drinking — have assumed so much importance. Meals are not occasions merely for showing off, for displaying the various status symbols that feature in other countries — foods and wines that are 'company fare' primarily because they are rare and expensive, table appurtenances that are costly and of historic interest; it is what goes onto the plate or into the glass that is the reason for devoting time and, usually, talk, to sharing a meal. People who, maybe for generations, have not known hunger or deprivation, cannot find it easy to understand the stress on food and drink in France and, even if they do, it may be that their attitude to hospitality is to provide large quantities, rather than more modest but finer qualities of refreshment, simply because the vast resources of France, coupled with her culinary traditions, do not exist in many other places.

There is also the odd attitude that, tough as the French can be — especially to anyone who does not manage to speak much of their language, alas! — they do not seem to envy or covet the acquisitions or experiences of those with more money to spend than themselves. Perhaps it is one of the civilizing and generous aspects of gastronomy, but I have been into the kitchens of some of the wine establishments and discussed with the staff there what they thought of such-and-such a banquet or much-publicized luncheon, in which, maybe, someone served the wines or somebody's cousin helped in the preparation. I have telephoned, from a workman's bar, to reserve a table in a world-famous restaurant and had good wishes and lip-smacking comments about possible dishes; I have been asked to come back from a new and very expensive restaurant to tell someone doing quite a humble job in a garage what it was like — all the comments charged with serious interest and 'One day I too may manage to do the same', without the slightest suggestion of resentment that a female foreigner was enjoying an experience not (yet) available to my interlocutor. This, to me, is as rewarding as when a great chef or a famous wine-maker talks to me, not as a customer or someone who writes about wine, but as another interested equal.

Because France is so big, it is, I think, important to stress that its resources are even bigger: it is not a matter of mere size — as when one flies across Australia and cannot grasp the way it 'goes on and on'. France is a *'nuancé'* country, one within which there are shades of gastronomic parochialism even within a few kilometres, where the wine one side of a track makes a huge price and a great name, while the wine made on the other side is never more than a good *'petit vin'*; where the bread of one baker 'merits a détour' even though the price of the petrol increases the cost of the loaf; where the cheese made by one man can be differentiated from that of somebody nearby; where a particular breed of chicken has an *'Appellation contrôlée'* and the pasture on which a lamb has been fed is stated on the menu as *'pré salé'*; where the circumstance of a restaurant's kitchen having an inspired pastrycook is mentioned as 'made in the house' at the sweet course section. It is not possible to generalize about France gastronomically, even now.

There are major splits within France, notably the old area divisions, that cling to many names of dishes, evocative of regional recipes that have become almost international. How many people today could differentiate between the various sorts of *cassoulet*? And some of the exported wines with famous regional names are, to my admittedly old-fashioned ideas, blandified down to a style that may please but has little to do with what the traditional beverage was — and can still be: people do not (really) care for the bone-dry Muscadets that used to scour the palate but went delectably with mayonnaise partnering a platter of seafood. These days, much 'Muscadet' is just 'fairly dry', just as much 'Anjou Rosé' is definitely sweetish and, it has to be said, some Bordeaux and Burgundy wines are adequate but unexciting, living on the renown of their labels. I have been presented with 'Chablis' that are mid-gold in colour and wholly untypical in taste, whether or not one could accept them as palate-pleasers; I have had Rieslings from Alsace that were pinched, mean, lacking in fruit, Vouvrays that were glutinous, red Burgundies that were sharp — as compared with the 'trafficked' Burgundies that were treacly. They let the French side down just as much as the ammoniac Camemberts, the frozen *'frites'*, the tea-bag and coffee-bag, the pizza, the 'hot dog' (no objection to 'le fast food' on my part, only when it substitutes for 'le real thing') and the elaborate presentations of fifth-rate food, accompanied by stale bread that wasn't good even when fresh, and 'butter' that seems remote from the cow and nearer to the long-time frozen pack, plus, of course, the 'olive' oil, with which one is presented in a cruet, that is a semi-medicinal lubricant rather than a dressing, and 'vinegar' that makes one long — and even ask — for the half of lemon that at least presents honest acidity, albeit of different calibre. These are the failings of our time. Alas, many travellers confuse attentive service and *chi-chi* presentôtion with French cooking. Many of the finest meals I have had in France have been quite simple, but the ingredients have been fresh and of prime quality, the cooking has been experienced and expert. The problem, today, is that travellers in France vary between those who really do require *'le grand chi-chi'*, for which they may indeed be paying vast sums, although they may not be able to tell the difference between something dolloped with tomato sauce (*'à la Provençale'*) and something where a reduction of fresh plum tomatoes has yielded its flavour to the ultimate food. These are the big spenders who revel in the bottle-sized glasses, even — *quel horreur!* — the brandy warmers, and think that because the *sommelier* wears a chain and has a *tastevin* he knows something about wine. If tourists enjoy theatricality, without really bothering much about what they taste, this is fine — let them have their fun. What is sad — and what may contribute to a decline in the great traditions of French gastronomy — is that their wishes and, let us be frank, their money, may often prevail and influence future gastronomy.

One should, though, persevere. You will not go wholly astray if, even with a few words (as indicated in the vocabularies here) you can convince a restaurateur that you do, truly, want to venture off the beaten track of well-known dishes. Assert, with the aid of this book, that you *do* want a tripe sausage (*une andouillette*), that when you ask for an *entrecôte*, and you say *'bleu'*, you mean — as I do — that you want it 'rushed through a warm kitchen' and not, certainly not, 'medium'. If you want baby eels stewed with garlic or a truly bitter aperitif — and if each member of a party wants to try a different wine, then these are what you should get, rather than the usually preferred 'safe' tourist fare. These days Anglo-Saxons abroad do not restrict their meals to endless omelettes and salad or steak and chips.

There can be no definitive book about French foods and wines — thank heaven! But I have tried to indicate some of them and ways in which they may be explored and enjoyed.

Great Names in French Gastronomy

There seems to be no end to the books published on the history of gastronomy in France. Yet, as some names on menus commemorate personalities and events of the past, it may be of interest to have an inevitably brief outline of the overall evolution of the traditions of eating and some of those who influenced it.

Placed as she is, France enjoys not only a variety of climatic conditions, soils and earth formations, but the influences of those who have in the past come across what are today's frontiers: refugees, political and religious; armies, and the aftermath of armies, bent on plunder; religious men and women travelling between the establishments of their orders; pilgrims, adventurers, spies, traders — and people just interested in seeing a new country. Many of these stayed on, enriching France, for they brought different ways of life that included new eating patterns, recipes and foodstuffs. Some of the French gastronomic traditions may have had their origin in northern Europe — although it is curious that the French never adopted the salting and curing of fish from the Vikings; however, that cradle of civilization, the Mediterranean, is a contributor of innumerable foods and the ways in which they may be used, as well as bringing the vine to many regions.

Some traditions may be far more ancient than anyone surveying a menu may suppose. For example, the great restaurateur, Raymond Oliver (of Le Grand Véfour in Paris) thinks that *'far'*, a term still in use in Brittany, may be traced to the staple diet of the Phoenicians — he thinks that, in this very early period, it was a type of hard-grained wheat. This would have been *durum*, used around the 'inland sea' and being the base of the bread baked for the Roman army's rations. The use of a substance as 'filler', often the main source of nourishment, is frequently a cereal. Bread made from this type of wheat-flour, still sometimes to be found, has no preservatives or additives and it does not go mouldy; it does harden — it becomes very hard indeed, so that the stone-like substance cannot be bitten. Hence such bread has to be softened — by dunking it in a liquid. The crusts on the top of *'soupe à l'oignon'* (onion soup) are one of the survivals of the way in which the 'staff of life' was eked out and the *'chapelure'*, the coating of crumbs on small pieces of meat or fish, is another way of stretching what was a precious and respected commodity, of which nothing should be wasted. Raymond Oliver also mentions that, in his own region of Guyenne — in the south-west — the world *'mil'* is still used for millet; he suggests that *'far'* may have been an early form of *'farine'* — flour. Being a practical country-man, he also reminds us why the different forms of fat as a cooking medium have become traditional in certain regions: oil is a natural resource anywhere that the olive can grow and is easier to keep and carry around than other fats, especially anything milk-based. Therefore, only in cooler regions could milk be skimmed and butter made. The cow, also, requires rich pasture, such as the lush meadows of the dampish north, and it prefers to remain in one place, whereas sheep and goats are less particular about their food and can accompany nomadic or semi-nomadic people. The US writer, Waverly Root, has pointed out (in *The Food of France*, Cassell, 1958) that France can be divided according to the fats traditional in regional cooking: oil, dairy produce, various forms of lard with the goose — source of fat in the south-west — also being an accommodating bird as regards food, willing to move around. The great trade and pilgrim routes across France, notably to Santiago de Compostella, in the north-west of Spain, meant that foods, drinks and recipes were often introduced via religious houses: these served as hostelries, schools, hospices and might be called on to take in the nobility, even royalty, plus their suites. Such an establishment might be more efficiently organized and self-supporting than a castle — stillroom, pharmacy, brewhouse, winery, the fishponds, dairy, larder and local pastures all benefiting when someone, perhaps returning from the Crusades, arrived with herbs, spices, any dried or preserved food, or a novel beverage. The clergy themselves sent one another gifts of food and drink so that there was a type of trade between monasteries, convents, abbeys. Once there was sufficient food to sustain life, man began to refine catering.

The early medieval religious and scholars, apparently poor by worldly standards, often enjoyed better health and lived longer than the well-to-do laity: they might eat frugally and have a diet high in vegetables from the garden, a more reliable source of nutrition than quantities of meat which, during the winter anyway, might have been rotten, as might fish. Most people suffered from various complaints associated with nutritional deficiencies: few sources of Vitamin C in the winter, very few of Vitamin B anyway, scant consumption of milk, except by children and invalids; the state of the teeth of a medieval man or woman is horrific to think about and the jokes about bad breath probably resulted from stomach upsets as much as non-existent dentistry. People from Mediterranean France, with its olives, various fruits and some wine, possibly suffered less than those from the north.

Kitchens, however, were well-planned in the large households, as witness the great one at the Abbey of Fontevrault (Maine-et-Loire), superior to anything similar surviving in castles or palaces. Even so, by the time a dish got from kitchen to table, it must have cooled off, so that even before the formal routines of service and any precautionary tasting (against poison), the dangers of food being polluted or infected are obvious. Recently experiments have been carried out at Fontevrault to see if the numerous fireplaces, each with its own chimney, would work satisfactorily and it was found that they do; so it is possible that soups, fish, meat, poultry were cooked separately but all in the same room. It may be that in some religious houses there were streams diverted from the local river and tanks for fish, with slabs specifically intended for the preparation of different foods, such as I have seen in Portugal. Ovens, for bread, would have been separate and soups and stews were cooked in a pot suspended over a fire. Top-of-stove cooking and the use of a grill are both latecomers to the kitchen.

In early times soup was eaten a great deal. The only 'cooking' an ordinary household might do would have been in a pot hung over the fire. The expression *'pendre la crémaillère'* means 'to have a housewarming', signifying that, when the big hook was fixed in the ceiling and the large pot — *la crémaillère* — was attached to a chain hanging from it, the household could move in. Jeanne d'Arc is said to have mixed several types of soup together — solids, such as meat, fish, pulses, would be incorporated as available.

People sitting around a table would eat any solid food put on a thick slice (*une tranche*) of bread — this is the origin of the world 'trencher'; when the food was finished, the bread, having absorbed any juices, would also be eaten, except in well-to-do households, able to have wooden or pewter platters underneath the trencher;

21

this bread would then be collected and distributed to the poor.

Bread has always been a precious thing in France. 'I'm a Frenchman, I cannot eat a meal without bread,' the late André L. Simon, founder of what is now The International Wine & Food Society, used to say. Even now, except on formal occasions, people in France mop up gravy or sauce with a piece of bread and sometimes also use bread to wipe cutlery that is not changed with each course. Another survival of former times is the use of *croûtons* in soup and, when soup is poured into a large tureen (*une soupière*), there may be several pieces of bread put in first.

In thinking about French food, it should never be forgotten that, although in the UK there were plagues and certainly many forms of nutritional deficiencies, at least in England and, often, in other parts of the British Isles too, the smallish population obliged the noble to feed what would be his fighting men, the merchant or small tradesman to feed his clerks and manual workers; there were not the terrible famines, invasions and depredations of roving bands of marauders recorded in French history — where the deerhounds kept in packs by the nobility might, in hunting, turn up the bodies of whole families dead of starvation, or when, during wars, cannibalism was rife. The French may sometimes seem obsessional about food these days but what many suffered in the past centuries explains the shrieks for 'Bread!' at the time of the Revolution and when today's Frenchman takes his family out for a meal that may appear extravagant to the Anglo-Saxon onlooker, he is, whether he realizes it or not, defying the past and resolving that starvation will not afflict him again.

Emperor Charlemagne (742 – 814) was definitely food and drink orientated: he promulgated many wine regulations, urged the inhabitants of the Palatinate to drink cider from Normandy and apparently effected a radical change in dining habits by allowing women to sit at table with men.

The first significant cook in French history is known, because of his long nose, by his self-adopted nickname — Taillevent (c.1310 – c.1395); he was chief cook to Philip VI of Valois, Charles V and Charles VI, all of whom esteemed him so highly that it is possible that they employed Taillevent on various secret diplomatic missions abroad. His *Le Viandier* is the first French recipe book. Later in the fourteenth century appears the first domestic cookery book — *Le Menagier de Paris* — by an unknown writer, instructions from a husband to his young wife, telling her how to cater for their household, including those who might 'come to the back door' expecting refreshment. And from the fifteenth century onwards there is much written evidence of the interest in cooking and the refinements of the table; rather oddly, books on wine and vine cultivation come much later. The royal mistresses seem to have had good cooks in their households and, as the Salic Law in France prevented women succeeding to the crown, wives, mothers and mistresses of the monarchs had to exert influence behind the scenes — in the dining-room as well as the boudoir.

When Catherine de Medici came to France in 1533 she brought Italian cooks with her and, ever since, historians have debated how much Italy influenced France gastronomically. Catherine sounds as if she enjoyed food; her secret cupboards supposedly containing poisons may well have held sweetmeats, spices and preserves. As a parting gift, Conte Cesare de Frangipani gave her a special confection of almond-paste, which is the 'frangipan' (marzipan) of today. The 'Florentine' tag for dishes made with spinach may also date from this time, athough this is only a personal theory. Herbs became more widely used and this may have been partly Italian influence — mountain regions usually produce a wide variety. A variety of birds featured on tables, also whalemeat, although the rich would only eat the tongue; there were, of course, many whales then in the northern seas, notably in the south-west.

Before forks were introduced from Italy, probably by Catherine de Medici, the only eating utensils were spoons and, for a man, a dagger to cut things up. Try eating most ordinary foods today with a knife and a spoon and you will see that the use of a napkin to wipe the fingers is essential — manuals of polite behaviour give many instructions as to the deployment of the napkin at table. It was Henri III (1551–1589) who made forks fashionable. The huge goffered and starched collars of the period made it difficult to convey anything to the mouth merely with the fingers or a spoon without staining the ruff or collar.

Marinades, baths of wine and vinegar (*vin aigre* — bitter or sour wine) were used to attempt to retard food from going rotten, and garlic began to be widely used. Henri IV, the Gascon who is credited with the wish that everyone in his kingdom should be able to have 'a chicken in the pot', is said to have had his infant lips rubbed with garlic and moistened with Jurancon wine. He is known also to have loved onions and was of amorous tendencies. 'Be thankful you're a king, sire,' commented one lady, 'otherwise no one would stand you — you stink like a carcass!'

In the sixteenth century, with the explorations of new countries, many vegetables were introduced. Michel de Montaigne (1533–1592) commented that salads were found everywhere.

Olivier de Serres (1539–1619), a famous botanist of the time, gave his name to the word for greenhouse — *une serre*. He advocated the large-scale planting of potatoes, but they were regarded with suspicion (except in Alsace, where they became valued food), though potato flowers seem to have been used as decorations. Like the tomato, the potato, when a novelty, was credited with aphrodisiac properties — and either condemned or only consumed in secret.

Louis XIII is perhaps the first French king to have shown a marked interest in food: said to have been a specialist in omelettes, he is reported to have known a hundred or more ways of cooking eggs, to have made soups when he was only ten years old and also to have concocted jams and preserves.

In 1651 François La Varenne brought out *Le Cuisenier Français*, a pioneer instruction in pastry-making. In 1665 Nicolas de Bonnefons produced *Les Délices de la Campagne*, stressing the culinary possibilities of vegetables and fruit. The wide variety of foodstuffs was beginning to be utilized. But cooking methods do not seem to have changed much since the Middle Ages, although I think that the use of the heated grill might have been introduced as a means of cooking meat, fish and poultry. Holding food over a fire, even if not on a spit (the best-known method of cooking it), must have then been in use. Denis Papin, born in Blois in 1647, invented the 'digester', a method of cooking by steam in a sealed pot — the first pressure-cooker; surviving examples of these can still be used. But, as with the potato, the French came late to appreciating this and, being a Huguenot, Papin had to leave France in 1685 at the Revocation of the Edict of Nantes (which had given religious toleration to Protestants) so that his writings were published first in England and Germany.

It was during the reign of the 'Sun King', Louis XIV, that food became particularly important in polite society. The monarch continued Cardinal Richelieu's policy of breaking the power of the nobles, who, their interests centred on Versailles and the trivia of court matters and etiquette, welcomed novelty on the table by way of a diversion. From the New World, exotic foodstuffs and beverages were coming in to France: coffee came from North America, tea from China and the little Spanish queen, Marie Thérèse, brought her fondness for chocolate with her when she came to France. This drink (from Mexico) became enormously popular (*see p.311*). These 'new' drinks inspired many of the beautiful creations of the manufacturers of china: the first teacups (as in China) tended not to have handles and chocolate cups were tallish, so that the special whisks used to whip up the froth could be used in the cup.

In 1687 a Sicilian, Francesco Procopio, opened the first Paris café — the Procope. His full name was dei Coltelli and in fact he was of noble birth but had lost all his money. After acting as a dogsbody in a shop kept by Armenian coffee-dealers, he opened his own establishment, the facilities including a 'real tennis' court and a bowling-alley, the premises being decorated with taste and offering patrons the chance to lounge elegantly around and glance at the newsheets provided. Even among the adherents of the court at Versailles it began to be smart to go to Paris for an ice or a drink in the café. Indeed, ordinary dining-rooms began to receive attention from decorators and became more attractive than the plain halls of former times. But precedence was important in deciding who sat where: royalty often dined alone at a table set just for one and, in private houses, the family would eat at small tables, caterers being called in to set up trestles should any large-scale function be planned. This is why, in what is otherwise a great period for French furniture, there are no big dining-tables — the privileged sat down to eat and anyone allowed to look on did just that — something not conducive to good relations between masters and men.

Now, wines began to be of great importance. The Benedictine Dom Pierre Pérignon rediscovered the use of cork as a stopper for the bubbly wine of Champagne and, even more important, evolved a system of blending the wines of different vineyards.

The croissant, supposedly first made after the defeat of the Turks besieging Vienna, became very smart and I think that this may have been when many French began to dunk their roll or croissant in their coffee or chocolate at breakfast and, even, to eat the softened bread with a spoon. One-time *maître d'hôtel* to the King and director of the household of Monsieur, the King's brother, the Marquis Louis de Béchamel gave his name to what is perhaps the best-known sauce in the world — although a jealous colleague commented that *he* had served *'crème cuite'* for the past twenty years.

Louis XIV made another innovation — though without realizing it. He was a big man and the post-mortem on his body showed that he had an enormous tapeworm in his gut — so no wonder that he ate voraciously (though he drank little) and he had a very sweet tooth. Up to this time, the *'entremets'* or courses served between the main dishes, were not necessarily sweet and sometimes consisted just of vegetables and salads; but, at the royal table, the

'in-betweens' tended to be sweet things, often elaborately concocted. The courtiers, although they tried to ape the King, simply
could not always eat more food after a dish of sweetmeats, so,
gradually, the *'entremets'* became the final food of a meal and, on a
French menu, the *'entremets'* means the sweet course, although,
as Raymond Oliver (op.cit.) points out, to this day the *'en-
tremetier'* working in a kitchen with a big 'brigade' (staff of
specialists in the various foods) is in fact the man who prepares the
vegetables!

In the Regency period and then in the reign of Louis XV (1715 –
1774) big banquets at court fell out of favour — well, they must
have been boring socially and dreary gastronomically by that time.
The *'petits soupers'* were the innovation of 'Louis the well-
beloved' and a very select company of courtiers and ladies would
be invited. On such occasions the King and the guests actually did
the cooking themselves. It has been sensibly pointed out that
most of the preparations could have been done in advance, so that
the only culinary skills required were to re-heat the foods in a
flambé pan. As to the tables that rose from the floor, they were
probably set with what we should call a buffet — the word in fact
signifies a sideboard or dresser.

Food was, however, becoming simpler and more stress was laid
on the details and ingredients of dishes. In 1739 *Les Dons de
Comus* was published and subsequently the author was found to
be Marin, *maître d'hôtel* to the Duc de Soubise, for whom Marin's
onion sauce gets its name. Marin stressed how important it was to
present and garnish food attractively — the rise of the merchant
classes, the interest beginning to be paid in smart circles in Paris
to fine wines, all emphasized that dining, for those who had
enough to eat, was a civilized occupation. In 1747 Menon's *La
Cuisinière Bourgeoise* said that even simple, everyday dishes
could be very good when made from quality ingredients. Cultivation of the appetite had become chic. This was the time when the
satyr-like Duc de Richelieu, at one time Governor of the Bordeaux
region, persuaded the French court to start drinking Bordeaux red
wines, instead of the Burgundy to which they had been traditionally faithful since the time when French kings needed the support
of the Dukes of Burgundy against the English. Richelieu (nephew
of the Cardinal) gets additionally into history books because his
chef was credited with 'Sauce Mahonnaise' to commemorate the
taking of Port Mahon; however, there are other theories about
this: André Castelot, in *L'Histoire à Table* (Plon Perrin, 1972)
gives two. In 1589 the Duc de Mayenne, on the eve of the Battle of

Arques, asked his chef to make a *chaud-froid* of chicken, which was such a triumph that the Duc forgot everything else and lost the battle next day. Prosper Montagné (q.v.) believed that the word 'mayonnaise' came from Mayons, in the district of the Var, where *'moyeu'*, a medieval word for egg, was applied to the egg-sauce by a local cook.

In 1765 a type of soup-kitchen, forerunner of 'le fast food', was opened in Paris by a man appropriately named Boulanger (baker) and in 1782 one Beauvillier opened the capital's first true restaurant. Food was talked about. A portly actor, who challenged a friend to a duel, had his opponent outline his huge stomach with a crayon, saying that hits outside this area wouldn't count — the affair was settled amicably around a dinner-table.

Parmentier (1737–1817), an army doctor and agriculturalist, made a serious study of the potato during his imprisonment in Germany and, realizing the usefulness of this cheap food, tried to popularize it in France. Although Marie Antoinette accepted a bouquet of potato flowers to decorate a headpiece, the tuber had little popular appeal. Ironically, although English farmers were also somewhat resistant to it, the potato plantations in England enabled the British to withstand the Napoleonic blockade.

Remarkable discoveries about the preservation of food were made by François Appert — *'le roi des conserves'* (the canning king) — at this time, but although he had hoped, by his researches, to assist Napoleon's armies, the secrets of his canning business fell into British hands — and *'boeuf bouilli'*, the first food satisfactorily preserved in a can, became 'bully beef', long-time staple of the British army.

One great name, of international repute, is that of Antoine Carême (1784–1833), a remarkably gifted man, author of many books, no mean artist and one who influenced dining throughout the polite world. His work is the foundation of *haute cuisine* as we now know it. He served a variety of masters — including the Prince Regent, later King George IV, King Louis XVIII, the Tsar of Russia and several ambassadors; perhaps his most important post was as chef to the wily Talleyrand, for whom Carême may have acted as some kind of special agent, who took him off to the Congress of Vienna in 1815, where delegates vied with one another about fine foods and wines and it was said 'Congress dances — but doesn't work.' Talleyrand (1754–1828) was definitely a gastronome. The one 'friend' he was said never to have betrayed was Brie cheese; he put on a theatrical performance when he carved meat, had a recipe with *foie gras* attributed to him and was witty in moments of crisis — such as when a waiter, tangled up with a guest's wig, hooked it off his head, at which Talleyrand cracked a joke. He discussed fine wines with Prince Metternich, owner of several great estates.

Napoleon, however, was not particularly interested in food — considering his impoverished early life and various internal ailments it is not to be wondered at — though he was well aware of the power of dinner-table diplomacy: 'If you eat sparingly, dine with me; if you like fine food in vast amounts, go to eat at Cambacérés', he said about his Chancellor, famous for magnificent dinners — and eventually dying of apoplexy. But Napoleon is supposed to have inspired *Poulet Marengo*, made by such ingredients as his chef Dunan could find on the eve of the battle. (This man must have had a somewhat trying time — Napoleon's uncertain time-keeping caused Dunan to have a chicken put to roast every quarter of an hour, so that one would always be ready if the Emperor wanted a meal, although the same story is told about Cleopatra catering for Mark Antony, *her* chef preparing relays of wild boar.) The Marengo recipe has also been hotly debated: could the cook really have found freshwater crayfish, ingredients in some versions? Was it the use of oil instead of butter — Napoleon gave Dunan no time to get any — that made the difference? And could Dunan have had tomatoes on hand? One story about Napoleon is that he was offered a sample of rye bread as suitable for army rations, but contemptuously called the stuff '*Pain pour Nickel*' (at that time his charger), from which pumpernickel got its name.

It was Napoleon's Minister of Agriculture, Comte Jean Chaptal de Canteloup (1756–1832), who, during a glut of sugarbeet, signed the decree permitting the addition of sugar to the *must* in wines unlikely to ferment satisfactorily without assistance — hence 'chaptalisation'. Chaptal was certainly food-conscious. Alexandre Dumas got from him a recipe for dressing salad that the Count said he had learned on one of his various diplomatic missions to northern Europe. (You season the vegetables, then put on the oil and only add the vinegar just before serving — superlative!)

The nineteenth century in France is rich in odd personalities. One of the strangest is Grimod de la Reynière (1758–1839). He survived the Revolution, though he sounds the sort of man whom many peasants would have liked to string up. He always wore gloves, saying that, as a baby, his fingers had been chewed off by a sow — although he always enjoyed pork dishes. Grimod was a friend of Anthelme Brillat-Savarin (1755–1825), famous for the wonderful dinners given for his friends and for his book *La Physiologie du Goût*. His family was very gastronomic: his aunt died while drinking a glass of wine and his mother, who invented the *pâté 'Oreiller de la Belle Aurore'* (using her own name Aurore), lived to be ninety-nine and then, towards the end of a meal, exclaimed, 'I think I'm going to die — quick, bring in the sweet!' and, as her brother remarked, 'She took coffee in another world.' Grimod de la Reynière wrote about food, bitterly disliked for so doing by Talleyrand and Carême — rivalry in gastronomic journalism is nothing new — but gave bizarre dinners: once he announced that he had died and, at the funeral feast, he suddenly appeared out of his coffin; later, he gave another dinner at which he invited those who had not turned up at the 'funeral' and who were obliged to dine sitting in individual coffins. Grimod died at the end of another dinner, whereas poor Brillat-Savarin perished of a chill caught while attending a friend's funeral in an icy church.

Two major influences now made themselves felt. Benjamin Delessert, *'Le roi du sucre'* (the Sugar King), established his huge refineries, making what had hitherto been a luxury food into an everyday commodity. And Prince Kourakine (1752–1818) started the fashion of people being individually served at a meal, instead of all — except for royalty or persons of very high rank — simply helping themselves. This is a *'service à la russe'*, mentioned even in comparatively recent cookery-books, and it eventually superseded the practice of setting all the dishes of a course on the table at once — old cookery books show diagrams of such settings. This change was particularly important. In many great houses, the kitchens, as already mentioned, were so far away from the dining-room that food was inevitably tepid when served; nor could any recipes be attempted when last-minute touches had to be given to the dish; the small-scale meals, such as those given in private houses by individuals such as Brillat-Savarin, were probably so much better than formal fare because of being hot and dished up immediately. *'Service à la russe'* was considered very advanced and it took some time to be adopted — one can imagine old-fashioned chefs and domestic staff stuck in their routines resenting the change — but eventually it prevailed. Many recipes could now show off the skill of an inventive chef.

Louis XVIII (famous from the unkind Daumier drawing which shows him as a pear) was very fond of eating; he and the Duc d'Escars would enjoy little gourmet meals together, after one of which the Duc died, the King remarking: 'Poor d'Escars — so, mine *is* the better stomach!' He seems to have been a catty man, saying of his brother, the soon-to-be guillotined Louis XVI, 'My brother goes to table with about as much enthusiasm as to his wife's bed.' The unfortunate Louis XVI actually delayed the flight of the royal family from Paris by insisting on stopping to have a meal on the way — they had a commode to relieve themselves in the carriage though didn't have the sense to take a picnic — but he is said to be the first person to make it fashionable to change from one wine to another in the course of a meal, instead of keeping to a single sort.

Charles X (1824–1830) revived the practice of royalty dining formally in public, gastronomy giving way to protocol; in his portraits he does not look as if he loved 'les bonnes chose de la vie' much. But the Second Empire, under Napoleon III, was the time for an outburst of experiments and discoveries in food and drink: now it was possible to cook by gas — exact control over every stage of a dish was easy. Many of the great Paris restaurants were founded at this period and gastronomic writing proliferated. The author François Châteaubriand (1768–1848) is credited with the invention of a steak recipe, the steak being cooked in between two others that are discarded (the Duc d'Escars had done this with cutlets 'À la martyre'), also a soup bearing his name, and his chef, Montmireil, is thought to have invented Sauce Béarnaise (though, as with other classic recipes, there will always be arguments as to its origin).

Alexandre Dumas the elder (1802–1870) used to say that he would rather be remembered for his cooking than for his novels and his Dictionnaire de la Cuisine is still delightful reading. When Dumas asked friends to luncheon, he apparently set each one down to finish the latest instalment of whatever story he was working on — which is how Les Trois Mousquetaires got finished in twelve days — while he did the cooking. Yet, rather oddly, wine gets only meagre mentions in his books — when the musketeers really want to treat themselves, they often order 'vin d'Espagne'.

Society now included many of the 'grandes horizontales' (the courtesans), as well as members of the stage, opera and ballet and artists. Restaurants attracted good custom and journalists wrote about where these celebrities dined. The original 'Lady of the Camellias', Marie Duplessis, is said merely to have taken a few meringues at luncheon — she probably had 'something on a tray' before going out. Dr Véron, made rich by a patent medicine, so that he could keep the great tragedienne Rachel, had a wonderful cook, Sophie — his friends were frequently trying to lure her away from him. Baron Louis Brisse (1803–1876) was one of the first gastronomic journalists, and Charles Monselet (1825–1888), author of the *Almanach des Gourmets*, composed a sonnet to soup. Food and, a little later, wine, were matters the man-about-town needed to know about.

In 1889 the first 'Concours Culinaire' was organized in Paris by Thomas Genin, known as 'the Gambetta of the kitchen' after the great statesman. Genin maintained what he considered to be the finest traditions of French cooking and he wrote with experience because he had cooked an enormous variety of animals, including rats, donkey (said to be good), dogs and a billy-goat (he said *no* method of cooking could make it palateable). At the Siege of Paris in 1870 the three hundred animals in the Zoo were killed and sold for food — the French never lost their sense of wit in matters gastronomic even when times were difficult and a famous banquet featured elephant as the main course! The delicately decorated menus are great fun.

In 1869 margarine was invented by a man called Henri Mège-Mouries; at first, farmers attacked this discovery but Emperor Napoleon III backed the man, seeing the possibilities. This was a breakthrough as regards a new fat, which began to be sold from about 1872. Food could be preserved, now it was about to be created in different forms.

Much publicity was given to various groups of gourmets who held various reunions in restaurants. The composer Rossini, who loved food so much that he married his cook, suggested to the *maître d'hôtel* at the Café Anglais that a new method of carving a steak could be tried. The horrified traditionalist protested that he *couldn't* do such a thing. 'Very well,' retorted Rossini, 'we won't look at you — I'll turn my back (*tourne le dos*)' and this is the origin of the *tournedos*, although Tournedos Rossini, plus *foie gras*, was in fact evolved at the Restaurant Magny, in the rue Contrescarpe Dauphine. Here, on 22 November 1862, the anatomist Dr Veyne Robin started a series of monthly dinners that were to achieve fame. Many well-known people dined at Magny's: Théophile Gautier (1811–1892), Gustav Flaubert (1821–1880), Georges Sand — one of the few women who were included (1804–1876), Renan (1823–1892), Turgenev (1818–1883), Saint Beuve (1804–1869), also the brothers Edmond and Jules Goncourt (1822–1896 and 1830–1870 respectively). Magny himself always maintained that his Châteaubriand was named for a Monsieur de Chambrillan and not the writer; he called his '*Bécasse à la Charles*' after Charles Labrau, his head waiter, and the much talked-about '*purée Magny*' was a potato baked in its jacket in the oven, then sieved and served with fresh butter — an interesting example of a simply prepared dish attaining the heights of gastronomy — although these days some cooks might not know enough about the basic ingredients even so. Many of the books about cooking from this period can still be consulted, notably *Cuisinier Practique* by C. Reculet and, in 1883, Paput-Lebeau's *Le Gastrophil*. The big name now in culinary history was that of Auguste Escoffier (1847–1935), the 'finest cook in the world' according to César Ritz, who employed him when the Paris Ritz opened in 1898. Escoffier later worked at the Savoy in London and cooked the monthly discussion lunches at the Paris Grand Hotel, organized for the Académy Goncourt by Léon Daudet — it was the reunions of this group of gastronomes that later made the reputation of the Restaurant Druant. Escoffier is famous for inventing Pêche Melba and Melba toast — when the soprano Dame Nellie Melba (1861–1931) was trying to slim — and he was frank that much of his renown came from the dishes he made for ladies. Another great cookery writer was Prosper Montagné, still much cited, who was born at Carcassonne in 1865.

The many great paintings of the late nineteenth century in France that show food indicate the real delight both artists and public had in it. Previously, only Chardin (1699–1779) seems to have made the viewer appear to take part in the wonderful pictures he made of food — until recently, any wine-trade trainee could have identified and used the implements shown in 'The Cellarboy'. But Manet, Renoir and others revel in the beauty and excitement of food and drink and also in the settings in which they show it.

The French novelists, too, went into details about this subject: Jane Grigson in *Food with the Famous* (Michael Joseph, 1979) indicates this: Émile Zola (1840–1902) may be chiefly remembered by Anglo-Saxons for his part in the Dreyfus case, but he gives wonderful accounts of food in his novels — *Le Ventre de Paris* (1873) describes the Paris Markets, Les Halles, now removed to Rangis. (When Zola came to England after the Dreyfus affair he suffered much from the cooking of the hotel where he stayed, near the Crystal Palace.) Proust, too, gives many details of food and drink, even though he apparently existed mainly on a milk diet. Burgundian Colette (1873–1954), often expatiates on food and wine — although she doesn't seem to know much about either.

The wine plagues of, first, downy mildew and then the *phylloxera* in the French vineyards from the middle of the nineteenth century have been admirably documented by my friend George

Ordish in *The Great Wine Blight* (Sidgwick and Jackson, 1987) and the different 'remedies' are amazing — although the Spaniards, settling in the New World in the sixteenth century, already knew about grafting to make a vine resistant to certain diseases. It is exasperating that so few menus of the period do more than list the wines by name and omit the vintages; a number would be served at a banquet, the great sweet wines often coming at the beginning of the meal.

At the turn of the century, in the *'Belle Époque'*, the fashionable courtesans vied with one another in the splendours of the entertainments as well as their jewels and this was naturally an incitement to chefs and caterers to compete too: Cora Pearl was once served up in a huge dish, clad only in a rose-coloured sauce (did she go and shower it off, I always wonder?), and at Maxim's Restaurant (the setting for Franz Lehar's operetta *The Merry Widow*), the ladies of the town would 'dance upon the tables, in and out among the spoons'. As 'queenly' figures and a portliness in men were fashionable, it was no wonder that the various spas, in which France is so abundant, did good business. Café life had, by now, become part of the routine of many, in the provinces as well as Paris. It is odd to think that the expression 'café society' has overtones of raffish stridency, for an entire family may still spend an hour or two in a café, enjoying modest refreshments.

After the 1914–18 war, though, French culinary traditions had to change: labour was difficult to get both in catering and private houses and people did not have time to recover from huge banquets by taking a 'cure'. Many chefs went abroad: Louis Diat went to the US and created vichysoisse from his mother's leek and potato soup. Marcel Boulestin came to London and, with his British colleague Robin Adair, set up the restaurant that still bears his name and wrote cookery books for the lady of the house who might still have a parlour maid but who was often obliged to do most of the cooking herself. The popularity of the automobile made it possible for the French provinces, not merely the resorts, to be explored, and travellers flourishing the fat *Guide Michelin* to know where to eat.

Between the two World Wars Maurice-Edmond Sailland (1872–1956) became famous as 'Curnonsky' — the tag 'Prince Élu des Gastronomes' being appended to his name. The 'Curnonsky' *nom de plume* comes from *'Cur non?'* (Why not?). He wrote *France Gastronomique* in twenty-eight volumes, founded 'France à Table' in 1934 and, stressing that 'Things must retain their own taste', held that *cuisine bourgeoise* and the dishes of the provinces were as important in their way as the *haute cuisine* of the capital; he ate one meal a day, usually having a boiled egg for supper, and forbade any commercial exploitation of his name.

Among the famous chefs of the period was Fernand Point, of the Restaurant de la Pyramide at Vienne (who also died in 1956). Proud that his staff called him 'Chef' rather than 'Patron' (boss), he influenced many notable chefs of today who have served an apprenticeship at the Pyramide and their menus may refer to this; Point's wife, who continued to run the restaurant until her recent death, was a judge of wine on whom he admitted he depended a great deal.

Many of the great French restaurants still strive to preserve the traditions of *haute cuisine* and to eat in one of them can be a memorable experience; but a change was bound to come. Michel Oliver, Raymond's son, made a gesture to the altered tempo of life when, in his writings and television programmes, he stressed the need for care, even when the cook is in a hurry. But it was someone else who altered the scene radically.

Michel Guérard, born in 1933, began his career as a conventional chef, progressing to be chief pastrycook and then chief sauce cook at the Hôtel Crillon in Paris. He then set up in his own restaurant — what a colleague has described as 'un petit bistrot' — where he evolved his now famous *'cuisine gourmande'* and in 1972 established himself at Eugénie-les-Bains, in the Landes. Here he brought to fruition his ideas about cookery and dishes to accord with the healthy life of today and he writes charmingly about this lifestyle, paying tribute to the lady who became his wife and who suggested he should lose a few kilos . . . describing the dreariness of the régime of grated carrots and *'grillade, haricots verts à l'eau'*. Then he introduced the concept of *'cuisine minceur'*. It is fair to say that several of the 'grands bonnets' I have heard speak on the subject (the mark of the true chef is that he wears the tall white cap) have commented drily that they cannot understand what the fuss is about — hadn't their fathers and grandfathers before them followed many of the same principles publicized as *'nouvelle'* and *'minceur'*? All require fresh ingredients, of prime quality, and certain dishes necessitate the fine chopping and purée-ing of ingredients by skilled hands; Fernand Point, for example, had special silver-meshed sieves made so as to achieve his aim in his *'mousse de truite en brioche'*.

In the 1970s, the Robot Coupe company introduced a remarkable device — the food processor — that enabled work previously requiring hours of skilled preparation to be done literally by the flick of a switch. In fact, the use of the purée and that of the salad was not a novelty — Voltaire had noted both in the eighteenth century — but now even the humblest housewife could achieve a vast range of dishes previously right outside her repertoire. True, there are few who can equal the quality and aesthetic balance that M. Guérard brings to his recipes and I admit that I am bored with being presented with several purées, resembling animal droppings, on a cold side plate. However, this phase will work itself out, like other fashions in food — at one time in France it was smoked salmon (generally of dreary quality), sweetcorn, regarded as mere animal food by some of my friends, raspberry vinegar, avocado pears (the only ones recorded as growing in France were in the garden of the late Somerset Maugham's villa), salads of 'oak leaves' (feuilles de chêne) and, after a much-publicized banquet at the Elysée Palace, soups covered in a pastry crust. All such ideas get copied but the tides of fashion merely wet the steps of a good restaurant and don't swamp the dining-room. The chef in the traditions of great gastronomy will continue to create, refine, and impress discreetly rather than stridently. There are still delectable experiences awaiting the traveller in France.

I breakfasted with the correspondents of two of your contemporaries. One of them, after a certain amount of hesitation, allowed me to help him to a leg of a rat; after eating it he was as anxious as a terrier for more. The latter, however, scornfully refused to share in the repast. As he got through his portion of salted horse, which rejoiced in the name of beef, he regarded us with horror and disgust. . . . During the siege of Londonderry rats sold for 7s. each, and if this siege goes on for many weeks longer, the utmost which a person of moderate means will be able to allow himself will be an occasional mouse. I was curious to see whether the proprietor of the restaurant would boldly call rat, rat in my bill. His heart failed him — it figures as a salmi of game.

HENRY LABOUCHÈRE, *Diary of the Besieged Resident in Paris*, 1871

3

How the French Eat

Generalizations about anything as individual as eating and drinking habits are risky. Anyone fortunate enough to enjoy a stay in some particular region may well find exceptions to the advice given here. But here are a few guidelines.

In France, breakfast tends always to be a light meal and is often eaten out. The midday meal is the main one and, although staff canteens are installed in some places of work or, at least, there is some means there for cooking or reheating food, many people still go home to eat luncheon. The evening meal is often lighter. Hours of eating vary somewhat according to where you are: in the north, restaurants may be full soon after noon, whereas in the south they will not begin to do much business until half an hour or an hour later and, near the Spanish border, two in the afternoon is not too late to eat. There are a number of public holidays: the religious ones are Christmas Day (25 December), Easter Monday, Ascension Day and Whit Monday, whenever these occur, also the Assumption (15 August), All Saints (1 November). The non-religious holidays are: New Year's Day (1 January), 1 May, Victory Day (8 May), Bastille Day (14 July) and Armistice Day (11 November). Restaurants and cafés will be crowded on these days, although in the mornings the pastry shops may be open, so that cakes, vol-au-vent cases, tarts, cream confections and chocolates and candies can be bought for serving at home or taking as gifts to friends. The same applies to Sunday mornings in many places. In the evenings restaurants and cafés may be less crowded but it is always wise to book if you have to eat out at such times. Saturday is when marketing is done for the weekend — on Mondays most big shops such as department stores are shut, so are those not concerned with food, although this can be up to the individual owner. Sunday is the great family day, when people enjoy getting together and eating out — booking anywhere is essential then. Realize, too, that anyone travelling alone and wishing to eat at a café or restaurant on such days may get a *'Complet'* (Full) reply at the door. If you are very keen on trying a particular establishment, at least get your hotel on the night before to attempt to make the reservation (*see p.89*).

Portions

Sometimes these may seem to be on the generous side. Usually two people can share one helping between them and, of course, if you order a dish such as a platter of seafood, it can be adjusted to the appetites involved — if you know that some of your company are small eaters, ask for one less than the overall number: *'Pour trois personnes'*, for example, even if there are four of you. If anyone is on a special diet, or has certain reactions to certain foods, state this clearly (*see p.114*). Usually you will find sympathy and willingness to cope — although it must be said that the French concept of 'a light meal' can be very much richer and more copious than what the Briton might expect! Most eating-places will arrange food for children, often composing a special small menu, either half portions of two simple courses. Soup, a little meat and vegetables and purée of potato are usually available and the charge will be fairly modest. French children are expected to behave like small adults in dining-rooms and the raucous or rampaging young person will be looked at askance.

Tips

If the service charge — which may be 12½ per cent or 15 per cent — is added to the bill, then it is not necessary to tip further, although, if there is some small change on the plate when the receipted bill comes back to you, it is a polite gesture to leave this if you have enjoyed yourself. The expression *'Prix net'* on a menu means that the service is included. Note this — do not tip twice.

Meals — getting what you want and value for money

Breakfast

This can vary. In an hotel it is usually taken in the bedroom, at no extra charge. If you come downstairs, you may be shown to a small salon or even the bar in which to breakfast, as the dining-room may be being cleaned at this hour. If the price of breakfast is included with that of the room, you will only be charged for any extras. If it is not, then you can go out to eat if you wish — it can be very pleasant to sit at a café table or eat outside in the sun. *Café complet* or, more accurately, *café au lait complet*, means coffee with milk and sugar, accompanied by bread or rolls and butter. Tea — not necessarily Indian tea, though — or chocolate can usually replace coffee, if you wish. Sometimes jam is included but it may be an extra — so ask in advance. (Jam in many French hotels is the dreary type, often in minute plastic pots. In the country you may get something better and more generously supplied.) Honey is seldom served, even in regions famed for it, but sometimes a request for it will be successful. Marmalade is seldom offered except in first-class hotels; take your own if in doubt. Unless you are in the country, when butter may come in a large slab, you may get somewhat meagre foil-wrapped portions — the French do not always use butter on their rolls. It is often unsalted, so take slightly salted butter with you if you prefer this type.

The different types of rolls and bread are detailed on pp.104—7. But there are a few caveats for the traveller staying in an hotel. Croissants are never cheap and may be stale; unless you are set on having them, opt for crusty bread. If you ask for 'toast', you may get hot buttered toast, made from *pain de mie* (crustless white bread). If you are more specific, you can ask for *'pain grillé'*, which is toasted crusty bread, either cut from a *gros pain* or diagonal slices of a *baguette* or *ficelle*, brought into contact with a hot grill; this is extremely crusty and is always my choice. Otherwise rusks (*biscottes*) are usually available or, of course, you can buy some. *Biscottes de régime* or *biscottes d'amidon réduit* are, respectively, diet rusks or starch-reduced rusks.

For more substantial breakfast fare, *oeufs au bacon* (bacon and eggs) can often be supplied, also *oeufs à la coq* (boiled eggs); with these, however, be specific about timing and remember that they may have to be brought from some distance — if you like your breakfast eggs soft-boiled you may be disappointed. Nor will they always be served in a *coquetier* (eggcup), so specify if you want one, otherwise you will have to make do with a plate. The simplest request, if you want more than coffee and rolls, is probably for a slice of *jambon de York* (cold boiled ham); if you say *'jambon'* you may get the local smoked variety.

Tea-time

The tea-bag dominates the service of tea today, but, in a good restaurant, you can usually also get China or Ceylon tea. Specify if you want it with lemon. Sandwiches, bread and butter are not often served, but, especially in a *salon de thé* (tea-room), there may be biscuits and pastries — also ices and fruit drinks, though do not forget that these can make the bill mount up. 'Cake' is fruit-cake of the slab kind, usually available in cafés, in individual slices in a cellophane pack.

Luncheon and dinner

Un lunch in French signifies a buffet meal. *Déjeuner* (literally 'to break one's fast') is luncheon. *Un cocktail*, of course, is a cocktail reception — although it may be wine and not cocktails at all. *Un vin d'honneur* is a reception with drinks — which may be wine or cocktails — on some important occasion.

Meals served in bedrooms are charged as extras, but it is worth noting that, if you are travelling with small children, it can be an overall saving to arrange this, because you can also give them food you have bought in — and keep them under control.

In most restaurants there will be a fixed-price menu — *prix fixe* — offering a choice of courses. There may also be a *menu touristique*, a little more elaborate than the *petit menu*, also a *menu gastronomique*, which is for the gastronomically robust. Some big restaurants and cafés may have several menus, some including wine. It is invariably better value to order a menu than to eat *à la carte*. If you wish to eat lightly, simple ask for one of the courses to be omitted — *'Annulez ce plat'*. You will not always get a reduction in price, though. The *petit menu* of a good eating-place

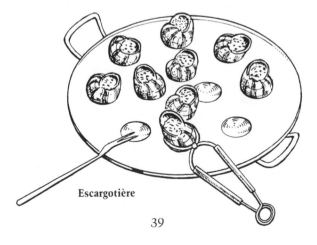

Escargotière

39

will frequently include either soup or a small *hors d'oeuvre*, a portion of fish and then perhaps a meat dish with vegetables and, maybe, salad to follow; then there will be cheese and a dessert — a fruit-tart or ice or piece of fresh fruit. Coffee will be extra. The fish course may not be included in a really small menu. Sometimes even the modest menu will have some form of luxury — a special *pâté* or, say, a lobster available at a slight extra charge, but there will be some alternative as well included in the overall menu price. The good restaurants pride themselves on the quality and value of the '*petits menus*'.

The letters 'SG' alongside a dish mean *selon grosseur* — according to size, the charge will be adjusted.

Inquire, when you order, if a dish is to be '*garni*', which means accompanied by some vegetables or salad. If it is, then, unless you are a dedicated vegetable eater, you may not want any more and, if you do order extra vegetables, remember that one portion may well provide for two people. Mayonnaise is usually specified when it comes with a dish, otherwise you will probably get an oil and vinegar dressing, sometimes made up, sometimes mixed for you at the table. Ask if you wish to do this for yourself. Grills are usually accompanied by chipped potatoes — *frites* — so do not forget to inquire if they form part of the garniture.

If you order consommé, this, except in a large establishment, may come out of a tin. Specify whether you want it hot, cold or *en gelée* — jellied consommé and cold consommé are not — or should not be — the same thing. With most *hors d'oeuvre* and with any of the versions of raw ham, butter will be put on the table — and then removed after you have had the course. Otherwise, you will have to ask for and pay for it. The *couvert* or cover charge, however, includes more or less as much bread as you wish to eat.

The *plat du jour* can be a great bargain. It may feature on the *à la carte* menu or form part of the middle course of a fixed-price menu. It is usually something in season and at its best. You should get something the locals come here to eat and that the chef does well. Do not be suspicious if it seems simple or out of place: once, down in the Landes, I hesitated about ordering the *caneton Rouennais* featured as the *plat du jour* — the little waitress urged me to select it. Only after enjoying something truly remarkable did I discover that the tiny restaurant, of the most modest appearance, was the property of someone who, in retirement, pleased himself about what he felt like cooking — and, as he had worked for years under Escoffier at The Savoy in London, he was a fine chef!

The *specialités de la maison* may be listed separately, although often one at least will be included in one of the fixed-price menus. If, however, you are staying somewhere and wish to try one of the local specialities, it is always possible to ask the cook, who may well prepare the dish for you or recommend a restaurant where a friend may do it well. Even if you are *en pension*, the management may arrange an adjustment of the regular menu so that you can sample the particular dishes of the region — do not hesitate to inquire.

Some foods, even on their home ground, will never be cheap. Do not assume, either, that because you are in the melon country, you will get the finest fruit — it may all go up to the Paris markets or for export. The same goes for many wines — people sometimes return from a tour grumbling that they can buy many classic wines more cheaply (and of better vintages) in the UK.

Useful phrases

Breakfast
À la chambre: In the bedroom.
Confiture d'oranges: Orange marmalade.
Un oeuf à la coque is a boiled egg (stipulate the number of minutes it is to be cooked). *Un oeuf dur* is a hard-boiled egg. *Un oeuf mollet* is a soft-boiled egg. *Un oeuf sur le plat* is an egg that is baked in a dish — the nearest you can usually get to a fried egg; to order this *au bacon* means with bacon.
Une tranche de jambon blanc: A slice of ham — stipulate *jambon de York* if you want plain boiled ham, as otherwise you may get smoked or raw ham.
Un thé/café simple is a cup of tea/coffee by itself.
Une cafetière is a coffee-pot.
Café noir/café nature is black coffee; *café crème* is coffee with milk already added; *café au lait* is coffee with milk added from a separate jug.
Une orange pressée/un citron pressé is the juice of a freshly squeezed orange or lemon. This is never cheap and can shock those who order it when they get the bill. If you must have fruit-juice first thing and ask for *jus d'orange* you may well get either orange-squash or some form of orange-juice out of a tin or frozen pack.

Tea

Thé de Chine is China tea. *Au citron* means with lemon.
Une tartine is a slice of buttered bread or bread and jam. *Tartiner* is to spread — hence, bread with something spread on it.

Luncheon and dinner

L'addition is the bill.
Avec service/service compris means that the service-charge is already included in the total of the bill — but ask, always, to make sure unless this is made quite clear. STC means *service et taxes compris* — *tout compris* means virtually the same as STC.
Un cadre soigné literally means 'a well-kept setting' and this, as applied to a restaurant, means 'airly luxurious décor and, inevitably, an expensive eating-place.
Un couvert is a place-setting, but the expression *pain et couvert*

When we left Le Puy . . . we saw . . . that it was a run of forty-five kilometres to Saugues. . . . We asked the waiter what we could eat. 'Trout and partridge'. . . . And the wine list? Chablis 1918 was our choice, and vin ordinaire to begin with. The waiter quickly brought us some home-cured ham as an hors d'oeuvre. It was not very good . . . the trout arrived, perfectly cooked, brown and delicious, with just the right accompaniment of butter and gravy . . . champignons arrives, a big dish, crisp and brown and succulent. . . . And then the waiter . . . brought in *not* the partridge, but . . . the most tender rabbit in the world, cooked with tomato sauce. . . . When the partridge arrived, we reminded the waiter that he had said something about potatoes, and could we have them at the same time? He . . . was genuinely distressed. 'You will see . . . that the flavours do not mingle well.' He was quite right. The potato savoury, with its delicate crust of cheese, was spoiled by being eaten with the partridge. . . . The next course was écrevisses . . . cooked in brandy. . . . The waiter . . . produced — flan he called it: a delicious pudding of white of egg and cream beaten up, and sponge fingers to eat with it. After that we merely had to cope with cream cheese, fruit, coffee, and four fines.

G.B. STERN, *Bouquet*, 1927

means the percentage you pay for the bread and the tablecloth — which may be paper but will be freshly set for each diner.

Un coussin is a cushion — usually available if someone wishes to sit higher at the table, or if a child needs to be propped up.

Ordering

D'abord means first — you say this when you order the first course; *ensuite* means next — what you are going to order after this.

Désosser means to bone (meat or fish). Do not hesitate to get this done for you with the more complicated fishes, unless you are adept already. It is boring to spend a meal taking bones out of your mouth. The expression *Enlever les arêtes* means to bone a fish — no one will despise you for asking for this to be done.

Les entremets is the sweet course (*see p.25*).

Éplucher is to peel — as with fruit and vegetables.

Le garçon is the waiter. *Le maître d'hotel* is the head waiter and this term is usually shortened to *Le maître d'*. *La serveuse* is the waitress. *Le sommelier* is the wine waiter.

La garniture is, literally, 'the trimmings' — signifying the accompanying potatoes, vegetables or salad to a dish. The query '*C'est garni?*' will reassure you that you are not only going to be served a piece of steak or slice of meat or fish.

Une lamelle is a sliver or tiny slice — say this if you want a very small portion of something that is carved.

La moitié is 'The half' — used of portions. Do not hesitate about asking for a half portion — you can always share it with another diner.

Partager is to share.

Un plat is a course (of a meal). *Un plat garni* is a course accompanied by salad or vegetables.

Un réchaud is a hotplate — where food you may not want piled on your plate can be left while you eat the initial serving.

Un rince-doigts is a finger-bowl.

Une salade panachée is a mixed salad, but this can also be *une salade anglaise*. *Une salade verte* is a green salad. If it is obvious that you are not French, then you may encourage the restaurant by saying if you want this merely of lettuce (*Que de laitue*), in case — like me — you cannot eat peppers, or else request the presence of onions (*avec oignons*) or, even, especially in the south, with garlic (*avec ail*). *Une salade de tomates* is a tomato salad.

Selon grosseur means 'according to size/weight' and is seen on menus where foods of different size may be featured, such as lobsters or crabs. It refers to the price of the item.

La table d'hôte is a conventional term for the *prix fixe* or fixed-price menu and is quite interesting historically. In the past, the 'host's table' was the table at which all travellers sat down, to have whatever food was available and had been prepared, except for the very wealthy, who would have private rooms and might order special dishes or even bring along their own cooks to cater for them.

Prévenir means to warn but, in restaurant terms, it means that you must reserve a table in advance: the phrase '*nombre de couverts limités — prévenir*' in a gastronomic guide means that the restaurant has only a limited number of places and advance booking is essential. (And do not count on waiting a bit and coming in later after a session in the bar — the French stay long at table once they have got there.) Also bear in mind that, if you risk being delayed, you should telephone — in a renowned restaurant or any eating-place in the high season or a feast day (including Sunday) your table will not be kept for you should you be even a few minutes late.

Réserver is the verb most used when booking an hotel room (*see* p.89).

4

French Food

France is a large and varied country. Within its boundaries there are several completely individual styles of cooking. Much, of course, depends on the natural resources: market garden country; the barren lands that are the birthplace of many of the greatest wines; the lush pastures favourable to dairy produce; the marshes and woods that are sources of game; rivers and inlets of the sea abundant in a variety of fish and shellfish. Sometimes it is the actual deficiencies of an area that produce certain culinary traditions: the slow, seasoned cooking of meat that may have started as being only fair in quality; the creation of stews that stretch the fish or fowl available; the transformation of vegetables into delectable dishes that eke out expensive meat. Necessity is the inspiration of many French recipes now world-famous. As already mentioned, the different cooking fats — butter in the north, oil in the south, animal fat, whether goose dripping or the lard of pork, in the east and parts of the south-west — affect the character of the dishes. So do the wines that may be incorporated: red Burgundy in a sauce or stew will not make *coq au vin* less enjoyable or more so than red Bordeaux, red Rhône, or any other red wine — but it will be *different*.

Since the earliest records were kept, France has received a multitude of foreign influences as regards culinary traditions. True, Vikings, Huns and similar marauders did not exactly travel with their chefs, but, after the Roman conquest of Gaul, settlements grew up along the great roads, and tradesmen arrived to cater for the needs of the military and their families. Merchants found it profitable to stop along the trade routes and, with the coming of Christianity, the schools and universities encouraged visiting scholars and students, whose travels were facilitated by the great religious houses, which acted as hospitals, places of education and provided accommodation. Even quite humble people might bring in foodstuffs and recipes, so that domestic cooking, such as it was, grew up alongside the more elaborate ways of what was to turn into *haute cuisine*. Today, in most towns and even many villages a huge range of foodstuffs is available, more are introduced as novelties, so that dishes and recipes that might formerly have been restricted to certain areas may have somewhat lost their regional character. Never hesitate to ask if you do not understand the style of a listed recipe. Here, some additional explanations are given. It is unlikely that anyone making use of this book will be narrow-minded about eating and drinking. If there is anything you really cannot eat — as the result of experience rather than prejudice — then explain (*see p.114*). It may be worthwhile reassuring people that the *boucherie chevaline* or horseflesh butcher, whose sign of the horse's head is unmistakeable, does not seem quite as active as in former times and maybe the sign will crop up in smart bric-à-brac or antique shops in the near future. However, real steak cannot ever be really cheap, so a suspiciously low-priced menu that includes it may well feature horsemeat, which, I hasten to say, can be excellent. I have eaten it many times. It is also rather odd that people who shudder away from offal or, as the US terms the food, 'variety meats', will nevertheless consume vast quantities of all types of *pâté*, which usually contains liver of some sort, and they may thoroughly enjoy the sort of local sausages that include tripe!

In the sections of this book dealing with the different regions, the local specialities and dishes will be briefly described — although bear in mind that some are so very much 'country cooking' that they are unlikely to feature on the menus of restaurants frequented by travellers. Nor is the reader likely to require explanations of terms such as '*Florentine*', '*au gratin*', '*flambé*'. There are numerous menu guides, should you be uncertain about this kind of thing. Here, there are accounts of the main foodstuffs, so that travellers can sort out the significance of what they may find both on menus and in shops — for these days self-catering holidays appeal very much even to people who do not need to budget too strictly; it is delightful to do one's own marketing, especially in a country town, and advice can usually be obtained from the locals about specific ingredients and recipes, even if you forget to bring a cookery book.

Shellfish

These are divided into shellfish proper — *coquillages* — and *crustacés* (crustaceans) — such as crab and lobster. All of them are also sub-divided into either *fruits de mer*, when they come from the sea, or *fruits d'eau douce*, which are from fresh water.

Huîtres (oysters)

The majority of French oysters and, for that matter, most European oysters as well, start life in Brittany. The adult oyster is much influenced by the place where it grows up; the baby or spat seems to thrive if it starts off in the cold waters of the north coast. There are two main types of oyster, the *plate* (*Ostrea edulis*), which, as its name implies, is flattish and is the sort of oyster that we British associate with Whitstable, Colchester, the Helford River — where spat from Brittany may have been *élevé* or brought up. This is the aristocrat of oysters and usually fairly expensive, also it suffers greatly from bad weather conditions when a shortage, after the sort of winter when the oyster-beds are frozen, sends the price rocketing. The *Portugaise* or Portuguese oyster (*Crassostrea angulata*) has a deepish shell, long and bumpily ridged, and this is cheaper. Oysters are usually sold tagged with the name of the place where they have been reared. The most flavoursome type of plate is the white-fleshed *belon*, which will be sold when it is three years old and has it own *appellation contrôlée*. It is also likely to be the most expensive. The *verte* or Marenne is an oyster greenish in colour, especially at what may be termed its hinges; this colour and its special flavour have been produced by contact with sea waters in which certain seaweeds and marine creatures are active. The oysters of Cancale, which are pinkish in tone, are sometimes referred to as *pieds de cheval*, because of their vaguely horseshoe shape.

The term *claire* refers to an oyster-park, where the creatures are reared, but sometimes the word is used to refer to the oysters as well. All down the west coast there will be a variety of oysters, sometimes merely termed *claires*, on market stalls. Near to the oyster nurseries people may eat them all the year round without ill effects, but otherwise the 'only when there is an "r" in the month' tradition prevails. Oysters are graded according to size. Usually, they are numbered from 4 downwards, to 0 and 00; the lower the number the larger the oyster. A five-year-old oyster can occasionally be as big as a fried egg! It is a matter of personal taste, not their flavour, that dictates the choice of size. As elsewhere, they are usually available by the half dozen, nine or dozen or more.

Crevettes grises are shrimps; *crevettes roses* are prawns, which latter are also referred to as *bouquets*, a term that can also suggest the presentation, where the prawns are gracefully arranged hanging from the edge of a dish or bowl. The term *à la nage* means that they swim *(nager)* in a *court bouillon*, not, as I once thought, that they are alive and swimming when served. Both types of *crevettes* are usually eaten with the fingers — how else, indeed, could you manage them easily?

Homard is lobster. The menu description often attached to it in France will be *à l'Armoricaine* (in Brittany style — Armorica is the old name for Brittany) and not *à l'Américaine (see p.222)*. A *langouste*, a smaller relation of the lobster, but without the big claws, is translated variously as crawfish, rock lobster, spiny lobster. The flesh of the body and tail is the best part, although one can dig about in the long legs. The *langoustine* is smaller than the *langouste*, like a giant prawn, its name being rendered variously as Norway lobster, Dublin Bay prawn or, even, scampi, an internationally accepted menu term these days.

Écrevisse is a crayfish — not to be confused with crawfish. These days crayfish are not often served in the UK, although they can be found in some British rivers. They range in size from prawn to almost *langoustine* proportions.

Coquilles Saint Jacques are scallops. They get their name from the time when, the body of the Apostle St James having been miraculously conveyed in a ship (without oars or sails) to Galicia in northern Spain, a wedding procession was passing and the bridegroom's frightened horse plunged into the waves. But both horse and man were restored to land and to life, covered with clinging scallop shells, at which everyone became Christian and, henceforth, pilgrims going to the great shrine of St James at Santiago (Compostella) wore scallop shells as a sign of their special (and protected) rôle.

Praires and *palourdes* are clams, but this mollusc is not wholly of French origin and sometimes the term clam is used as well. In the south the word is *clovisse*. They can be eaten raw, as part of an *hors d'oeuvre* or platter of seafood, or cooked in ways similar to recipes for mussels. *Coques* are cockles (sometimes also called *bucardes*) and *bigourneaux* are winkles (because of their shape, the word is the same for a hair-curler). *Moules* are mussels, eaten raw, or stuffed, or, of course, in the soup-like recipe *moules marinières*.

Poulpes, seiches (also sometimes called *chiprones*, especially near the Spanish border), *calmars* and *encornets* are, respectively, octopus, squid, inkfish, cuttlefish. They are found in the Atlantic as well as the Mediterranean; indeed, in these days of polluted waters, the best probably come from the ocean. *Oursins* are sea urchins, which are variously described as sea chestnuts or sea hedgehogs. They may be eaten raw, sliced open and scooped out, or in various recipes and the flavour is slightly similar to that of the *écrevisse*.

Escargots (snails) have been a delicacy in France since Roman times. The consumer may find two sorts: *hélices vigneronnes*, the snails that fatten on the vines, especially in Burgundy, where they become very fat, and the *petits gris*, smaller and to be found in many gardens everywhere. The most usual way of serving them is to poach them and put them back into their shells, with garlic butter. You can order them, like oysters, in sixes, nines or dozens, and they will arrive in an *escargotière*, a snail plate made with hollows to hold the snail-shells. (*See illus. on p.39*) Special thin-tined forks are usually set for pulling the snail out of the shell, while a clamp held in the other hand keeps the shell steady. Do not be shy about sopping up the garlic butter with a piece of bread; if someone is not eating the snails and has no objection to garlic, it is obligatory to do this because then, as everyone around the table will have tasted garlic, no one will find the smell obtrusive. Some people are, understandably, a little hesitant about snails as something to eat. Try one, from a neighbour's plate — as with oysters — before making up your mind. The best description of their flavour is my late husband's — 'Something between grilled mushrooms and liver, plus garlic.' They are neither slimy nor fishy.

Grenouilles are frogs and it may surprise some people to know that it is possible to find French people who have never eaten them and others who do not like them! It is only the *cuisses* — thighs — of the frogs that are eaten, usually with the fingers, because it is virtually impossible to manage to get the meat off the little bones otherwise. They may be lightly fried or sautéd, there are recipes involving them *au gratin, en brochette* or *en beignets,* or in a sauce. The flavour is very delicate, something akin to the slivers of meat between the leg and wing-bones of a young chicken. Sometimes, like snails, frogs get comic names on menus, 'nymphs' being one I have sometimes seen.

Freshwater fish

Anguille is eel, delicate in flavour when it comes from a stream or river rather than the muddy waters of a pond. It can, of course, also be fished from the sea and methods of cooking are numerous. Sometimes I have thought its flavour evokes a combination of young rabbit and herring — but you must decide for yourself.

Piballes are elvers — tiny eels. They are an esteemed seasonal delicacy and may be served in the south-west. Looking like silver threads, they are cooked in oil with garlic and brought to table so hot that you will be given a wooden fork with which to eat them, as anything metal would burn the mouth of the diner.

Brochet is pike, a fish popular in the eastern European countries, but not often served in the UK. The most famous gastronomic recipe is *quenelles* — the apotheosis of fishballs — made of pounded pike, in a usually rich sauce. The *barbot* or *lotte de rivière* is a fish that seems to be translated as eel-pout; in fact it has a certain likeness to an eel and may be prepared in similar ways. There is also a *lotte de mer*, a sea fish, which is also referred to as *baudroie* — monkfish.

Saumon (salmon) and *truite* (trout) are easy to identify, although the trout may come from a fish-farm rather than a stream these days. Other freshwater fish that may be featured include *tanche* (tenche); *goujon* (gudgeon); *perche* (perch); *ombre* (grayling), and *ombre chevalier*, which is a speciality of many of the lakes in the east of France; *carpe* (carp), often prepared with beer in the recipe and also with red butter; *brème* (bream); *barbeau* (barbel); *fondre* (pickerel) and *alose*, which is shad and, like the salmon, goes up rivers; apart from numerous bones, shad has a very delicate flavour and is particularly a speciality of the Gironde estuary. *Sandre* is pike perch. *Gardon* is roach and can often form part of a mixed fry — *friture* — when it may seem a little like whitebait.

Sea fish

Colin is hake; *daurade* is sea-bream; *éperlans* are smelts; *merlan* is whiting — not served with its tail in its mouth in France — *mulet* is grey mullet; *rouget* red mullet. *St Pierre* is John Dory, getting its name because of the supposed 'thumb-mark' of the Apostle Peter, who took the tribute money from the mouth of the fish. *Cabillaud* is cod, but it can also be *morue fraîche*, whereas *morue* is salt cod. *Merluche* is stockfish; *barbue* is brill; *bar* is bass, a white fattish fish, somewhat like salmon; *grondin* is gurnard; *églefin* is haddock; *flétan* is halibut; *hareng* is herring. *Limande* is lemon sole. *Plie franche* or just *plie* or *carrelet* are all names for plaice. *Raie* is skate; *thon* is tunny fish — used in *hors d'oeuvre* and *salade niçoise* as well as being served hot; *espadon* is swordfish, which is a fleshy fish, somewhat like tunny. *Laitances* are soft roes. *Loup de mer* is sea perch, often grilled over fennel sticks and a great feature of the south of France. Sole and turbot are the same as in English. But it is worth bearing in mind, unless you are an experienced fish cook, that sole is 'the game of the sea' so, ideally, it should not be cooked when it is quite fresh, but be allowed to 'rest' in a cool place for twenty-four hours, when the flavour will have intensified and the flesh be tender and succulent; it can be eaten as soon as it is caught, but will not be quite as good.

Une chaudrée is a chowder of fish-stew, named for *la chaudière*, the cauldron in which it is made. A *matelote* is also a fish-stew and a *pochouse* the type of fish-stew for which Burgundy is especially famous (*see p.229*). Best-known of all, of course, is *bouillabaisse*, from the south (*see p.300*).

Charcuterie

The word *charcuterie* comes from *chair cuite*, literally, cooked meat (*see p.95*). Even quite small shops often have an enormous variety of what we might term *delicatessen*, plus prepared take-away dishes. Somewhat strangely, there is not usually a huge range of cooked meats on the *hors d'oeuvre* trolley, but some regions do have their own specialities that come into this category. This section is likely also to be of use to anyone shopping for a picnic or having a self-catering holiday (*see also p.102*).

Various *pâtés* and *terrines* (strictly, a *terrine* is in some form of case or holder — made of *terre cuite* — baked earthenware) and meats *en croûte* — in a pastry case — are likely to be familiar. Anything *truffé* (with truffles) or *aux pistaches* (with pistachio nuts — the bright green ones) may be expensive. *Andouilles* and *andouillettttes* are types of tripe sausage, often made to regional recipes. *Rillettes*, a Touraine speciality but made elsewhere, are potted pork sausages; *rillons* are slightly different as the shredded pork is not cooked until it is soft, as for *rillettes*, but remains firm.

A *saucisse* is a larger version of a *saucisson* and may be made of various kinds of meat; a *saucisson sec* is a hard sausage, somewhat akin to salami; *rosette*, a type of *saucisson sec* special to the Lyonnais, is the same sort of thing. *Cervelat* is a type of pork sausage, getting its name from *cervelle*, brains; the English word saveloy comes from this. *Boudins* are puddings, *boudin noir* being what we might call blood sausage, *boudin blanc*, made from chicken and/or veal, a paler version. Since the arrival of many *pieds noir* — the settlers from what was formerly French Algeria — there is also a spicy sausage, called *merguez*, often seen on menus or advertised as being the *plat du jour* in little restaurants. *Jambon de York* is plain ham — nothing to do with York; it is sometimes also called *jambon de Paris*. Various forms of *jambon fumé* (smoked ham) or *jambon cru* (raw ham) are also found — ask if the curing of these is very strong, unless you already know and like this kind of ham. Butter will be served with it. *Jambon persillé* is a Burgundy speciality, but may be seen elsewhere: it is ham in parsley jelly, sliced so that the pinkish-red meat and green form a pattern rather like tiles. *Hure* is a type of brawn — what some might call head cheese of pork. *Pieds de porc* are stuffed pigs' trotters. *Jambonneau* is the foreleg of pork, or knuckle, looking like a small pyramid with the bone sticking up, vaguely similar to a Bath chap.

The *confits* of the south-west are rich, usually expensive. The term isn't easily translatable, but a *confit* consists of joints of either pork, duck, goose — or anything else available and suitable — pickled and then preserved in their own fat, from which they are extracted when ready to eat.

Légumes (Vegetables)

The size of France means that, these days, many vegetables are available for a very long season. *Les crudités* are raw vegetables, often part of an *hors d'oeuvre*. Some of the slightly confusing names of vegetables are *céleris* (celery) and *céleri-rave* (celeriac). The most topsy-turvy of all is *chicorée frisée*, which is endive, and *endive* or *Witloof*, which is chicory; then, also in the chicory section, there is *barbe de Capucin*, which is apparently a type of dandelion, which is a bitter variety of chicory looking rather like feathery-topped chives. *Chicorée scarole* or *maraîchère* is a bunchy vegetable, somewhat resembling ordinary endive but with fatter, flatter serrated-edged leaves. *Chicorée rouge* is radicchio, the red-leaved bunched salad vegetable. Other salad vegetables include dandelion leaves — *pissenlit*. (They do not have this effect on the eater and are agreeably bitter, often being combined with diced bacon.)

Laitue is lettuce — of which there are many kinds. *Laitue romaine* is what the British call cos lettuce; *laitue batavia Beaujolaise*, crisp and curly, resembles the Webb's Wonder lettuce of the UK. *Mâche* is what Britons call lambs' lettuce or corn salad. *Feuilles de chêne* is a lettuce somewhat recently in vogue, having brownish-red leaves (rather like oak leaves) that are crisp and slightly bitter.

Cresson is cress; *cresson de fontaine* is watercress. (If either are a garnish to a dish, it is up to you whether or not you eat them — I usually do.)

Oignons are onions, the red-skinned type being *oignons d'Italie*. *Échalotes* are shallots; *une ciboule* is a spring onion, *les ciboulettes* are chives. *Rocambole* is akin to a shallot. *Haricots verts* are French beans; *fèves* are broad beans; *haricots* or *haricots blancs secs* are dried white beans — butter-beans; the tiny variety are known as *soissons* — sometimes mentioned on menus and often used for *cassoulet* recipes (*see p.280*).

Petits pois are the tiny peas, cooked in butter, with a little onion and, sometimes, diced ham; the British know them via the canned versions and, as French regulations prohibit the use of additional green colouring, the dull green is inevitable — though the flavour is not affected. If, when self-catering, you prefer to cook peas *à l'anglaise* with mint, there is nothing to prevent you — and if you find that French peas are deficient in colour, add a few drops of *crème de menthe* at the last minute to remedy this. *Pois mange-tout* are the type of peas that are cooked and eaten pods and all. *Pois chiches* are chickpeas.

Asperges (asparagus) is usually fatter than the slender British variety. *Argenteuil* asparagus is very pale, greenish only at the tips, *Lauris* also has green tips with fat stems. *Cavaillon* is rather similar. There are various types of *asperges blanches*, all pale yellow; these may be served hot, with melted butter or an Hollandaise sauce, or cold with a vinaigrette. Ready-cooked asparagus is often found in *hors d'oeuvre* and also at a *charcuterie*. (For the devotee of English varieties of asparagus and, certainly, sprue [for which I can find no French equivalent], it may be wise to opt for French asparagus either with an Hollandaise sauce or a vinaigrette; oddly, in this vegetable-rich country, the delicacy of the thin, dark green stems of best Evesham, so delectable served hot with melted butter, is not found — the fat-stemmed varieties do not seem to have the same flavour.) *Artichauts* are globe artichokes, Jerusalem artichokes are *topinambours*. *Fonds d'artichauts* are the bases of globe artichokes, found in tins and often featured in *hors d'oeuvre*. *Panais* is parsnip; *navet* is turnip (usually much smaller than in the UK); *carotte*, of course, is carrot; *rutabaga* is swede — although I do not think I have ever seen this featured on menus and many people probably regard it as only animal fodder. *Piments doux* or *poivrons* are sweet peppers. *Aubergine, courgette, concombre, tomate* probably do not need a translation — although remember that it is the irregular tomatoes seen in southern markets that make delicious salads and the plum tomatoes, which are not so good for eating raw, that make the finest sauces. *Betterave* is beetroot; *gourde* and *courge* (pumpkin) may sometimes be seen on menus in the south; *cardon*, which is a cardoon, may be known in the UK as chard. *Radis* are radishes, which, served with butter, sometimes make a first course. *Salsifis*, an odd vegetable, looking somewhat like braised celery, is getting known outside France these days under its own name. *Poireaux* are leeks.

Chou is cabbage; *chou-fleur* is cauliflower (sometimes served with a vinaigrette cold); *choux de Bruxelles* are Brussels sprouts — although I don't think I have ever eaten them in France! *Chou rouge* is red cabbage. As anywhere else, there are many varieties of cabbage, from the pale, tightly-packed leaves of one sort to the curlier leaves of others — on a menu this is not likely to be a problem, but if you are shopping, it is probably easiest to point to the type you require — and register the local name for it. *Oseille* is sorrel — it is cooked like spinach and is delicious as a soup as well.

Pommes de terre are potatoes — available in a greater variety than is usual in the UK. When you are shopping for them, specify what you are going to make of them — there is a violet-skinned variety, admirable in salads, and there are other waxy types. *Frites*, of course, are chips or fried potatoes — *pomme allumettes* are the finer stick-like version. *Purée de pommes de terre* is just that — a purée, made with milk and butter, light and creamy, very pleasant for anyone wanting a rather 'comforting' vegetable accompaniment, or for serving to children. ('Mashed' potatoes do not seem to be a version known to the French.) A few peeled and boiled potatoes are often the accompaniments to fish dishes, served with the food instead of later, as with some vegetable courses. *Pommes de terre en robe de champs* are potatoes baked in their jackets ('in a field coat' is the literal translation), but the refinements of menu language have changed this to '*en robe de chambre*', which means 'in a dressing-gown'. They have become popular in recent years for simple fare. Terms such as *sauté, dauphine, gratiné* are fairly obvious, though the varieties of *gratin de pommes de terre* are indicated on *p.331*.

Champignons (mushrooms) are the subject of many books. The word itself can also signify 'fungus' so that, when wine-growers talk about 'noble rot', they may use the term *champignon* to indicate the formation of the condition. Many pharmacy windows or inside displays may include pictures or a chart of different sorts of mushrooms — especially when they are just coming into season — and the poisonous type will be clearly shown, with the addresses of '*Centres Anti-Poison*' in the vicinity. However, the soundest advice for anyone picking mushrooms in the wild is 'If in any doubt — leave them alone'. The ordinary field-mushroom is a *champignon*; *champignons de Paris* are button mushrooms. Among others that may be proudly featured on menus are: the *morille* (*Morchella*), a thick-stemmed mushroom, with a closed, pointed, crinkled cap. It grows in the spring. There are several types of the *morille*. Another spring mushroom is the *pezize*,

which can be *ecarlate* (scarlet), also the *pleurote* (*Pleurotus cornucoiodides*), which has cream-coloured caps and grows in layers under trees; it, too, features in many recipes. Summer mushrooms include the *bolet orangé*, with a tawny cap — like the pictures of mushrooms in fairy-tales — and the *chanterelle*; another name for this last may be *girolle*. The *roussotte* is cream in colour and like a trumpet in shape; the *lactaire* (*Lactarius deliciosus*) is a bit like a pale field mushroom; and the *polyphore* (*Polyphorus umbellatus*) is flat-topped and cream in colour, giving out a delicious aroma in June and July. There is a huge family of mushrooms called *russules*, though French gastronomic writers do not seem to rate them very highly, but they praise the *truffé d'été*, also called the *truffe de la Saint Jean* (because of being associated with Midsummer, St John's Day), which is a pied mushroom, found at the roots of various trees (not only oaks) between June and October. In the autumn mushrooms abound. You may be offered a mixed dish of them, which, in spite of seeming like a 'witches' brew', all odd shapes in an almost black sauce, can be delectable. There is the *armillaire de miel*, which has a frill around the stem below the cap; many *bolets* (*Boletus*) grow in various regions, including those abundant in conifers. The *cèpe* (not to be confused with *cep*, which is a vine shoot), is the speciality of the south-west and is very rich. Other autumn varieties are: *litocybe, craterelle,*the *fistuline hépatique,* with its scarlet surface, various types of *helvelle* with ridged stems, the oddly shaped *hydne,* the tall stemmed *lépiotes,* the bulbous capped *lycoperdon.* Many have a delicious smell, even when raw. Members of the *pezize* family, *pholitotes, polyphores, psalliotes* and the seaweed-like *sparessis,* are also to be found. Try to note which are which if you visit a market.

Even in winter there are plenty of mushrooms: there is the astonishingly convoluted *oreille de Jusad (Auricilaria auricula judae),* also the *collybie,* the *hydne* again and the *pleurote en forme d'huître;* this last is now often a commercial rather than a wild crop and the mushrooms do look rather like oyster-shells.

Many mushrooms are kept preserved in oil, vinegar, or may be frozen *(congelé)* or made into an essence *(concentré).* A good shop should be able to tell you about the various kinds available in these forms.

Some Herbs and Spices

Ail is garlic, a single clove being *une gousse d'ail,* the whole head *une tête d'ail.* You can sometimes find the dried, powdered variety, but fresh garlic is usually available all the year round.

Basilic is sweet basil.

Cannelle is cinnamon.

Câpres are capers.

Cerfeuil is chervil.

Ciboulette is chives.

Estragon is tarragon.

Fenouil is fennel.

Genièvre is juniper.

Gingembre is ginger.

Girofle is cloves, a single clove being *un clou* (literally, a nail) *de girofle.* Do not confuse the word with *giroflée,* which is a carnation or gillyflower.

Grains de capucines are nasturtium seeds, sometimes used in salads.

Marjolaine is marjoram — but a *marjolaine* on the sweet-trolley is a rich confection, something between a cake and a pastry.

Mélisse is lemon balm.

Muscade is nutmeg.
Persil is parsley.
Romarin is rosemary.
Sarriette is savory.
Sauge is sage.
Thym is thyme, *serpolet* is wild thyme.

A few more vegetable matters:
Un cornichon is a gherkin — usually served with *pâté* and cold cuts.
Raifort is horseradish.

Orange bigarrade is a bitter orange — what the British might term a Seville, used in some recipes for sauce with duckling.

Pasta

The overall term is *Les pâtes*. *Nouilles* are noodles, *riz* is rice, *orge perlé* is pearl barley. Otherwise the Italian terms are used.

Salads

As already noted, *une salade panachée* is a mixed salad, *une salade verte* a green salad. If dressed with a special oil, this will usually be mentioned on the menu. (*See also pp.43, 98.*) *Le mesclun* is an expression I owe to Monsieur Roger Vergés, who explains that it is some of the packages of mixed salad herbs, rather like an extension of the *bouquet garni* — ready assembled and, sometimes, available in supermarkets as well as on market stalls. Originally, according to M. Vergés, it was made up of wild herbs: *riquette* (rocket), *pissenlit* (dandelion), *mâche, pourpier* (purslane) and, sometimes, *séneçon* (groundsel — beloved of canaries). It seems as if it can consist of whatever is available in season.
   Mayonnaise is not served with green or mixed salads and is generally the accompaniment to eggs and *hors d'oeuvre* or certain fish dishes or of course a *plateau de fruits de mers*. *Aioli* is the

garlic mayonnaise of the south. A *salade Niçoise* is another South of France dish that is frequently a first course; it can vary, but usually includes lettuce, hard-boiled eggs, tunny fish, anchovies and black olives, with a vinaigrette dressing.

Meat

Meat

The big joint is seldom seen in France and the cuts of meat are different from those in the UK — frequently more economically prepared, so that there is no waste.

Beef

A *contrefilet* or *faux filet* is about the same as the end of the rib, or the boneless uppercut of the loin, the larger part of the T-bone or porterhouse steak. The *aloyau* is the entire sirloin, of which the filet is virtually the same as the English fillet. *Un entrecôte* is either a piece of the rib meat or a cut from the fillet and it is worth remembering that it is usually larger in France than in the UK, so if you want a small one, ask for an *entrecôte minute*. A *Château-briand* — usually priced for two people but often ample for three — is a thick double fillet. *Côtes de boeuf*, or *côtes* of anything, are chops, *côtelettes* are cutlets.

Any type of steak tends to be cut thicker in France than in the UK. When ordering, you will be asked how you like it cooked and the terms are: *Bien cuit* for well done; *à point* for medium; *saignant* for rare or underdone. If, like me, you like steak almost raw, the term is *bleu* — but sometimes waiters find this difficult to credit — so insist plainly! Beef from Charollais cattle will probably have this mentioned on the menu.

> The most portable and useful condiments for a traveller are — salt, red pepper, Harvey's sauce, lime-juice, dried onions, and curry powder. They should be bought at a first-rate shop.
>
> FRANCIS GALTON, *Art of Travel*, John Murray, 1872

Lamb and mutton

As the French like lamb cooked so that it is pink inside, it may be wise to say that you must have a portion *bien cuit* if you want it medium to well done. *Gigot d'agneau* is leg of lamb; *carré d'agneau* the best end; *épaule* is shoulder; *selle* is saddle. Sometimes the whole of the hindquarters, *un baron d'agneau*, may form part of a special meal. *Pré salé* lamb, from the salty pastures alongside the sea, will usually have this quality indicated on the menu.

Pork

Carré de porc is loin; *filet de porc* and *côte de porc* are types of chop. There is no 'close season' for eating pork.

Veal

French veal — *veau* — is usually of high quality. *Escalope de veau*, the flattened slice, and *côte de veau* — a chop — are probably familiar terms, but *ris de veau* is veal sweetbreads, another delicacy. *Tête de veau vinaigrette* is calf's head, served cold.

Offal

These 'variety meats' are *les abats* and much esteemed. *Foie* is liver; *rognons* are kidneys; *cervelles* are brains.

Poultry

The *poulet de Bresse* is a famous type of chicken, with its own A.O.C. However, a *poulet de grain* (maize fed) chicken, yellow in colour, can also be very good — and cheaper. A *poularde* is a large hen, a *chapon* a capon. In some regions there are local breeds, such as the *géline de Touraine*, a smallish black fowl.

Pigeon is the same word, *oie* is goose, *dindonneau* is a young turkey, *dinde* a hen turkey — the word '*d'Inde*' indicates where the bird is thought to have originated, although in fact it seems to have come from Mexico. *Caneton* is duckling; *col vert* a type of wild duck; *un sauvage* is a mallard. The Nantais breed of duck is an esteemed variety. *Palombe* is a wood pigeon; *pintade* or *pintadeau* are names for guinea-fowl. These speckled birds, which are excellent eating, are named 'painted' (in French) because of the classical story of how the sisters of Meleager wept at his death, after which Artemis changed them into birds, the spots on their feathers representing their tears. For those doing their own marketing, it is worth remembering that the innards and feet and heads of poultry will, usually, be included; if you want a bird cleaned, the term is *'effilé'*, but the liver etc. will be left. Pre-packed birds are often on sale these days, minus their insides. A *poulet de ferme* is a free-range bird.

Game

The overall term is *gibier*. This is divided into *gibier à poil* (with hair) and *gibier à plume* (with feathers). *La chasse* is very popular and all sorts of game will feature on menus, including — to the horror of many Anglo-Saxons — song-birds, although they do seem to be in decline. Game birds are not always hung, as they might be in Britain; the term is *'faisandé'* — that is, 'gamey'. *Faisan* is pheasant; *perdreau* is partridge; *coq de bruyère* is capercailzie; *bécasse* is woodcock; *bécassine* is snipe; *pluvier* is plover; *caille* is quail and *carcelle* is teal. The French are great admirers of *'le grouse'*, but I am assured by friends who should know that the grouse does not thrive in France and, when attempts at rearing it there have been made, they have been unsuccessful.

Venaison is venison, *chevreuil* is roedeer, very delicate. *Basse venaison*, however, signifies *lièvre* (hare); *lapin de garenne* (wild rabbit, whereas reared rabbit is *lapin de clapier*); *Râble de lièvre* is saddle of hare; a *civet* is what the British might translate as a 'jug' or type of stew.

> The common cookery of the French gives great advantage. It is true, they roast everything to a chip, if they are not cautioned: but they give such a number and variety of dishes, that if you do not like some, there are others to please your palate. The dessert at a French inn has no rival at an English one; nor are the liqueurs to be despised. We sometimes have met with bad wine, but on the whole, far better than such port as English inns give.
>
> ARTHUR YOUNG, *Travels in France*, June, 1787

Little birds that may sometimes be mentioned on menus include *alouettes* (larks, often made into *pâtés*), *grives* (thrushes) and *merles* (blackbirds) — either made into *pâtés* or, sometimes, roasted, like quails. *Ortolans* (wheatears) are now, I think, protected birds. The *becfigue* — literally, figpecker — is described on *p.310* among the regional specialities. We should remember that our ancestors were also quite prepared to eat all of these things; the handsome plates, decorated with ears of wheat, with hollows to hold the *ortolans*, are still sometimes to be found. With such things and also quails, the only satisfactory way to secure even the small bits of meat is to eat the birds with the fingers. You are supposed to scrunch up the bones and even eat the head, said to be the best bit, although I admit I have never been able to do this, somewhat to the surprise of waiters. You are likely to need a *rince-doigts* (a fingerbowl) to clean your hands afterwards.

Alouettes sans têtes need not provoke a shudder — it is a euphemism for beef olives.

Some General Menu Terms

Un hachis is 'a chopped-up dish'; *un hochepot* is French for 'hotpot'. *Le jus* is the juice or gravy from the meat — not to be confused with '*un peu de sauce*', which is definitely sauce.

The terms *ragoût*, *salmis* and others are likely to be familiar, the latter, strictly, referring to game.

Une assiette anglaise is a plate of cold cuts (with the inevitable gherkin), the sort of dish you may be able to order in some cafés.

The '*pain et couvert*', priced on the menu, refer to the basic charge and even if you ask for more bread, this will not usually be extra.

Anyone keeping to a special diet will probably have worked out the relevant terms beforehand, but to be *végétarien(ne)* is to be a vegetarian and, although there do not seem to be many conspicuous in France, a request for a vegetarian meal can usually be complied with. The '*jours maigres*' or fast days, involving abstention from meat, do not appear to affect the French menu a great deal these days, although on the major church fasts, restaurants may cater for '*pratiquants*'.

The keen student of the French language should note that the names of dishes can be given in shortened, even ungrammatical forms — such as, for example, *Pommes Lyonnaise,* instead of what should read *Pommes à la Lyonnaise.* If the significance is understood, this is one occasion when the slight distortion of the language doesn't matter.

Cheese (*see p.65*). In France it will be offered before the sweet.

Fruit

This forms part of most meals. *La corbeille des fruits* simply means a piece of fruit taken from a basket of assorted fruits. *Fruits rafraîchis* or *compôte de fruits* are fruit-salads of varying types; if these have the addition of a liqueur, such as *kirsch*, this will usually be mentioned.

Pomme is apple; *poire* is pear; *banane* is banana; *abricot* is apricot; *citron* is lemon; *orange* is orange; *pamplemousse* is grapefruit; *ananas* is pineapple. A *grenade* is a pomegranate, the juice being much used in grenadine; the bomb — *grenade* — gets its name from the fruit because of a resemblance in shape. *Une prune* is a plum; *un pruneau* is a prune; *une prune de damas* is a damson. *Une reine-Claude* is a greengage, getting its name from Queen Claude, wife of King François I, who loved the new type of fruit that the gardeners of her time evolved. There are many types of plum (including one named after Monsieur, the pervert brother of Louis XIV), but the two most likely to be found in tarts and similar pastries are *mirabelles,* rosy-yellow golden small plums, and *quetches,* which are small purple plums. *Une groseille* is a gooseberry; French gooseberries tend to be smaller than those seen in the UK. *Une groseille rouge* is a redcurrant; *une groseille noire* or *un cassis* is a blackcurrant (the fruit that makes the famous liqueur). *Un raisin de Corinthe* is a currant; *un raisin sec de Smyrne* is a sultana.

There are many varieties of melon, the main orange-fleshed variety being the family of *melons brodés,* of which the Cavaillon and Ogen are the best-known; there are also many types of *melons cantaloups.* Water melon is *melon d'eau.*

Fraises are strawberries and *fraises des bois* wild strawberries; you will not get them served with cream unless you ask — but try them with a little red wine sprinkled on instead. *Framboises* are raspberries, *cerises* are cherries. *Une pêche* is a peach — usually the yellow-fleshed variety (do not confuse the word with *un péché,* which is a sin). *Une nectarine* is, as you might expect, a nectarine. *Une figue* is a fig, but *une figue banane* is a plantain (more of a vegetable) and *une figue de Barbarie* is a prickly pear.

Ices

Une glace is an ordinary ice, what we might term ice-cream, whether or not it contains any dairy product. *Un sorbet* is a water-ice, *une cassate* a cassata. There are many different ice-puddings, ices made with fruit, ice-cream gâteaux: the following are made with ice-cream, in various forms and with many different ingredients: *biscuits glacés, bombes, mousses, parfaits, poudings glacés* and *soufflés glacés*. The following are made with types of water-ice: *granitas, marquises*. Every ice-cream kiosk has a variety of different ices, bearing alluring names. *Une omelette norvégienne* and *un soufflé en surprise* are both slightly different versions of baked Alaska — meringue surrounding sponge-cake and ice-cream. Sometimes they are sprinkled with liqueur and are brought *flambé* to the table.

When the waiter asked '*Quel parfum?*' if you order an ice, he means 'What flavour?' The most usual are: *vanille, chocolat, café* or *moka, fraise, framboise, cassis* and *praliné*, which last is caramelized nuts. *Une glace panachée* is a mixed ice-cream; you may get two or three scoops of different flavours.

Sweets

Les entremets (*see p.25* for an explanation of the term) are not always very extensive, unless you are in a large restaurant. Usually fresh fruit, a fruit pastry, (*tarte maison* — often of apples) and ices will feature on a menu. If the establishment is proud of its pastry, it may mention that the *pâtisserie* is made there in the kitchen, not bought in. Soufflés and crèpes (pancakes) must be ordered in advance and, if they include a liqueur (Soufflé Rothschild features several, for example) they will not be cheap. Yoghurt (*yaourt*) is often available, useful if you have children with you or want a light meal. The fruit-flavoured kind may be offered but if you want a plain one ask for *une yaourt nature*.

5

The Cheese-Board

Most people will be familiar with the French saying — often used in advertising — that 'a meal without cheese is like a beautiful woman with only one eye'. There are certainly hundreds, maybe thousands, of French cheeses and the cheese-board of even a modest restaurant will usually provide quite a selection. (Remember that the cheese will be eaten before anything sweet. It is up to you to decide whether you take your cheese with any salad or after this.)

There are many variations on the great regional cheeses so, if you are doing the shopping, explain the basic type you require — it may have a different name in various parts of the country. Anglo-Saxons tend to be hesitant about goat cheeses — goodness knows why. The goat, a most useful animal all around the Mediterranean, is somehow associated with the Devil in northern countries. Also, people may have been unfortunate in trying goat milk or goat cheese that really is 'goaty' — often because the animal hasn't been kept clean — and so one bad experience has put them off. But good goat cheese is excellent with many wines and need not necessarily be strong.

There are some hard, matured cheeses, so much the specialities of the UK, but the range of soft and semi-matured cheese is extensive. Any good cheese-board should have several distinct types and, when you order cheese, no one will object to your trying several — although you may find that anyone serving will give you a substantial chunk, so it is wise to warn them you want only *une petite tranche* (a small slice) or *une lamelle* (a sliver) or, if a large portion has been cut, *la moitié de ça* (half of that). You will not be served butter, unless you are in a restaurant accustomed to catering for people who do order it with cheese — there is a saying that good cheese brings its own butter, bad cheese needs none. Of course it can be ordered. Bread is the usual accompaniment, not biscuits, and there may be a tiny pot of caraway seeds or cumin on the table for you to season the cheese if you wish. A knife and fork will be provided and it is usual to eat the cheese with these. Cheese is traditional with wine. But people do not always realize that some white wines, even the big sweet white wines, can be very good with certain cheeses. It is a constant gastronomic argument as to whether some cheeses swamp delicate fine wines but this is a matter for the individual to decide; just as certain crisp Loire white wines go agreeably with many slightly creamy cheeses, fruitier dry whites with some goat cheeses and even with the well-known creamy cheeses, such as Brie, so the hard cheeses and even the creamier blue cheeses, can be pleasant with the definitely sweet white wines.

What, to me, makes a great difference is the fat content of the cheese as well as its actual assertiveness or pungency. Many cheeses indicate the degree of *matière grasse* on their labels and, in very general terms, the higher the fat content, the better seems the partnership of such cheeses with delicate fine red wines. The alkalinity of the cheese should be balanced against the acidity of the wine for maximum pleasure: for example, a cheese that is 45 – 50 per cent *matière grasse*, or one of the little goat cheeses, will go well with a fairly light-bodied red wine, itself possibly high in acid. But with a subtler red, a cheese that is slightly higher in fat — 65 – 70 per cent, or even 80 per cent *matière grasse* will not only balance itself against the wine's acidity, it will also smooth away any tannin, such as may be present in a classic red wine that is far from attaining its prime. You must think of what the cheese will do to your palate, in conjunction with the wine: the alkalinity and fatness, more or less, against the acidity and tannin. This is why the wine trade say, 'We buy on apples, sell on cheese' because a crisp apple will tune up the palate and reveal the wine ruthlessly, whereas the cheese will smooth away any hard edges and make the wine taste much better. The cheese-board is a wasteful element in any restaurant. As you will know, if you have watched anybody propping up a Brie that is literally running away and has to be kept within bounds by means of little wooden or plastic stays, some cheeses are only *à point*, at their very best, for a matter of hours; it was years before I could understand the charm of Camembert, having had so many that were hard, ammonia-redolent, or some other cheeses that were raspingly salty. If you see that a cheese-board has a somewhat *passé* appearance, opt for any fresh-seeming cream cheese and, if you are drinking a robust red wine, anything that is hard.

A Little Directory of Cheeses

Abondance: This creamy cow-milk cheese comes from Savoie, and is one of the round flat cheeses, pressed into shape. Sometimes it is called *tomme d'abondance*, like other cheeses of this shape, especially those made in the mountains.

Aligot: A cow-milk cheese, made in the Rouergue region in the south-east, a bit like the hard cheese, Cantal (*see p.72*) and, because it is good to grate, often used for cooking and making into various dishes, such as *gratins* and cheese pastry.

Amou: This is a ewe-milk cheese from the south-west, the Landes and Gers regions supposedly making the best. It is a round, flattish cheese, fairly firm in texture and can be used, when old, for *gratins*.

Annot: This comes from the region round Nice and can be made either from ewe or goat milk. It is round and flat, not as large as some of the flatter cheeses. It still seems to be made as a cottage cheese up in the mountains.

Ardi-gasna: This is a Basque cheese, made from ewe milk, and has a thickish round shape. It can get quite hard and may be grated when it reaches this state. The name, according to the great authority on cheese, Monsieur Androuet, is Basque for 'country cheese'.

Arômes: There are various types of *arômes*, which come from around Lyons, some made from cow milk, some from goat milk. White wine and *marc* are incorporated in some of them.

Banon: This is a Provence cheese which may be made from goat, ewe or cow milk, or a mixture of two or all three. It is a rather small, round, flat cheese, wrapped up in chestnut leaves, good when fresh, although apt to be on the salty side. There are various forms of Banon, some of them wrapped in other leaves, all of which are supposed to impart some additional flavour.

Beaufort: This is a cow-milk cheese from Savoie, and like a large wheel, with slightly convex sides. As, according to Monsieur Androuet, its other name is Gruyère de Beaufort, its nature may be imagined from its name — medium firm in texture, moderately fat and usually satisfying. Beaumont is also a Savoie cheese, some-what similar to Beaufort, but made from pasteurized milk, there-fore rather more unctuous and without the same definite charac-ter.

Belval: This is a Picardy cow-milk cheese, made at the Abbey of Belval. It is a round, pressed cheese, and seems to resemble St Paulin (*see p.77*).

Bergues: This is a cow-milk cheese made in Flanders. It becomes hard and therefore is used in cooking as well as raw. It comes from the town for which it is named and is either round and flat or a flattened bulgy shape. It is not high in fat and therefore it seems to have become popular with the beer drinkers of the locality.

Bethmale: This is a cow-milk cheese, sometimes called Oustet, coming from a region in the south, the best supposedly from Bethmale itself. It is a round cylindrical cheese and seems to be, like many of the mountain cheeses, medium fat and a pleasant one to try on the spot.

Bleu de ... or Blue Cheeses

These are the cheeses which have blue veining, either fairly definite in outline or else somewhat spotty in appearance. They may otherwise be creamy or dead white. Monsieur Androuet's great reference book lists eighteen of them as main types in France and there are certainly more, with local names, in certain regions. They tend to come from the mountainous areas, and can be of different sizes and shapes, although the majority are usually disc-like, of varying thickness. Although a number of them are made from cows' milk, there are notable exceptions — the great Roquefort (*see p.80*) being the most obvious, as it is made from ewe milk.

Most blue cheeses in France tend to be creamy, slightly piquant when at their best — after being matured for several months in cheese caves if they are not the factory-made versions. When you are buying a blue cheese, make sure that it is fairly firm to the touch because, if it is very soft, it may have become salty and rather sour in taste. The cows' milk may sometimes be augmented with a little goats' milk which firms the texture and, as with all cheese made from goats' milk, gives a whiter colour.

Bleu de Corse: This is a ewe-milk blue cheese, fairly strong, although not aggressively so.

Bleu de Bresse: This is one of the most famous blue cheeses and comes from the Ain. It is a small, dumpy, round cheese and was apparently first made in the 1950s, from pasteurized milk, so as to

popularize the purchase of little cheeses, because the large ones are difficult to cut in small quantities and somewhat wasteful because they crumble easily.

Blue cheeses from Auvergne, the Landes, Quercy, Savoie and Dauphiné may all be found on cheese-boards in the different regions.

Bondon de Neufchatel: This is a cow-milk cheese from Normandy, small and cylindrical in shape and rather soft. It is one of the pleasant, slightly unctuous cheeses from this pasture-rich region.
Bossons Macérés: This goat-milk cheese from Languedoc is really more in the nature of a cheese relish, because it is mixed with oil, *marc* and white wine and is presented in a little pot after it has matured. You may be lucky enough to try one of these — the strength will be rather obvious — if you are in the country or if a restaurant is able to buy directly from a farm. This type of cheese is good as a spread when picnicking.
Boulette: There are several cheeses bearing this name, often with the suffix of their region. Some are made in the north of France. As

the name implies, they are spherical and are cow-milk cheeses of fairly light, creamy consistency.

Bressan: This cheese from the Bresse region in the Ain is made from goats' milk, which may be mixed with other milk. It is soft, shaped like a small cone, which marks it out on the cheese-board, and is fairly strong in flavour.

Brie: This is certainly one of the great cheeses of the world. There are, however, various kinds, although all are made from cows' milk. The Brie province is east of Paris along the lower valley of the River Marne, the chief town being Meaux, from which the best cheeses are supposed to come, although there are other regions: the descriptions *fermier* (farmhouse) and *laitier* (dairy-made) differentiate them. The various types of Brie de Melun and the Brie de Montereau are round and flattish, of quite large diameter; Brie de Provins is smaller and thicker. The cheese has been famous at least since the thirteenth century. The poet duke, Charles d'Orléans, gave Brie as presents to his friends. Henri IV said it was the best cheese he knew (but he said that about quite a lot of food and drink); Condé celebrated the victory of Rocroi with red wine and Brie; Queen Maria Leczinska filled her *bouchées à la reine* with cheese; Rabelais praised Brie; Saint Amand wrote a whole poem to it.

Large, round, thin and, at its best, unctuous without being actually runny, Brie is a cheese that combines richness with delicacy and when good it is difficult to think that any cheese of this kind could be better. Unfortunately, the 'king of cheeses' is not always served when it is at its best: it should be unctuous without being actually runny and never too salty. Once the huge disc of a whole Brie has been cut, however, the interior may begin to flow away from the main part and, in order to keep it within bounds, small props of wood or, nowadays, plastic, are inserted to shore up the cut sides. There is a lot of discussion as to whether, if a Brie is served in a single pointed slice, it is correct to cut another slice alongside the whole length of this or whether you should cut from the point, some people being as firm about the one practice as others about the opposite. It would seem, however, that, with a very ripe Brie, to cut the point would be to take the ripest bit and therefore prevent the cheese running away, as might happen from the remaining section if a sliver is taken off the sides.

From Melun, in the Île de France, there is a type of Brie that is lightly dusted with wood ash. Brie de Montereau has a slightly reddish exterior.

Brillat-Savarin: This round, flattish cow-milk cheese is made in

Normandy and is 75 per cent *matière grasse*. It was given its name by Monsieur Henri Androuet.

Brindamour: This is a rectangular goat-cheese from Corsica, flavoured with rosemary and the herb savory.

Broccio or *Brocciû*: Another Corsican cheese, made from ewe milk. Varying in size, it is usually slightly rounded and slightly piquant in flavour.

Brousse: There are various types of this cheese, which is made in Provence, sometimes from ewe milk or goat milk. It is a fresh, creamy cheese, the type that can be eaten with fruit as well as after a meal.

Cabêcou: This is a country cheese from various regions in the south-west, made from various types of milk, or goat and cow milk mixed. It is small, flat and rounded and pleasant when fresh. The name is supposed to come from the old Languedoc words signifying *petit chèvre*.

Caillebote: There are several types of cheese found bearing this name, some made from cows' milk, others utilizing goat or ewe milk. Usually it is a fresh, light cheese, one that can be served with fruit.

Camembert: This is one of the most famous cheeses in the world. It has certainly been made from the beginning of the eighteenth-century, possibly before then, but was brought to fame by Madame Marie Harel, wife of a farmer at Vimoutiers, near Camembert, at the end of the eighteenth century. She transmitted the secret of the special excellence of her cheese to her daughter, married to a man called Paynel, whose name was attached to what many considered to be the best Camemberts. The original Harel recipe produced a cheese with a bluish tinge, but after the mould used was changed, Camembert became pale lemon in colour. Another native of Vimoutiers, a Monsieur Ridel, invented a little wooden box in which the cheese could be sent to other countries without deteriorating, although nowadays the boxes in which the round cheese is presented are usually cardboard.

Before the war there was a statue of Marie Harel, erected at Vimoutiers by an American specialist who claimed that Camembert and Pilsen were responsible for many cures of stomach complaints in his clinic; this statue was destroyed in the war but a subscription from private individuals in the US enabled another one to be presented to the town in 1956, when the Prefect presiding was actually a gentleman with the tactlessly rival cheese name of 'Gervais'.

Camembert-like cheeses are made in other parts of France, as well as in many other countries. The 'real thing' is a seasonal speciality, at its best at the beginning of the year and really only to be served from November to June. One gourmand sniffing a fine specimen, said it smelled like 'the feet of God'.

Cancoillotte: This is a cow-milk cheese made in Franche Comté. But it is more of a cheese spread, as it is put into a little pot, mixed with salt water and gently cooked, with fresh butter added. It can be served warm on toast and it tends to be extremely strong. If offered any, take a small quantity unless you are sure you really like it.

Cantal: This is one of the great cheeses from Auvergne and made from cows' milk. It is a pressed cheese, matured for some months in a cool, damp place, such as a cave, meanwhile being regularly turned and brushed, rather like Cheddar. It is large, round, similar in shape to Cheddar, and quite tall. A good Cantal is a wonderful cheese but it can, unless well made, have many cracks in it, which spoil the appearance and it may also be too salty. The type of Cantal made in a mountain farm is superior to most of the Cantal produced by creameries.

Caprice des Dieux: This is a cow cheese, made from pasteurized milk in Champagne. It is soft and creamy, oval in shape, pleasant in flavour but not especially distinctive.

Carré: There are several cheeses referred to as *carré* because they are square in form. The most famous is certainly *Carré de l'Est*, made in Champagne and Lorraine. The milk is pasteurized cows' milk and there are two types, one described as *fleuri* after the yellow-orange colour of its rind or skin, the other *lavé*, meaning that the rind of the cheese has been washed.

Cendré: There are several cheeses bearing this name, the implication being that it is covered with ash — cinders. These cheeses are a speciality of Burgundy and Champagne and are made from cows' milk, some of them being like a stumpy tower or flattened round.

Chabichou: There are two types of this Poitevin cheese, which is made from goats' milk, one of them is a farmhouse cheese, the other a dairy product.

Chaource: This is a cow-milk cheese made in Champagne, round in shape, soft and creamy.

Charolais: This is a Burgundy cheese. It can be made from cow milk, goat milk or a mixture of both. It is a small cylindrical cheese, fairly definite in flavour; some people find it slightly nutty.

Chaumont: This is a cow-milk cheese from Champagne, cone-shaped, with a reddish skin, rather like a small tower with its top cut off. Similar cheeses are those of Langres, Époisses, Soumain-train, Munster and Gérome, some of which can be definitely strong, so make sure that you like such cheese before taking a large portion.

Chavignol: This small, round, pellet-like cheese comes from the Sancerre region in the upper Loire and, as it is made from goats' milk, it is often referred to as a *crottin* (dropping). M. Androuet's invaluable reference book says that a true *crottin* is a matured goat cheese, brownish in colour and rather dry, possibly having been macerated or steeped in white wine. But the more ordinary *crottins de Chavignol* are firm, tasty and, indeed, can be excellent cheeses for the person suspicious of the goat to start changing his or her mind about this maligned animal.

Chester: It is necessary to include this, because the name is often given to cheeses in large cylindrical shapes, made from pasteu-rized cows' milk. Also, the French often confuse *le Chester* — which I often have to explain does not exist in England — with le Cheddar or, even, le Cheshire, two great English classic cheeses. Chester is a mature cheese but I do not think it is particularly distinguished as to quality. It is said to have been first made in France immediately after the Second World War, its name presum-ably aimed at attracting the Allied forces.

Chèvre: Goat cheeses are made in many regions and can be of various shapes — rolls, rectangles, little balls — bearing names indicative of their origin, such as Chèvreton, Chèvrette and so on. If you hesitate, ask whether the cheese is *'Tres fort'* (very strong), *'Cremeux'* (creamy) or whether it is *'salé'* (salty), which will usually be known.

Comté or *Gruyère de Comté*: This is a cow-milk cheese, from Franche Comté and the Jura. It is a fine cheese and somewhat resembles a Gruyère in texture, although a little lighter in flavour. It is made in a large mould and is pressed, matured and brushed, being, in its finished version, like a wheel, with the sides slightly convex. Very often Gruyère or even Emmenthal are passed off as *Fromage de Comté*, because of the similarity, but if you can see the whole cheese, from which the portion will be cut, it is the convex edge of the 'wheel' that gives the clue as to whether it is genuine or not.

Coulommiers: This is, as might be expected, a type of Brie, made in the Île de France from cows' milk, but it is usually slightly cheaper than 'the king of cheeses'.

Demi-sel: This cheese, now known throughout the world, is made from pasteurized cows' milk and was first produced in Normandy.

It is mild in flavour and lightly creamy, put up in square packs.

Époisses: This is a cow-milk cheese, made in Burgundy, matured (in cheese caves) for three months and, apparently, washed down with *marc de Bourgogne* during one month. It is a flat, circular cheese, somewhat similar to the cheeses of Langres, St Florentin and Soumaintrain, and it can be enjoyed both in its matured form or as a fresh, creamy cheese. Napoleon is said to have liked it.

Excelsior and *Explorateur*: These cow-milk cheeses, very creamy, are made in Normandy and Île de France respectively. They are round, fairly small and usually presented in boxes. They are mild in flavour and can be extremely enjoyable. Related to them are branded cheeses such as Brillat-Savarin (*see p.70*), Boursin and Le Magnum. High in fat content (about 75 per cent *matière grasse*), they are good with most fine wines.

Fondu au Marc/Fondu au Raisin: This is a Savoie cheese of cows' milk, round and fairly thick in shape, with its skin consisting of impressed grape-pips. It is what one might describe as a *'fantasie'* cheese, of no particular distinction but pleasant enough. M. Androuet notes that it must not be confused with the Tomme au Marc which is not only different but protected by an *Appellation Controlée* (*see p.143*).

Fontainebleau: This is a light creamy cheese from the Île de France, made from cows' milk, very delicate in consistency, as cream is beaten into it. There are a number of similar versions.

Fromage Fort: This version of cheese quite often appears on the board today, usually in a little pot, and it therefore may be described as potted cheese. Recipes vary, but it can be a mixture of grated cheese plus oil or stock, brandy, wine and various herbs — the result looks creamy and fairly neutral, but the flavour can be intense and strong. It is best to inquire about this before you help yourself to a pot of anything with the word *fort* (strong) in its name. The same applies to any *fromage en pot*.

Fourme d'Ambert: This Auvergne cheese, made from cows' milk, gets its name because the word *fourme* signifies the mould in which it is made. It is lightly pressed and matured for about three months and has a greyish exterior. There are a number of *fourme* cheeses made in both farmhouses and dairies, all fairly definite in flavour, although some people find certain of them a little sharp.

Galette de la Chaise-Dieu: This is a flat, thin cheese (hence the name *galette*) made from goat milk and fairly pronounced in flavour, but not necessarily strong, according to descriptions, although as I have never had it I cannot be definite. It comes from the Auvergne.

Gaperon/Gapron: This is an Auvergne cheese made from skimmed cows' milk, like a ball and firm in shape, tasting vaguely of herbs and dry rather than fatty. It traditionally has a flavour of garlic.

Géromé: Cow-milk cheese from Lorraine, round and rick-shaped, reddish on the outside and definitely strong. A *Géromé Anisé* has aniseed pressed onto the outside.

Gournay: This is a Normandy cheese made from cows' milk, small, round and flat. There are several varieties, but in general it is slightly salty and mild in flavour.

Guéret: This is a cow-milk cheese, made from skimmed milk, from the Creuse. It is round and flat, firm even when first made, later becoming hard, so that it can be used in cooking.

Jonchée Niortaise: This is a fresh goat-milk cheese, getting its name from Niort in Poitou, although it is made in other regions in the west of France. It is fresh, moderately creamy, delicately flavoured.

Laguiole-Aubrac: A Rouergue cow-milk cheese, pressed and matured, sometimes for as long as six months, made in the mountains of the south-west. It is large and round, with a greyish skin, firm and somewhat assertive as to smell. If you like Cantal you will probably like Laguiole.

Laumes: A cow-milk cheese from Burgundy, bearing the name of where it is made. It has a dumpy squared-off shape and is apparently somewhat similar to Époisses, Soumaintrain and Saint Florentin in taste.

Roquefort cheese may be excellent eating — it is not pleasant to the nose. I left Marvejols on my way to Paris. Three little parties were in the same carriage with me, all prepared for a night journey. We left Marvejols at 3.10 p.m. and were to arrive in Paris at 5.15 the following morning. All the three little parties were provided for the night — for supper, collation at midnight, early breakfast with supplies of Roquefort cheese in an advanced condition of ripeness, exhaling a very emphatic odour. I held out till shortly before midnight, and then fled — to an hotel at Clermont, to continue my journey next day, sans Roquefort cheese.

SABINE BARING-GOULD, *The Deserts of Southern France*, Vol.I, 1894

75

Livarot: A Normandy cheese made from cows' milk, sometimes referred to as *Lisieux*. It ripens for about three months, when its flavour becomes really assertive. It is cylindrical, bound up with reed-like bits of vegetation and can be quite large and fat in some presentations. It is said to be one of the most ancient of Normandy cheeses.

Mamirolle: A Franche Comté cheese made from pasteurized cows' milk, pressed and matured for about eight weeks, on the strong side, with a slightly rubbery consistency.

Maroilles: This cow-milk cheese is brownish-yellow on the outside, deep yellow within, square and substantial, with a very pronounced, rather rich flavour, and really comes from the edge of the Champagne region. It has been made at least since the twelfth century, when the Abbot of Maroilles decreed that the four villages nearby should make cheese from the St John's Day (24 June) milk and give it to their parish priests on St Rémi's Day (1 October), to be sent later to him. Even today, Maroilles is the cheese traditionally provided for the vintagers in the Champagne vineyards. It is a matured cheese, the flavour deriving partly from frequent brushing of the rind and washing it with beer. This, as might be supposed, gives the cheese a very distinctive taste. All sorts of famous people have sung its praises, including Philip Augustus, François I, Fenelon and Turenne. Maroilles is also sometimes referred to as Manicamp. Other types of Maroilles are: Sorbais, Monceau, Mignon, Quart, Maroilles Gris or Gris de Lille, Fromage fort de Béthune, Vieux Puant or Vieux Lille, which is a rindless cheese, very strong; le Dauphin, which is shaped like a crescent and is flavoured with tarragon and cloves and is said to have received its name after being presented to Louis XIV's son; Boulette d'Avesne, or Boulette de Cambrai, shaped like a pear; Baguette de Thiérache, like a little loaf, and Losange de Thiérache. Le larron, or *fromage d'ours*, is a skimmed milk-cheese of the same type.

Meilleraye: From Brittany, this cow-milk cheese gets its name from the Trappist establishment where it is made. It is thick and rectangular with a yellowish skin and resembles some of the other cheeses made in religious establishments.

Metton: This skimmed milk cow-cheese comes from Franche Comté and is generally used to make Cancoillotte (*see p.72*). If you do find it on the cheese-board, where it will look like largish pellets, remember that it is extremely strong in flavour.

Mignot: A Normandy cow-milk cheese, sometimes square, sometimes round, with a reddish skin. It may be either fresh (*blanc*) or ripened (*passé*). I have not tried it but apparently it is somewhat similar to Livarot (*p.76*).

Monsieur/Monsieur Fromage/Fromage de Monsieur: A Normandy cheese, made from enriched cows' milk, round, flat and quite plump, fairly small. It is quite creamy, pleasant with fine wines. Its name comes from a farmer called Fromage, who evolved it at the end of the nineteenth century.

Montoire: A goat-milk cheese from the region around Vendôme. It is like a small tree-stump in shape, with a definite but not too strong flavour.

Montrachet: This goat-milk cheese comes from Burgundy but must not be confused with the more famous wine. It seems to be of moderate character, cylindrical in shape. Unfortunately, I have never tried it but M. Androuet says that it is somewhat similar to many other goat cheeses that are slightly creamy.

Munster: This is possibly the most important Alsace cheese, taking its name from the region around the town of the same name. It is made from cows' milk, the farmhouse type being produced up in the mountains, although large quantities are now made in dairies. It is round and flattish, but there are both small and quite large versions, and it has a reddish outer skin. It is kept for a few weeks to ripen — to gather its strength might, in this context, be a more appropriate term! — and during its conservation in cheese stores it is washed down several times. Apparently it is of considerable antiquity and was probably first made in the various religious establishments of the region. Anyone not already familiar with it should be warned that, although it may look soft and even creamy, it is very strong indeed, making its presence definitely known if you buy some and take it in a railway carriage or a car. If you put it in the boot of a car, make sure it isn't near anything to which it may impart its smell, such as a raincoat or canvas luggage, however much you swathe it in apparently impermeable wrappings. Do not let it get overripe, when it becomes violently acrid and unpleasant. The smaller versions are slightly milder in flavour and smell.

Nantais/Nantes/Fromage du Curé: A cow-milk cheese from Brittany supposedly evolved by a parish priest in the Vendée during the nineteenth century. It is square with rounded corners, apparently resembling other cheeses made in religious establishments such as St Paulin, is pressed but not matured, has a yellow skin and is lightly creamy in consistency.

Neufchâtel: This Normandy cheese is made from cows' milk, can be square, cube-like, rectangular, even heart-shaped or other fancy shapes, and is supposed by some to be the best cheese produced in the Pays de Bray. It may be eaten when it has been kept for only a few days, in which case it is creamy, soft and mild, and is called Neufchâtel fleuri; if allowed to ferment and ripen it is known as Neufchâtel affiné, and is fairly strong. It is always a small cheese, but may be of different shapes: one like a little roll may be simply referred to as a *bonde, boudon* or *bondart*. A cheese that is square will be *le carré;* a heart *le coeur; le Gournay, la briquette* and *le Malakoff* are others. Bourgain is a fresh Neufchâtel cheese, very soft and light, Ancien Impérial or Petit Carré are other fresh cheeses, and Carré affiné a mature cheese. Incheville, Rouennaise, Villedieu and Maromme are local names for the same type of cheese.

Oelenberg: This Alsace cheese is made of cows' milk, pressed and matured for about two months. It is a small, thickish round shape, resembling the cheeses made in other religious establishments. The Abbey d'Oelenberg is the only place where this particular cheese is made and apparently — because I have never been able to try it — it is rather more distinctive in character than most.

Olivet: There are two versions of this cheese, which is made in the Orléanais region from cows' milk. Olivet bleu has a bluish rind and is in season from October to June. Olivet cendré has an ashy skin and is in season from November to July. It is flattish and rounded in shape. The cheese is somewhat elastic in consistency, but can have a good, slightly Coulommiers-like flavour (*see p.73*).

Passe-l'An: This Languedoc cheese is made from pasteurized cows' milk and I gather from M. Androuet that it was evolved in France when imports of Parmesan from Italy were stopped, so, although I have never tasted it, I imagine it being similar to this Italian cheese. It is made in a large mould, becomes hard and therefore can serve for many culinary purposes, as well as being eaten by itself. It seems to be wheel-shaped, with convex sides.

Persillé: There are several types of this cheese, which can be of goats' milk or a mixture of cow and goat. It is matured for about two months generally and is usually cylindrical in shape, with a greyish rind. It tends to have a slightly sharp flavour and the 'parsley' of its name refers to the slightly greenish speckles in the flesh of the cheese. The east of France, especially Savoie, seems to be where most Persillé cheeses are made.

Petit Suisse: This cheese, made nowadays throughout France, is the product of cows' milk plus cream. It is fresh, light in texture and agreeable, if not particularly distinguished in taste. It was evolved by a farmer's wife, Madame Hérould, at Auchy-en-Bray, near Gournay, about the middle of the nineteenth century. Her cheese achieved a wide reputation because, instead of selling it locally, she sent it straight to the Paris markets. Her Swiss cowman suggested that it could be improved by adding a little cream to the fresh milk, and because of this it got its name. A clerk in the Paris offices of the purchasers of the cheese saw the possibilities, and went into business with Madame Hérould; this was Monsieur Gervais who persuaded her to start a cheese factory at Gerrières, and arranged the distribution of the cheese in Paris by means of cabs having yellow wheels, which naturally attracted great attention. There are two sizes of Petit Suisse. Pommel is another brand name for a similar type of cheese, and *demi sel* and *double crème* are the general types of fresh cream cheese and richer cream cheese respectively. Mesnil, Castel, Suprême, Excelsior, Parfait, and le Curé de Bonneville are other types of fresh cream cheeses, all excellent when really freshly-made. In France they are often served with sugar and/or thick cream and eaten with a spoon.

Picodon: There are several cheeses bearing place-names prefaced by this word. The cheese seems usually to be made from goat milk, the cheeses being slightly firm in texture and similar to small goat cheeses from other regions.

Pigouille: This cheese comes from the west side of France, made from cow, goat or ewe milk, rounded and flat in shape and is a light fresh and creamy version of other fresh cheeses.

Poivre d'âne: This is a Provençal cheese which appears to be made from whatever milk is available, matured for about a month, wrapped in twigs of savory. It is very similar to Banon (*see p.67*).

Pont l'Évêque: A Normandy cow-milk cheese and a famous one. It is oblong in form with a yellow skin, rather strong in taste, and is supposedly of very ancient origin.

Port du Salut/Port Salut: This is a little outside the strictly Norman cheeses, but is bound to be met with in the region. There are two sorts of cow-milk cheese involved: Port du Salut is that made by the Trappist monks at Entrammes, near Laval, who produce 200,000 cheeses a year. Other Trappists, however, also other cheese makers in France and throughout the world are able to make and market a cheese under the name of Port Salut, which, unlike Port du Salut, is not a trademark.

Puant: Any cheese which has this word as part of it or that is described by the waiter as *'puant'* should be approached with hesitation — the term means 'stinker'. There is one which appears to be Maroilles soaked in brine and beer.

Reblochon: A cow-milk cheese from Savoie, lightly pressed and kept for a few weeks. It is now enormously popular and rightly so, because the high pastures from which it comes make good cheese, like those from the lush meadows in the north of France. It is rounded and flat in shape. The flavour is mild, the texture lightly creamy. At its best a good Reblochon can be very good indeed. The origin of the name is interesting: in former times the shepherds in the mountain pastures would not milk the animals dry on the day when the bailiff came round, keeping back this milk or *'rebloche'* for their personal perks. Although the cheese has been made for hundreds of years, it is because of this slightly underhand method of production that it has only recently become widely known. Some cheeses similar to Reblochon are now made, including one called Chambaraud.

Rigotte: There appear to be several sorts of this, the one I know being the goat cheese of Auvergne, a round, flattish mixture of cow and goat milk or, when it appears in a rectangular shape, La Brique or Chevrotin Cabion. The Rigotte de Condrieu is a cylindrical cheese.

Rocamadour: This, in my experience, is a goat cheese, but it can apparently also be made from ewe milk. It is a small, round, flattish shape similar to many of the little goat cheeses found throughout France.

Rogeret des Cevennes: This is a Languedoc goat cheese which I have never tried, although Lamastre, where it is apparently famous, should be a name well known to lovers of great restaurants. It is another of the small, round goat cheeses typical of many regions.

Roquefort: This ewe-milk cheese, from the Rouergue, is one of the great blue cheeses of the world. The milk is collected during the lambing season and after being heated is mixed with rennet from the lambs' stomachs; the curd coagulates and is drained, then it is interspersed with crumbs of bread on which the culture of *Penicillium glaucum Roqueforti* is growing and which makes the blue veining. The cheese is then salted, pressed and brought to the Roquefort caves for maturing in the cool humidity. It cannot be made anywhere else, though the milk can be drawn from ewes throughout the region and even from animals of the Pyrenees and Corsica.

Tradition says that Roquefort was discovered by a shepherd who left a piece of bread and ordinary cheese forgotten in one of the caves and, coming on it later, ate it and found it delicious. Cheese appears to have been made in Roquefort for about a thousand years, kings of France from Charlemagne onwards having praised it, its fame spread widely. Good Roquefort is not like any other of the great blue cheeses, but it is only fair to say that, when a chunk of it has been either bought at the wrong time or left far too long on the cheese-board of a restaurant, it may be a disappointment. People who are not in general amateurs of blue cheeses should not dismiss Roquefort after a single disappointing experience — I myself never liked any great blue cheese until I was fortunate enough to be given four of the famous ones when each was absolutely as it should be; from then on, I saw why the fame of such cheeses has spread. Roquefort at its best is great!

Ruffec: This is a Poitou goat-milk cheese, small, round and flat, very pleasant, lightly soft and creamy.

Saint Benoît: A cow-milk cheese from the Orléanais, possibly originally made at the great Benedictine abbey, the name of which it bears. It is a circular dumpy shape, soft in texture, somewhat similar to Olivet (*see p.78*), and its surface is rubbed with salt and charcoal.

Sainte Maure: This goat-milk cheese comes from Touraine, and is a long cylinder in shape. It has a blue-grey skin and is white and slightly assertive in flavour — very good with many wines. There are two types of Sainte Maure, the farmhouse or *fermier* and the *laitier* made in dairies.

Saint Florentin: A Burgundy cow-milk cheese, round and flat, somewhat similar to those of Époisses, Langres and others of the region.

Saint Marcellin: This is a cow-milk cheese from the Isère region, matured for several weeks, round and flattish in shape, with a bluish grey skin. It is a slightly lightly creamy cheese, fresh enough in flavour to be a good accompaniment to fine wine. Nowadays it is made in dairies, although it used to be a goat-milk cheese, very much a peasant product. There are proud traditions associated with it, especially from the time in the fifteenth century when the future King Louis XI, then the Dauphin, got lost out hunting and was given refreshment by peasants, consisting of bread and cheese — the poor man was obviously in need of succour, as he had previously been confronted by a gigantic wild boar; the wood-cutters, who had driven off the animal and shared their picnic with him, were rewarded with titles and promised a large sum of money — which they never got. However, it is a pleasant story to associate with a good cheese.

Saint Nectaire: This cheese comes from the Mont Dore region, the finest farmhouse version from pedigree cows of the Salers and

Ferrandaises breeds. A semi-hard cheese, it is matured on mats of rye straw, often in cellars below Clermont-Ferrand, during which process it often develops a yellowish-red crust. It is round and flattish in form and sometimes apparently the crust can be greyish. Murol is a type of this cheese, with a hole in the centre of its rounded disc shape. Vachard is another type.

Saint-Rémy: This is a Lorraine cow-milk cheese, squarish in shape and somewhat similar to the cheeses of Munster, Geromé and Langres — in other words, strong.

Sassenage: This is a cheese from the Vercors, usually made of cows' milk, sometimes mixed with that of the goat. It is a blue cheese somewhat similar to certain other blue cheeses.

Soumaintrain: A Burgundy cow-milk cheese, round and flat with a brownish skin similar to Époisses (*p.74*) and Langres, therefore strong, made in the regions of the Aube and Yonne. There is also a fresh creamy type.

Tomme: There are many types of 'Tomme' (which term refers to the mould in which the cheese is made). It is not usually very large, but is rounded and fairly thick. The type of milk used, like the character of the cheese itself, depends on where the cheese is made, up in the mountains or in more lush grazing country. It tends to be a cheese of eastern France. Sometimes the exterior is washed with *marc* or impressed with cumin or grape-pips.

Tournon-Saint-Pierre: This Touraine cheese is made from goats' milk and is cone-shaped, the skin being greyish.

Vacherin: There are several sorts of *vacherin*, which, as the name implies, are cheeses made from cows' milk. At its best, it can be a delicious fresh-tasting cheese, of slightly creamy texture and delicate after-taste. These are the cheeses made by mountain people, wishing to make a creamy, slightly solid but unctuous and light-textured cheese. Those made in the high pastures are thought to be slightly aromatic. This type of cheese should, ideally, be eaten when fairly fresh: when drying, its texture risks becoming rubbery, its flavour dull or just vaguely 'cheesy'.

Valençay: This is a cheese from the Indre region; made from goat milk, it is like a stunted pyramid in form, sometimes grey-skinned, occasionally orange, very white and firm in texture. It has a particularly keen fresh flavour and, when at its best, is definitely something to eat when finishing fine wine. Opt for the farmhouse rather than the dairy-made product if any choice is possible.

Vendôme: There are two cheeses from the region around Orléans, the blue variety and a '*cendré*' (ash-looking rind), both made from cows' milk. The shape is a thickish round disc, the flavour slightly sharp, more so than one might expect from a cow cheese. It is particularly suited to accompanying the crisp red wines of the Loire.

Some of these cheeses, including all the great names, actually have their own *Appellation d'Origine Contrôlée*. This, of course, means that the area and method of production are subject to definition, but it also means that the price of the product may be a bit higher than something not exactly the same, not possessing the AOC, but nevertheless — if you can get an informed shop-keeper or waiter to recommend it — being as good (if not even better). But for that you must rely on the knowledge of the locals and their benevolence to the traveller.

So Louis XVI built her (Marie Antoinette) the famous dairy . . . in which she could play at milkmaids, making cheeses in porcelain pots, while he returned to his own 376 moutons, imported from Spain, on the trotter, for stock breeding. Louis XVI was not to know that he was creating a line more enduring than his own, for the Rambouillet coat of arms bears a sheep to this day (and an interesting motto), and the descendants of those merinos still live on the estate at the Bergerie Nationale. . . . I really wanted to know what sort of cheese Marie Antoinette made in her dairy, and what it tasted like . . . she probably made a soft cheese like Camembert or Brie that did not require a great deal of pressing, rather than something like a Cheddar where the physique of the milkmaid is important (. . . "the bigger the dairy-maid, the better the cheese"). Though I suppose she could always have called a footman to put his foot on it.

TOM VERNON, *Fat Man on a Bicycle*, Michael Joseph, 1981
[The 'interesting motto' on the coat of arms is *"Semper erecta"*. P.V.P.]

6

Where to Eat — What and How

French catering establishments may often bear names similar to those in other countries, but be somewhat different in style and as regards what you can eat where. It took me some while to sort out the difference between a bar, a café and a buffet — and to stop being surprised at seeing a French mama ordering *'un porto'* when with her family in a *salon de thé*.

Un bar without qualification is a place where one goes for a possibly quick drink, maybe standing up at the counter (*le zinc*). *Un bar comptoir* is precisely this — a place for a drink where you stand up. *Un bar dégustation* may have tables and chairs, so may an ordinary bar. In large bars you may be able to get a snack or sandwich, although a French bar is not really an eating-place. Large bars may also serve coffee, although bars in general are not where one goes for this. The sign 'American bar' seems vague: you might get a cocktail there — but it might not be the version you are accustomed to. It might also be somewhat smart — or not. One can always telephone from a bar, although the instrument may not be arranged so that your conversation cannot be overheard. If it is actually on the bar, people will unashamedly listen.

Un buffet is a restaurant primarily for quick meals, sometimes including both a snack counter and tables. The term is mainly used for eating-places on stations and at airports, although the big terminals may also have restaurants as well.

Une brasserie originally meant a brewery — hence the name implies somewhere serving beer, together with sandwiches and snacks. This is a place where you may find draught beer (*bière sous pression*), seldom available in ordinary bars. A *brasserie* may also serve light meals and other drinks, including wines and coffee. Some brasseries are fairly smart — and, therefore, not cheap.

Un café is a place where families may go to eat and drink, or anyone may have a single drink. If there is a menu posted outside and the place describes itself as a café-restaurant, full meals will be served and, according to its size, it may also serve ices, snacks, sandwiches and feature several different menus, plus an *à la carte*. The term *vin compris* on a menu signifies that wine is included in the price of the meal, either *en carafe* or from a bottle, when you may help yourself. Families go to meet friends in cafés; cards and various games, such as backgammon, may be played and the waiter can usually supply writing materials for people catching up with their correspondence. Cafés range from the simplest sort to the large, smart, expensive kind, such as the Café de la Paix in Paris, where food can be first-rate. The charm of the French café is that a soft drink or cup of coffee can be made to last for hours, while the untroubled customer watches the world go by.

Un restaurant serves meals, not drinks only. Usually, too, food is only served within the midday and evening meal-times, although a café-restaurant may have snacks and other food available most of the time it is open. *Casse-croûte* (snack) *à toutes heures*, or *repas à toutes heures* implies service of some form of food at any time. *Repas rapide* is another sign, sometimes put up on the side of main roads. On autoroutes, the larger stopping places usually have both a restaurant and a snack-bar. You can imbibe with your food or simply have a drink — but use discretion, because spot checks are frequently set up by the police on main roads.

In towns, there may be seen the sign *déjeuner homme d'affaires* — businessman's lunch; this implies a meal that is good value and will not take much time; although, of course, apart from the mere

---

Arles. Hôtel du Forum in the Place du Forum. Garage. Tourists should insist on having rooms on first, second, or third floors, ... and having dinner served hot. Sanitation modern, but service poor. A first-class modern hotel is much needed. [Annotation in pencil: 'Hôtel du Nord excellent, 1925.]

ROSE G. KINGSLEY, *In the Rhône Country*, 1910

---

snack or sandwich, a meal in France invariably does take longer than the Anglo-Saxon might expect.

Although I have not noted the 'minimum charge' practice in France, it should be borne in mind that any restaurant (as opposed to a snack-bar) will be reluctant to serve you with a single dish unless this is fairly substantial and includes salad and other trimmings. And such a single course can cost as much as a small *prix fixe* (*see p.39*). If you do want just a snack, then go to a café or bar, or ask if the restaurant has a section for this sort of fare. There is a tremendous variety of cafés and restaurants, but most display menus, both the set menus and the *à la carte*, outside, so that you can get an idea of the sort of fare and the price involved.

Un salon de thé — unless it really is an English tea-room, kept by ex-patriots — is somewhat akin to what we might call a coffee-house. Sometimes it is an extension of a *pâtisserie* (pastry shop). Tea, coffee, soft drinks, ices, sometimes sandwiches and small savoury snacks, may be served and sometimes alcoholic drinks too — often sweetish ones. A *salon de thé* can be an elegant meeting-place for prosperous ladies and their families — if so, it won't be cheap.

Une buvette is a place where you can get a drink. One often sees the sign out in the country. Mineral water, beer, *vin ordinaire* and, sometimes, tea, coffee and ices may be available. Occasionally there may be some form of sandwich. Essentially a *buvette* is for the traveller's casual refreshment. Sometimes, either on a *buvette* or small café, there may be a sign *Ici on peut apporter son manger*, or *On reçoit avec provisions*: this signifies that you can bring your own food and eat it at their tables, with cutlery and tableware supplied, as well as chairs. You only pay for the drinks. This is a great convenience for travellers wishing to be spared the major chores of a picnic and can be a considerable saving of time and trouble for those travelling with small children.

Un bistro(t) is a small restaurant. The theory is that you can get a meal quickly. The word originates from the Allies' occupation of Paris after the Battle of Waterloo in 1815, when the Russian soldiers would call for quick service — the Russian word being 'bistro'. Today, however, there are bistros and bistros, some of them definitely chic and expensive.

Une guinguette is a refreshment pavilion, usually with music and, sometimes, dancing. There may be a sign *'guinguette'* along-side a well-equipped swimming-pool; it is a snack eating-place. The name is supposed to derive from a type of grape formerly grown in the suburbs of Paris and from which a sharpish cheap wine was made, on sale in the taverns outside the city walls. This is why the dictionary indicates that a *guinguette* is in the suburbs of a city. The term *bal* means a public dance — what we might term a hop — and the word *sauterie* is definitely a down-market dance, sometimes used instead of the international 'disco'.

The words *estaminet* (which might be translated as pub), *hostellerie* (hotel), *taverne* (tavern), and *auberge* (café hotel) are all somewhat archaic terms, although they are still in use. But beware — the use of any one of these terms can mean that the establishment is definitely expensive, possibly luxurious and is cultivating a clientèle who like a touch of the 'olde world' atmosphere and are prepared to pay for it. *Auberge*, however, can also mean a truly modern eating-place. Note, too, that the term *rustique* need not mean 'simple' — it can imply costly country-style décor and fare.

Un cabaret means a small drinking place, rather than the sort of thing Anglo-Saxons may understand by the word. For a night-club the term is *boîte de nuit*. A *cabaret* can also be a rather smart informal eating-place. *La terrasse*, in connection with anywhere to eat or drink, means that tables and chairs are set up in the open — although the *terrasse* need not be a raised, paved terrace. *Volière*, when seen as part of the description of a restaurant, means that there will be an aviary or pen for ornamental birds.

Un hôtel does not invariably have a restaurant, although hotels are usually able to supply continental breakfast. If there is a restaurant then there is usually — but not always — a bar of some

---

À propos the 18th century, he comments 'Lady Blessington writes that a bad inn "where the sleeping and sitting room are destitute of all comforts" can generally be relied on to produce a passable meal. In England . . . it is precisely the opposite.'

Quoting the nineteenth-century Colonel Pinkney – 'In no country but America and England have they any idea of that first of comfort to the wearied traveller, a clean, well-made bed. I speak from woeful experience when I advise every traveller to consider a pair of sheets and a counterpane as necessary a part of his luggage as a change of shirt.'

RODERICK CAMERON, *The Golden Riviera*, Editions Limited Honolulu — originally Weidenfeld & Nicholson, 1975

sort, although this may not be a place to sit and you may have to order your drinks from the table. The sign *chambre d'hôte* outside a house means 'bed and breakfast', but do not confuse this with the phrase *chambre garnie* — which you are unlikely to see written down; *une chambre garnie* does not mean an attractive room, but one which is provided with a person of the required sex to enhance its appeal.

Even a little experience can prompt the traveller wondering where to eat, although there are some exterior signs to beware. Unfortunately, a crowd of cars bearing British or US registration numbers can mean that the place caters indifferently for those who want omelettes, steaks and salad, or over-elaborate second-rate supposed *haute cuisine*. It can be useful to see certain credit card and gastronomic societies' signs outside, but it is significant that the *Michelin Guide* never permits itself to be advertised in this way. Cars with the regional number-plates indicate that the locals patronize the establishment, which is a good sign; ask at the garage or postcard shop or even a policeman where they take their fiancée/wife/family to eat and convince them that you do want to enjoy typical fare at modest cost. Some things that make me hesitate — especially when I don't want to spend too much — include: obvious 'handcrafted' furnishings, menus written on the back of old parchments, wine lists with velvet covers, lots of wrought-iron in the décor, red and white tablecloths and elaborately folded napkins and the red, blue and white faïence de Gien, plus staff in vaguely archaic uniforms. These are the possible clip-joints, whose walls are covered with framed menus of elaborate meals served on occasions of which one has never heard to supposedly important persons whom one will never meet. There may well be hunting-prints in the bar and slightly 'naughty' eighteenth-century pictures in the cloakrooms. Indeed, the description *'anciens meubles'* (antique furnishings) can mean a definite tourist trap — or, sometimes, a place where people go discreetly to meet each other. It is not necessarily unpleasant to be the only *bona fide* diner or family party in such places, but it can be extremely expensive. One friend adds to the list of danger signals any furniture of the Louis XIII or Louis XV (mock or genuine), another says menus that unfurl like scrolls over the table and, certainly, a wine-list that is long in illustrious names but gives no information as regards vintages or shippers — and may well have been subject to revisions of price that the unwary will not discover until the bill arrives. My personal detestation of background music (often badly reproduced) and 'atmospheric' (which signifies insufficient) lighting are, I know, shared by many as well. For it has to be admitted, alas, that today it is possible to eat indifferently, even badly, in France as anywhere else. The easy availability of junk foods and the advent of tourists who really know little about gastronomy, have lowered many standards; chefs get ideas they cannot always realize, hoteliers cater for the big spenders who are impressed by vulgar décor and piped music — dining-rooms drenched in Strauss waltzes are unlikely to be temples of gastronomy — *sommeliers* impress by their *tastevins* and not by their knowledge of what is in the cellar.

So — if possible, try to eat either at the very top establishments (which may often have modest and very worthwhile menus), with serious traditions and reputations to maintain, or, as most of us must do, eat where the locals go. And, in addition to thanking those responsible for giving you pleasure and even a meek 'experience', write your impressions to the gastronomic guides. A recommendation, personal or by letter (and you need not write in French) can achieve much by way of encouragement to those who are trying to maintain their gastronomic standards. They need this as much as they need a full restaurant — and, with luck, they will have a few appreciative customers who may well become *anciens amis de la maison* (friends of the house).

Making Reservations in Hotels and Restaurants

If you wish to eat at a particular restaurant, it is always as well to book. Indeed, at a weekend and even more so on any public holiday (*see p.44*) it is essential. The solitary traveller, male or female, is very often turned away with a brusque '*Complet*'. If you are in any doubt, get wherever you stayed the night before to telephone and make the booking for you — if they can. It may be necessary for you to ask them to make you up a picnic or for you to buy one early in the day.

Any hotel that has a restaurant will probably inquire, when a booking is being made, '*C'est pour diner?*' ('Will you be dining here?') before they will agree to give you a room. Unless you can say, in good French, that you are having dinner with friends elsewhere — and ideally give a high-sounding name to back this — you had better eat where you sleep. This is understandable, although it can be tiresome if the place has an interesting local restaurant and the hotel is of the somewhat insipid 'international cuisine' category. If, of course, you really are dining with friends, get them to deal with the reservation for you and explain. Being on the spot, they will be able to convince the management.

Even many of my French friends carry with them an alphabet that facilitates telephone and spelling out proper names. I found this in the General Post Office in Mâcon years ago, when I decided, during a session when I was trying to ring up an hotel in the next *département*, that, what with the traffic and the reactions of the switchboard lady, it would probably be easier to place a reversed charge call to the Kremlin! Here it is:

Anatole
Berthe
Célestin
Désirée
Eugène
Émile (use this when spelling any French word with an acute 'é')
François
Gaston
Henri
Irma
Joseph
Kléber
Louis
Marcel
Nicolas
Oscar
Pierre
Quintal (if this is misunderstood as 'Cantal', try 'Quimper — *comme en Bretagne*')
Raoul
Suzanne
Thérèse
Ursule
Victor
William (pronounced 'double vay')
Xavier (say this like 'Zavier')
Yvonne
Zoé

Shopping — including Le Pique-nique and 'Le self-catering'

It was Napoleon who said that an army marches on its stomach and I certainly travel on mine. Before I leave, I make lists of things that it may be worthwhile to bring back — but I also take the means of sustaining life along with me, whether I am going by car or travelling via boat, train or plane, in the form of iron rations. Ports and airports may have a good selection of food and drink, but prices can be high and queues long.

What to Bring Home

Check, in advance, as to what you may *not* bring home — potatoes, uncooked game, which risk being confiscated in the UK, and, in other countries, raw meat, seeds and flowers or plants are also prohibited. Contact the Customs Officers *before* you go if you have plans to bring back, say, some special seed potatoes, fruit or have been invited to a 'shoot'.

Markets out in the country will usually have stalls selling kitchenware and pots, dairy produce, honey, vegetables and herbs. Airport shops in France can be attractive — but, as already mentioned, prices can be high, although sometimes, if you are buying gifts, the pretty packaging can make this worthwhile. If you buy hand-made chocolates, remember that these may not contain preservative — keep them cool on the journey and do not wait too long before eating them. You will probably buy bread but, alas, the delicious *ficelles* and *baguettes* and rolls lose their crispness rapidly, although country bread and certain loaves do remain freshly crusty for several days and, even after this, merely go hard, not mouldy. (*See p.103*). Airport shops and ports, also the various shops at service stations on autoroutes, are sometimes useful for buying local produce, such as pâtés, sweets and biscuits and various things in cans and bottles — but again, these are seldom cheap.

What About Buying Wines and Spirits?

See *p.157* for advice about these. Check on what you may bring in free of duty before you go and, if you have a fondness for a particular French spirit, this is possibly worthwhile importing within your allowed duty-free bottles. Should you buy in quantity, then be sure to get a detailed bill and declare what you have. Remember, by the way, that although Britain is now a member of the EEC, this does not mean that your French friends can send you wines and spirits regardless — it can be embarrassing to get a large bill for 'duty' and a great inconvenience if you have to go and fetch the present from a port or airport, even more so if you have to pay for its delivery to your home. If somebody wishes to send you something alcoholic as a gift, ask them to do this care of someone in the wine trade, who will know the form.

Buying Drinks for Consumption in France

You should take your own corkscrew. If you buy quantities of bottled water, you may want an opener — *un décapsulateur* — although sometimes you get this with the bottles. The same applies to branded fizzy drinks, tonic and soda water. (*See pp.191–3* for the French table waters — you may pay more for the world-famous branded varieties, even when these are made under licence in France.) If you buy large bottles of such non-alcoholic beverages, it is useful to have one of the stoppers that seal in the fizz. You can buy these at virtually any supermarket and they work by a lever being pulled so that a rubber band expands and seals the bottle. They are cheap — and they will seal not merely a bottle of Champagne but a magnum — which the 'push on and clamp down' rather smarter *'bouchons de Champagne'* will not do. In fact, although no one can explain why, a teaspoon handle, inserted in the open neck of a bottle of any fizzy drink, will keep it fizzy until you have drunk almost all of it. So, shop at the co-op or the sort of local country shop that has everything and, if you run out of stoppers, remember the teaspoon (metal).

Drinks in litre bottles may have stars marked on their sides. These and some other bottles of inexpensive beverages are *bouteilles consignées* — returnable bottles on which you will get a small sum *'pour la consigne'*. If bottles that you buy have only the metal capsule and then a plastic stopper, use an ordinary cork or the sort of 'stopper cork' (for which I can find no French equivalent — it probably doesn't exist in France) such as is often used for port and sherry: it is a tapered cork with a metal top, which can be used to seal up a bottle of wine.

Many supermarkets have a *'tirage'* or serve-yourself drinks department, to which you can take any starred bottles, hold them under a dispenser and get them filled with whatever inexpensive wine is on sale. You will then need a cork or some form of stopper. You are not likely to discover any astonishing wine experience by drinking such beverages, but they are convenient and, if you and whoever is with you drink a fair amount of wine, the refund of the *bouteilles consignées* can mount up agreeably.

How Much is What?

Many people will now be accustomed to the metric system — it really is so much simpler than the remnants of medieval measures that are inflicted on some still at school. If you can't easily adapt, however, the following may simplify shopping in France:

1 kilogramme (abbreviated to 1 kilo or 1 kg.) is about 2.2 lb. (UK) so a kilo of anything is a generous 2 lb.

100 grammes is equal to about 3¾ oz. — or a 'short quarter of a pound'.

1 litre is a very generous 1½ pints (UK) and 1.759 of a UK quart.

You can usually indicate how much of a food you want by pointing — a slice, which is *une tranche*, which will willingly be cut as required. With fruit and vegetables or dry goods, *une poignée* (a handful) can be a guide, although the person serving you may have a large hand. If you are wanting to buy something for a specific number of people, state *pour quatre/cinq/six personnes* or more. But remember, your appetite and those of your friends may not be as robust as that of the French supplier — it may be prudent to allow a slightly lower quantity if in doubt, especially if you are buying fish or anything quickly perishable.

Shops

Faire les achats or *Faire les emplettes* is to do the shopping — of any sort. In general: *un magasin* is a shop or store; *un grand magasin* is a department store; *un supermarché* or *une grande surface* is a supermarket.

Un débit is a retail shop — hence *un débit de tabac* is a tobaconnist, who may also sell stamps. (*See also p.96*).

Débiter is to sell retail.

Une boutique is a small shop — not necessarily a fashion or clothes shop.

Un boutiquier or *un marchand* are both expressions for a shop-keeper.

Le quartier commerçant is the shopping centre, whereas *Le marché* is where the market is held.

Une boulangerie is a baker's shop. The word *Viennoiserie* means that fancy breads, *brioches* and possibly plain cakes, such as madeleines, may also be stocked.

Un blanchisserie is a laundry; *un nettoyer à sec* a dry-cleaner. The sign *'Stoppage'* means invisible mending.

Une bucherie is a butcher's shop.

Une pharmacie is a chemist — but this sort of shop may stock a variety of products, such as herb teas and certain seasonings, that would not be found in an ordinary chemist in the UK. Mineral waters may also be bought here.

Une herboristerie is a herbalist, who may also be able to provide advice about the use of plants and herbs, both for medicinal and culinary purposes. If you are likely to require any specific medicament while travelling, it is as well to take it with you or, otherwise, take the prescription or formula; the French pharmacist is usually well qualified and knowledgeable, even in out-of-the-way towns and villages, but for some preparations a prescrip-

tion — *une ordonnance* — may be required, even for something that need not involve getting such a thing from your doctor at home.

Une crémerie is a dairy, but nowadays butter, eggs and milk may not only be stocked in the supermarket, but in the sort of general store that also stocks cheese.

Une charcuterie may be translated as *delicatessen*, although, in addition to cooked foods and prepared dishes, it will also stock canned goods and many staple commodities. The word derives from *'chair cuit'* (cooked meat) and, up to the fifteenth century, the *charcutiers*, who did good business when, for other people, the only means of cooking was a pot hung over the fire, were not allowed to slaughter and prepare animals for cooking — that was the prerogative of the butchers. Later, the *charcutiers* were allowed more freedom in what they sold and, today, even a small *charcuterie* may stock a wide range of cooked meats, fish, salads and sometimes cheese.

Une épicerie is a grocer — in a small village it may be one of those shops that stock a variety of dry goods, plus vegetables, fruit and kitchen equipment.

Une drogerie is a hardware shop but, in the north of France (and in Belgium), the more usual word tends to be *une quincaillerie*.

Fruits, primeurs, légumes on a shop-front means a greengrocer, who usually stocks some canned goods as well.

Une fromagerie is a cheesemonger, who may also stock butter and milk.

Une poissonerie is a fishmonger.

Une librairie is a bookshop, where magazines, postcards and, sometimes, postage stamps and stationery may be on sale. *Un bibliothèque* is either a personal library or a public library but, in a wine context, it can mean the reserves of past vintages kept by the estate owner.

Une pâtisserie is a pastry and cake shop and, sometimes, a type of tea-room. It may also sell confectionery of a generally superior sort. It is therefore worth noting that the sign '*Chocolatier*' means that the establishment specializes in chocolates, probably of its own make, plus special biscuits, candied fruits and fruits in brandy. The chocolates can be delectable — but the first-time visitor may well be astounded at how much even a single chocolate of this sort will cost and the boxes and wrapping papers and ribbons that may be used if you answer the question '*C'est pour offrir?*' (Is this for a present?) will be enchanting — and very expensive indeed.

Un tabac, which has a red, cigar-shaped metal sign outside, not only sells cigarettes and tobacco, but postage-stamps. Even a small *tabac* can also stock postcards and a few magazines or newspapers and a large shop will retail maps, books, stationery and writing accessories.

Foodstuffs

For some of these, see the sections in other parts of this book, dealing with menus and dishes:

Herbs and spices (*see pp.57–8*)

Shellfish, crustacea, fish in general — salt and freshwater (*see pp.47–51*)

Meat of various kinds, poultry, game (*see pp.59—62, also pp.102—3*)

Cheese (*see pp.65–83*)

Basic provisions

Dairy produce

Beurre is butter and even a small shop usually has several sorts. These will mostly be unsalted, but *'Salé'* or *'Mis-salé'* on a packet means slightly salted. Regions such as the Charentes and Normandy, famous for butter, have various well-known brands that are available in many shops. *Beurre fermier* is farm butter, usually cut off a huge chunk according to requirements and generally stocked by a shop that specializes in butter and, probably, cheese. Farm butter is not necessarily richer than commercial butter, but it seldom contains any preservative, so do not buy more than you need at a time — and, as it can vary in taste, make sure that you do like it before you buy, because it is seldom cheap.

Margarine is margarine. The diet-conscious, cutting down on fat, should look for the word *'Allegé'* (lightened) on a label of this type of fat, which will contain less *matière grasse* (fat) than butter, although it may actually have some butter in the mixture. There is no one French term for 'spread' as the UK understands the word, but I can recommend a *'Spécialité laitière diététique'*, which is sold under the name *'Sylphide Table'*, and there is another one called *'St Hubert'*, both of them, to my palate, better than UK spreads and praiseworthily not trying to imitate the taste of butter at all.

Fats

Graisse literally means fat — *graisse de rôti* is meat dripping, often on sale in packet form in the dairy section of a shop or supermarket. The fresh type can usually be bought from the meat department of a supermarket and from a butcher, but not from a dairy.

Saindoux is lard — but, as *lard* is French for bacon, be careful you are not misunderstood if using the term. *Lard de poitrine* is pork-belly fat; *lardons* are the bits of pork fat used for inserting in meat in various recipes. *Couenne* is the skin from a pork joint. As the French do not sell pork joints with the skin on, they are unaware of the joys of crackling — if anyone wants the skin, it will be necessary to explain carefully (and you might take the co-operative butcher a chunk of crackling afterwards to provide an example). *Couenne*, in small quantities, is used to enrich the gravy from joints of meat. *Gras dur* is the fat immediately under the *couenne*.

97

Milk and Cream

Lait is milk. If you buy it from a farm, you may be asked whether you want the milk from the morning or evening milking — according to what you are going to use it for. There is no such person as a milkman in France, so people buy milk as they require it. Commercial bottled milk is as follows: the full cream type has a red capsule, the skimmed variety a blue capsule. Longlife milk is very popular — because of the non-existent milkman — and, although I would not go as far as a friend who says that 'UHT' on a carton of 'milk' signifies 'utterly horrid taste', for many years I thought that the odd taste of much French coffee (and, I suppose, tea, which I do not drink) was because goats' milk was used!

Crème is, of course, cream — but there are various kinds. *Café crème* is just white coffee, not necessarily coffee with cream. *Crème stérilisée* is what most people will find useful as either single or double cream. *Crème fraîche*, which has disappointed many supposing it to be similar to Devonshire or clotted cream, is made by allowing the cream to thicken and ferment slightly, hence the sharp, almost cheesy flavour; this is delicious with much cooked fruit and fruit-tarts, but can be somewhat off-putting to anyone supposing it to be thick fresh cream and who finds it 'on the turn'. But *crème fraîche* can be used for most recipes, it won't curdle even if boiled for a short time — but it is a rich form of cream, so bear this in mind if you adapt a recipe and make use of it. Nor does *crème fraîche* contain preservative, although you can keep it, refrigerated, for five to seven days as a rule. For making what the Anglo-Saxon understand by 'whipped cream', use *crème fraîche* with either milk or iced water, one-third of the thinning-down agent to two-thirds of the cream. *Crème Chantilly*, the accompaniment to many pastries, ices and sweet dishes, is not as rich as *crème fraîche* and is just lightly whipped cream, that becomes fluffy in the process.

Les condiments (seasonings)

Huile is oil — and a large variety will be available. *Huile d'olive* is olive oil and that labelled *vierge* (virgin) will have the most definite flavour, although the taste can vary according to where the oil comes from. Olive oil is not cheap so, if you are watching the bills, try others for various culinary purposes. *Huile d'arachide* (peanut oil) is blander than olive oil and *huile de tournesol* (sunflower-seed oil) can be useful in the kitchen, such as for frying. *Huile de noix* is walnut oil, while *huile de noisettes* is hazelnut oil, both expensive and, when put on a salad mentioned on a menu, probably described as such; even a little of either, combined with olive or, even peanut oil, can make a great difference to a salad. *Huile pour frire* is frying oil, *huile pour assaisonment* is a general term for salad oil — probably rather undistinguished. Always wipe the lip of any bottle or can of oil immediately after use — the remaining drop of oil can go rancid and will affect any oil subsequently poured over it — which is why many people think 'all that oil' is so unpleasant. (But, as the entire olive crop of Spain goes into the world's most famous baby foods, it is foolish to suppose that vast numbers of people cannot take oil at all.)

Sel is salt, *sel blanc* being what the British would call table-salt (for pouring); *sel gris* has slightly more flavour even if it does look a bit grubby; *sel marin* is sea salt and *gros sel* is a coarse-grained type of salt, which is in particles that have to be ground up if you want to pour it. This last is the sort of salt that is often put in a small dish at table, for people to take a pinch with their fingers. *Sel épicé* is spiced salt; *sel de céleri* is celery salt. You will, of course, pay slightly more for these last two — and it is not difficult to make your own versions anyway.

Poivre is pepper. It is available as black or white or, as *poivre en grains*, in peppercorns — which can be bought at a pharmacy as well as in the grocery shop. *Poivre de la Jamaïque, toute épice,* is allspice; *quatre épices* is a mix of pepper, nutmeg, cinnamon, cloves, in which sometimes ginger is substituted for the cinnamon. *Poivre de Cayenne* is Cayenne pepper — very hot.

Moutard is mustard — an important and fascinating commodity. It first came to France with the Romans and was especially popular in Burgundy — some people even think that its name derives from the motto of the Ducs de Bourgogne — '*Moult me tard*', but more probably it comes from the Latin, *Mustum ardens,* the term used for pounded mustard-seed. Early in gastronomic history Dijon mustard began to be famous and, in 1756, the painter. Naigeon made it in its present form by grinding mustard-seed in a mill and then blending it with *verjus,* the sharp, acid juice of unripe grapes (*vert* signifying green or sharp). The popularity of this type of mustard is one of the reasons why mustards made in wine regions are publicized, because of the ingredients ready to hand.

French mustards are all in paste or cream form. Sometimes, as in the Gironde, the '*must*' of wine is included for the luxury types, but generally the mustard is ground up with *verjus,* red or white wine, cider, vinegar or simply water, or maybe a blend of several of these; the resulting paste is milled again, then the mustard undergoes maturation, the vats in which it remains being regularly stirred, so as to get rid of any air. A decree of 1937 is precise about what mustard is: the name can only be given to products obtained by milling (and, if preferred, subsequently sifted and/or screened) the seeds of *brassica nigra* (black mustard) or *brassica juncea* (brown mustard) or a blend of the two. Strong mustards are made with sifted or screened products, whereas mild mustards are made with non-sifted products; it is the seed coat that provides piquancy, so, if this is removed, the mustard is more 'mustardy'. About 50,000 tonnes of mustard are made each year in France and, of this, around 90 per cent comes from Dijon. It is carefully controlled. *Moutard fort* is somewhat more aromatic than English 'strong' mustard, but not very strong; *moutard douce* (mild mustard), comes in various forms — *jaune, brune, verte*, even *violette* and each maker will have an individual style. Maille, Grey Poupon, Amora are only a few of the great mustard firms. In a village *épicerie* you may see a locally made mustard, which can be well worth trying. *Moutard à l'ancienne* is the type made with the coarsely-ground whole mustard-seeds and, although it looks as if it would be strong, it isn't. Mustards described as *'aromatisées'* or *'aux aromates'* have additional flavourings: *fines herbes* (herbs), *à la ravigote* (slightly piquant), *à l'estragon* (tarragon), *au poivre vert* (green pepper). Mustard is usually served in pots — a pot is *un moutardier* — and many pots are attractive enough to keep after use. There are a few brands of mustard in tubes, useful for picnics.

If a dish on a menu is marked as containing mustard, do not suppose that it will be very strong or piquant. For years I deprived myself of many good things by supposing this would be so.

Vinaigre is vinegar — literally *vin aigre*, bitter wine. Orléans vinegar is famous and there are many kinds of wine vinegars, also cider vinegar and some vinegars flavoured with herbs. I have never seen a malt vinegar on sale. Do not assume that red wine vinegar is 'stronger' in taste than white wine vinegar — it isn't. The British associate chips with vinegar, and malt vinegar at that, but up on the Franco-Belgian border *frites* (chips), which are often sold at street stalls in paper cornets, will have a dollop of mayonnaise on the top, not vinegar.

Fish
(see pp.47–51)

Meat

Viand means meat; *viand rouge* means beef, lamb, mutton (which does still exist in France); *viand blanche* means veal, rabbit, poultry; *viand noire* is game (but *see pp.61* for the various types of this as well). Cuts of meat in France are rather different from those in the UK. You may manage by pointing to parts of your own anatomy, but sometimes it will be simpler to buy a cheap French cookery book that has diagrams of the various portions. Specify what you are going to cook: either the butcher or, often, several other people in the shop, will help you to get what you want and be generous with recipes. (Also *see p.59*).

Terms in General Use

Haché is mince, cut fresh from the requisite animal and minced while you wait, so it is quite fresh.

Une farce is a stuffing — you may want some minced meat for this.

Jus is gravy — I do not think there is a French equivalent for gravy powder. If you wish to thicken the meat juices, use some flour and, if you wish, *couenne* (*see p.97*).

Arroser is to baste — as with a joint.

Dégraisser is literally to 'de-grease' or get rid of surplus fat, which is often done by setting the dish containing it alight, often with *rhum*, but other spirits may be used too.

Côtes de ... are ribs and, when the term is used in association with pork or lamb, the equivalent is chops. *Cotelettes* are cutlets.

Ris de veau is calves' sweetbreads.

Pied de porc is pig's trotter.

Une bavette may be literally translated as 'bib' in English, but in fact is what the British would call skirt of beef. *Un anglet* is part of the stomach of the cow. Both are fairly cheap cuts, mostly intended for braising, the *bavette* often being used for *pot-au-feu*.

Mouton is, literally, lamb, but from a slightly older animal; what the UK would describe as 'baby lamb' will be called *agneau*. (With its provenance stated if this is important, as with lamb reared on a salty pasture — *pré salé*.) Matured lamb is not really mutton — so seldom found in the UK these days — but anyone longing to try a recipe for this former delight may find it acceptable.

At the Charcuterie

Jambon d'York, as already noted, is ordinary mild ham, such as some Britons like as an addition to a continental breakfast. It varies in quality but usually is adequate. The other sorts of ham, however, can be more distinctive in taste and these are *jambons crus* — raw but cured hams; sometimes they are thinly sliced, rather like Parma ham, but they may be in thick slices too. Bayonne, where the ham is cured by burying it in the earth, the Morvan region of Burgundy, are other well-known types of ham that usually form part of an *hors d'oeuvre* or else make a robust type of sandwich. *Un jambonneau* is a mild ham, rolled in crumbs, to form a pyramid shape, with a point of bone sticking out of the top.

Un boudin is literally a pudding — but in the savoury sense. The British may forget that many of their 'traditional' dishes started savoury and only lately became sweet. *Boudins*, in fact, are types of sausage and, as they can be good served either hot or cold, you should ask the shop if what you buy needs to be cooked or can be served sliced as it is. *Boudin* slices can be an excellent cocktail snack or, with a salad, provide part of an *hors d'oeuvre* or a first course. *Boudin blanc* can be very choice, made from pounded or minced chicken, veal with delicate flavourings and sometimes being enhanced with truffles. *Boudin noir* is a slightly coarser version, often served with apples. If you think of it as 'blood-pudding' or 'black pudding' of the north of England, some hearers may shudder — but it is the same sort of thing, with the haggis of Scotland a kissing cousin. Indeed, there was a recent occasion when, in a French-organized contest to see who made the finest *boudin*, it was a British-made black pudding that took the first prize!

Fromage de tête is brawn. *Hure* is a type of brawn, which has more jelly around it.

Museau de boeuf is ox muzzle, often served, with a vinaigrette, in a salad.

Sausages

Une saucisse is a sausage — and you should ask as to whether it should be boiled, grilled or fried. EEC regulations prohibit the import of the traditional British 'banger' into France — because of the 'rusk' or filling. As the ex-patriot can pine for the traditional sausage, it was reported that, at one time, the BBC's Paris office had their refrigerator crammed with pounds of the delicacy — and you may well consider using some as a gift to friends in France whom you are flying to see. But French sausages are not like bangers — usually too meaty to face at breakfast. *Chair à saucisse* is sausage-meat; *crépinettes* are cakes of sausage-meat held together by threads of caul (*crépine*) — delicious, but remote from the British banger. *Un saucisson* is sometimes referred to as a *saucisson sec*, or sausage that is already cooked — it can be served sliced or cut up in chunks, rather like salami. A *saucisson* can sometimes be improved by heating, but ask about this when you buy one — it may contain largish lumps of fat or whole peppercorns, which can get lost if you fry or grill the *saucisson*. *Une andouille* is a tripe sausage, not to be confused with its near relation, the *andouillette* (a chitterling), because the *andouille* is — usually — ready to eat as it is, whereas the *andouillette* must be cooked. Different regions have their own versions of both. *Cervelas* (the 'saveloy' of UK Victorian songs) is meant to be eaten cold, with potato salad. But these are only a few of the great range of sausages. Some resemble Italy's salami, some are more like German *würst*. If they are not labelled in the *charcuterie*, ask about them, especially as to whether they should be cooked or can be served as they are.

Bread

French bread at its best is wonderful — though, alas, the use of mass-produced steam baked and, even, sliced loaves is increasing. The *boulangerie* is an important shop and Marcel Pagnol's delightful play, *La Femme du Boulanger*, shows how precious this commodity is. Sometimes a bakery may double as a *pâtisserie* but not always, although there may be a few packets of madeleines or biscuits available. Very small villages will have a sign *'Dépôt de pain'* where a baker's van will regularly leave bread — if you plan on buying some in such a place, do not leave it too late, because supplies tend to be quickly exhausted.

A sign outside a bakery saying that the bread is cooked *'au feu de bois'* means that the oven is fuelled by wood, the resulting bread being especially good, superior in crust and texture to bread baked in gas or electric ovens. Most regions have their own local names for the different types of bread and rolls.

Most French bread has a substantial crust, although obviously a large loaf will also have plenty of crumb. The long, thin *baguettes* and *ficelles* become rock-hard when only a few hours old, but the bigger loaves, especially those made in wood-fired ovens, will remain fresh for several days, though they do harden. When you buy bread, you can select a particular loaf — if you want one with a crust that is well-done, the expression is *'bien cuit'*. If you are helping yourself to cut bread at table and want the crusty end of a loaf, the word for this is *le coin*. The majority of breads and rolls are white, although you can now find several varieties of brown.

Different loaves

Un pain is a loaf, usually fairly large, of virtually any shape. *Un pain de campagne* is the long, thickish crusty loaf and this may be either the *pain de deux livres*, or the *gros pain*, both of them the workers' basic bread. The *gros pain* is enormous, the *pain de deux livres* only slightly smaller. *Un bâtard* is a smaller version of the *pain de deux livres*, a useful family size, as it can be utilized for a picnic or, for a more elegant occasion, sliced thinly.

Une baguette is the long, thinnish loaf that most people mean when they say 'French bread', although, because of the difference in the flour used, this, when you find it in the UK, is only a very distant relation to the genuine French article. *Une ficelle* is a thinner, crustier version of the *baguette*, not quite as long. It is the bread to buy if you want to split it lengthways, to make a French type sandwich.

Un pain polka may be round or long, slashed across the top, slightly less crusty than the *baguette*.

Un joko is a longish, moderately crusty loaf, slashed across the top, rather like what the British call a Vienna loaf.

Une couronne is circular, with a fairly crusty top. *Une couronne Sarthoise* is rather like a large, open-ended croissant, but with a firmer crust.

Un pain provençal is a very light, crusty round loaf, with a twirly-looking crown on the top.

Une tresse or *une natte* are shiny plaits of bread, made with a slightly sweet dough and sometimes sprinkled with sesame seeds or cumin.

Un pain boulot is a fattish, long loaf, with a slight crust.

Other unusual shapes include the *épi de Charente*, which, as its name implies, is rather like a sculpture in bread of a thorny

branch, the thorns sticking out at intervals along its length. *Une palette* is flattish, with a little piece rather like a handle extending from one end. *Un bagnat* is a stumpy little loaf, with a prong of bread sticking out from one side — a little like a hand making a rude gesture. But there are many, many more.

Special Breads

Pain au levain (*levain* is leaven or the raising agent) has a slightly coffee-toned crust, made in various shapes, and is useful because it stays fresh for several days.

Pain de mie is a longish loaf, rather like the British tin loaf, and it is the bread from which crumbs (*chapelure*) are made.

Pain bis or *pain de son* is brown bread. It is not always easy to find, although most supermarkets will stock various forms of 'diet' breads, including the Vogel Three Grain. (*Bis*, meaning twice — what people shout when they want an encore — is the origin of biscuit, i.e. twice cooked.)

Pain de seigle is rye bread, although sometimes it is taken to mean any bread with a light brown crumb.

105

Pain d'avoine is oatmeal bread, sometimes to be found.

Pain Russe is black bread — not the same as pumpernickel, which is the same word (*see p.28*).

Pain brioché is spongy bread, with a slightly sweet dough, delicious when toasted and pleasant to eat with butter and jam; a good choice for anyone who finds the crust of the *baguette* and *ficelle* a bit too hard.

Pain d'épice is sometimes translated as 'gingerbread', but I do not find it predominantly gingery — 'honeycake', slightly spiced, might be a more accurate description.

Pain spécial croustillant is crispbread, although it is usually easier to ask for this by brand-name, such as Ryvita. *Biscottes* are rusks, *biscottes d'amidon réduit* are starch-reduced (crispbread or rolls).

Rolls

Un petit pain is the general term for a roll, but usually means one with a fairly hard crust, round or long in shape.

Un petit pain au lait is a milk roll, soft in texture: what a Briton would call a bridge roll.

Un pain sandwich is a long, light-textured roll with a soft crust, a little like a Scots bap.

Une galette is a round roll.

Un pistolet is a small round roll, with a hardish crust — what would be called a dinner-roll in the UK.

Un petit pain opéra or *grand opéra* are both rolls, longish in shape, with a fairly hard crust, slashed across the top. They often accompany meals.

Une brioche is rather like a small, shiny-surfaced cottage loaf, light in texture, with a slightly sweet yellowish crumb. It is usually a better choice for breakfast or tea than an indifferent croissant and sometimes *brioches* are stuffed with savoury things — notably mousses and *foie gras*. Raymond Oliver has a theory that the word derives from Brie (the cheese) and the verb *hocher* (to shake or stir up), because, in the days when butter was difficult to make and keep, cheese was often worked into this sort of dough (as indeed it is for some of the Easter breads of Cyprus).

Un croissant is the roll that most people know and think of as 'French' — although there are seldom really good ones unless you are very near a good bakery. In former times, relays of servants would go to fetch croissants because, even after an hour or so, they are stale and, in my opinion, not worth eating. Ideally, they should splinter as you touch them — and you should lick your fingers. If your hotel does its own baking or is near a good baker, then it may be possible to get a decent *croissant au beurre,* the true, featherlight roll that is almost a twist of flaky pastry. As mentioned earlier, the vogue for the croissant originated when the Turks, whose emblem the crescent is, were defeated at the siege of Vienna. The use of chocolate as a filling is not restricted to biscuits and *brioches* and croissants may be bought filled with it — pleasant for breakfast and at tea-time.

> French bread is like love — essentially transitory, and what lies at the heart may be rather lightweight: but the crackle of the crust is worth the long-time sog of the sliced loaf any day.
>
> TOM VERNON, *Fat Man on a Bicycle,* Michael Joseph, 1981

Basic Shopping

Un filet is a string bag; *un sac* is a bag; *une poche plastique* is a plastic bag — some of these may be supplied at a supermarket, rather superior ones may be on sale and they can be pretty enough to bring back as small gifts. *Une pochette* is a bag, or paper bag. If you are buying food to eat on a picnic, say that it is *'Pour emporter',* and it will be wrapped up.

Un casse-croûte is a snack or, if you see the sign in front of a small eating-place, perhaps a type of stand-up snack bar in a supermarket, it means snack-bar. *Casser la croûte* is to have a snack. *La fortune du pot* is potluck.

En boîte is in a tin. *Un ouvre-boîte* is a tin-opener.

Une bouteille consignée is a returnable bottle *(see p.93)* and the statement *'00 centimes pour la consigne'* means the amount you get back when you bring back the bottle.

Un ouvre-bouteille is a bottle-opener; *un tir bouchon* a corkscrew. *Un décapsulateur* is a bottle-opener of the type that is used for 'crown' corks — the ones with frilly edges. *Un limonadier* is the flat 'waiter's friend', comprising a knife (for cutting capsules), corkscrew, crown cork opener and, sometimes, a tin-opener as well. *Un bouchon de Champagne* is a stopper to keep the fizz in all types of fizzy drinks *(see p.93).*

Une fermeture à vis is a screw stopper, sometimes used for cheap wines.

Produits diététiques are dietetic foods, available at a pharmacy as well as in an ordinary shop. *Produits naturels* are health foods — seen much more these days.

Tartiner is to spread, hence *une tartine* is a slice of bread and butter or bread and jam — useful when buying ingredients for sandwiches.

Chocolat à croquer is eating-chocolate.

Cake is always fruit-cake — as mentioned earlier, in a bar or café it will be a slice of fruit-cake wrapped up in cellophane. Other cakes will have specific names — madeleine, *palmier* (the very light pastry twist), and so on. With packets of biscuits and cakes, there is usually a picture of the contents on the wrapping.

Location de vacances

This expression literally means 'rented holiday' and implies self-catering. As other people's kitchens are never quite as satisfactory as one's own, here are some things you may wish to buy — some owners of holiday homes or returning visitors in '*gîtes*' find it pleasant to make a present of some gadgets and equipment to the house or flat where they have enjoyed themselves.

Un couteau à découper is a general purpose cook's knife.

Un couteau à éplucher is a paring knife.

Un couteau à pain is a bread-knife.

Un couteau scie is a saw-edged knife.

Une palette is a palette knife.

Une pelle à tarte is a serving slice — useful for turning hot things.

Une casserole is a saucepan.

Une poêle à frire is a frying-pan.

Une marmite is what the British would call a casserole.

Une cocotte is a stewpan.

Un couvercle is a saucepan lid.

Un fait tout is a type of skillet or shallow pan with straight sides and a lid.

Un grill is a grill.

Une cocotte minute is a pressure-cooker.

Une rape is a grater.

A Final Word

If you go into a shop and find the patron or patronne enjoying a long telephone conversation or engaged in talk with one of their more verbose old friends — and you are in a bit of a hurry, the truly French way to get attention is to say *'S'il vous plaît'*, in a rather plaintive but wearily strong tone. Even if you are then told that what you want 'doesn't exist in France', you'll get attention at once — and it makes you feel that you have mastered at least some of the nuances involved in speaking French!

> The people of this country dine at noon. . . . I and my family could not well dispense with our tea and toast in the morning, and had no stomach to eat at noon. For my own part, I hate the French cookery, and abominate garlick, with which all their ragouts, in this part of the country, are highly seasoned. We therefore formed a different plan of living upon the road. Before we left Paris, we laid in a stock of tea, chocolate, cured neats tongues, and saucissons or Bologna sausages, both of which we found in great perfection in that capital, where indeed, there are excellent provisions of all sorts. About ten in the morning we stopped to breakfast at some auberge, where we always found bread, butter and milk. In the meantime, we ordered a poulard or two to be roasted and these, wrapped in a napkin, were put into the boot of the coach, together with bread, wine, and water. About two or three in the afternoon, while the horses were changing, we laid a cloth upon our knees, and producing our store, with a few earthen plates, discussed our short meal without ceremony. This was followed by a desert of grapes and other fruit. . . . The wine commonly used in Burgundy is so weak and thin, that you would not drink it in England. . . . I believe all the first growth is either consumed in the houses of the noblesse, or sent abroad to foreign markets.
>
> TOBIAS SMOLLETT, *Travels Through France and Italy*, 1766

8

Keeping Well

Even before I married a doctor, I was usually the one who went round ministering to those succumbing to various maladies while abroad. It is sensible to know how to deal with what may be routine ailments and to travel with certain medicaments that can make a great deal of difference to your recovery and comfort. Of course, there are the times when any doctor would advise bed, rest and a light diet, but when life has to go on and one simply has got to catch a plane, attend a dinner, make a speech — so therefore cannot 'be sensible' — I know that my advice has sometimes been helpful in such instances.

Before You Go Away
Check that you are adequately covered as regards insurance, including possible additional expenses that may be incurred during illness, also transport home.

It is obligatory in France to carry your identification papers at all times. It is wise to attach to your passport the following, written clearly on a card: blood-group; any inoculations, adverse reactions to specific drugs, any habitual condition, such as diabetes, epilepsy, a heart condition. Also state whether you usually wear contact lenses or a pacemaker.

First-aid equipment must be carried in the car. To the basics I add: a big roll of cotton-wool, an extra supply of gauze and bandage, plus a large clean towel and plenty of tissues, all of which are invaluable if you have to clean up after even a minor accident. A pack of damp 'wipes' are useful in the car anyway. Check any made-up first-aid kit for sufficient bandages, dressings (large as well as small), scissors, disinfectant, tweezers (for extracting thorns and splinters), and smelling-salts — it is surprising how few people carry these and how many have been glad that I do so. Your own toiletries will probably include a thermometer, aspirins, health salts, travel-sickness remedies and one of the good propriet-ary branded preparations for tummy upsets. Sun-lotion can usual-ly be bought anywhere, but, in the first stages of a trip, it is wise to have some with you and, if you or any of your family find it difficult to sleep when travelling, arrange with your doctor to have something in the way of a mild sedative.

Can You Drink the Water?

Almost certainly yes — although, from the average tap, it may not be any more agreeable than the recycled liquid that pours from the taps of many cities anywhere. If you are camping or picnicking, then it may be unwise to drink from even the most attractive bubbling stream — you do not know what may have flowed into it from higher up its reaches.

Any place where there is a record of tourists being upset as a result of drinking the tap-water will usually be only too ready to warn you if it is unsafe for you, albeit perfectly all right for them. If you cannot always get bottled water (see pp.191–3 for the various types) then equip yourself in advance with a supply of the sort of tablets that will make doubtful drinking-water safe for you and that any chemist can supply. These tablets can also be useful in hot water for washing fruit or salads bought for picnics — any café and sometimes even a garage will be able to refill a vacuum jug with water for you. If you want to mix up baby foods, however, you are probably best advised — mainly for your own peace of mind — to buy a still, bottled water for this.

I shall not, I trust, be accused of wishing to lure the younger generation to drink, but it is worth remembering that the tradition of French children diluting their drinking-water with a spoonful of wine, or the other way round, has a sound reason behind it: should the water supply of past times have been doubtful, then the drinkers 'cut' it with a dollop of whatever wine they had, for wine is the second oldest disinfectant in the world.

Do also remember that you may have been firm about drinking only bottled water, you may have washed your salads and fruit in water purified with appropriate tablets, but with what — if you are self-catering or camping in a region where it is just possible that the water supply is a vague risk to the visitor — do you wash up your dishes and glasses and cutlery? It is worth putting some purifying tablets in the washing-up water as well, even if you use strong soap or detergent, because, if you rinse your glasses in plain water, you may run a slight risk of picking up whatever might upset you, even after the obvious precautions. Personally, I have never bothered — but then I have never coped with self-catering in remote regions. I drink so much water anyway that, fortunately, I have seldom been unwell when abroad. But it is better to have peace of mind — the digestion is often much influenced by this.

Tummy Upsets

These are often caused by people who, tired at the beginning of a holiday, then eat and drink far too much, especially indulging in the British habit of taking food and drink between meals. Any fruit bought in an open market should be washed before you eat it and, if you notice the slightest 'beeriness' in the taste, throw it away — this touch of prickle indicates it has begun to ferment and it will go on fermenting inside you. Do not buy large quantities of food and keep it in a knapsack, plastic bag or boot of the car if you are anywhere hot: food will decompose quickly in such places. If you cannot transport perishables in an insulated bag or box, buy them only as you need them.

It cannot be over-emphasized that any radical change in climate, diet and domestic routine can affect the digestion — don't, while travelling, overload the stomach. As any minor upset can dehydrate you, the prime consideration is to take plenty of water and, if it is really hot, lick up additional salt to guard against a mild form of heat-stroke. One wise friend makes it a rule always to drink as much water as he does wine with any meal. If you do get a gastric upset, avoid actual iced drinks and anything very hot or very cold, but keep up your liquid intake. Do not take fruit juice or fruit, salads or anything acid — this will make matters worse as you are adding to the excess acidity in the stomach. Very slightly gassy mineral water will disperse any gas in the stomach and can stop you feeling sick. When you do feel like food, opt for consommé and a rusk.

Should you have a tendency to diarrhoea when you travel, get your doctor to give you a suitable prescription before you leave — and write this down. When the need is great, you may not be able to remember its name or the formula. And I do not think that anyone has laughed at my suggestion that some soothing ointment for the sort of anal split or irritation that 'the trots' can bring on, should also be carried.

If you have to call a doctor, make sure you and he understand each other — get someone to interpret if you are in any doubt. And follow his instructions *exactly* — much trouble is caused by people feeling better and ceasing to take the prescribed medicine.

Never take aspirin without plenty of liquid with it and never, with any tummy upset or internal pain, take an aperient — this can be dangerous if you have, for example, a grumbling appendix or perhaps an incipient ulcer.

If you are looking after an invalid, be scrupulous about washing your hands and keeping personal effects, tableware, towels quite separate. Disinfect the telephone if the invalid uses it.

Things You Cannot Eat

Sometimes people only imagine they cannot eat or drink certain things — but for their own peace of mind it is better to be on the safe side. It is now accepted that some people are definitely unable to take red wine. Anyway, do not think that white wines are 'light in alcohol', nor *rosé* wines either; unless the strength is stated on the bottle, realize that you cannot tell strength just by tasting — until you have tasted too much!

Tourists sometimes shudder about 'all that oil', but it must be accepted that, in many parts of France, oil will be the cooking medium. And why the British, whose liking for fish and chips (usually cooked in inferior oil anyway) have this odd notion, I have never been able to understand. After all, one of the greatest manufacturers of baby food in the world, whose products are shovelled into British infants, dominates the olive oil crop of Spain — unlubricated babies are unhappy and I sometimes reflect that the contemporary 'English disease' (constipation) would be much reduced if people did not think that oil was bad for them.

In almost all country places out of England it is impossible to avoid the greasy dishes which are apparently preferred by all except our own countrymen; and a frequent consequence is rancid indigestion, with nauseous taste in the mouth, and flatulence or diarrhoea . . . Another article of cuisine that offends the bowels of unused Britons is garlic. Not uncommonly in southern climes an egg with the shell on it is the only procurable animal food without garlic in it. Flatulence and looseness are the frequent results.

THOMAS KING CHAMBERS, *A Manual of Diet and Health and Disease*, 1875

Garlic tends to be something that many find 'loosening' but, again, if you go to the south — unless you restrict yourself to hotels where 'international' food is served — you are likely to find it in many recipes.

If you simply cannot eat a particular thing, say either '*Il m'est defendu de manger . . .*' (I've been ordered not to eat . . .), or, '*Je suis allergique à . . .*' (I'm allergic to . . .).

Hangovers (*Gueule de bois*)

Prevention is certainly better than cure, but we have all been caught at least once by inadvertently taking too much alcohol. If in the slightest doubt, take plenty of water before you retire for the night, plus some health salts and aspirin — with more water. When you wake up, repeat the treatment and have breakfast — even if you feel utterly disinclined to do so. A cool shower and a brisk walk will usually complete the cure but, if your eyes still don't seem to fit in your head, you can try France's answer to Italy's Fernet Branca, which is Arquebuse (*see p.172*)

Drinking and Driving

It must be stressed that police checks on roads and motorways are frequent and penalties severe. It is not a bad idea always to have a chilled bottle of water in the car and, if in the slightest doubt, give yourself a glassful before you set out after any meal.

Cloakrooms

Visitors to France often cling resolutely to their coats in a restaurant or café. But it is usual to put these in the *vestiare* or get the waiter to take them from you, plus cameras, large bags, sticks and so on. Except in very large establishments, male and female property is put in the same place and the tip you give when you collect your things need not be large. If you really must keep a bag or valuable camera with you, the waiter will usually put a chair alongside yours for them.

The Water Closet

Everyone can interpret the letters 'W.C.' but the polite phrase a woman can use is '*le petit coin*'. It should not surprise anyone to know that, in some '*toilettes*', even in these days, there may be separate entrances for ladies and gentlemen, but a common set of closets and urinals inside. If there is an attendant, then you tip should you use the soap and towel. Unless both sections of a lavatory are being used, there is nothing to prevent ladies using

114

the gents, should people be travelling in a group and if they are in some haste. There are, of course, water-closets of various kinds. I like the comment of the late Freda White, who, being told that the section on lavatories in one of her admirable books was 'non-U', retorted: 'I've yet to be introduced to the traveller whose digestion is more U than that of common mortals; and believe me, you will not enjoy either a Roman arena or a Romanesque abbey if you are desperately in need of a lavatory.'

The most treacherous type of water-closet is that known as 'Turc', which has a hole in the floor and two places for one's feet. Be ready to leave this place at once when you activate the flush — it can rush around you like a flood.

Anyone who does not feel well can usually find either *la patronne* (the lady of the restaurant or café) or simply another person to give assistance. But it can help to be able to explain what is wrong.

First-aid phrases
(The English is put first, for quick reference at need.)
I feel faint/unwell — *Je ne me sens pas bien*; I'm not very well is *Je suis fatigué(e)*; to be *souffant(e)* is to be in pain; to be *malade* is to be ill.
I feel sick — *J'ai mal au coeur*.
I have become unwell (euphemistic way of saying you are having a bad period) — *Je suis indisposée*.
I am pregnant — *J'attends un bébé*.
I need ... *J'ai besoin de* ...
The lavatory does not work/is blocked — *Le lavabo est bouché*.
(*Le lavabo* means washbasin as well as lavatory pan.)

I fancy it must be the quantity of animal food eaten by the English which renders their character insusceptible of civilisation. I suspect it is in their kitchens and not in their churches that their reformation must be worked, and that Missionaries of that description from hence (France) would avail more than those who should endeavour to tame them by precepts of religion or philosophy.

THOMAS JEFFERSON, Letter to Abigail Adams from Paris, Sept. 25, 1785

The water does not run — *L'eau ne coule pas.*
The water does not run away — *L'eau ne passe pas.*

Some items you may need:
Adhesive dressing — *Un pansement adhésif.*
A bandage — *Une bande.*
Cotton-wool — *Le coton.*
Disinfectant — *Un désinfectant.*
Lavatory paper — *Le papier hygiénique* or *Le paper de toilette.*
A nappy — *Une couche* (*'disposable'* for the disposable kind).
A safety-pin — *Une épingle anglaise* or *de nourrice.*
A sanitary towel — *Une serviette hygiénique;* the plural is *Garnitures périodique* — add 'soluble' if you want the soluble type, and *'Un Tampax'* for the internal sort. A sanitary belt is *Une ceinture périodique.*
Smelling-salts — *Les sels volatiles.*
Sticking-plaster — *Le taffetas gommé.*
A towel — *Une serviette.*

> We drove . . . to the Hôtel du Lion d'Or, at Langon, in the Sauternes district . . . the girl . . . brought in two bottles of wine . . . the gentleman whose name was on the card, he had chosen our wines for us. She poured out the Cheval Blanc, a Graves Saint-Emilion of 1923, and then left us to it. It was hopelessly sweet, of course, sweeter even than our apprehensions. . . . With the poulet en cocotte, the second bottle was opened for us — Sauternes Sigalas-Rabaud 1922. Perhaps the best way of describing it would be to state that by force of its sweeter sweetness, it made the first wine seem quite dry . . . that fatal year 1847, in which vineyards which might have produced wine fit for gentlemen to drink . . . produced instead this clinging, highly-perfumed, luscious and full-blooded horror, known as the great wine of Sauternes!. . . . We talked, in low subdued voices, about the niceness of vinegar and sharp apples and olives and anchovies. . . .
>
> G.B. STERN, *Bouquet,* 1927
> [The four self-styled 'connoisseurs' reveal their ignorance. What the 'sweet' Cheval Blanc was I have no idea! P.V.P.]

9

The Social Scene: Les Bonnes Manières

No one reading this book is likely to need a lesson in good manners or etiquette. But various conventions have developed in countries with different ways of life from our own as regards everyday procedures and it can be a tactful gesture to know something about these prior to a visit.

Remember, first, that 'Paris is not France'. You may know Paris or any other capital city well, but this knowledge and your experience of staying in large hotels in the capital will not give you much insight into the ways of life in the provinces; French society can be very closed indeed, although the 'grapevine' is something of a built-in passport. The French are a proud people, intensely individualistic, tolerant as regards those who are not familiar with their ways, but not always indulgent to those who oppose their conventions. (Dare I say they somewhat resemble the British in this?) They can be quite outspoken and adamant: if a café proprietor says it is too late to serve you — even if the regulars and the family owners are all placidly eating soup and there is plenty to spare — do not press the matter. It is, simply, too late. They will not bother. If a saleswoman in a shop says she hasn't got what you ask for — even if it is sitting on the shelf behind her — she'll announce blandly that '*Ça n'existe pas en France*'. Should you point to it or even go and get the required item, the response may merely be a shrug. Olivia de Havilland, having lived in France for many years, relates in her autobiography with what glee she made this reply — 'It doesn't exist in France' — to a rather tiresome tourist who had mistaken her for a shop assistant. I have to admit that sometimes I'm on the point of starting the Hundred Years' War all over again. . . . But in France Jack really is as good as his neighbour unless there is a very great difference in rank, title and ability. (The importance of that little 'de' in front of someone's name is a bit of snobbery that I do not think the ordinary Briton will ever understand.) Still, the casualness that has infiltrated British conventions is often difficult for others to understand and, alas, the former tradition of *'parole d'un anglais'*, meaning that an English person would keep his word, is in decline.

If you are ever fortunate enough to be entertained in a great French restaurant or to enjoy the hospitality of a French household, the experience will be unforgettable; it is a glimpsed moment of being 'royal' when one arrives at, for example, a great wine estate and the staff as well as the owners smile with more than routine welcome. This sort of thing should naturally never be taken for granted and it eases your way if you are aware of what may please those who have taken the trouble to please you. Nor should it ever be forgotten that, when abroad, even the humblest individual is an ambassador for his or her country.

What to Wear
People on holiday sometimes forget that a town is not a beach. Swim-wear or very casual attire can be out of place in cities such as Bordeaux or Beaune; country wear is not quite the same thing. Do not be surprised, though, if you see French friends wearing thicker clothes than you do — if they live in the south they will feel chilly earlier in the autumn. For men, a jacket and a tie — which your host may sometimes thoughtfully urge you to remove — and, for women, a dress or at least well-cut trousers, are always acceptable, although do not forget that stone buildings, such as cellars and many French houses, can be cool inside, so a cardigan or wrap of some kind may be a good idea. In Champagne the cellars are very deep and definitely chilly — you will see the guides button and belt their coats, so do not be too proud about taking a jacket or thick sweater to keep you warm. This also applies to children, who, if merely wearing sandals and short-sleeved attire, can get really cold in such places.

For vineyard visits, stout walking shoes or sturdy sandals are essential. If you visit such regions outside the high summer season, then waterproof footwear, an umbrella and even a mackintosh are useful accessories. If you are visiting cellars, remember they may be damp — do not risk slipping — and, in places where one spits wine on the floor, do not don light-toned expensive shoes: even if you manage to avoid spitting on your own feet, someone else's splashback may still stain them. The same applies to light-coloured clothes, which may get dusty or stained. Do not forget, though, that the stain of a red wine can be lifted as if by magic if you immediately dowse the mark with white wine. Outside the summer season, it is also worth bearing in mind that restaurants and the public rooms of hotels can be, to the Briton, unbearably hot and stuffy; the argument about fresh air recurs! So although you may arrive wearing a winter coat, it is prudent to wear something light underneath, or else you may find your head bursting during dinner.

Routine Courtesy

France has been called *'le pays du shake hand'*. I do not know whether it is still routine to shake hands with every single member of a class at school or university or in the office, but one certainly should at least offer to shake hands with anyone known even slightly. Shake hands with the nice man at the hotel's reception desk, or the patron of the restaurant you have revisited; shake hands when you — a woman — go to the *salon de coiffeur*, or when the garage man has performed some satisfactory service; remember that whenever you shake hands at the outset of some social meeting — somebody you have vaguely met before perhaps — then you must shake hands again when you leave. If somebody has been doing some form of work that has dirtied their hands, they may extend their forearm for you to grasp — don't avoid doing so.

Introductions

A man makes a gesture of kissing the hand of a married woman or lady of some seniority, although the actual kiss does not usually land except between great friends. Unmarried ladies do not usually get their hands kissed — the man greeting them bows and inclines his head; more might be a familiarity. Or, these days, hands may be shaken all round.

Verbal introductions are as expected — a man to a woman, unless the man is of great importance or a member of the church, when it is the other way round. What is said isn't difficult: *'Mes hommages'* or *'Mes respects'* is said by a man to a woman, with the addition of *'Madame'* or *'Mademoiselle'*. The woman can simply smile and say *'Monsieur'* or *'Madame'*, with an inclination of the head. When a man is introduced to a man, he will give his name — 'John Smith' — while shaking hands. If anybody is of great importance, listen to whatever title they have and repeat it — *'Monsieur le Comte'*, *'Monsieur le Préfet'*, *'Docteur'*, *'Professeur'*, *'Monsieur le Curé'*, *'Monsieur le Deputé'*, *'Monseigneur'*, and so on, likewise for ladies of title and importance. Listen to how the introduction is made and copy it or, for any very formal occasion, ask advice in advance.

Other Grace Notes

Throughout the day you say *'Bonjour'* and, from around six in the evening, *'Bonsoir'*. *'Bonne soirée!'* is the farewell to people going out to dinner or a night on the town, *'Bonne nuit'* is 'Goodnight'. When saying goodbye, *'Adieu'* is somewhat formal: say *'Au revoir'* or *'À la prochaine'* (Till the next time). If people are travelling, say *'Bonne route'* or *'Bonne continuation'*, as alternatives to *'Bon voyage'*. (*See also p.12*)

Please and Thank You

When asking for anything — in a shop, a garage or a restaurant — preface your request or order with *'S'il vous plaît'*. Alas, it is said with some justification that the unfriendly reaction provoked by many tourists from the US is because the simple 'Please' and 'Thank you' phrases are not always used by them. When you get what you want, the acknowledgement is *'Merci'* or *'Merci bien'*, although, as you probably know, the word *'Merci'* when you are being offered anything, such as a second helping, means 'No thank you.' If you do want the second helping, *'S'il vous plaît'* is what you say. Always, in a shop, make use of the prefix *'Madame'* or *'Monsieur'* or *'Mademoiselle'*. (Look for the ring finger of a woman's hand.)

Do not use the second person singular — *'tu'* — unless you really are on very friendly terms with the person to whom you are speaking. You will hear it used to children, but, if in doubt, don't. There are even households where children say *'Vous'* to their parents!

When you have been introduced to someone, you may feel you have got to say something. Well, some people will say *'Enchanté(e)'* to you, but others shudder at the very idea — it is rather like saying 'Pleased to meetcher' in England for, although there's nothing basically amiss with this, it does have a slightly 'down-market' association. I have never got a definite answer about this tiny problem, but it is certainly in order for a woman to say *'Enchantée de faire votre connaissance'* if she is pleased to make someone's acquaintance, and a man can fling in an *'Enchanté'* to another man to show willing.

If you have to push past someone or jostle them, the phrase is *'Excusez-moi'*, or simply *'Pardon'*, to which the automatic and correct reply is *'Je vous en prie'*. You say it back if they say *'Excusez-moi'* to you.

When you have met someone they will usually ask *'Comment-allez vous?'*, to which the reply is *'Très bien, merci — et vous?'* whether you are in fact well or not. And should French friends greet you at any time before noon, they are pretty sure to enquire *'Vous avez bien dormi?'* to which you answer *'Très bien, merci'*, even if you have just passed the worst night of your life. Sending a greeting to another friend, you say *'Dites-lui bonjour de ma part'* or, more formally, *'Donnez mon meilleur souvenir à Madame Dupont'*, signifying 'My best wishes to Mrs Dupont'.

When saying goodbye to someone you have met for the first time or to whom you have been presented, say *'Très honoré(e)* or *privilegié(e) d'avoir fait votre connaissance.'*

Having a Drink

The query *'Vous voulez prendre quelque chose?'* means 'Would you like anything to drink?' This needn't mean anything alcoholic — order a coffee or mineral water if you wish. Friends greeting you may clink their glasses with yours — the verb is *trinquer*. You may hear them say *'Chin chin'*, a salutation that tends to surprise foreigners, but it is quite in order to say *'Santé!'* (Your health!) or *'À la vôtre!'* (To your health!)

═══════════ *Being a Guest* ═══════════

If you are invited to a meal, be punctual — if the food has been carefully ordered a delay may ruin the menu. But do not always assume that you will get an aperitif — you may go straight to the table, whether in a private house or in a restaurant, and, even if you are invited to have something to drink first, do not be put off if your hostess or other women guests refrain, while having a social chat before a meal. Sometimes, as a compliment, you will be offered '*Un petit whisky*' — when many friends from France visit me I have to remind myself that they may want this drink, whereas we do not always think of it as an aperitif, especially before any fine wines.

At table, be careful when picking up your napkin — it may conceal a roll or chunk of bread and to send this flying isn't an elegant beginning. There may not be a side plate — the French will put their bread on the cloth, as we British used to do.

Now for a curious divergence in manners from those across the Channel: in France, well-bred hands must rest on the table, up to the wristbone, on either side of the place-setting. '*Tes mains!*' from Maman makes children plonk their hands on the table, whereas 'Hands in your lap!' is the British command. No one seems to know why there is this difference, although many theories are put forward, but it is worth warning your children if you are travelling with them that this is what they will see at table.

Dishes are usually handed round twice, so avoid taking too large a helping first time round. However, sometimes — invariably when one wants a second helping — the dish doesn't reappear. Play safe, but give yourself enough. Glasses are set above your plate, cutlery on either side, forks with tines down. It is not usual to have all the cutlery set at once — the French visiting Britain are often surprised by the array of silverware in front of them — and utensils are generally supplied with the courses. But, except for very formal meals, you will probably have a knife rest set to the right of your plate, against which you prop knife and fork when you are helping yourself to a second portion or when the same implements are to be used for another subsequent course. One French manual of etiquette is firm that this *porte couteau* must never be used when the plates are to be changed — then one leaves the knife and fork on the plate. But I think that you are in a situation where you can never count on winning: you may have had fish and put the knife and fork on the plate — with a scornful air the person serving will take them off and put them on the *porte couteau*. You may have had meat and see that asparagus is coming, so you use your *porte couteau* — and the domestic removes them and puts them on the plate being cleared. Even French friends tell me one can never be sure. Keep an eye on the hostess (although she will probably be served last) if in any doubt.

Soup is eaten from the point of the spoon, not from the side, as in Britain. The use of the fork, with the knife put to the side of the plate, as in the US, is now fairly common. It is quite usual to pick up the shells of oysters or mussels and drink the liquid from them, also — except on very formal occasions — to use your fingers to get the little bits of meat off small game birds. Finger-bowls (*rince doigts*) usually arrive after such foods and they are also often put on the table when fruit is served at the end of the meal. Cheese will be served before the sweet course and dessert (fruit) and eaten with knife and fork. Sometimes, where a sauce is of great importance in a dish, such as with *moules marinières*, you will be given a spoon to scoop it up with.

Wine Meals
When there are several glasses set at your place for different wines, it is wise to keep a little of each wine in them. This enables you to take part or at least listen attentively to any conversation about them. Those who drain their glasses quickly may not get any more of what may be a rare wine.

Washing the Hands
It is not usual, unless your hosts are very cosmopolitan, to ask visitors if they wish to visit the cloakroom when they arrive at a private house or restaurant for a meal. Nor will you automatically be offered the chance of 'washing your hands' afterwards. So, if you wish to go to the bathroom, ask '*Voulez-vous m'indiquer le petit coin?*' Do not ask about 'washing your hands' — you may get shown a tap, with a yellow oval of soap on a spike, in a corridor. Nor, as far as women are concerned, is it really polite to attend to make-up over the dinner-table.

Smoking
Although sometimes you will find ashtrays set and, especially towards the Spanish border, hosts — even in the wine trade — may light up before the end of a meal, I think this shows a disregard for the food and the wines. Do not do it unless you are encouraged.

Afternoon Invitations
To be asked 'to tea' can be an informal or formal occasion. 'Le five o'clock' may be as late as six in the evening and is quite different from *goûter*, which is the meal children have when they arrive home from school. Be cautious, too, about avoiding the expression '*cinq à sept*', because it means an illicit rendezvous.

'Tea' with French friends may include an aperitif, especially *le porto*, drunk in enormous quantities; it sometimes turns out to be sherry. There are also the *vins doux naturels* (*see p.186*) which are sometimes offered. The refreshments may be biscuits, small cakes and, sometimes, pastries — with which you will get a pastry fork (seldom seen these days in the UK) so as not to get your fingers sticky. Tea itself may be served with hot or cold milk, or with cream — possibly American influence — and also with lemon. Sometimes you may be offered a dash of one of the fragrant French Caribbean *rhums* in the cup.

Staying with French Friends

Breakfast will probably include tea or coffee served in a big cup — called *un bol* — which may or may not have a handle. There will probably be a big spoon, larger than a teaspoon, for you to use if dunking your bread or croissant in the tea or coffee.

Saying Thank You

It is always pleasant, as well as indicating that one has been well brought up, to write a thank-you note. The French expression for this is *'la lettre du château'* and, although one famous friend of mine, whose knowledge of France is great, admits sending telegrams to avoid the nuances and complexities of the *'formules finales'* (correct endings) to letters, which are infinite, an expression of thanks in English, even if written on one's visiting-card, is a routine form of politeness. Even if you wait until you have returned home, do not omit this courtesy.

As regards tipping, if you stay in a private house, follow the same routine as you would do in your own country — make the gift in person, with an expression of appreciation. Even if you cannot make the tip lavish, the good wishes will be understood.

What About Flowers?

If your friends are country people, these may be superfluous, but a small basket of fine fruit or some of the exquisite candies and chocolates in which the French excel will be much liked. (Do not forget that any special cartons or boxes used for such a gift may cost as much as the present itself.) You can usually arrange with a shop for hosts to receive such a gift after they have entertained you — and the accompanying card need only say 'Thank you' or *'Merci infiniment pour une expérience inoubliable'* (Thank you for an unforgettable time) plus your name. Naturally, for friends you already know, you may have already brought a small gift. If the exigencies of travel have meant that you have put this in your luggage, do not forget that a shop where you buy, say, a small item such as a few sweets or a souvenir, may be able to gift-wrap the present at modest cost. The French still seldom mix flowers in bunches — to do so identifies you as a foreigner. But the florist will probably advise and, still, may counsel that it is conventional to send white flowers to a young girl (such as your host's daughter on her birthday), but that a white bouquet is a sign of mourning to an older woman. Red roses imply love. Something that can be much liked is if you bring a small piece of china into which a flower arrangement can be fitted — combining something British, something French.

Presents

Friends will always appreciate even a small gift — I have heard rapturous reports of an English lady who visited several French friends bearing lavender-bags and pot pourri made from the produce of her own garden. Anything typical of the donor's country or region will give pleasure. If you do not know the tastes of your hosts, consult the section overleaf for possible gifts.

La Celle, M. de Vindé's Country House, 4 June, 1820. We have coffee brought to us in our rooms about eight o'clock, and the family assemble at breakfast in the dining-room about ten: this breakfast has consisted of mackerel stewed in oil; cutlets; eggs, boiled and poached, au jus; peas stewed; lettuce stewed, and rolled up like sausages; radishes; salad; stewed prunes; preserved gooseberries; chocolate biscuits; apricot biscuits — that is to say, a kind of flat tartlet, sweetmeat between paste; finishing with coffee. There are sugar-tongs in this house, which I have seen nowhere else except at Madame Gautier's. Salt-spoons never to be seen, so do not be surprised at seeing me take salt and sugar in the natural way when I come back. . . . Dinner at half-past five; no luncheon and no dressing for dinner. . . . Wash hands at side table; coffee in the saloon; men and women all gathering round the table as of yore. But I should observe, that a great change has taken place; the men huddle together now in France as they used to do in England, talking politics with their backs to the women in a corner, or even in the middle of the room, without minding them in the least.

MARIA EDGEWORTH, *Letters*, 1800

As regards people in the wine-trade, it is now possible to present a bottle of an English wine, or, of course, any British liqueur, or — for lovers of 'le whisky' — a bottle of one of the straight malts.

Traditional foods are often overlooked. The shortbread 'petticoat tails', with its associations with Marie Stuart and *'petits queues de taille'*, biscuits for cheese, sweets and toffees (in households where there are children), a truckle of a British cheese or, certainly, portions or a side of smoked salmon are usually greeted with delight. More modestly, fine marmalades and jams and relishes (I sometimes take those I make myself) are gifts most people like anywhere. The French often love tea for breakfast, but take them Indian — in a traditional-looking tin or pack if possible. If you can find Dundee cake, Madeira cake, gingerbread and parkin in pretty tins, these are other ideas. The attractive packs of honeys, Gentleman's Relish, potted fish and meat are also possible gifts for anyone able to keep them cool along the way. (An hotel may put them — and smoked salmon — in their refrigerator overnight but don't forget them!) Another idea could be a special sort of cake. A friend of mine took a traditional British wedding-cake to France (by air) and it was greeted with much delight; the icing had been slightly damaged in transit, but the local *pâtissier* was charmed to repair it. A Christmas cake or christening cake might also be the focal point of a party buffet.

Other ideas — one runs short of inspiration sometimes when packing — include: small silverware, such as decanter labels, grape scissors, antique meat skewers (for use as letter openers), any little dishes or bowls; also cut-glass, British or Irish, and English bone china: remember that the *'service de table'* is still much in use, so that fruit-knives, dessert plates (or a single plate), bonbon dishes, comfit boxes, a pin-tray (useful for today's *petit fours*) or a platter will be gratefully received. Do not forget pewterware, either. Linen and tableware are other good — and easily packed — presents. The French tend to use cloths rather than mats on their tables, but mats can be an idea for anyone with a holiday house. Linen drying-cloths are a universal useful and acceptable gift. Another item that French friends of mine like are the heatproof mats, often with traditional scenes on them, that can be used at table or singly for plant stands. Otherwise, remember the charm of anything with a tradition behind it — the piece of pottery from some 'stately home'; an oddment from an antique shop, such as a napkin or potato ring; a pair of cordial glasses; a coaster or, of course, the latest gadget as regards extracting corks and serving wine.

10

Speaking French

The French are proud of their language and sensitive about its use — unlike the British: our sloppy diction, muttering through almost closed lips and the repetition of meaningless phrases and sounds, with a tiny vocabulary, is deplorable, considering the heritage of our literature. In France, people will comment with appreciation on the delivery and turn of phrase of anyone who speaks well. So, although in some countries you can get by with a few words and phrases, a smile and a 'How to say it' book, this does not apply in France where, even if you speak French fairly fluently, you may be stonewalled from time to time with a bleak *'Je ne comprends pas'* ('I don't understand'). But the charm and subtlety of the language is great and, once you have listened to the music of the French as spoken in Touraine, you will probably make an effort to brush up your pronunciation. To hear a conversation coruscating around a luncheon table is stimulating, even if you cannot take much part in it — do not expect anyone to slow down and translate just for your benefit. This can be the place for only a few prudent counsels. If yours is the French of the schoolroom, it may be innocent of terms and phrases current on French radio and television, but do not strain to make use of these — nothing is as odd as misplaced or out-of-date slang. Even if you are pretty sure you are speaking in a very 'antique' way, this, with an acceptable accent, may be understood more easily than interpolated 'pop' words and, possibly, argot (which is not always suited to polite conversation and — seldom realized — is not the same thing as dialect).

Beware of using expressions that, in English, now mean something slightly different from what they do in French: to a French person, to make a *'faux pas'* is to go astray — taking a step out of line; the expression to use is to make *'une gaffe'*. Similarly, a *'cul de sac'* is an *'impasse'*; a *contretemps* is *un malentendu; sensible* means sensitive and *demander* is a polite way of asking, not demanding; *aider* is to help — as you might help someone into a bus (which is *un car*), whereas *assister* means to give pecuniary help, as might be asked by someone planning to buy a horsebox (which is *un van*), or a van (which is *un camion* or *une camionnette*). See?

In gastronomy, however, things are simpler. *Rôtir* is to roast, *bouiller* to boil, *une forchette* is a fork, *moutard* is mustard, and so on — the Normans brought many such words along with them in 1066. Because of the 'Auld Alliance' between France and Scotland there are some similar words shared there too, such as *ashet* for a dish (*assiette*).

Many French will have learned their 'English' either in America or from someone who did not speak with a usual 'English' accent. This can be charming, but it can also be disconcerting for, as readers will know, some US words and phrases have also taken on meanings different from those they bear in England. Spelling can be a problem (see the postal alphabet on *p.98*), and remember that the French 'i' is pronounced like the English 'e', whereas the French 'e' is usually sounded like English 'er'. Accents, with which we have dispensed, indicate pronunciation and, these days, are often put on capital letters, such as on signposts. Nor does the double-barrelled name seem easy for the French to use — I speak with experience here! — which is rather odd, as they will cheerfully string together several noble-sounding surnames, linked by the highly regarded 'de'. If you have a surname that is really difficult for the French to pronounce, it can be a friendly gesture (and simplify introductions and telephone conversations) to make use either of part of the surname, or, as I often do, simply use the first name with a prefix.

Although French is not an easy language for many of us, the study of it can be very rewarding, and praise, when one has achieved accuracy in using terms and sounding words, can be outspoken and flattering. (Few Anglo-Saxons would say, about another, 'How well he/she speaks!' alas.) And some definite sensitivity to the French language is of importance in relation to wine and food. Winston Churchill could mangle the language of La Belle France — but his doing so didn't endear him to Général de Gaulle.

11

Visiting Vineyards

Many people try to plan a trip to a wine area at vintage time. But it does not occur on the same dates every year — to the surprise of many! In France the picking may start in the middle of September and last until the end of October or, in the more northern vineyards, begin a week or two later and even go on to the end of November. So this can be awkward if anyone is circumscribed by school or college vacations. In fact, though, vintage time is not ideal for exploring a wine region. Of course, you will see grapes being picked out in the vineyards. But many installations, working long hours while the weather is propitious, will not be able to receive and show around visitors who just turn up — many of the great estates definitely do not want casual tourists at this time. Producers will usually have many visitors from all over the wine world, who occupy such time as they may have with hard business and, certainly, hotel accommodation in any locality where a vintage is taking place may be difficult to find: some firms take rooms from year to year for their business clients. (This also applies to the major wine festivals, such as the sale of the Hospices de Beaune wines in November.)

Then — are you seriously keen on trying very young wines, not yet ready for drinking, that will have to be spat out? Many people are disillusioned about this but in fact some great estates now do not permit the more ordinary visitor to taste wines of this sort — one great Bordeaux property estimated that, in a few months, an entire cask of what would eventually have been a priceless fine wine would be spat onto the floor or into the spittoon if everyone arriving were offered a sample! It can be more interesting to see the vineyard, and possibly go round such parts of the winery as may be open — and then to enjoy a bottle of the wine that is ready to drink when travellers sit down to lunch later on. But, if you are accustomed to trying young wines, get an introduction if you seriously wish to taste any where they are made.

Another basic reason why vintage time isn't ideal for sampling very recent earlier vintages is that then, and at the flowering of the vine in the spring, wines can be somewhat off colour; the curious link between wine and vine is evident then and even wines long in bottle can seem less than at their best at such times. So do not condemn a wine sampled during the height of vintage and at the spring flowering if you find them less interesting and exciting than you expected.

Among the best times to visit vineyards, in my opinion, is, first, the high summer, when the grapes are filling out and, possibly, changing colour; this means June and July, for in August most workers go on holiday and offices and cellars may only keep a skeleton staff, so that there may not be anyone to meet you and show you round. The beginning of September, just before the vintage, is another possible time, when excitement about the forthcoming crop will begin to be felt and you may see the preparations starting on the various presshouses, where equipment will be cleaned up and got ready. If you do not have to do your visiting in warm weather, then another good time is after the vintage, in the late autumn. Then the vine leaves turn colour before they fall, and the vineyards present a panorama of gold, yellow and crimson. Where only a single variety is planted, such as in the red wine vineyards of Burgundy, the brilliance of the Pinot Noir is spectacular; along the Loire the white wine vineyards are shaded from yellowish green to a soft gold.

In some regions, such as Alsace, the central areas of the Loire, Bordeaux, Burgundy and the southern Rhône there are, at all times of the year, many things for the wine-minded visitor to see: museums devoted to wine and sometimes special regional tastings and wine fairs. Bear in mind that, after the summer, many small hotels and restaurants at what can be thronged resorts, have their 'fermeture annuelle' or closing; others take this break soon after Christmas.

Some returned travellers express disappointment at not seeing stocks of cobwebbed bottles of old vintages when they visit châteaux — and several also find it surprising that they are not always offered a free drink! But, with the exception of the private reserves of the owners of an estate, wines should have been sold, either direct to customers or through the shippers, so that, ideally, no old wines ought to be still in store where they are made. Usually, when wines have been bottled, they will leave their home cellars. As for free hospitality — the larger Champagne houses and some of the big co-ops often conclude their organized tours with a glass of wine, but, especially on properties where the wines may need some time to mature to being enjoyable drinks, there are not facilities or space for offering drinks. The finest wines may, eventually, be sold at high prices — they are, understandably, in short supply for quaffing, even by serious wine-minded visitors.

Organized Wine Holidays and Tours

There are a number of firms who offer tours in wine regions these days and this sort of 'package' can be convenient to people who do not have much time and who prefer to be driven rather than drive themselves. When appraising their brochures, note whether there is anyone knowledgeable in charge, who can answer questions, not merely a paid employee of a firm who will promote their wines. Also, if this is taken as a holiday or part of one with a husband, wife or friend who is really not 100 per cent serious about wine, it can be a tedious matter to see vineyard after vineyard, winery after winery, tasting only young wines (when allowed to do so) that are not ready to enjoy. If a tour is centred on a city or some place where it is possible to go off and shop, see the sights, swim or otherwise pass the time, this enables the non-wine-minded to have an enjoyable day or half-day. Check the time-table — it takes longer to travel in a mini-bus or coach than a private car and, especially if there has been a 'gastronomic' lunch, people may find this really tiring. Ideally, make sure that there is even an hour or two free, for exploring and maybe simply sitting in a café and absorbing the local atmosphere.

In most wine regions the independent traveller will find some 'routes du vin' signposted — the local Syndicat d'Initiative will probably have brochures showing them. Along the way most of the great estates will be indicated and there are usually signs to any salons de dégustation (tasting-rooms). If these are run by the local growers' association, they are generally worth visiting, for you can sample wines, see maps of the region and pictures of the vineyards. Sometimes a small charge is made for tasting, sometimes you contribute what you wish. There may be bottles on sale, but no pressure to buy — but the tasting-rooms of individual growers, with placards saying '*Visitez!*' or '*Dégustation gratuite*' may well expect you to buy wine as well as sampling a few — and such firms are not likely to be able to provide general information.

For those who have not done much vineyard visiting, I would advise concentrating on one of the more important regions: Bordeaux, Burgundy, Alsace, Champagne, the Loire and the Rhône Valley. A famous estate is always of interest, a small establishment may not be typical — and the large concern may have multi-lingual guides.

Introductions
Ideally, get your own wine merchant to suggest and possibly arrange some contacts for you. Of course, any appointments should be scrupulously kept — no one should be kept waiting for your arrival. Telephone or get someone to ring up on your behalf if you are delayed. But if you do not want too circumscribed a time-table, suggest to whoever is making the contact to inform their principal as to when you will be in the area and say that you will then telephone to arrange a specific appointment. Do not forget the sacred 'lunch-hour' — from midday until two in the afternoon or sometimes from one until three; during this time the switchboard may be closed. Should you not be able to make an introduction of this sort, your hotel or a restaurant may be able to arrange something on the spot. But do not make any schedule of visits too tight — in the country, one appointment may take far longer than is anticipated and you may be so interested that you linger.

Saying 'Thank you'
Usually it is made obvious if you are expected to tip any guide who shows you round a wine establishment — the hat will be doffed and the hand held out. If, though, it is a member of the firm's staff who shows you round, you should only shake hands and express verbal thanks. In the country, especially at vintage times, this sort of 'guide', in *bleus de travail* (overalls) and espadrilles, may be far more than a mere workman — possibly the *maître de chai* (cellarmaster), *régisseur* (bailiff), or one of the directors of the concern, maybe even the millionaire owner. Shake hands and express appreciation — the very idea of tipping the *maître de chai* of an historic estate shocks traditionalists, who may well be

correct in supposing that such persons could buy up the majority of visitors, but one friend of mine in the Bordeaux wine trade did admit to tipping this character on one occasion — 'He was a huge man, with a cauliflower ear and he loomed up suggestively.' But this is not usual. Nor should you suppose that anyone who conducts you round a vineyard or winery is ignorant of English: they may have had a British nanny, been to a British school or university — and will therefore pick up any phrases in English you may mutter among yourselves. Be polite and tactful — even if they pay you the compliment of letting you speak French to them.

Festivals and Parties

Bear in mind that for many of these the places where they are held will be crowded with local and other visitors and accommodation may be difficult to find. (*See p.335.*)

At the end of vintage, there is usually some sort of party on the estates, but this is only rarely a 'picturesque' occasion, such as may attract the traveller. Those involved with the picking have completed a hard task — now they want to enjoy themselves among themselves. Unless specifically invited by owners of properties, outsiders are not always truly welcome. In the major wine towns there may be some sort of public celebration, such as a vintage Mass and procession of the local dignatories and the wine order — traffic comes to a standstill and every restaurant and bar will be crammed.

And here we were, at Château Lafite-Rothschild. It was just a house, really; a house surrounded by vineyards . . . (he) then exhibited proudly the famous 'vin bibliothèque' of the Rothschilds: a cellar containing over one hundred thousand bottles of every notable claret of every year, as far back as 1780. . . . We walked the whole way down the cellar . . . and then the whole way back again, speaking in whispers. . . . Had I been a child, I would have . . . said out loud as we neared the door: 'Yes, but isn't he going to *give* us a bottle now? Aren't *we* to drink any of it?' Apparently this was not part of the ceremonial. I decided, not without cause, that the Rothschilds had too much good wine, and I too little.

G.B. STERN, *Bouquet*, 1927

133

What About Working at Vintage Time?

This can sometimes be arranged through student organizations or, of course, a personal contact. Remember that picking grapes is as hard work as lifting potatoes and teams of vintagers may have to work long hours under the hot sun or, even, in the mud after any rain. The odd day or two of work is not required — you must agree to work throughout a determined period, else you are not paid. Meals — with wine — are provided, also, sometimes, accommodation, though this can be somewhat primitive. The regular bands of vintagers can be tough characters, so if you cannot speak even a little French you will be at a disadvantage. It can be very hard work to help with vintaging, though those who manage to do so get to know French life as it truly is and may have a merry time as well. But it is not for the delicate and, certainly, no easy way of paying for a trip to a more luxurious resort!

Cellars, Tasting-rooms and Tasting

Wear comfortable clothes and walking-shoes, preferably of material that will not be spoiled if wine or damp earth gets in contact with them. Take a jacket for going round any cellar, a coat for the cellars of Champagne and where sparkling wines are made — they really are cold. Once inside, you may not suddenly be able to run back and get a sweater. It should be realized, too, that some cellars, especially in Champagne, are very deep and, although adequately lit, they are dark; anyone who dislikes being underground for any length of time should remain in the reception-room or outside. Women are also advised that they may have to go up and down ladders, winding stairs and, sometimes, across open-work grids — do not wear high heels.

In a *salon de dégustation*, the host or person in charge will probably offer a visitor wine that is ready to drink; each visitor will have a glass. But you are under no obligation to finish the wine, although, if it is anything special, make a gesture of drinking some. If you are offered a range of young wines, spit them out. They are unlikely to be pleasant drinks and may upset the stomach. If there is a spittoon or sink, use this. In a cellar, if there is nowhere obvious to spit, either go outside or spit on the floor. One would not do this in the impeccably kept *chais* of the great Bordeaux châteaux or anywhere else that is meticulously kept free from any spilt wine but, if casks are standing on wooden props above earth or gravel, spit between them onto this — it tends to splash too widely if you spit onto a stone floor. If in doubt, see what other people do and copy them.

The procedure of tasting, wherever you do it, is the same: tilt the glass slightly away from you, if possible over something white or light coloured, so as to see its colour; swing it round in the glass to release the bouquet and sniff this, then take a little into the mouth, plus, if you like, a little air — this seems to intensify the taste. Pull the wine around in your mouth, spit it out — or, of course, swallow if it is ready for drinking — then 'huff' through nose and mouth so as to get the after-taste or echoes of smell and flavour that circulate in the cavities of the face.

Glasses are usually held by the stem or the foot, as this prevents the hand making the bowl of the glass greasy and you will find it is easier to swing the wine around.

In a professional tasting-room a range of wines, with a glass in front of each, may be offered for you to taste. Do not be hesitant about sharing the glass with everyone else, unless, of course, you have a cold or mouth infection, when you can ask for a glass to yourself. In such a place, it is thoughtful not to arrive smelling strongly of scent, hair lotion, sun-cream, after-shave, anti-mosquito spray or anything similar. Nor it is considerate to light a cigarette in the tasting-room, even when work is finished — the smell may take hours to disperse. As a firm's turnover depends on the people who select and buy the wine, by smelling and tasting, it is only right that your presence is not a distraction, even when they are not working very seriously. If your host offers you a cigarette — and many of the wine trade smoke — then of course it is in order to accept if you wish. Do not, however, assume that the small saucer-like metal cups that may be standing about are ashtrays: they may be *tastevins*, carefully kept for professional use. True, souvenir shops do sell *tastevins* that can serve as ashtrays — but make sure that wherever you put your ash is not a cherished tasting-cup.

The Wine Orders

From early medieval times most French wine regions had specific fraternities concerned with wine, just as those in other forms of trade and business had their guilds. Sometimes these fraternities were almost the governing bodies of the locality: the Jurade of Bordeaux was virtually the town council. Anyway, the wine orders established certain procedures, attempted to maintain quality, assisted with trading in all its aspects and, in addition to celebrating at particular festivals, looked after members and their families who fell on hard times. One of their most important functions was to proclaim the vintage — by means of what is referred to as the *'Ban des Vendanges'*. Before it was announced when this might start, no one could pick the grapes — something that still applies in Alsace — and, by making the wine early, get a start on competitors. Of course, this sort of thing could result in unripe grapes and sour wine, but sometimes the growers who could offer visiting buyers wine earlier than anyone else, did profit — and quality could decline.

One of the most widely-known of the surviving orders, as opposed to those created or re-created in modern times, is the second oldest of all, the Jurade of St Émilion, founded in 1199. The *'jurats'* or officers of this were at once magistrates, tax collectors, administrators and, if necessary, military leaders. They surveyed the quality of their wine, destroying any judged inferior. Their importance and influence was considerable. With the unification of France at the end of the Middle Ages, the government was established in Paris, the capital; the wine orders fell into decline and many ceased to exist. But their traditions were not forgotten. In 1904 the wine growers of Anjou, anxious to encourage interest in the wines of their region, founded the first of what are termed the 'bacchic associations' of today. This was the Chevaliers du Sacavin. Then, in the time of the great depression between the two World Wars, the Confrérie du Chevaliers du Tastevin was started at Nuits St Georges in Burgundy, to stimulate interest in wine. Its activities proved so successful that 'chapters' of sessions were set up in a number of countries where Burgundy wines sought to keep and extend their sales. Eminent people and 'personalities' from all over the world are invited to Tastevin ceremonies today. In 1944 the Chevaliers du Tastevin bought the Château du Clos de Vougeot, the historic Cistercian building, where the banquets and installations — *intronisation* — of new members of the order now take place. The order makes a selection of wines each year, which are marked with its special seal — *'Tasteviné'*. The example of wine-growers and makers of spirits has also been followed by the cheese-makers and the oldest gastronomic fraternity in the world, the Guild of Goose Roasters, founded in 1248, was revived in 1950 and is now the Chaîne des Rôtisseurs, concerning itself with improving the standards of spit roasting.

Any ceremony of these fraternities is worth watching, with the officers in medieval-style robes, speeches and often some tasting and, for very special occasions, feasting. The work in publicizing and promoting the various products with which they are concerned is of importance and to be invited to become a member of any gastronomic order is an honour. It should not be assumed, however, that ordinary members are necessarily authorities on the wines or products, although in some instances it is necessary to be fairly experienced in knowledge of them.

(A list of the wine and spirit fraternities is given on *pp.141—2*.)

Although the public manifestations of the wine fraternities may take place at almost any time — except August — throughout the year, they usually hold some ceremony at the *'Ban'* or proclamation of the vintage in the autumn; indeed, in Alsace, this is official permission to pick — no one can start earlier! The other big moment is in the spring, the *'Fête de la Fleur'* or flowering of the vine. The vintage usually takes place one hundred days after the flowering. It is possible to see any processions or public events by simply arriving early and getting oneself a place of vantage along the ceremonial route, but for the *'intronisations'* or installations of members and of course for any formal meals, a ticket is necessary for admission — wine firms can sometimes arrange these but, if you are trying to buy one (perhaps through your hotel), be warned that the occasion can be fairly expensive, though it may well prove memorable.

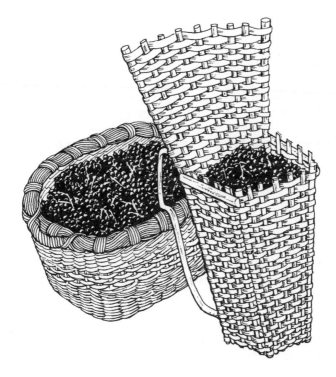

The Year in Vineyard and Cellar

Although activities vary, according to the location of the vineyard, there is usually something going on, both out of doors and within the installations, throughout the year of interest to visitors. The following calendar basically refers to the Bordeaux region, which is not only extensive but is visited by many wine enthusiasts; add on a week or two for vineyards further north, subtract the same time for any in the south. But do not forget that in regions where the area is broken up by many micro-climates certain activities, such as harvesting, may be a week or more apart even from inside quite a small region.

January: Wines made in the previous autumn — the vintage — will be carefully watched. Any in cask will be regularly topped up, the bungs cleaned and inspected. Out of doors, it is traditional for spring pruning to begin on St Vincent's Day, 22 January, but nowadays the process may be started in December. Watch is kept should it be very cold and, sometimes, smudge pots may be hit in any exposed vineyards or the vines may be sprayed to keep them encased in ice so as not to be frozen and destroyed.

February: The process of racking begins — transferring the wine into fresh casks, leaving the lees or deposit behind. In installations where the previous season's wines have been made from different grape varieties or separate plots have been picked at different times from others, the process of *'assemblage'* may start, when the contents of all the previous year's wines are put together in a vat or vats, prior to being run off again into separate casks or vats, each 'collection' of wines being appraised while this is being done. In the vineyard, cuttings for grafting are now taken and, when necessary, the grafts are put to the rootstocks of vines and kept indoors, in boxes of sand.

March: 21 March, the spring equinox, is when the vine seems to be particularly in contact with the wine — the second stage of fermentation is traditionally supposed to begin when the sap is rising in the vines, but of course the fermentation starts again anyway with the beginning of warmer weather. Now the spring rackings should be completed and the casks, to which the wine has been returned (if it doesn't go into a vat), must be topped up. Any wines that are scheduled for bottling immediately after the fermentation has finished are put ready for the bottling line. This is also the time when trade buyers begin to come visiting and sampling — some may start making purchases earlier, but when the spring rackings have been finished, it is possible to have a more definite idea of the quality of the wine. Outside, the vineyard workers go along the rows of vines, opening out the soil at the base of each vine, so as to aerate it.

April: The stress shifts out of doors, although casks are still carefully watched and any stocks that have not yet been bottled are observed and, when required, put to the bottling line. Now the vineyard has to be ploughed and generally set in order. Any young cuttings should have been planted. This is a slightly uneasy time, because, if vegetation comes on too fast, due to very fine weather, the young shoots of the vines are still at risk.

May: Wines in cask should be racked off for the second time. The vineyard, meanwhile, must be weeded, sprayed against any vine pests and the surplus shoots have to be trimmed off while the sap is still rising. The mid-May period is that of the 'Ice Saints' (Pancras, Servatius, Boniface, Sophid), whose feast days occur then — and so do any late frosts, which can literally destroy vines at this time. Even the wealthiest owners may not sleep easy until the dangerous season is past and the warmer weather sets in.

June: Indoors, the second racking of the wines in cask should have been completed and older wines still in wood or vat will also be racked. Now everyone watches for the flowering of the vines, which, ideally, takes place within a few days, so that the 'set' is satisfactory — and so that an idea as to when the vintage will take place, one hundred days later, may be worked out. The delicate fragrance of a vineyard in flower is something any traveller should try to remember — it lasts such a short time but is so charming.

July: The vines are sprayed against pests and they are also trimmed or topped, the shoots being lopped away in case they take nourishment from the minute bunches of grapes which may be seen forming after the flowering. Vineyard workers will be spraying and weeding frequently.

August: The big holiday month — and many people go away and even big establishments close, although a skeleton staff will keep watch. The vines must be supervised, although now it is a matter of watching them — and hoping! Any wine not bottled must be inspected and watched, in case any high temperatures during the summer may affect it adversely.

September: All the equipment used during the vintage (often the only time of the year it is used) must be cleaned and put ready. Casks are prepared — filled with water to swell the staves; vats are cleaned, workers insert themselves into them, one arm and one shoulder first, to prepare them for receiving the *must*. Anyone who has got too plump to get in receives much teasing! Outside, the grapes are filling out and the black varieties will begin to turn colour. The ripening fruit attracts birds so, in some regions, nets go over the vines and bird scarers are put into use. Everyone now hopes for fine, warm weather, not necessarily a very hot time, and perhaps for a little light rain, possibly at night, which can plump out the grapes and give a bigger crop. But heavy rain or, of course, hail is damaging as it can split the skins of the fruit and batter the stems of the vines. People watch the skies (and telephone the meteorological stations).

October: Vintage has usually started throughout the vineyards of France and, in some regions, especially where mechanical harvesters are in use, can go on almost all round the clock, because, by harvesting in the cooler night hours (but before the heavy dews), the grapes can come into the winery without risking the heat causing fermentation to start even *en route*. Stress is on picking the grapes and making the wine but, when labour can be spared, the vineyard is tidied up and, often, manured. Work on any new plantations of vines may be started, ploughing can take place and plans are made by those primarily concerned with the vineyard rather than the wine for what is going to happen next year. In the winery the grapes are crushed as they come in, then they are left so that the fermentation can start and, after it is complete in this initial stage, the wine is run off into casks or stored in other vats; the process continues until all sections of the vineyard have been picked and, in those regions where 'noble rot' (*pourriture noble*) may develop, the vintagers may have to pass through the vineyard many times, long after the ordinary vintage has been picked, so as to use their skill and experience in selecting the tiny bunches or, even, single grapes on which the *botrytis* has acted. It is not unknown, in some northern vineyards, for the last days of the picking to take place when snow has fallen! At the end of the vintage, the wines of the previous year's vintage are racked for the last time and then the bungs in their casks are driven home firmly and the casks turned so that the bungs are on one side, held tight by the pressure of the wine within. Then these casks will be removed to the section of the cellar or *chai* where they will remain for the second year of their maturation. The wines of the new vintage go into cask — or vat — and, if in cask, the bungs are only loosely inserted, so that any gas given off during the continuation of the fermentation can escape through the bunghole on the top of the cask.

November: The furious type of fermentation dies down as the weather gets colder and the yeasts cease to be active. Mature wine, intended for bottling, is racked off if it is now thought to be ready and it may then be fined, although in some vintages it may remain on its lees a little longer. Outside, the vine shoots are finally trimmed off, manuring is finished and the soil around the base of the vinestocks is ploughed or raked up to provide protection against frost.

December: Equipment and machinery in use at vintage time should now be cleaned and put away — most of it is needed only once in the year and it must be protected while not in use. Plans may be made to replace or invest in new machines — if the vintage seems likely to be profitable. Oldish wines not yet bottled may now be put finally to the bottling line. Some pruning may be started before Christmas. Those concerned with sales begin to think about the quality as well as the quantity of the wine just made — and prepare their reports to customers. Because this is the season of the year when many people buy wine, publicity is augmented by those who can motivate it and cautious estimates of prices begin to circulate.

Wine and Spirit Fraternities

Confrérie de St Étienne d'Alsace
Connétablerie de Guyenne
Commanderie du Bontemps du Médoc et des Graves
Jurade de St Émilion
Les Compagnons du Beaujolais
Confrérie des Chevaliers du Tastevin (Côte d'Or)
Confrérie Saint Vincent des Vignerons de Mâcon
Les Piliers Chablisiens (Chablis)
Commanderie de Champagne
Ordre Illustre des Chevaliers de Méduse (Côtes de Provence)
Les Mestres Tastaires du Languedoc
Ordre des Chevaliers du Cep (Montpellier)
Ordre de la Dive Bouteille et Confrérie Albigeoise de Rabelais
   (Gaillac)
Viguerie Royale du Jurançon
Confrérie des Chevaliers de la Chantepleure (Vouvray)
Confrérie des Chevaliers du Sacavin (Angers)

141

Ordre des Chevaliers Bretvins (Nantes)
Confrérie Vineuse des Tire-Douzil (Vienne)
Sabotée Sancerroise et Comité de Propagande des Vins A.O.C. de Sancerre
Confrérie Saint Vincent des Vignerons de Tannay (Nièvre)
Confrérie des Chevaliers de la Canette (Deux Sèvres)
Confrérie des Chevaliers des Cuers de Baril (Loches)
Ordre des Fins Palais de Saint Pourçain en Bourbonnais
Paierie des Grands Vins de France (Arbois)
Compagnie du Sarto (Savoie)
Compagnie des Mousquetaires d'Armagnac
Principauté de Franc Pineau (Cognac)
Commanderie de l'Île de France des Anysetiers du Roy (Paris)

N.B. The names in brackets indicate the town or wine region with which the various organizations are chiefly concerned, should this not be clear in their names.

My companion in the cabriolet of the diligence was a young wine-merchant of Bordeaux, who was going to look after the affairs of his house at their entrepôt at Bercy, the suburb on the Seine, outside the barrier of Paris, at which all the wine from the south destined for the consumption of the capital arrives ... he told me several anecdotes of prices almost incredible given for choice wines; but mentioned none so high as that which another merchant told me of, upon another occasion. He had recently sold, he said, a thousand bottles of Chateau Margaux to the emperor of Russia, at thirty-six francs a bottle. It was forty-four years old, and had a bouquet, which the owner assured me scented strongly the whole of a large room as soon as ever it was opened.

T. ADOLPHUS TROLLOPE, *A Summer in Western France*, Vol.II, 1841

12

Some Basic Wine Background

Certain terms are sure to crop up in wine talk, so it is helpful to have a précis of what they imply. Unless you are truly well versed in wine, I advise being cautious about expressing too many opinions on matters about which your French friends may hold strong views. The same need for discretion applies to voicing criticism of wines you may have tasted at different establishments — your host of the moment will prefer to concentrate on *his* wines and you may not always be aware of his relationship with, say, somebody you visited on the previous day — it may be a competitor, it can be some family connection; the word 'grape-vine' is full of significance, so that what you may have said on one day can be quoted in another house, another region, even another country the day after! Even praise, unless you know for sure that your host is both a friend and colleague of whoever you are talking about, can be undiplomatic. Intelligent acquaintance with some of the expressions to be seen on labels and referred to in wine conversation will always be received with respect.

Appellation d'Origine Contrôlée/Appellation Contrôlée/A.O.C./A.C.

This is a control or series of controls exercised by the Institut National des Appellations d'Origine des Vins et Eaux-de-Vie, which is often referred to by its initials INAO. It is a government-appointed body, supported by a levy exacted on every hectolitre of wine vintaged in France and keeps a strict watch on all wines and spirits distilled from wine grapes to which an A.O.C. has been or may be granted. It is in some sort the equivalent of a pedigree, preventing the famous names of some wines from being exploited;

it does not only say what the wine is, where it comes from and how it is made, but relates it to its traditions and capabilities. It is, as may be imagined, a prized acquisition. INAO grant an A.O.C. after an application is made, taking into consideration the requirements of the local syndicates of the relevant wine trade. In brief, the A.O.C. rules define:

(a) The exact area within which the wine may be grown and made.

(b) The types of grapes planted and the way they are cultivated. (Pruning and training.)

(c) The amount of vines planted per hectare (a hectare is 2.471,05 acres).

(d) The minimum amount of sugar in the 'must' (unfermented grape-juice).

(e) The minimum degree of alcohol in the finished wine.

(f) The maximum production of wine per hectare, in hectolitres. (A hectolitre is approximately 22.4 gallons UK.)

The A.C. is also subject to the granting of the 'label', which signifies something rather more than the English word 'label'. It is awarded each year as the result of the tastings organized by the local wine committees.

The essential thing to remember is that the A.O.C. — which doesn't apply only to wine, for some cheeses, and 'poulets de Bresse' also have their A.C.s — implies but cannot *guarantee* quality. No piece of paper can. Only those who make the wine and handle it can do this. But in general all A.O.C. wines should be good. All the fine wines of France are now A.O.C., being obliged by law to have the words '*Appellation Contrôlée*' printed clearly on labels, either above or below the name of the wine. The one exception is Champagne, which may use merely the phrase '*Vin de Champagne*'.

The A.O.C. regulations apply, first, to an area, such as Bordeaux, Côtes du Rhône, Beaujolais; or they apply to a smaller region within that area — Médoc, Graves, Châteauneuf du Pape, St Émilion, and so on. The type of wine — *rouge, blanc, rosé* — is often added. Then, within this sub-division, there may be others: Moulin-à-Vent within Beaujolais, Gigondas within Côtes du Rhône, St Julien within Médoc. Obviously a great estate in the Bordeaux region could, by someone who did not realize the significance of the A.C. regulations, be thought of as 'Bordeaux', or 'Bordeaux Supérieur' or 'Médoc' or 'Haut-Médoc' or, coming down to the exact parish, 'Pauillac' — and this might be the great first growth, Château Latour! The significance of the A.C. is essential if people are to know exactly what they are getting: in the overall Bordeaux region, there are sixty-one 'Château La Tour something or other'. There are seven 'Châteaux Latour' properties. But there is only *one* Château Latour of which the A.C. is Pauillac — the great first growth. This is why knowing what the A.C. is enables a potential purchaser to know what the price should be — a cheap 'Château Latour' might be a perfectly good claret, but by no means of first growth quality.

In Burgundy, the A.C.s are somewhat more complex, but they too fit inside each other, each superior A.C. being subject to more demanding requirements by the authorities. Sometimes the A.C. is the same name as that of a parish or commune. The tip of the pinnacle is probably Château Grillet, in the Rhône, which is within the parish of Saint Michel, this having the A.C. Condrieu; but Château Grillet, making only a few casks of wine per annum, has an A.C. all to itself.

The traveller may hear all sorts of arguments about these regulations. Suppose in one year a vineyard produces, quite legitimately, more than the permitted amount of wine? (The *rendement.*) The maker will not be able to put the usual A.C. and the authorized name on this extra and, of course, if the wine cannot bear this, it will not fetch as high a price if it has to be sold under a lower A.C. To 'declassify' a wine to a lower category, or maybe use it in one of the firm's blends or as part of a general wine, can involve a serious loss of prestige as well as money. Suppose a vineyard is actually on the boundary of the limits of a particular A.C. — how can it be possible to divide the wine, which may be made in the same *cuverie?* One can give as an example of the problems involved by too much being laid down in regulations, the circumstance of the dry wines of the Sauternes region today: when the A.C. controls were established, these wines all had to be sweet — which means that, now, the dry versions made by some great estates can merely bear the *A.C. Bordeaux Supérieur.*

All these are much debated matters and the visitor will be wise not to take sides — although, of course, the more a wine-lover can learn from hearing such things discussed on the spot, the more the wine can ultimately be appreciated.

V.D.Q.S.

Vins Délimités de Qualité Supérieure or V.D.Q.S. wines are also subject to controls as regards production, though slightly less rigorous ones than for the A.C. wines. The initials denoting them must be on the label or a separate stick-on label. This category is likely to be phased out in the future, but meanwhile the wines offer both interest and, usually, quality.

Vins de pays
Vins de pays were legally defined in 1979, the category coming between that of the V.D.Q.S. and that of the *vins de table* — although, slightly confusingly, the term *'vin de table'* may also be on the label of a *vin de pays*. *Vins de pays* are subject to quite strict controls, including the judgement by a tasting panel, and the amount allowed to be produced from the defined vineyards is restricted, so as to maintain quality. There are a large number of *vins de pays* and apparently they are the only E.E.C. wines to bear the names of the regions where they originate. Usually, *vins de pays* are quite interesting, sometimes even more so — in their essentially regional style — than V.D.Q.S. wines. Some bear pretty names — Île de Beauté, Jardin de la France and many more.

Remember that, when you want a local wine, do not, these days, ask for a *'vin de pays'* — the expression you employ is a *'vin de la région'*.

Vins de table
Vins de table are wines in a slightly lower category than *vins de pays* but, as is mentioned above, sometimes the label can use both categories. *Vins de marque* are branded wines, sometimes non-vintage blends put out by the large wine concerns and intended as *vins de consommation courants* — wines for everyday drinking. In some regions, certain of the registered brands of reputable shippers and, even more important, certain growers, can be distinguished in style, in spite of the seemingly modest labels they bear. Should an estate or specific vineyard make more wine than permitted in the legal *'rendement'* (return), this may be sold under a different and less high-sounding name and, of course, at a lower price. It can then be quite a bargain for it will actually be the *'grand vin'* under another name or, sometimes, the wine of young vines. But here it is the name of the grower or shipper that should give you a clue.

Things to Note
In certain regions, especially Burgundy, you may see the wines of individual growers, as well as those handled by the shippers; the differences in style, even between wines of the same vintage, bearing the same overall vineyard name, can be considerable and

interesting. Do make notes of any label details, should you wish to report on the wines you try or are likely to mention them to your merchant at home; this sort of information is always important. The address of the firm who did the bottling is also relevant, if bottling is not done at the place where the wine was made. Every single bit of information on a wine's label is subject to controls and, except for the cheapest wines, so is the shape and colour of the bottle; with the finest wines, the controls are strictest of all.

Strength

It is impossible to determine alcoholic strength merely by tasting, but all wines fall into certain categories as regards this, so you do not risk quaffing a 'high strength' wine with a meal by mistake! Do not be misled by a wine with a flowery bouquet and full flavour and suppose this to be 'heady' (*capiteux*) or alcoholically strong. It may be lower in strength than a thin beverage from a carafe.

Here are the approximate strengths of the main French wines and spirits, expressed in percentage of alcohol by volume, a term usually referred to as 'Gay Lussac', after Joseph Gay-Lussac (1778-1850), the chemist who made it famous:

Red, white and rosé still wines	8–12°
The great Sauternes	12–14°
Champagne and most sparkling wines	12–13°
Vins doux naturels	15–20°
Vermouth and many aperitifs	16–20°
Liqueurs and fruit cordials	30–60°
Brandy, including Cognac, Armagnac and *marc*	45–55°

Sometimes you may hear a wine particularly praised for being at the top limit of the alcoholic content; this can make it more resistant to infections and the hazards of travel but, especially in its homeland, it need not always be obviously superior in quality. Of course, the workman who sinks his litre or so of '*gros rouge*' (the term used for very ordinary red wine) when he wants a quick lift at the end of the day, will appreciate a wine that is slightly higher in strength, but this is not presumably why you drink wine. If you are buying wine of ordinary quality in a supermarket, you may discover that, after a wine of 12° or 13.5° in the lower price ranges, you feel sleepy and disinclined to drive after using it for a midday picnic and therefore you will do better with a wine of 11° or 11.5°. But this is wholly personal.

147

Wine Vocabulary

Here are some of the words you will probably hear — the significance of which may not always be easy to grasp. And you will not find many of the definitions in even a good dictionary anyway. But if you are trying to follow someone explaining a process, some of the words may be helpful. Bear in mind that, from wine region to wine region, there may be special words and expressions that will not, perhaps, be understood elsewhere. But the following will enable you to get by.

People

Être dans le vin: To be in the wine trade.

Un courtier is a broker; *un fermier* is a peasant farmer; *un propriétaire* is the owner of a vineyard — large or small; *un régisseur* is a bailiff, estate manager or, even, a director of the whole concern — a very important person.

Un marchand de vin is a wine merchant; in France he may be a small-scale distributor, not quite the same sort of person as 'merchant' implies in the UK.

Un négociant éleveur is a shipper; *le négoce* is a term for the shippers in general.

Le maître de chai is the cellarmaster, in charge of making and generally seeing to the wine — another very important person.

Une caviste is the term used for a cellar worker, but, especially in Champagne, this is someone far more important than a mere 'hand' — he will be somebody skilled in looking after the wine.

Un oenologue is a wine specialist.

Un vigneron is a vineyard worker; *un vendangeur* a vintager.

Places

Un château is a house — large or small — to which a vineyard belongs, but it is a term also used to signify the vineyard or the property in general. It can be used anywhere, but is chiefly associated with the wine estates of Bordeaux — although there is not necessarily a 'Château' on all the properties.

Un clos is an enclosed property. It is used in wine regions in general, but is often associated with Burgundy, where several owners may have holdings within the same 'Clos'.

Une propriété is a property; *un vignoble* is a vineyard; *un climat* is a particular site — a term often used in Burgundy.

Soils

Le terroir is the soil and *Le goût de terroir* is the taste given by the vineyard to the particular wine — but this term should be used with caution because it can be pejorative, signifying that the wine tastes unpleasantly earthy.

Le sol is the soil and *Le sous-sol* the sub-soil; this is particularly important because the tap-root — *Le pivot* — of a mature vine may go down twelve to fifteen feet, so that the sources of its nourishment can be influential.

Argile is clay; *calcaire* is limestone; *craie* is chalk; *graves* is gravel; *graveleux* is gravelly; *gravier* is gravel by itself; *sable* is sand. *Alois* or *Aliotique* is a type of sandstone peculiar to the south-west of France, the Pauillac region virtually sitting on a layer of it.

Vines

Le raisin is the grape; *la grappe* is the bunch of grapes.

Le pépin is the pip (used of any fruit); *le pellicule* is the (grape) skin. *La sève* is the sap; *la tige* the stalk.

Le cépage is the variety of vine.

Le fleuraison is the flowering of the vine.

La greffe is the graft; *le porte-greffe* is the vinestock that carries the shoot grafted onto it.

Une pépinière is a nursery garden, used to refer to where young vine shoots are grown.

La souche is the vine root. To buy wine *'sur souche'* is to buy 'on spec', before the vintage, banking on expectations and the wine's reputation.

La taille is the method of pruning; *tailler* is to prune or train.

Vineyard work

La charrette is the cart used to take grapes to the presshouse — nowadays a tractor is often used.

La douille is the small wooden tub used in much vineyard work, but today often superseded by plastic.

Épluchage is the term used for the sorting out of grapes according to soundness that is done in the vineyard in Champagne in certain circumstances.

La hotte is the tall, bucket-like basket carried on the back to hold grapes — today often plastic and lighter in weight. (*See illus. p.137*).

Un panier is a basket used for transporting grapes by individual vintagers who, when it is full, tip its contents into a larger

149

container. It can be lifted by an inserted pole. Such baskets have often been replaced by easy-to-clean plastic. (*See illus. p.235*)

Un refractomètre is a refractometer, an instrument that takes a drop of juice from a ripe grape and then gives a reading as to the sugar content therein; valuable for estimating not only the degree of ripeness but any possible chaptalising or treatment that may be required when the grapes are picked.

Un sécateur is pruning shears; *la serpette* is the knife used for cutting grapes at vintage time, but it can also refer to a pruning knife; *une vendangette* is a mechanical pruner that tops off and cuts away the side shoots of the vines.

Une tracteur is a tractor.

Une machine à vendanger is a mechanical harvester or picker.

Trier is to select; *faire le triage* is to do the selecting — the sorting out of grapes after they have been picked but before the wine is made.

Les vendanges is the overall term for the vintage, although it can also be used in the singular. It does not mean the date — vintage — of a wine.

Making Wine and Cellar Work

Un alembic is a still (for distilling).

L'assemblage is the process which takes place in the spring after the vintage, when wines made from different grapes or from different plots and at slightly different times are then 'made up' or assembled in a vat. Between cask and cask and vat and vat there can be great variations before this is done, so that tasting a wine before *l'assemblage* is not only difficult but unwise.

La bande is the bung; *bande dessus* is bung up — when the casks have been filled and the bungs are uppermost; *bande dessous* is when the cask has been topped up and turned to one side, so that the bung is driven home tight. *Le linge de bande* is the bung cloth.

Un casier is a wine-bin.

Le cave is the cellar, but, in the Bordeaux region, the above-ground wine store at an estate is known as *Le chai*.

La chaine embouteillage is the bottling line — alas, big installations are invariably proud of whatever equipment they have here, so that you may be required to stand alongside the procession of bottles and make polite and impressed comments for far too long.

Le chapeau is the mass of grapeskins and pips that rise to the top of the fermentation vat.

Chaptaliser is the process of adding sugar to the *must* (unfermented grape-juice) so as to provide food on which the wine yeasts can feed and to increase the alcoholic content of the ultimate wine. This is strictly controlled and although the process is now carried out in many wine regions, it is specially associated with Burgundy. As mentioned earlier, the process gets its name from the Comte J. de Chaptal, Minister of Agriculture to Napoleon I (*see p.28*).

Un chariot élévateur is a fork-lift truck.

Coller is to fine — the process of clarifying wine in cask. It is not possible to taste wines that are '*sur colle*' — i.e. on finings.

Un conteneur is a container — the type used for bulk shipments. It can vary greatly in size, it may look like a giant petrol-can or even be a container lorry or the hold of an entire ship. *Un camion citerne* is a container lorry. The size may be from 2,500 – 6,000 litres for a whole lorry or the hold of a ship.

Couper is to blend, the process being *coupage* — a skilled test of the wine-maker and in no way a pejorative term.

Le cuve is the vat; *la cuvée* the contents of the vat, which, therefore, is a term sometimes used to signify the assembly of wines, as in Champagne, where to '*make the cuvée*' is to compose a particular blend. There are various types of *cuve*: *une cuve en acier inoxydable* is a stainless steel vat — the term usually being abbreviated to 'Inox'. *Une cuve en béton armé* is a reinforced concrete vat; *une cuve en acier emaillé* is a vat made of enamelled steel; *une cuve vitrifiée* is a vitreous enamel vat. *La cuverie* is the vat house; *le cuvier* is the overall place in the wine installation where the wine is both made and stored.

Debourbage is literally 'cleansing', the process often used for dry white wines, whereby they are put into a stainless steel vat as soon as the crushing is complete; they remain there for about twenty-four hours, plus sulphur dioxide (SO_2), before being 'finished' in the usual way. The process removes all the solids in the wine and prevents there being any risk of premature oxidation.

Dégorger is the process whereby the first cork of a sparkling wine is taken out and any dosage put in, prior to the insertion of the second cork.

Le dosage is the sweetening added to sparkling wines before the second cork is inserted.

L'égrappoir is the device that strips the grapes off their stalks. *Un égrappoir-fouloir* is a stripper plus crusher — *fouler* is to crush. Some installations use a machine that does both.

Un entonnoir is a funnel.

Fermenter is to ferment, but, should a wine continue to ferment after it is either in bottle or is presented for tasting, the verb is *travailler* — to work. A wine that is still 'working' cannot fairly be tasted.

Filtrer is to filter, usually done before bottling.

Gazéifier is to make a wine sparkling by pumping gas into it.

Les lattes are the lathes on which bottles are laid on their sides or binned in cellars. But the expression *'sur lattes'* has recently come into prominence in relation to Champagne — the Champagne houses may, in certain years when their stocks have been depleted and the vintages of recent years have not been abundant, buy in wine already made, lying in the cellars of small makers or co-ops — in other words, *'sur lattes'*. Of course, the house that then buys the wine and inserts the second cork and any dosage (*see p.151*) may not have supervised the making of the wine in the first place. But it is fair to say that, before making substantial purchases that will go out bearing its own label, any Champagne establishment will satisfy itself that the wine is worthy of bearing its name. And, as has been pertinently commented, the wine bought from the *'sur lattes'* stocks, may in fact even be superior to what would otherwise have been used. Do not enter into this discussion!

La levure is yeast.

Macération carbonique is a process that originated in the Rhône Valley. It is the means whereby wines that might otherwise require long maturation are rendered agreeably drinkable within months, but retain their regional attributes. The grapes are piled up when they are brought to the winery, the juice begins to run because of their pressure on each other and, at the same time, a type of fermentation starts within each grape or berry. The grapes are subsequently pressed as usual. Many agreeable wines are now made by using this method or incorporating a proportion of *macération carbonique* wine in a blend. It makes many pleasant wines in the southern regions.

Méthode Champenoise is the method used to make Champagne and by which all the finer sparkling wines of France (and elsewhere in the world) are made. Its use will probably be proudly mentioned on the label of the wine. But it is to be restricted to the wines of Champagne alone within the next seven years.

La mise (*en bouteilles*) is bottling.

Le moût is the *must* — unfermented grape-juice.

Une palette is a large wooden tray, in which bottles come from the bottle maker and are stacked prior to use.

La pipette or *la sonde* is the vessel, often referred to as the *velenche*, a large metal or glass siphoning device, whereby wine is drawn out for sampling from cask or vat.

La pompe is the pump.

Le pressoir is the press. It may surprise many visitors to wine regions to note that the old-fashioned type of press that came down to squash the grapes by sheer weight is seldom in use today, nor do people stamp about on the grapes. In Champagne there is a basket type of press, which holds the grapes and then is raised so that a weight 'presses' them — this is called a *maie*. There are various other presses, some merely breaking up the grapes by means of a continuous screw — an Archimedes screw, which crushes the fruit as it turns, the amount of pressure regulated as to whether the screw turns fast or slowly. There is another type of press that has chains inside, which break up the grapes as the whole cylinder revolves and the juice runs out between the slats of the cylinder. There is yet another type, also long and cylindrical in form, in which the grapes are crushed by the swelling of an inflatable bag inside — when a gentle pressure is required. The type of press used depends on the grapes, some of which have thin skins, some thick ones, also on the type of wine to be made. There are now few places where *un pressoir* of the old type, usually with a huge, heavy screw, turns to exert pressure on the grapes. Modern presses are often referred to by the names of the best-known makers — you can refer knowledgeably to '*une presse Seitz*' when you are shown one of the type with chains inside (it will usually have the name on the side anyway), or '*une presse Wilmes*', which is the type with the inflatable bag inside. But there are many others.

Le récolte is the crop — in the US the term 'the crush' — i.e. the amount of grapes harvested — might be used.

Remplissage is the process of topping up casks of young wine — so that the air cannot affect the wine.

Soutirer is to draw off (wine) and is a term often used for racking, the process by which wine is pumped or drawn off from cask or vat, leaving behind its lees (*Les lies*). This is done several times in the life of most fine wines.

Viner is a verb meaning the adding of alcohol to wine, so *un vin viné* is a wine with its strength increased by the addition of alcohol, which is usually an illegal process. So it is wise to avoid this term — even if you do suspect that the wine you are criticizing has been somehow 'hotted up'. A fortified wine is something different. The French do not have such things and the term '*fortifié*' is somewhat pejorative; indeed, the French managed to establish at Brussels that the expression might not be used and substituted '*Vin de liqueur*' — which, as may be imagined, caused furious disagreement from the UK and countries that do make 'fortified wines'. In fact, in Britain a fortified wine still means a wine that is 'stronger' by the addition of spirit than a table-wine — such as port or sherry. Unless you can really cope with an animated technical discussion in French, it might be wise to keep away from the subject. Though of course you can get both port and sherry in France — and the local *vins doux naturels*, which *are* higher in strength than table wine but not made in quite the same way as the fortified wines of other countries. (*See below.*)

Vinifier is the process whereby grape-juice becomes wine.

Un vin de garde is a wine worth keeping. *Un vin de presse* is such wine as is made after the first free-run juice and early pressings have been drawn off; wine made after these stages may be kept for domestic use at the property or sold for distillation. *Un vin muté* is, literally, a 'stopped' wine — that is, a wine with the fermentation arrested by the addition of some form of grape spirit — in other words, *this* is what most Britons understand by the term 'fortified wine'. But the expression is seldom heard and use it only if you are driven to distinguishing between, say, '*un porto*' and '*un vin doux naturel*' and need to be precise.

Casks

Une barrique is a cask, but it may vary in size according to local usage. The Bordeaux *barrique* holds about 214–223 litres (47–49 UK gallons), the Burgundy *pièce* is about 218–232 litres (48–51 UK gallons), when the casks refered to are those for maturing and storing the young wine. But a *barrique de transport*, for moving bulk wine, will contain about 218 litres (48 UK gallons).

A container — the same word, *un conteneur* — such as is used for shipping bulk wines, may be either a vessel holding 2,432.16 litres (535 UK gallons) or a stainless steel porter cask, of 2,659.47 litres (585 UK gallons). The word 'hogshead' may be generally used for an English expression signifying a cask or its contents, but remember that, nowadays, most fine wines are bottled where they are made and only medium and inexpensively priced wines are shipped in bulk — for which the expression is *en vrac*.

Un demi-muid is a very large cask, varying in size as to the region.

Une feuillette is a name often used for the Chablis cask, holding about 132 litres (25–35 UK gallons).

Un foudre is a general name used for a large cask.

Un fût is a cask of any kind — but the word is often used to refer to one that is empty. *Expédier en fût* is to ship in cask. *Expédier en vrac* is to ship in bulk.

Une pièce is a Burgundy cask.

Une pipe is a large cask, not necessarily one for port, and sometimes used for spirits.

Le porte fût is the scantling — the wooden props and trestles that support the casks.

Une tonne is a very large cask — and the term is not used nowadays. It is a measure of capacity, originating in the Middle Ages when a ship's load (of wine) was appraised as to how many tonnes its hold could accommodate. Hence, to this day, a ship is referred to as so many tuns — from the time when the Bordeaux wine fleet supplied England with wine. (*See p.212.*)

Un tonneau is a cask that holds approximately four *barriques* or hogsheads — it is still a term used to indicate the production of an estate, especially in the south-west of France, although many statistical reports will now quote production in *caisses* (cases) of a dozen bottles of wine.

Un tonnelier is a cooper.

Tasting

Avaler is to swallow down or gulp, whereas *boire* is to drink. The expression *Avaler le bon Dieu en culottes de velours* (to swallow the good Lord in velvet trousers) is a fairly common phrase in wine regions when someone wants to express high praise for a red wine. *Sabler*, however, is to swig or swill — such as '*Sabler le Champagne*' at a lavish party.

Charnu is fleshy — the sort of wine that is very full. *Un vin de mâche* is a wine so substantial it seems almost possible to chew (*mâcher*) it. *Charpenté* is literally 'built', so that to say a wine is '*Bien charpenté*', is to signify that it is well constructed. A wine that is *Bien equilibré* is one that is well-balanced. *Corsé* is full-bodied. *Bouqueté* is fragrant.

Déguster is to taste. *Humer* is to smell. *Cracher* is to spit and *un crachoir* is a spittoon.

Une gorgée is a mouthful.

Vider is to empty. *Vider d'un coup* or *Vider d'un trait* is to empty (a glass) at a single draught or gulp.

Une jolie robe is an expression used to describe a wine with a beautiful colour.

Un grand cru means a great growth — used for fine wine from an individual vineyard. *Un vin fin* is almost impossible to translate — it signifies a wine of distinction, high quality, rather more than 'a fine wine'.

Il se laisse boire is, literally, 'It lets itself be drunk', a phrase of understatement, implying that a wine is highly drinkable — 'moreish'.

Bottles

Une bonbonne is a large container, used often for small quantities of wine or a spirit — i.e. a carboy.

Le bouchon is the cork; *bouchonné* is corked (in the bad sense).

Une bouteille fantaisie is an unusually shaped bottle, such as is often put up for tourist souvenirs.

La capsule is the covering for the cork. *Étain* is the metal type, plastic often being used nowadays.

Décanter is to decant, but this need not be into a decanter, only into another container.

L'emballage is the packing (of the wine bottle).

L'étiquette is the label; *l'étiquette de collier* the neck label; *l'étiquette du millésisme* is the label giving the vintage — if this is not on the main label; *la contre étiquette* is the back label, which often gives additional information. *Le passe partout* is the strip label — this gives the name of shipper or supplier when this information is not on the main label.

Le goulot is the neck of the bottle; to drink *au goulot* is to drink directly from the bottle.

Un millésisme is a vintage date. The term usually applies only to wines of fair quality. *Un vin millésismé* is a vintage wine. *Un grand millésisme* is a great vintage.

Un tastevin is a tasting cup, now in use only sometimes in the Burgundy region.

Un tir bouchon is a corkscrew. *Un décapsulateur* is a bottle-opener.

13

The Wine Label and the Wine List

The more you know about French wines, the more you are likely to enjoy them. As dozens, possibly hundreds of books have been written in English about them, it is downright lazy not to do even an hour's 'homework' looking up the wines of where you are going to be in France and, ideally, you should take at least one of the many good paperbacks along with you. Do not count on buying a wine book on the spot, even if your French is fluent: some of those available may be of the 'prose poem' type, enthusiastic about the wines but omitting facts about them, and even in major wine towns it is sometimes difficult to find anything except some collections of vineyard pictures. Another important point — you may see a beautifully produced book, in English, on certain wines. When was it written? Even within five to ten years, the information in it may be wholly out of date and, in consequence, misleading to today's wine lover. (Do not blame the author — he or she may have not been allowed to update the book, for corrections and additions can be costly.) Check the qualifications of the writer and also see whether he or she is actually in the wine trade, when, valuable though this can be, the 'interest' may also be rather too obvious. Wine information given in brief in even good general guidebooks is seldom of much use and, if you haven't even a small reference work with you, try the local Syndicat d'Initiative [ESSI] (tourist office) who may have useful leaflets, with maps and indications of wine estates and museums open to the public.

Buying Wine
Nor should you look forward to buying wonderful and rare bottles

on their home ground. A shop may be importantly entitled an *'Oenothèque'* and contain picturesque wine accessories of many kinds, from the practical to the *chi-chi*, such as mats, aprons, glasses (some of them horrifically gigantic), various thermometers and decanting devices and the latest type of cork extractor. But the bottles on sale may be extremely expensive, they may have been standing under bright display lighting or been in the window and, when you compare prices, you may realize that you are likely to get better value from a good merchant in the UK. Supermarkets these days can have impressive displays of wine, including imported wines and spirits: I remember one range of different types of Scotch that would have been impressive even in Scotland, far more so in the outskirts of Bordeaux! You can often find wines and spirits that are 'fun' drinks, to consume at picnics or in any self-catering house — and you will not risk spending vast sums.

'Cellar door' sales are a recent and rather smart way of buying wine in France. There is nothing wrong in following the example of any French friend who recommends 'his' particular grower — although sometimes enthusiasm for the locality and euphoria engendered by a good lunch can lure you into lavish expenditure on something that is really no more than pleasant. Sometimes special tasting-rooms or the local Maison du Vin will have wines available by the two or three bottle carton; these will be ready to drink, whereas young wines bought where they have been made will probably need additional maturation. You may be quite sure that, whatever you find, it is highly unlikely to be a valuable treasure — the wily wine trade will have been exploring before you. But it can be fun to discover wines in this way — though remember to get a detailed bill if you are going to bring back any quantity. I know that there are people who advocate taking plastic dustbins across the Channel and filling them with the wine available at the dispense taps in a number of supermarkets — but I do not think that this sort of wine is more than an adequate beverage even before it has been brought home, and the duty paid on a quantity. As for buying in bulk and bringing home a quarter cask or so with which to have a bottling party — I say firmly *'Don't'*. You are not likely to get anything of quality in this way. Are you able to buy the necessary equipment for bottling and can you put right anything that may go wrong? Even a small amount of wine that has 'gone off' can be a great quantity of vinegar, and even an adequate wine bought in bulk (with the expense of bottles, corks, etc. costed in) is at best a rather boring buy and not much of a bargain these days. No one in the wine trade does it — and they have all the facilities. I am not being chauvinistic, then, in saying that, on the shelves of wine merchants of all types throughout the UK, there is a better selection of wines, in all price ranges, from all over the world, than you are likely to find anywhere else.

Explore and have fun with 'local' wines — but do not arrive home and pester your favourite merchant to ship something unknown for you; you may find it just isn't as enjoyable when you drink it in the UK as when you quaffed it on some vine-wreathed terrace. That is the sort of wine that tends to be less popular outside its homeland — nothing to do with being a 'bad traveller' — and can fill up the list of 'bin ends' that are offered at sale prices later.

The Wine Scene

Wine is an important part of the French economy. Vast numbers of people are engaged in the wine and spirit trades or within the peripheries; those living in wine regions cultivate their own patches of vines before and after their regular hours of work, children engage in this as well. Of course, the classic wines of France have established standards respected throughout the world and the great oenological institutes and wine schools, notably those of Montpellier and Bordeaux, are famous.

What some first-time visitors may find surprising is that there are few 'wine merchants' in France, as the term is understood in the UK. There are some, such as the well-known Nicolas establishment in Paris. Otherwise, as previously mentioned, wine is bought at the local grocer, from a supermarket, or at a 'cellar door'. Do not expect that anyone selling wine is likely to be a specialist — the fortunate French have been able to take wine for granted! Indeed, the inhabitants of one wine region may have scant knowledge of the wines of another — it is not so long since someone in Bordeaux asked me if it was true that 'quite drinkable wine' was made in Burgundy! Not even a Frenchman springs from the womb knowing everything about wine — indeed, many take wine somewhat for granted and treat it in a way that some visitors may find casual: in some small country cafés, for example, you may be expected to drink out of a chunky tumbler — even a tinted one — and the wine may simply be the red, white or pink of some well-known brand.

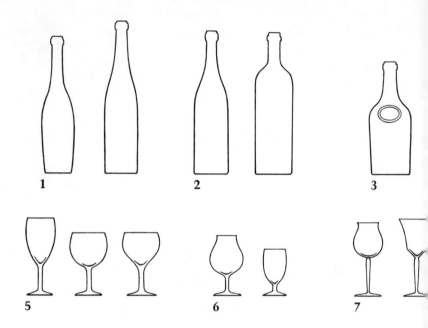

1 *Left*, Beaujolais 'pot', holding half a litre; right, the 'Flûte d'Alsace', a pale green bottle. The same shape is also used for Tavel and also, plus ridges or rings around the neck, for Muscat de Beaumes de Venise. In plain glass it may also be used for some other *rosé* and white wines, although those of the Côtes de Provence are sometimes 'waisted' and bulgy at top and base.

2. *Left*, the traditional bottle for red and white Burgundy. The same basic shape is also used for Rhône wines (but for the 'Rhodanienne' shape *see p.325*) and for wines from the Loire and other regions — though in fact the Loire bottles are very slightly shorter and fatter, though seeming similar unless put side by side. On the right is the classic bottle for red and white Bordeaux, with the 'shoulder' that facilitates long-term laying down on its side, that also holds back from the neck any deposit that comes up from the bottom when the wine is decanted.

3. The clavelin, a bottle used in the Jura for *vins jaunes*, such as Château-Chalon. It sometimes has a seal on the side, as shown here. It holds about 63 cl. or 22 fluid ounces.

4. The Marie Jeanne on the left is mainly associated with the Côteaux du Layon region of the Loire, but it can also be used — in these days of the popularity of big bottles — for claret. It holds about 1¾ bottles. The magnum of Champagne on the right holds 2 bottles — magnums of still table wines, red and white, are also now often seen.

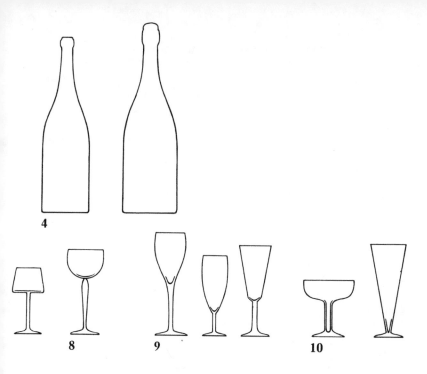

5. Three suitable glass shapes for drinking wine — still or sparkling. In Burgundy they may be slightly larger — but the storm-lantern' giant glasses should be avoided. The tulip shape is on the left, the 'Paris' goblet centre. Sometimes a slightly smaller sized glass is set for white wines.

6. Two glasses that are suitable for brandy of all types and also for *alcools blancs*. A smaller version of the one on the right may be used for liqueurs. The left-hand glass shape is in fact similar to the International Standard tasting glass and, if of a reasonable size, is also suitable for most table wines.

7. Traditional Loire glasses — although these days ordinary wine glasses may be used. *Left*, the glass for Chinon reds, the Bourgueil glass being slightly more globular; *centre*, the glass for sparkling Vouvray; *right*, the Anjou glass, used for red, white and *rosé* wines.

8. Alsace glass, usually with a green stem.

9. Three forms of glass suitable for sparkling wines — traditional tulip, with the bowl ending in a point so as to encourage the bubbles to rise from this; elongated tulip, sometimes used for the various versions of *vin blanc cassis*; modern version of the 'flûte' glass.

10. Two types of Champagne or sparkling-wine glass in use in the past: the deepish saucer glass has a hollow stem, through which the bubbles rise — pretty but extremely difficult to clean; *right* the 'flûte' glass that is sometimes shown in old pictures.

Remember that the world-famous wine estates and great shipping houses are only the tip of the wine pyramid. Fine and rare wines make the news — seldom do they make enough money to enable their owners to continue in business; it is the inexpensive and branded wines that are the 'bread and butter' of the wine trade. Nor will you often find the greatest wines on lists, except in the top luxury hotels and restaurants — when the prices charged may certainly seem surprisingly high by comparison with even similar establishments in the UK and, even more so, with prices of the same wines in British merchants' stocks. What can be of great interest, when eating out in France, is to sample the sort of local wines that may not often be exported (because of insufficient production and the necessity for keeping the immediate customers supplied) and the *sommelier* or whoever takes your order may recommend something unusual, if convinced of your wish to experiment. Do not, though, expect that a modest catering establishment will have a list of wines other than French.

The Service of Wine

The French tend to drink even those wines that benefit by long-term maturation rather younger than the Anglo-Saxons — this can be a useful way of keeping track of what your carefully laid-down stocks may be doing at home!

There is seldom much concern about decanting even a fine old red wine. In a luxury restaurant, decanting may be done — but possibly with the maximum *chi-chi* and possibly merely involving tipping the contents of the bottle, deposit and all, into the decanter. You are not likely to get an obviously 'warmed-up' red wine — but I have known imposing *sommeliers* argue even with the proprietors of well-known properties as to whether a particular wine really is corked or not — so be prepared to justify the complaint about any bottle you are going to reject.

White and *rosé* wines are, sometimes, served rather colder than the British prefer — for over-chilling a wine deprives the drinker of much of its bouquet and taste. American tourists do like very cold drinks, so it is up to the customer to take the bottle out of the ice bucket if necessary. Remember the tradition of serving young Beaujolais, even *en carafe*, from an ice-bucket — agreeable, especially on a stuffy day.

Glasses

These vary. In hotels catering for many tourists, it is, alas, a risk that you may be given the 'storm-lantern' type of huge glass for red wine, within which the liquid has to crawl towards your lips and the size of which risks over-aerating the bouquet of most wines. But the sensible wine drinker will request an ordinary glass or goblet, which will be perfectly suitable. The same applies to any glass for brandy — Cognac, Armagnac or another local brandy — which should certainly not be the 'goldfish bowl' size, nor should it be warmed over a flame — a glass of a size to be cupped in the hand is what is correct. For certain *'alcools blancs'*, however, the glass may be chilled by having ice-cubes put into it, swirled around and then tipped out. No glass should be too small, just as no glass should be too large.

For anyone staying in an hotel, it is worth remembering that, if a bottle of wine is ordered but not finished, this can always be put aside for subsequent drinking, marked with your room number. (Remember, approximately, how much you have consumed.) The contents of such bottles will not usually suffer — indeed, many rather ordinary wines can improve enormously by a little aeration. Wine is usually available by the glass, the carafe or half carafe — though do not expect anything outstanding — and, in a wine region, there may also be wine that can be ordered in the *carafon* (small carafe) or *pichet* (little jug).

Bottles

Outline shapes of some of the more widely-used regional bottles are given on *pp.160—1*. Both shapes and the colour of the glass are subject to controls, although sometimes a special wine may be put up in a *'bouteille fantasie'*, for an attractive presentation. As some tourists like to compile a record of their trips, with labels of wines tasted, it is always possible to ask a wine firm to spare a label or two, although new labels are not usually handed out by the owners of the great estates — for fear that they might be put onto something less worthy by unscrupulous persons.

14

The Great French Spirits

There are very few products that cannot be distilled — as many former inhabitants of P.O.W. camps discovered! Since the procedure of distillation, discovered by the Arabs, came to France from Spain — more strictly, from Catalonia, probably via the great Arnaud de Vilanova — an extensive and increasing number of distillates have been made. In virtually all the regions of France some form of 'strong drink' is produced, utilizing produce that probably might otherwise have been wasted; before sugar became cheap, sweetening had to be done mostly with honey and, therefore, fruits and berries were not easily converted into jams and preserves, except as luxuries. Of course, these days stills are licensed and controlled but, as some of my Alsace friends have related, during the Second World War many of them got out old stills from their farms and put them to work on the local produce — 'We knew the customs officers wouldn't come investigating into the mountains.'

Many of the great places of pilgrimage and, certainly, the major religious establishments, also made forms of 'strong drink' in their stillrooms, for medicinal and social purposes. Visitors to many such places today will probably find local 'liqueurs' in the souvenir shops. But the world-famous spirits are very big business and such is their influence that there are even versions of famous brands made, under licence, in other countries. What is important to understand is that there are several main types of these spirits. The main aperitif drinks are described on *p.185*. I have added a short section on vermouth on *p.186*, because there is still some confusion as to what 'French' really means in this context.

In the following section, there are notes on: the great brandies of

France — Calvados, *rhum*, brandy in general, Cognac and Armagnac in particular, *marc, fine*; then there is a section on 'liqueurs', according to the regulations that govern them in France; finally, there are the *alcools blancs*, the true 'fruit brandies', of which those of Alsace are specially renowned. Although the travellers should certainly not 'play safe' and stick to advertised brands of all these drinks, some of the more obscure ones may prove a somewhat taxing experience — perhaps, if you wish to try something unknown, it is wise to order a single helping, from which friends and family can sip to start with. Nor is it fair to reject as 'horrid' a drink that has been poured from a bottle that may have been standing open for months, even years; true, spirits do not 'go off' as wine does with exposure to air, but they do change and you may be getting something stale, flat — and certainly unprofitable. Try the drink again fresh if you can.

Brandies

Calvados
This is peculiar to Normandy, in which province apples have been extensively grown at least from the twelfth century. A distillate from cider, *eau-de-vie de cidre*, is something of a rarity unless you are in the region, but Calvados itself seems to have originated in the sixteenth century, when one of the Norman nobles had a visit from a friend in Touraine, who described how fruits were used in distillates in the Loire. The result was that, at Mesnil-au-Val, the Sieur de Gouberville got his blacksmith to build a still and started making apple-brandy. The spirit seems to have remained rather a peasant product, made up for the use of individual farms and manor-houses, until the Région de Calvados was defined in the nineteenth century. Calvados makers, however, were keen to produce a quality spirit, insisting on a seven-year apprenticeship for anyone wishing to qualify as a distiller, with strict rules governing the training period. In 1946 the Institut National des Appellations d'Origine started to control Calvados production and the Institute's stamp henceforth must be acquired before the spirit can be sold. The Bureau National Interprofessional des Calvados et Eaux-de-Vie de Cidre et de Poires (BNICE) also plays a supervisory role in its production.

Calvados is distilled from a mash of apples, fermented with

yeast, the distillation being done twice. After this the spirit is matured in oak for a period varying between six and ten years. It must then be submitted to an official tasting committee before it can gain the certificate that will allow it to be sold. The Calvados of the Vallée d'Auge has its own specific A.O.C. There are many brands of Calvados on sale today, but home-made Calvados can still be found, although the tourist should be warned — it can be very much stronger than the commercial product.

Rhum

This is the word the French use. All rum is the distillate of sugar-cane, but it may surprise many people to know that the spirit is by no means sweet — although it can, of course, be sweetened to suit particular markets. French *rhums*, made in the Antilles, are rather different from British rums, being more aromatic and as according to French law the *eau-de-vie* of sugar-cane, distilled in a single operation from the juice of the cane or in the form of syrup of molasses of cane, can be made *only* in the country where the cane is grown, this is why *rhum* is not made in any part of mainland France. Nor may it be flavoured or rectified once it leaves the Caribbean.

Rhum has a long tradition in the French army. In the Crimean War (1854–6) the troops were issued with *rhum* instead of wine or any form of brandy. In 1916 the British as well as the French forces in the trenches had a regular rum ration.

There are several sorts of *rhum*: *rhum agricole* and *rhum de sirop* both being specialities of Martinique; the former takes on its colour from the wooden casks in which it is matured. *Rhum vieux* must have been matured for at least three years in oak, although many *rhums* sold as *vieux* will have been aged in this way for longer, taking on a delicate, penetrating fragrance that makes a fine *rhum* a truly distinguished spirit. The great name in *rhum* is Bardinet. It was in 1857 that Paul Bardinet set up as a producer and distributor of *rhum* at Limoges. It was he who first presented his *rhum* in a bottle with a partial outer casing of white raffia, which is the way Rhum Negrita, the dominant brand, is still marketed today. (It has been estimated that at least 70 per cent of French housewives keep this particular *rhum* for kitchen use, where, as well as flavouring sweet things and being used in pastry-making, it is invaluable for flaming and 'degreasing' both fish and meat dishes.) Bardinet's white *rhum* is marketed under the Old Nick brand. The gigantic establishment, formerly at Bordeaux, is now part of the Cointreau organization and is being re-established at Le Havre.

Brandy

The two greatest brandies in the world, Cognac and Armagnac, are both produced in France, although, as brandy is a distillate of wine, grape brandies are also widely made in many regions.

Cognac, in the south-west of France, has produced a variety of wines for almost as long as records have been kept. Distilling seems to have begun there in the sixteenth century, although there are various theories as to why this started: a popular one is that the over-abundance of wine — a 'wine lake' of the time — resulted in the Cognac growers heating up the wine to make it into some form of spirit, which did not take up so much space when being moved or exported. The trade with the Low Countries led to the adoption of the term *brandewijn,* from which the British term 'brandy' has derived, but in French, although you are certainly likely to be understood if you use the word 'brandy', the correct term is *eau-de-vie.* If brandy as such is not intended, then there will be the additional word or words qualifying the description, such as *eau-de-vie de cidre.*

The area within which Cognac may be produced was defined in 1909 and consists of Grande Champagne, where the finest brandies originate, Petite Champagne, Borderies, Fins Bois and Bons Bois. The word 'champagne' merely means open countryside in this context and has nothing to do with the Champagne region in the north of France, although this of course is open and undulating, with few forests. Each one of the different Cognac areas produces a different type of brandy and it is the skill of the blender that results in the harmonious balanced spirit, made according to the style of whichever house is responsible. Several different types of vines are used for making the wine from which Cognac is distilled, mainly the Folle Blanche, St Émilion and Columbard. The white wine, although it is something to drink on the spot, is very little more than pleasant. The great Cognac houses do have some holdings in vineyards, but they also buy in wines or spirits from the local peasant growers or co-operatives.

All Cognac is made in a pot still, the process taking place twice: the liquid from the first distillation is known as the *brouillis,* the second distillation, called the *bonne chauffe,* produces Cognac. Every stage of the process is strictly controlled and, although the contemporary distiller has many instruments and much scientific knowledge to assist him, it is still not uncommon for a man to sleep alongside the still, because, once the distillate is running, the still's operation must not be stopped and only great experience can determine the precise moment when the impurities coming at the beginning and end of each distillation should be diverted away from what will eventually be the heart of the distillate. The whole process takes about eight hours, then the still must be thoroughly cleaned. The colourless liquid is then ready for subsequent maturation in wood, after which it will be sampled and put into the great blends by the blender. It is not surprising to learn that all the skills involved in making Cognac tend to be passed on within families, so that the up-to-date technician you see in his laboratory in one of the great Cognac establishments may be the seventh or eighth generation of his family to be engaged in the work; the same applies to those out in the fields with their small stills. Equal skill is involved with the making of the casks, for which oak is the perfect wood. Trees from the Limousin and Tronçais forests are used and, although the oaks are not identical, both seem to produce satisfactory results. The Cognac coopers are world-famous — in Australia, for example, I was frequently told the exact source of many a cask of fine wine, the name of the maker — often from Cognac! — being mentioned with pride. All the wood has to be seasoned, for up to six years ideally, and the wood for the staves must be cleft, not sawn. If you go round a Cognac house, try to visit the cooperage so as to see the fascinating way in which a cask is put together, a fire being lit under each one when the staves are assembled so as to draw into tight association all the pieces of wood fitted into the hoops that hold the end or head by the action of the heat, making the wood contract.

Cognac is not only expensive to make, it is expensive to keep, because the evaporation in the stores of brandy are up to 4 per cent annually (see p.254).

Contrary to what is often supposed, Cognac does not go on indefinitely improving in wood, so the producers must constantly sample the contents of the casks, drawing up the brandy with the aid of a small cup on a wire, known as une preuve, which can be easily passed down through the bung-hole. To walk through a brandy establishment is rather like being inside an enormous Christmas pudding or trifle, because of the atmosphere! Some of the brandies, especially those of great age, may be removed from their casks and put into large glass carboys, known as bonbonnes. In the blender's tasting-room there will be several hundred samples in bottles; this collection is known as the bibliothèque or library, because it is from these that the master blender will make up his 'marks'. The finest Cognacs may be kept in a special enclosure, usually very well secured, in which a fortunate visitor may be allowed to have a tot of something very special: this is known as the paradis.

Although French law no longer permits a vintage Cognac to be made, you may, as a guest, sometimes be offered one which does come from a particular year. Otherwise, the quality of Cognac varies according to the quality of the brandies that make up the blend: any entitled 'Fine Champagne' are obliged to consist of at least 50 per cent Grande Champagne. Another thing that people do not always realize is that, once brandy goes into bottle, it will not necessarily improve; it is not quite true to say that it will not change, but it will not get appreciably better, even if you do not draw the cork. It should, of course, be kept standing upright, not lying down, when the spirit will eventually rot the cork. Old, cobwebby bottles, often decorated with hand-written labels on parchment, are a piece of *chi-chi* aimed at the ignorant tourist, so there is no need to be impressed by them or waste money on such things. Buy Cognac from a good house, made according to the style you yourself prefer, in the quality category you require or can afford.

Armagnac

This comes from what was formerly Gascony, which is why it is sometimes referred to as 'the brandy of the Gascons'. It has a long history, many references suggesting that a spirit was distilled in this region about a century before distillation began in the Cognac area, but controls did not determine the area where it could be made and other particulars until 1909 (*see p.167*). A variety of grapes may be used and there is a special Armagnac still, in which a single distillation is made. Of course today the great establishments will have their own large installations, but there are also travelling stills in the region.

Armagnac must be distilled by the end of April after the vintage of the original wine and its age is worked out from this, starting with a rating of zero then gaining an extra number each succeeding September. Maturation is done in wood, ideally from the local forest, although nowadays other oak must inevitably be used too.

When you look at an Armagnac label, the marking of three stars or XXX means that the spirit will be three years of age, a VO marking that it is from five to ten, VSOP from ten to fifteen. *Hors d'age* means that the brandy is twenty-five years old or even older. Like Cognac, Armagnac does not go on indefinitely improving in wood and seems to be at its best after about thirty years, when the finest brandies will be bottled.

The three regions where Armagnac may be made are Ténarèze, Bas-Armagnac and Haut-Armagnac, the use of any of these names on a label requiring that the Armagnac in the bottle must be 100 per cent from that region. Otherwise it will be a blend. Various types of bottle are in use, the flagon-shaped one is known as a *basquaise*; there are tall bottles and a square-shouldered one, rather like a Bordeaux bottle, which is called the *pot gascon.*

Many people suppose Armagnac to be 'weaker' than Cognac, but this is quite wrong. It may be exactly the same strength, but it is different in character and, of course, the styles of the different producers vary too. Armagnac may perhaps be described as having a slightly gentler and more aromatic style than Cognac.

Marc

This is the distillation of the debris of the pressings of grapes when wine is made. In former times wine-growers would distil this after a further hard pressing, so as to make spirit for their own use, but nowadays it is usually simpler to sell the mass of pips and skins to a distiller who will use it for making industrial alcohol. Some spirit, however, is still made in the old way. The most famous *marc* is probably *marc de Bourgogne*, but there are others, including a *marc de Champagne* and, in Alsace, a *marc de Gewurztraminer.* A properly matured *marc* can be a good digestive, but if it is a raw immature spirit it tends to stun the palate. Again, do not be taken in by any pretentious hand-written labels and odd-shaped bottles closed with sealing wax; the contents may be quite ordinary.

Pousse Rapière

This is a drink evolved fairly recently, probably as part of a campaign to publicize Armagnac and consists of a measure of this brandy, topped up with the harshly dry white sparkling wine of the Gers region, plus a little zest of an orange. It makes a delicious mixture, but if you make it up yourself do not put in too much Armagnac or else you may find that you are unable to finish your wine at the subsequent meal! Packs of the orange-flavoured Armagnac, together with a bottle of the sparkling wine, are now sold in the region, although the drink is easy enough to make from scratch.

Une fine

This is the general term for any brandy distilled from wine. In the ordinary way, a *fine à l'eau* (brandy and water) may be made with ordinary grape-brandy or, in a fairly smart bar or restaurant, Cognac will be used. Sometimes, however, there may be a specified origin of the *fine*, such as *fine Marne*, from the Marne region, or *fine Bourgogne* from Burgundy. The thing to remember when you are ordering is that if you simply ask for an *eau-de-vie*, you may be offered a range of drinks, including liqueurs and various digestives, but if you specifically require a brandy, then you ask for *une fine*.

Liqueurs

According to French regulations, a liqueur is a sweetened spirit which must contain 200 grams of sugar per litre; a *fine* is 49° proof, a *demi-fine* 40° proof, a *surfine* about 52° proof. The *surfine* is the sweetest and the *demi-fine* the least sweet. The term *double*, which you will see, for example, on bottles of *cassis*, generally means that there are double quantities of the flavouring ingredients used, although sometimes there may only be 50 per cent more, because using twice the quantity would unbalance the ultimate drink. It is important to note that it is the flavourings that concern the use of the word *double*, not the alcoholic strength, for a *double* liqueur is generally about as strong as a *surfine*. The word *crème*, followed by the name of a particular spice, flower or herb, means that this will be the principal flavouring of the drink.

French law requires that on the label the fluid content of the bottle and the strength of the liquid should be stated: the letter 'A' means that the bottle contains either an aperitif based on wine that is lower in strength than 18°, or spirits that are flavoured with aniseed below 45°, or bitters below 30°. The letter 'D' means that the contents are liqueurs and spirits higher than 15°, except for aniseeds, bitters and any wine-based aperitif higher than 18°. But, as will be noticed, there is no sharp differentiation between the type of drink that is consumed in France between times, even as an aperitif, or after a meal, by way of digestive. It is astonishing how versatile some of these drinks can be and I never forget how, when I was the guest of the Distillerie de la Côte Basque, the directors and their families took me to the beach at a week-end, where, in the intervals of swimming, we consumed vast quantities of Izarra (*p.176*), poured over crushed ice and sipped through straws. It was surprisingly good.

Abricot

Apricot liqueurs are popular, Marie Brizard's Apry and Garnier's Abricotine being well known. Cusenier, who make an apricot liqueur, also make a peach brandy and one called Prunellia, which contains plums and other fruits, mainly greengages and sloes.

Aiguebelle

Discovered by a Trappist monk at the beginning of the twentieth century when he was going through the papers of a monastery in Normandy, this is now known as *Formule de la Liqueur du Frère Jean*. It is supposed to contain about fifty different herbs, mainly those local to the great monastery of La Grande Trappe, with an ancient formula from which the recipe originated.

Angelica

These liqueurs are not very prevalent these days, but there is one, made at Niort, called *Liqueur d'Angelique*, based on old Cognac.

Anise Liqueurs

Most liqueur establishments make an *anise*, which has been famous since very early times for medicinal purposes as well as flavourings. The most famous, however, is that of Marie Brizard & Roger, founded in rather charming circumstances in the eighteenth century. Marie, the third child of a carpenter, in the parish of Sainte-Croix, Bordeaux, devoted much time to looking after the poor and sick, one of whom, a West African native, who had presumably arrived through the busy port of Bordeaux, gave her a recipe for a drink which he said would not only cure many stomach complaints but act as a preventive medicine. The basis of this was *anise*. Marie Brizard followed the recipe and had so many appreciative patients that she eventually founded her own firm in 1755, taking into partnership Jean-Baptiste Roger, who eventually married her niece, Anne Brizard. The firm, now very modern, is still a family business and they make a number of liqueurs in addition to their *anisette*.

Arquebuse

This is a digestive produced by Cusenier, white in colour and once recommended to me as 'the French answer to Fernet Branca'. Several firms make it and it is a very efficient digestive or remedial drink. A number of herbs are incorporated.

Bénédictine

This very well-known drink is made at Fécamp in Normandy, a Benedictine foundation since AD 988. It was in the sixteenth century that Dom Bernardo Vincelli, one of the religious, made up a highly successful cordial, incorporating the juices of twenty-eight plants — the sort that he used to gather as he wandered about the countryside and Normandy coast. The fame of this drink attracted the attention of the French court and the foundation prospered as a result. In the French Revolution the religious establishment was closed, the Benedictines expelled and many of the Abbey's treasures and records were scattered among loyal friends, one of whom, Alexandre Le Grand, managed in 1868 to make up the Bénédictine elixir from old manuscripts and, at the end of the nineteenth century, started to sell it, also building an incredible house for the distillery and offices, on the site of the former Abbey. This is an amazing establishment, surpassing in appearance anything that even the most ambitious film-producer could possibly imagine. Tours of it are well organized, the collections of works of art and many other objects made by Monsieur Le Grand being included in the visit. The liqueur still bears the wax seal of Fécamp Abbey and the Benedictine initials DOM, which signify 'To God most good most great'. The Le Grand family still own the secret formula for the liqueur; it is based on herbs and matured in oak, with fine brandies, including Cognac, subsequently added. In 1938 'B & B' was made, which is a mixture of brandy and Bénédictine. The Benedictine establishment today own the firm of Revel of Toulouse, which produces the rather curiously named Pipermint Get (pronounced 'jet').

Cassis

This is a blackcurrant spirit drunk as a liqueur, used in ices, sorbets, and in many other ways, although the most famous is probably in *vin blanc cassis* (*p.185*). It should not be confused with *sirop de cassis*, which is non-alcoholic, or Cassis wine from the south. Burgundy is especially famous for its blackcurrants, the plant being mentioned as early as the sixteenth century for medicinal purposes, and most *cassis* is made there. In 1923 *cassis* received its A.O.C. defining where it may be made, also stating that only *cassis* with a minimum strength of 15° and a certain sugar content was entitled to the description *crème de cassis*. A number of firms make good *cassis*, although naturally not all can put the description *cassis de Dijon* on their labels. Frequently several different strengths are made, 14° for more ordinary and kitchen use, 15° or more for *crème de cassis*, 20° for what the house of Védrenne call *supercassis* and some firms refer to as *double crème*. Védrenne make a *cassis* of 25°, but this really is a very intense liqueur. Trénel, of Charnay-lès-Mâcon, put a vintage on their *cassis*, because, as they rightly say, with time the beautiful brilliant purple colour becomes brownish as the spirit 'eats' the fruit of the drink and although the liqueur remains perfectly fit for consumption it is less enjoyable. A warning — the term *liqueur de cassis* refers only to a drink which is described as 'sugar or glucose added to blackcurrants macerated in brandy' and therefore, anyone shopping should look closely to make sure that an apparent bargain is a true one.

Chartreuse
This is not only one of the world's best-known liqueurs but it is the only one in large-scale commercial production that is still entirely controlled by a religious order. The source of the original recipe has a confused history, but it began to be available to the laity from 1765, and it has always had a reputation for being a preventive medicine, which is why it is sometimes called the *liqueur de santé*. In 1838 a yellow version of the liqueur was made, being slightly sweeter and not quite as strong as the original green type. In 1903, when all the religious orders were expelled from France, the Carthusians of the Grenoble house where Chartreuse had first been made went to Tarragona in Spain and began to distil the liqueur there. Chartreuse was meanwhile made in France in a version that was not successful and the company producing it went bankrupt. The Tarragona distillery continued in production, the brothers referring to the liqueur made here as *Une Tarragone*. In 1931 they were able to return to the original establishment at Fourvoirie.

The distillery at Voiron, where the brothers moved after a landslide had destroyed the original building in 1935, is still strictly controlled by the religious: only since the 1960s have visitors been allowed to see inside at all: they can only look through a glass window at the stills and every detail of the publicity is under the direction of the religious, which is why the advertising is of an austere, factual type. The formula is a secret, known only to three of the brothers, the only persons allowed in the 'Hall of Herbs' above the distillery. Chartreuse is claimed to be the only French liqueur that is made with completely pure ingredients, with no colourings or additives being permitted except those deriving from the components of the formula. This is why it is inevitably expensive — about a hundred and thirty herbs are used plus fine brandy and mountain honey.

In addition to the yellow and green versions of Chartreuse, the Elixir Végétal is also produced, put up in tiny bottles each within a wooden container: it is 140° proof, very strong indeed. The traditional way of taking it is by shaking a few drops onto a lump of sugar, which is then eaten as a digestive.

Cherry Brandies
These must be differentiated from the *alcools blancs* (*p.180*). Most big liqueur houses make a type of cherry brandy, including Marnier-Lapostolle, Dolfi, Cusenier and Rocher. Around Angers, in the Loire valley, a special type of cherry known as a *Guignolet* is grown and many liqueur establishments also make a Guignolet liqueur.

Cointreau
This is the most important and powerful liqueur establishment in the world. The firm makes an enormous range of liqueurs and is now in association with the giant establishment of Bardinet. But it is for its Curaçao that it is best known. Cointreau was founded by Edouard and Adolph Cointreau at Angers in 1849 and although the liqueur became enormously popular, winning many prizes and medals, it was not until the period between the two World Wars that the name was changed from the generally used term *triple sec* to Cointreau, to be marketed as a unique Curaçao. The firm today also controls the liqueur establishment of Regnier. Robert Cointreau — for the firm is still a family concern — is also involved with promoting the wines of the region and much respected for his knowledge of them.

Cordial Médoc
This is made at Cenon and is another herb-based liqueur, based on claret, slightly sweet.

Crème de cacao
Most of the great French liqueur-houses will have something equivalent to this, which may be also called *crème de café* or *crème de mocha* or *mokka*. They are definitely sweet but can be delicious at the end of a good meal and I have known distinguished members of the wine-trade pour a measure over a meringue glacé which I was eating, then demand spoons for themselves and dig in. Two that I have tasted with pleasure are Kamok, made by

Vrignaud, a firm founded in 1812 at Luçon, and one called Baska, made by the Liqueur Giffard concern, which was founded in 1885 at Avrillé, Angers.

Curaçao

This was originally made from the bitter oranges growing on the island of Curaçao off the west coast of Venezuela, but nowadays the peel and other ingredients are produced in many other places. This is why some liqueur houses will specify 'orange Curaçao', indicating that the orange variety is made with the peel of the bitter orange, not just any orange. *Triple sec* is this type of Curaçao, though slightly sweeter, and it is not a brand-name — people often assume that Curaçao and *triple sec* are registered but they are not. The liqueur need not be coloured — in fact, it is often white, although blue and green Curaçaos exist as well (*see also Cointreau, p.175*).

Grand Marnier

This is made by the firm of Marnier-Lapostolle, founded in 1827, and the orange liqueur was made for the first time in 1880. There are now two kinds, Cordon Rouge and Cordon Jaune, the yellow one being slightly lower in strength. Cordon Rouge is based on Cognac, not just brandy.

Izarra

This is the Basque word for 'star'. Made from herbs and flowers gathered in the Basque regions of the Pyrenees, blended and mixed with Armagnac, the distillation is then combined with the region's honey and more Armagnac, before being aged in wood. Izarra was first made by Joseph Grattau, who founded the Distillerie de la Côte Basque and evolved the liqueur in 1835. There are two types, the green version being slightly stronger than the yellow.

Mint Liqueurs (Menthe)

These are made by most drinks establishments, some of them being white as well as green. They are often served over crushed ice and drunk through a straw.

Nut Liqueurs

These are made in several country regions, including the Perigord liqueur, *Eau de Noix*, made from walnuts. *Crème de Noix* is a sweeter version of the same thing. *Crème de Noisettes* is made from hazelnuts. These are all interesting to try when you are in the area that makes them and, if you really can't stomach them as a drink, then the ideal thing to do is either to dilute them with soda or water, or, perhaps, to pour them over a vanilla ice cream, which many of them make delicious. Other nut liqueurs include *Noyau*, made from almonds, although Cusenier's *Crème de Noyau* in fact is made from apricot kernels.

Parfait Amour
This is a lilac-coloured drink, made by several liqueur establishments today, although its great vogue was at the turn of the century. It is essentially a sweetish liqueur, highly scented, and, as Cusenier say in a press release, 'brightly coloured'.

The Great White Spirit
This, in France, has various names, but the two that are best known are the brand Pernod and the generic *pastis*. Pernod has an aniseed flavour, whereas *pastis*, which is a southern French drink, made by several firms, is in fact liquorice-flavoured, although many people suppose it to include aniseed. Both of them originally contained absinthe, the foundation of vermouth, from which the German word *wermut* (hence vermouth) got its name (*see p.186*). But absinthe has been banned in France since 1915, so that only aniseed or liquorice can be used to flavour these drinks today. The associations of absinthe with narcotics and the high strength of the original formula for Pernod contributed to this, but it was the other versions of the original Pernod (which only ever contained a very small amount of absinthe) which may have resulted in the origin of the word *pastis*, because the word for imitation is *pastiche*; however, the Provençal verb for stirring, or 'troubling' a drink, is *se pastiser*, so that it is thought that the word *pastis* may have derived from this.

Pernod has a fascinating history, having first been made by a Dr Pierre Ordinaire while in exile in Switzerland from the French Revolution at the end of the eighteenth century; he bequeathed the recipe for his special drink to his housekeeper, who marketed it, as she thought that it might be an aphrodisiac. In 1797 the recipe was bought by one of her customers, whose son-in-law, Henri-Louis Pernod, opened a small factory in Switzerland, extending this to one across the border at Pontarlier in 1805. Very soon Pernod became enormously popular and the distillery, alongside the River Doubs, was in full production. One day a cask of the liquid burst and the spirit flowed into the river, turning it bright yellow!

Pastis, the south of France version of the same sort of drink, is commercially the invention of Paul Ricard, who obtained a recipe from an old Provençal shepherd, went into business with enormous success and whose firm eventually amalgamated, in 1971, with that of Pernod. Paul Ricard owns the Island of Bendor, off the coast near Cassis, where there is a wine museum, and the firm, from which he has now retired, controls many other wine establishments.

Both these aniseed-flavoured drinks are fairly high in strength and the traditional way of taking them is with water. The dilution is traditionally five parts of water to one of the spirit. Ice should not be put in the drink, say locals, spring water being preferable. The old way of drinking is for a perforated spoon to be propped across the glass in which the measure of spirit has been poured. Then water is poured through this, clouding the colourless liquid; or the water may be poured through a lump of sugar propped on the spoon. There are, of course, many different brands of *pastis* on sale, the Corsican brand, Cazanis, being rather lighter and, to my taste, a little fresher than some of the others.

Pineau des Charentes
This is a drink evolved in the Cognac country — hence the regional suffix — supposedly when some new wine or *must* was tipped into a cask in which there had remained some brandy. Legend has it that it was enjoyed by Henri IV and Louis XIII — some of the publicity claims that it was the aphrodisiac which was responsible for the birth of Louis XIV — and that the latter king took it as a stomach settler. *Pineau des Charentes* got an A.O.C. in 1935; it must be made from fresh juice of the grapes cultivated in the Charente region only, to which is added a Cognac of the previous year, in the proportions of one of Cognac to two of grape-juice. It is a pleasant, slightly stimulating drink and another that comes into the category of 'holiday tipples'. *Floc de Gascogne* is similar, but here Armagnac is used with the unfermented grape-juice.

Sapindor
This is a Jura liqueur, greenish in colour and piney in smell and slightly in flavour — quite often it is put up in bottles which resemble a chunk of tree-trunk.

Selestat
This is a herb-based bitter, usually made in two strengths.

Sénancole

This is a bright yellow liqueur, smelling very fresh and originally made by the monks of the Abbey of Sénanque, at Salon, in Provence, a Cistercian foundation established in 1148. The monks still own the secret formula, but the liqueur is made in a modern distillery which has been in private ownership since 1930.

Suze

This brilliantly yellow-green drink is the best known of a number that are based on gentian. It is a drink that you either like very much, as the sort of aperitif that can make it possible for you to face a large meal when you do not want anything of the kind, or else you cannot bear it. In one of his Maigret stories, Georges Simenon says that Suze is popular with commercial travellers because it is light in alcohol. In the Auvergne, a good bitter drink of this kind is Arvèze, less sweet than Suze.

Toni-Kola

This is based on the kola nut and was first evolved by a Monsieur Gaboriau in Guinea. The drink is slightly sweeter than most other bitters.

Trappistine

Based on Armagnac, this is greenish yellow and contains herbs from the region of the Doubs, according to a recipe in the Abbey of Grâce Dieu.

Verveine du Vélay

This is a slightly bitter herb-based liqueur, made by the firm of Pagès, in the south-west, in both green and yellow versions.

Vieille Cure

This is made at Cenon, across the river from Bordeaux, and is a liqueur made with herbs with both Armagnac and Cognac involved in its preparation.

Alcools Blancs

It is difficult to work out a satisfactory English translation for this category of spirit, but some explanation is necessary. These colourless spirits — they are indeed 'white alcohols' because they are kept in glass, and therefore do not take on any colour, as occur when a spirit is matured in wood — are true *eaux-de-vie*; this means that they are a distillate of fruit — the mash of the fruit or, sometimes, the fruit being macerated in alcohol, and the resulting mixture distilled. Sometimes, with soft fruits, the kernels are included.

Do not, however, think that an ordinary liqueur, such as a cherry brandy or colourless Curaçao, is an *alcool blanc* — for it is not. In the preparation of these drinks, various processes are involved and various additives and sweetenings may be employed. With a true fruit-brandy of the *alcool blanc* type it is just the distilled essence of the fruit that makes the drink — nothing else. This is why *alcool blancs* are not sweet; they have no more sweetness than the fruit on which they are based, and this is why such spirits are admirable digestives. For obvious reasons, such distillates are most often made in mountains, where berries and fruits of various kinds are available in the wild state.

Traditionally, the way to drink these spirits is by pouring a small quantity of the colourless liquid into a medium-sized glass that has either been previously chilled or has had a few ice-cubes swirled round in it, then tipped out. The coldness of the glass releases the wonderful smell of the liquid.

An enormous range of *alcools blancs* are made in Alsace, although such drinks can be found elsewhere: for example, in the Dordogne Valley there is an *eau-de-vie de prune*, this particular *prune* being a type of greengage. Sometimes this spirit is combined with one of the local liqueurs made from walnuts, the result being called Mesclou. It is an odd drink, by no means disagreeable, but I have not found it in any other region. It will be appreciated that many of the *alcools blancs* are peasant or home-made products of great interest to the traveller and often of high quality, but few of the oddities compete with the well-known types on sale in shops.

Mountain regions are often places of production for *alcools blancs*: this is because of the availability of the ingredients in wild form. Alsace is by far the most important area, and its *alcools blancs* are famous. As Peter Hallgartern, in his authoritative book *Spirits and Liqueurs* (Faber, 1979), points out, these fruit-brandies tend to be bottled at a higher alcoholic strength than the usual liqueurs and it is rare for them to be aged before bottling. He also states that the best-known *alcools blancs*, as they are commercially made, are produced 'by distillation of the fermented fruit, but many are previously prepared by maceration in neutral *eau-de-vie* for several weeks to extract the delicate flavour, which would be destroyed by the heat of the distillation process'. The main distilled *eaux-de-vie* of Alsace are *kirsch, quetsch, mirabelle, poire Williams* and *prunelle*. Those made by means of maceration are *framboise, fraise, mûre, sureau, sorbier, baie de houx* and *aubépine*.

It will be appreciated that, in a region where the long hard winters meant that, in former times, most of the animals would have been slaughtered in the autumn, little outdoor work could be done for most of the winter, and, as soon as the use of the still became known, the farm household would get busy making use of such produce from the countryside that could not otherwise be used for human or animal foodstuffs; before sugar was cheap, jams and preserves would naturally not be widely made.

Alisier
This is the true rowan, or mountain ash, and the *alcool blanc* evokes the smell of marzipan to some people.

Aubépine
This is the hawthorn. It is rarely found today, because the berries have to be picked after the first frost and, therefore, if you do discover it, it will probably be a home-made product.

Baie de houx
This is the holly berry, which, as an *alcool blanc*, is very fragrant and crisply fresh.

Bramble or brimbelle
This is the true bramble, not the blackberry. (The English-looking version of the name is pronounced 'bromble'.) In former times it was often recommended as a reviving and stimulating drink.

Coing
This is the quince, and is perhaps best known for making *cotignac* (*p.290*) but is sometimes found in *alcool blanc* form as well.

Eau de vie de pommes

This is made from apples and I have no idea of the taste, except that an authoritative writer says it is in no way similar to Calvados. It would appear to be rather a neutral drink and seems to be often used as the base of *tutti frutti*. This last is a mixture of fruits, possibly peculiar to Alsace, because I have not seen it elsewhere. Obviously it was a way of using up small quantities of produce in a mixture at the end of the season, thereby utilizing windfalls. It is not particularly interesting, but is worth trying.

Eglantine

The wild or briar rose, this is also sometimes found as a white alcohol. One reference informs me that it can make *Un schnapps* (which I presume means a liqueur) which may be referred to as *gratte cul*: I have only once known anyone essay this strangely-named beverage, but the report was that it was in no way exciting.

Fraise or fraise des bois

This is made from strawberries, ideally the wild ones. The smell is delicious.

Framboise

This is made from raspberries and is highly rated by amateurs of *alcools blancs*. It tends to be expensive, because it is rather difficult to make and is also usually slightly higher in alcohol than similar drinks.

Gentiane

This is the attractive mountain plant with dark blue or yellow flowers. The root is used in various drinks, including several aperitifs, notably Suze (*see p.179*). There is an *alcool blanc* made from *gentiane* but I have never tried it, although I should suppose it to be rather bitter.

Kirsch

This is certainly the best known *alcool blanc* of all, probably because of its versatility in cooking, but it can also be used as a digestive. Although it is made from cherries, do not confuse it with any kind of 'cherry brandy'. The kernels go into the mash of the *kirsch* and it is distilled twice. It is often poured over pineapple, fruit-salad or used for *flambé* pancake recipes.

Kirsch Peureux

Some people suppose this to be a sweetened version of ordinary *kirsch* but in fact it is made by the firm of August Peureux, of Fougerolles in the Haute Saône. It is, in my opinion, not as distinguished a spirit as true *kirsch* made by any of the reputable Alsace establishments and, although interesting to sample, probably not worth trying more than once.

Mirabelle

This is made from *Mirabelle* plums, small and golden in colour. It has a delicious flavour, lightly luscious and this drink and *quetsch*, made from a small purplish plum, are often recommended as the ideal drinks to take with the beautiful fruit-tarts made from the same plums that glisten like jewels from the sweet trolleys of restaurants.

Mûre or mûre sauvage

This is the wild blackberry and it is found in the form of an *alcool blanc* simply because the French housewife does not make as much use of this fruit in the kitchen as her British counterpart.

Myrtille

Made from bilberries, this is often considered to be a particularly good digestive, probably because its flavour is rather assertive.

Nèfle

This is the medlar, which, in a cold region, has to ripen to the point of partial rottenness before it can be used. It is somewhat like a quince.

Prunelle or prunelle sauvage

This is the sloe or blackthorn. This makes a very good *alcool blanc* and anyone who has read the Maigret stories of Georges Simenon will recall that, because Madam Maigret comes from Alsace, the *prunelle* bottle is often brought out after dinner.

Reine-Claude

This is a greengage (*see p.63*). The *alcool blanc* is slightly similar to the plum liqueurs.

Sapin

This is the pine-tree buds in distilled form. Again, this is not often found, and one writer on Alsace drinks says that the pronounced resinous taste of the *alcool blanc* has to be cut with neutral alcohol to make it palatable.

There are probably many other 'cottage liqueurs' in the *alcool blanc* category, but the only one I have ever seen in addition to those made from berries and fruits was *cumin* or cummin. This, although I was not able to try it, would probably have had some flavour of caraway.

Sorbier, baie de sorbe

This is the fruit of a type of mountain ash, the rowan. The only English name I can trace is 'service tree'. The fruit makes a somewhat assertive and slightly bitter liqueur.

Sureau or Baie de Sureau

This is the elder, the fruit of which is often distilled. Although, in the nineteenth century it was elderberries that were much used to give colour to port and, for all I know, other wines that might have been light in tone in an indifferent vintage, the fruit can today be occasionally found in the form of an *alcool blanc*.

Williamine, Poire Williams, Poire

This is made from the William pear. It can be found in various regions of France, although the Alsace version generally seems superior to me. It has an amazing smell, instantly evocative of a pear, and is very popular.

15

Other Drinks

Even quite a small bar will have what seems to be a huge range of bottles, although close inspection may reveal that these often consist of several different brands of the same drink — such as *rhum*, vermouth, anise (*pastis*) and, these days, 'le whisky'. But, as one who has explored many of these can say, I now realize why certain of the world-famous brands of drinks *are* world-famous: they are usually better than others.

Wine By the Glass

This is usually available, although it may be poured from the already open bottle of some branded blend. This is likely in any region that does not make wine. Champagne by the glass may be available in a rather smart bar or hotel-restaurant. If you like wine as an aperitif, it is sometimes worth asking if you can have a bottle or half bottle; they will usually serve this at the bar or café table.

Ice is usually available, but you may be asked if you want it actually in your drink. If so, say *'Avec des glaçons'* (with ice-cubes). Plain water is brought on request, although sometimes just a single glass instead of a carafe. If you want soda or 'a splash' ask for *'Eau de seltz'* or *'Avec du siphon'*; the waiter may bring the siphon and squirt it for you, or you may have to buy a split of Perrier.

Vin blanc cassis is likely to be available almost everywhere, made with the local dry white wine. In Burgundy, it tends to be stronger than elsewhere — a deep almost purple pink. Vermouth *cassis* is a different version and, in sparkling wine regions, you can often get *cassis* in a glass of this. The term *'Un kir'*, colloquially used for *vin blanc cassis*, refers to the late Canon Kir, Mayor of Dijon, a great hero of the French Resistance. He did not invent but greatly enjoyed this Burgundy drink, traditionally based on dry white Aligoté. Kir Royale is *cassis* and sparkling wine.

Vins doux naturels are the wines of several of the southern regions, which are slightly higher in alcohol than table-wine and, usually, slightly sweet as their name implies. Some of the best known include Muscat de Beaumes de Venise, Muscat de Frontignan, Banyuls and the Grands Roussillons. They should be served chilled. Although Britons may associate ordinary Muscat wines with the sweet course of a meal, these *vins doux naturels* are very pleasant between-times refreshment.

Vermouth

Vermouth is widely drunk between times too, or as an aperitif. If, however, you order by brand, especially 'Un Martini', it may be advisable to indicate definitely that it should be 'sans gin', unless you want a cocktail. There are many different branded vermouths, so this can be an opportunity to sample some that may not be as familiar as Martini, Noilly Prat or Chambéry vermouth.

Vermouth has fairly been described as 'the oldest wine in the world', because, in very ancient times, aromatized wine, with additives of herbs and spices, was well-known, both for social and medicinal purposes. Wormwood, which comes into many vermouth recipes, was a frequent ingredient, hence the name.

Vermouth can be made wherever wine is produced and, in the past, often utilized the rather ordinary common wines that, now, are able to be pleasant everyday drinking in their own right. The methods vary from establishment to establishment, but involve the processes of infusion, maceration and distillation — utilizing the local herbs and spices, as well as the local wines. Peels, barks, plant derivations and various flavourings can all go into vermouth and at each stage it is important that the additives are allowed time to combine satisfactorily with the base wine, whatever it is. Originally, vermouth was made in Italy but, at the beginning of the nineteenth century, Louis Noilly started his business in Lyons, taking his son-in-law, Claudius Prat, in with him and they were so successful in making vermouth, using the southern wine and local herbs, that they moved to Marseille in 1843. Noilly's daughter, Joséphine Prat, remained a director of the firm after her father and husband died. Her granddaughter, the Vicomtesse Vigier, went into the business before 1939 and directed it until in 1970 she died — being then more than a hundred years old! Noilly Prat extended their premises to Marseillan and Sète, where the huge casks of vermouth mature in open-air enclosures, the action of the sea air on the vermouth being important. (It is this maturation that is one of the differences in production between French and Italian vermouths.) There are many other vermouth establishments in Marseilles and the south.

Chambéry vermouth, however, is different again. It was first made in 1921, by Joseph Chavasse, 'Pharmacien, Herbaliste et Distillateur', using the dry white wine of Savoy. These days, the base wine for Chambéry comes from various regions. Chambéry is made by two main companies — Comoz, who market their vermouths under the names Boissière and Comoz, and La Grande Distillerie Chambérienne, who make Dolin and Gaudin Chambéry. There are various versions, including an extremely attractive one, Chambéryzette, flavoured with wild Alpine strawberries. But Chambéry, which got its A.O.C. in 1932, is strictly controlled, must be made in Chambéry and cannot contain extracts or concentrates — unlike other vermouths. Although Chambéry vermouth from time to time enjoys a certain vogue among the dry martini drinkers, essentially it is intended to be drunk straight, without additives or diluents. Very light and in fact distinctive, because of its ingredients, it should be served chilled.

Other French vermouths will be found in great variety and it may be worth stressing that 'French' does not mean 'dry', any more than 'Italian' means 'sweet'. All the great vermouth houses make a range; it is the style of the house that gives each one its individuality. So, when you order, specify whether you want a 'Vermouth *sec*' or '*doux*'. (For other vermouth-type drinks, see *p.188*.) Another point to stress is that, should you spy some unknown brand of vermouth and wish to try it, see whether you are being helped from a bottle that has been open for ages — vermouth, based on wine, deteriorates with exposure to air and, although it will not harm you to drink an oxidized vermouth, it will not give you much pleasure either.

Some Other Drinks

Dubonnet is one of the best-known French aperitifs, the basic version being deep pinkish crimson. There is also a dryer, golden version. It was created by Joseph Dubonnet in the middle of the nineteenth century as 'blended quinine wine', the use of quinine being of great importance in the expanding French colonial countries.

Lillet or Kina Lilet is the same thing — the second spelling is more usual in the south. It is aromatised white wine, made in the Graves region. St Raphaël is another drink making use of quinine. It is named for the Archangel Raphaël because, in 1830, a man named Jupet who first made it had recovered his sight and Raphaël is patron of the blind. It comes in white (sweetish), very pale (dryish) and red (sweetish and fruity) versions. Byrrh is a wine-based vermouth type drink, said to have been evolved by a Roussillon shepherd in 1866. It also contains a little quinine. Cap Corse, reddish-brown and rather sweet, is the great aperitif of Corsica. Ambassadeur, made by Cusenier, includes oranges, herbs and barks and gentian, the bitter herb of the Vosges. It was first made in 1858. There is a red and a pale gold version.

Amer Picon is spirit-based, flavoured with gentian, quinine and oranges. It was first made by Gaeton Picon in Algeria in 1835. It is not actually very 'Amer' but, if you want to sweeten it, add fizzy lemonade or orangeade instead of soda.

Suze is the bright yellow drink incorporating gentian, which can be taken neat or with soda and ice. (*See p.179.*) It is light in alcohol and can be a good preprandial digestive, but it is somewhat bitter.

Beer

Most French beer is like lager in style, generally made by the low fermentation method, with a higher proportion of carbonation than most British beer. It is served chilled and you can order it anywhere, even in a smart restaurant. Draught beer (*bière sous pression*) is not always available, unless you are in a *brasserie* (*see p.84*) or in a town where there is a brewery. Alsace is the great beer area. These days well-known brands of beer from many different countries may be available.

Sizes of beer glasses vary. *Un bock* is a somewhat dated term, but, if you order one, you will probably get a fat-stemmed goblet, containing about four decilitres. The *demi* is 250 decilitres; *un distingué* is 500 decilitres; *un formidable* is one litre.

Hot Drinks

Tea, coffee and chocolate are of course widely available, though the 'bag' dominates many tea and coffee pots. Specify coffee '*sans chicoré*' if you do not like chicory to the extent that many French do. It is also worthwhile specifying if you want hot milk with your coffee and cold milk with your tea — you may get the reverse!

188

the reverse! Decaffeinated coffee — *'Décaf'* — is usually available in restaurants. Sugar is always served with coffee and sometimes (though not on 'polite' occasions) people will dip the corner of a sugar-lump into the coffee and then eat it. The procedure is known as *'Faire le canard'*.

Milk, for those who ordinarily drink a lot of it, can be a problem. The bulk of French milk is pasteurized but, as deliveries are only able to be made in cases of special need, a great deal is also sterilised; this is what many visitors dislike (*see p.98*). In the country, milk may come straight from the cow, and children, notoriously conservative about some foods, may find this unpleasant, so, if in doubt, take a supply of powdered milk.

Un grog is hot water with either *rhum* or brandy in it — an agreeable warming drink. It is also quite common for people to augment their tea with a spoonful of *rhum* on a cold day.

Infusions or tisanes are traditional in France for many semi-medical purposes. Sometimes they come in little bags, which can be attached to the lid of a teapot or simply dunked in a large cup; sometimes, when in loose form, you must use a strainer (*une passe*) to pour the resulting liquid. You can buy sachets of infusions in supermarkets or at an herbalist — there are still plenty of these in France — shops specializing in health food products and, of course, at the pharmacy. Some of the better known are listed here — travellers will often find them refreshing and restorative:

Camomile is a sedative for the nerves and the digestion.
Fleurs d'Oranger is another mild sedative, especially calming for the digestion.
Mélisse (Balm) is helpful with fevers and colds.
Menthe (Mint) is digestive and refreshing.
Pensées sauvages (Pansies) is a general soothing, cooling drink.
Queues de cérises (Cherry stalks) is a useful preparation for anyone suffering from fluid retention, as it is *'pour faire pipi'*.
Sauge (Sage) is recommended for the brain and for headaches.
Serpolet (Wild thyme) is a mild stimulant, for lungs and digestion.
Sureau (Elder) is an overall soothing and healing herb.
Tilleul (Lime) is good for sleeplessness and *Tilleul-menthe* is a very popular soothing digestive.
Verveine (Verbena) is another soothing drink.

Soft Drinks
Jus d'orange and *Jus de citron* are orange or lemon fruit squashes. If you want 'the real thing' you must ask for *orange pressée* or

189

citron pressée — and, if you want more of a drink than just the juice of a single fruit, you should remember also to ask for water or soda. As mentioned earlier, real fruit-juice is never cheap.

Jus de raisin is grape-juice. In wine regions at vintage time you may be offered the fresh juice of the grapes — but be careful about drinking it copiously, as it may have slightly aperient properties. *Jus de pamplemousse* is grapefruit squash.

Grenadine, one of the most traditional casual drinks, is pomegranate juice, slightly sweet. It is generally diluted with water or soda.

Sirops are sweet, flavoured concentrates, also usually diluted. Some of the most popular are *citron, orange, cassis* (blackcurrant but not to be confused with the blackcurrant liqueur), *pamplemousse* and *ananas* (pineapple). Otherwise there are numerous fizzy sweet drinks, including the ubiquitous 'Coke'.

Table Waters

There are hundreds, possibly thousands of springs in France, their waters being appreciated for their refreshing qualities as well as for any medicinal properties. The thrifty French did not take to drinking them because of any doubts about the tap-water, but because their tuned-up palates prefer such waters. (If you are camping or caravanning, then a supply of water-purifying tablets is obviously essential, but the ordinary traveller will risk nothing by drinking the tap-water anywhere else.)

Many table waters are now bottled in plastic. If you have problems about disposing of these containers, the method — which I learned from the label of a container of Volvic — is to fill them with boiling water and then, after a few minutes, the plastic will become soft, so that you can empty and stamp on them.

Most of the better-known varieties will be available in chemists as well as general shops and supermarkets. If ordered in a restaurant, the bottle should arrive chilled. (If you buy one for a picnic, remember that any gassy variety ought to be cool, else it can seem very bloating to the consumer.) The most important thing to know about any table water is whether it is *gazeuse* (fizzy) and to what extent, or *non-gazeuse* (still). It can be useful also to know of any medicinal properties — once, I consumed vast amounts of an Italian mineral water after a continuing tummy upset and it was only when my doctor husband read the label that we found I was taking a type of aperient!

The following are the best-known table waters:

Badoit: This is mildly salty with a slight effervescence that is more a *pétillance* than a sparkle, which can be very refreshing. It comes from St Galmier, in the Loire, and has been known since the thirteenth century; the bottling room is kept at the same temperature as that of the spring, so that Badoit comes off the bottling line naturally *pétillant*.

Charrier: This is another water suitable for those on salt-free diets, often recommended as the purest water known in its natural state.

Contrexéville: This is a still water, with a slightly earthy taste. It is mildly diuretic so that 'Contrex' is used by people who suffer from fluid retention. The water comes from a spa in the Vosges and began to be famous when the physician of the exiled King Stanislas of Poland (father-in-law of Louis XV) investigated the spring, commenting, 'What happiness for the human race!' The little town hence became fashionable, thanks to subsequent recommendations of Dr Thouvenel, physician to Louis XVI. In the nineteenth century the spa was very smart: the Shah of Persia visited it in 1900, the Queen of Spain and many English aristocrats also going there.

Evian: This comes from Evian-les-Bains, overlooking the Lake of Geneva. It is a still, neutral water, publicized as the best-selling table water in the world, being from the Cachat spring that is fed from the rainwater and melting snow of the Mont Blanc range. Analysis of the water shows that it has not changed throughout a century and it is this purity that makes it often recommended for mixing with baby foods. Evian is very slightly diuretic, useful for anybody on a salt-free diet as it contains no sodium, and these days it is also recommended as a type of skin moisturiser in spray form. Evian became famous when the Marquis de Lesert, a sufferer from kidney stones, took a drink from a running spring near the garden owned by a Monsieur Cachat, in 1789: his trouble was cured and although Evian as a spa didn't get really organized until after the French Revolution, it attracted many celebrities and today is an enormous concern.

Perrier: This spring is at Vergèze, near Nîmes, and the waters may have been used by Hannibal: certainly the Romans built a bathing place there for their legions. Originally, carbon dioxide gas, rising from the limestone, combined with the spring waters to result in a natural carbonation, but today, so as to ensure continuity of the amount of bubbles, the fizz is removed from the water and then put back, in an agreed amount, when bottling is done.

In about 1863 a Dr Perrier became interested in promoting this spring, Napoleon III giving him the rights to develop it; but he had no luck until, in the early 1900s, A.W. St John Harmsworth, brother of newspaper tycoon Lord Northcliffe, visited the region with his tutor during a university vacation and met the doctor. As a result, Harmsworth bought the spring, though he agreed that it should always bear Perrier's name. He marketed the water in a dynamic way, coining the slogan that it was 'the Champagne of table waters' (a description that, nowadays, would have the Champagne establishments going for him in the courts!) After a car accident, Harmsworth became paralysed and exercised with Indian clubs to regain the use of his limbs — which gave him the notion of designing the Perrier bottle in a club shape, which it still has. Perrier has become chic, notably, recently, in the US and, as it has no flavouring of any kind, it is an ideal water to use as an additive or in a mix.

Vals St Jean: This is another slightly sparkling water.

Vichy: This table water gets its name from the Latin *vicus calidus* — 'hot town' — the Romans having made a big settlement there. In the fourteenth century the town enjoyed a revival of prosperity and the Convent of the Célestins was established there. Unfortunately, Vichy changed hands and suffered much privation during the various troubles of the time and it was only in the seventeenth century that prosperity was restored there, especially after the Marquise de Sévigné took two sessions of the cure. During the Second World War, Vichy attracted the undesirable set of 'the Vichy Government', but today the place is smart, elegant — and very big business. The springs belong to the French Government, who direct their working.

There are four main sources of water. Vichy Célestins is the best known of the springs, lower in mineral content and with a very slight sparkle. As the Célestins spring runs too slowly to keep pace with demand, Vichy Boussange augments the supply — it is very slightly more sparkling. Vichy St Yorre, Bassin de Vichy is the slightly sparkling, faintly salty water. Vichy Grande Grille and Vichy Hôpital are medicinal waters, only to be found at the chemist and not particularly pleasant as drinks.

Vittel: This Vosges spring has been known for its medicinal properties for centuries and the Romans had a big settlement here. It was in the nineteenth century that a lawyer, Louis Bouloumié, became ill and tried various cures without success; a friend told him of a spring in a nearby field, called the Fountain de Gérémoy, which achieved his cure. Subsequent analysis has shown that the water is high in calcium. In 1854 Bouloumié bought the spring and founded the spa — and his own fortune.

There are three main springs at Vittel. The still water, slightly earthy, is Vittel Grande Source. Vitteloise is advertised as *'L'eau qui chante et qui danse'*. Vittel Hépar is unlikely to come the way of the ordinary traveller, although it is on sale at the chemist. It has laxative properties and is recommended for use by children. Vittel Délices are fizzy fruit-flavoured drinks.

Volvic: This comes from the Auvergne and is quite still.

Table waters are usually available in several sizes but, if you only want a small bottle, ask for *'un petit'*. You may have to buy a small bottle of a fizzy version if you want, say, a 'splash' in a drink, as no siphon may be available.

193

16

Alsace and Lorraine

Although Belgium, Luxemburg and Germany are the external boundaries of these two French regions, both Alsace and Lorraine have remained independent and original as regards gastronomy, taking in many traditions and recipes and foods, but transforming them. Those who live in mountain regions tend to evolve robust dishes and the thrifty utilize the berries and herbs of the slopes, in addition to the wines, to incorporate in dishes. In addition, the terrible sufferings, notably in the Thirty Years War, caused the inhabitants of this part of France to develop a great respect for food; all religious occasions were celebrated by feasts, some of which went on for several days. Birthdays, weddings and anniversaries, victories or their anniversaries, reunions of students, army veterans — and the killing of a pig — were all occasions for lavish eating and drinking. At funerals, the corpse would often be present in his or her coffin and each dish would be formally offered to the defunct person, before being distributed to the poor.

It should always be realized that Alsace and Lorraine, in spite of the latter having given France her most loved saint — Joan of Domrémy — and the former having, even under the most severe conditions of German and other occupations, kept its local traditions and language alive, are sometimes considered not really 'French France'. Indeed, some ill-informed writers still refer to Alsace as being Germanic. In former times the mercenaries of Lorraine earned themselves a reputation for being brigands. But there is no doubt that, even though both regions are as firm as ever in their regional pride — justly so — they *are* French and the large number of famous restaurants in the area demonstrate some of the finest traditions of French cooking at its apogée. It is worth remembering that, with some dishes, a portion for one will probably satisfy the appetite of three visitors to the region as well!

The area received a great gastronomic boost in the eighteenth century. Stanislas Leczynski, exiled King of Poland, was the father of Louis XV's wife, Maria, and when François II, Duc de Lorraine, decided to exchange his duchy there for that of Tuscany, the King of France made his father-in-law Governor of the region in 1738. Stanislas did not have much 'ruling' to do and his courts at Nancy and Lunéville, where he was surrounded by people who were charming and accomplished in many things, were obvious nurseries of culinary delights. For an account of the agreeable life they led, see the late Nancy Mitford's *Voltaire in Love* — one may deplore the superficial attitude of many of these people, but it would have been fun to have been one of them. Delicious foods streamed from Stanislas's kitchens, often being forwarded to the court at Versailles or the gastronomic nobility in Paris. *Bouchées à la reine* (cheese puffs) were named for Queen Maria; it would be pleasant to think that this lady was even greedy but, alas, according to historians and her portraits, she was an adequate breeder, but otherwise of unamusing bovinity, the sort of plain woman who everyone says is wonderfully good and cannot wait to escape from. Stanislas's cook Madeleine, however, was the first to make the little orange-flavoured sponge-cakes to which she gave her name and Stanislas himself is supposed to have had the idea of soaking the *kugelhopf* (the light yeast cake, usually with a hole in the middle, traditional in Alsace) in *rhum*, hence the rhum baba.

In the eighteenth century too, a boy, Claude Gelée, was apprenticed to a Toul pastrycook; he grew up to become the painter Claude Lorraine — and is also credited with the invention of puff pastry. As he did work for a time in Italy, where the Italians claim they first made it, it is possible that he did introduce it to France. During the same period, the Maréchal de Contades became the military governor of Alsace in 1762; he settled in Strasbourg and his personal chef, Jean-Joseph Close (who may have been either a Norman or a native of Lorraine), came with him. Close devised a special way of serving goose liver — a dish praised by Horace, Pliny, Martial, Rabelais and Montaigne. Close's version was prepared with truffles and cooked in a pastry case. This '*Pâté de Contades*' became so popular with the Maréchal and his associates that a sample was sent to Louis XV, who liked it so much that he bestowed a Picardy estate on Contades and money on Close — the latter married the widow of a Strasbourg pastrycook and set up

195

in his own business there, making *pâté de foie gras truffé,* for which, rather oddly, he did not use the local truffles, but those of Périgord. This culinary creation became famous and it is said that Maréchal Rapp, then only a lieutenant, got onto the staff of Géneral Desaix and the first rung up the ladder of promotion, by presenting a Strasbourg *pâté* to his commander in chief. There are supposed to be forty-two different versions of this *pâté* today and the making of it is an important industry in Strasbourg; only recently, however, have Alsace truffles been used. During the German occupation in the nineteenth century (after the Franco-Prussian war, 1870–71) it was forbidden to use the pig for truffle hunting, so spaniels, pomeranians and poodles, breeds with a keen sense of smell, were trained to search for the delicacy.

Food is copious in this part of France, whether it is *haute cuisine* or the more homely *cuisine bourgeoise* or *cuisine paysanne.* There is much use of cream and many sweet things to tempt the traveller. But it is also possible for tourists to get snack meals — almost impossible to find, except for 'le sandwich' or on auto-routes elsewhere; plates of cold cuts and salad are easily obtainable and the *weinstub* or café will prove a boon to people who, especially while sightseeing, do not want to spend several hours and a lot of money on an elaborate meal.

Food in General

Lorraine is a great source of salt. Many place-names — Salival, Château Salins, Salins-les-Bains — indicate this. Alsace is dominated by the pig and the goose, so that there are many different sorts of sausage, salted meats and recipes involving goose or pork fat, whereas butter tends to be the cooking medium in Lorraine.

There are many fish in the lake, although the river trout these days are scarce and trout featured on menus probably come from a fish farm. The *carpe* (carp), *brochet* (pike) are often served, also *écrevisses* (crayfish) and *sandre,* which last is a cross between a pickerel and a perch, very delicate in flavour, and *ombre* (grayling). The description '*à la juive*' may be seen applied to many recipes; there seems always to have been a fairly large Jewish community in these regions and their use of certain spices and herbs is interesting.

The great vegetable is the cabbage — a special type, *chou*

quintal, is used for *choucroute*; this dish, it may be fairly said, is to the German sauerkraut what caviar is to lumpfish roe! Until quite recently, each village had a man who, with a special shredding cutter, did nothing but prepare the huge white cabbages for pickling and there are endless different recipes and stories about the vegetable. Tons of the stuff are consumed at the annual *choucroute* festival in Colmar. *Chou rouge* (red cabbage) and many types of salad vegetables are common — the people of Alsace have always appreciated these — and, of course, the potato, which is recorded as a food as early as 1625. *Jets de houblon* (hop sprouts) are sometimes to be found.

The numerous sweet confections are often a legacy from the time when, before the French Revolution, the great religious establishments of the area were proud of their cooking and entertained important persons travelling in the region; the names sometimes give indications of this. The *bretzel* or *pretzel*, a salted twirl of biscuit, is a regional accompaniment to beer and many aperitifs.

Specialities and Dishes

Although there are some dishes peculiar to Lorraine and others to Alsace, these days restaurants may feature them without too much regard to the dividing Vosges Mountains, so I have not separated them here. *Choucroute*, the dish of the region, is said to have been first brought in by the Romans — but historians claim it to have been invented by both the Tartars and the ancient Egyptians. Essentially, it is pickled cabbage plus. The ingredients vary, according to whatever is available, but they can include ham, smoked loin of pork, various sorts of sausage, maybe a pork chop or a chunk of goose or game, all prepared with wine, onions and various seasonings, usually accompanied by boiled potatoes. A *choucroute garnie* is a formidable dish — but one to be enjoyed at a country restaurant, rather than anywhere smart; these days a version of it, called *choucroute royale*, arrives with a split of *Crémant d'Alsace* poised on the top, to be squirted over the whole just before serving. I do not know that the last-minute drench does much for the flavour, but it looks luxurious. *Cervelat* is a smoked pork sausage; *mettwürst* a sausage mainly made of beef; *saucisse de Strasbourg* is a mixture of pork and beef, lightly smoked, containing caraway seeds; *knockwurst* is blood sausage; *saucisses de Montbéliard* (which come from Franche Comté) are somewhat akin to the British pork sausage, though with more pork and having been lightly smoked.

197

Schifela is shoulder of pork with turnips. *Porcelet farci à la peau de goret* is stuffed suckling pig. *Civet de porc* is a pork stew. *Baeckeoffa*, or *beckenoffe*, is a stew of mutton, pork, beef and potatoes. *Pikefleisch* or *boeuf salé*, a Strasbourg speciality, is smoked brisket of beef. *Derentifleisch* is smoked rib of beef, a Lorraine recipe.

Grenouilles à la Bouley are frogs' legs, rolled in crumbs, shallots and parsley, then fried. This dish dates from 16 November 1821, when an accident caused the Metz reservoir to break open and there was a sudden glut of frogs, which the thrifty housewives felt obliged to use up in various ways. Frogs are not as plentiful these days as they used to be and the storks, which bring good fortune to the buildings on which they build their huge nests, have suffered from the decline in the frog population, as well as from the industrial effluent in the rivers, so nowadays there have to be stork parks in which the birds are reared — and where some seem content enough to stay throughout the year.

Knepfl are small dumplings, served on toast either with gravy or grated cheese. *Grillade à la Champagneules* is a speciality of Lorraine and has been described as the French version of Welsh rabbit. It is fried ham on toast, covered with a sauce made with cheese and beer.

Zewelwai or *tarte aux oignons* — an onion tart — is a country dish that is often among the starters in good restaurants today. Tarte Lorraine is a tart of pork and veal, plus onions and spices, with an egg and cream filling. Quiche Lorraine is the world-famous tart of bacon with a filling of eggs and cream. Local variations may include the addition of onions and/or cheese. In some regions it is referred to as *féouse*. Culinary historians say that these pastry dishes are descendants of the Roman *'torta'*, various things combined with a custard and served on a base of pastry. *Quiche aux chanottes* is a poppyseed and onion tart.

Tarte flambée, however, is not like any of the usual 'tarts'. Very much a country dish, it is something that can be announced as being made that day on boards outside little restaurants, where locals will flock if the reputation for *tarte flambée* is good. It is bread dough, smoothed out wafer-thin on a wooden shovel, topped with eggs and possibly with bacon and onions, which is then briskly cooked to crispness in a wood-fired oven. Relays of *tartes flambées* will be brought to the table to be eaten in your fingers.

Fromage blanc, another very pleasant dish, is white curd cheese, which is brought to diners accompanied by dishes of chopped parsley, onions, garlic, shallots, boiled or baked potatoes, which customers then mix up according to taste. You are unlikely to get either this dish or *tarte flambée* except out in the country.

Poisson à la gelée du vin is usually carp or pike, poached in red wine and allowed to cool, when it looks as if it were in a pinkish aspic jelly.

In general, the term '*à l'alsacienne*' implies that the dish is served with or cooked with cabbage or *choucroute*, possibly also with sausages and potatoes; '*à la Vosgienne*' implies that onions and, possibly, *mirabelles* are in the recipe. When fish or poultry are cooked in wine, this is usually specified — e.g. *coq au Riesling* or, in Lorraine, *coq au vin gris*.

Bar-le-Duc is the name given to the red or white currant preserves made in this town, which are sometimes served with a fluffy fresh white cream cheese. Bar-le-Duc is expensive, because each currant has to be separately pierced, so that, when cooked, it will plump out correctly.

Mirabelles de Metz au sirop are *mirabelle* plums in syrup — very rich and luscious. Metz has always been famous for fruits and the local *silvanges*, a type of fragrant pear, were sent as a regular order to Grimod de la Reynière (*see p.28*).

Vacherin glacé is a meringue and cream and ice-cream concoction. *Tarte alsacienne* is a large open tart with fruit arranged on a type of custard — the variations of this bejewel many a fruit trolley. *Eierkuchas* are pancakes, usually served with raspberry jelly. *Tarte au Mengin* is a tart made with fresh white cheese, eggs, cream and sugar. *Talmouses* are a puff-pastry-and-almond sweet; *krapfen* are little doughnuts; *nonneferzlas* is a type of fritter-cum-cream-puff; *kaffeekrantz* is coffee-cake; *macarons des soeurs* are Nancy's speciality and have been made by the 'good sisters' since the twelfth century; *chanoinesses* are honey-cakes from Remiremont; *birewka* is a rich fruit and spice cake. *Bergamots de Nancy* are sweets flavoured with bergamot.

Drinks

Much beer is drunk in this area and the big breweries, under their patron, Saint Arnould, the twenty-ninth Bishop of Metz, who lived in the seventh century, are interesting places to visit. Travellers should ask to see round the establishments of Kronenbourg at Strasbourg, Le Pêcheur at Schiltigheim, La Meuse at Champigneulles, and others at Metz and Thionville. Hops may be seen growing on many of the flat cultivated lands throughout the area.

Wines

The vineyards of Lorraine have been much reduced in size. Today, the best known is the *vin gris*, a pale pink, which is produced around Toul, Metz and Vie-sur-Seille.

Alsace wines, however, are of increased importance. More than one bottle out of every three drunk in the French home is from Alsace, and West Germany takes vast amounts, people coming across the frontier to load their cars — because, say the Alsaciens rather wickedly, Alsace wines are more easily drunk and one can take more. Certainly more Alsace is drunk in Germany than any other A.C. French wine. Exports to Belgium, the UK, the US, Switzerland and many other countries reflect the quality of the wines, backed by the determination of the people to provide the sort of wines that both the everyday drinker and the connoisseur require.

Perhaps the most important thing to bear in mind about Alsace wines — 'Alsatian is ze dog,' the late André Simon, founder of the International Wine & Food Society, used to growl — is that, unlike the delicate light wines of many other regions, they are sufficiently robust to stand up to even the most substantial food — of which, in Alsace, there are numerous typical recipes. They are named for the grapes that make them: Riesling, Gewurztraminer, Pinot Gris or Tokay d'Alsace (efforts were unsuccessfully made to stop the use of the word 'Tokay'), Muscat, Sylvaner, Pinot Blanc; a blend will be called Edelzwicker. Pinot Noir is used to make the red wines, which are deep pinkish-red in colour. The *Crémant d'Alsace* wines are the sparkling wines made according to the Champagne process (and more strictly the makers say), and there are also sparkling wines made by the sealed vat process.

Some special wines will bear specific vineyard names, but, overall, the important thing to remember is that the wines of each establishment will follow their makers' own individual house style, so that, even if made from the same grape within the same area, each will be different. Even within villages there may be different micro-climates as well, all affecting the wines; of course, the northern part of the Alsace vineyard will produce wines of slightly different character from the south. Wines that are late picked, therefore of additional, concentrated quality, are categorized as *'vendange tardive'*; it should not be assumed that these are invariably sweeter than the more ordinary wines — some producers ferment them so that they are dry, although with more intensity. The term *'Sélection de grains nobles'*, which signifies that the grapes have been picked individually, berry by berry, in particularly favourable vintages, is an even higher category, wines of great force and impressiveness.

Although the Riesling ('Heaven on earth in the glass' is a saying about it) is the most esteemed noble grape of Alsace, the Gewurztraminer is probably the 'when in doubt' choice for many people. This, the 'spicy' Traminer, does not, in French, have the umlaut — the two little dots — on the 'u', as in the French language the sound does not represent the contraction 'ue' as it does in German. The Sylvaner grape makes wines that are light and refreshing, the Pinot Gris wines that are somewhat complex, agreeably aromatic, whereas the Pinot Blanc wines tend to be somewhat four-square and robust, very dry. The Muscat makes dry wines here but the distinctive fragrance is something that people either like very much or not at all — it is perhaps the only wine grape that produces wine unmistakeably 'grapey'.

Alsace is also the most prolific French region for *alcools blancs* — the white spirits distilled from a huge variety of fruits, berries and even herbs; they are quite distinct from liqueurs, which are also made here and are excellent digestives after a rich Alsace meal (*see p.181*). Some of those that are seldom found outside the region should be tried by travellers — the *baie de houx* (hollyberry), *alisier* (rowan), *coing* (quince), *prunelle* (sloe), *nèfle* (medlar), *sorbier* (sorb apple), *sureau* (elder), *eglantier* (rosehip). The *mirabelle* (plum), *kirsch* (cherry), *framboise* (raspberry) and *fraise* (strawberry) are, though, perhaps the ones most likely to please those unfamiliar with them.

Marc de Gewurztraminer is distilled in the region and should also be tried — it is, however, something of an acquired taste, as its flavour is very definite.

Serving Drinks

The Alsace glass is rather like an onion with its top chopped off and on a long stem, which may be green. The device of the Grandes Maisons d'Alsace, a group of eight important producers, adroitly combines the stork and the Alsace glass. The Alsace bottle, strictly controlled, is tall and green, but for the sparkling wines the more bulbous type of bottle is used. The *alcools blancs* are often served in a chilled glass, which some people find brings out the flavour advantageously, but there are others who think they should be served at room temperature — it is for the individual to decide.

Things To See and Do

Alsace in particular is rich in works of art and in most cities there are important collections of items relating to past life. In Strasbourg, at the Musée Alsacien at 23 quai Saint Nicolas, there are reconstructions of various rooms, including a kitchen and a pharmacy and a section devoted to wine. The Maison Kammerzell, now a restaurant, dates from 1467. In Nancy, there are important china and handicrafts exhibits in the Ancien Palais Ducal et Musée Historique de Lorraine, plus a pharmacy museum and, in the Galerie des Cerfs, a series of tapestries, *La Condamnation du Banquet*, showing the shocking consequences of overindulgence at table. At Thann there is a small folklore museum. Colmar, centre of the Alsace wine trade, is where the annual *Foire aux Vins* is held in August. The centre of the town is a pedestrian precinct and here, in the Place de l'Ancienne Douane, one can admire the statue of the mercenary, Schwendi, holding up the vinestock (supposed to be Tokay) he brought back from the wars in Hungary. Here, too, is the wonderful Musée d'Unterlinden, which has a reconstructed wine cellar and museum of wine, with decorated casks, wrought-iron inn signs and equipment used in wine-making, and all types of kitchen utensils. Nearby, the Maison des Têtes, dating from 1609, is a restaurant, with the tables divided from one another by pew-like partitions, just as it might have been a century ago or more. At Mulhouse, the Musée Historique in the sixteenth-century Hôtel de Ville, has reconstructions of rooms of different periods, plus exhibits of equipment used by *vignerons* and coopers.

Langres is famous for its meringues and the Musée de Breuil de Saint German has exhibits of china and cutlery; Diderot, son of a cutler, was born here. The Château du Haut-Koenigsbourg is a medieval castle burnt in 1633 but rebuilt for Kaiser Wilhelm II; visitors can see the cellar, kitchen and dining-room and there is a superb view over the Plaine d'Alsace and the Rhine.

The *Route du Vin* is very well planned so that even travellers with only a short space of time to spare can see at least a section of it. It runs for about ninety miles from Thann in the south to Marlenheim west of Strasbourg, although there is plenty to see even further north, if you can go up to near Wissembourg, almost on the German frontier. It would be possible to drive the length of the *Route du Vin* in a day, but this would not allow for stopping, which would be a pity, as virtually every village has something delightful to look at even in addition to its wines, and the views as the road winds through the vineyards are very beautiful. Highlights might be a stop in Riquewihr — 'the pearl of Alsace' — with a visit to one of the many establishments and, certainly, a walk up the main street; over 90 per cent of the houses here date from the sixteenth century. Eguisheim is another enchanting little wine town and these towns are largely pedestrian precincts, so that one can wander about appreciatively. Kaysersberg, birthplace of Albert Schweitzer; Turckheim, where the night watchman still makes his rounds; Kintzheim, where at the headquarters of the wine order, the Confrèrie de St Etienne holds its ceremonies in the château, plus a wine museum, and Obernai are all of particular charm, but these are only a few.

The Comité Interprofessional des Vins d'Alsace (C.I.V.A.) at 12 Avenue de la Foire aux Vins, Colmar will supply good brochures, including a map of the *Route du Vin* giving details of wine establishments open to visitors. In London, tourist offices can often provide or obtain information via either The French Government Tourist Office, 178 Piccadilly, W.1., or Food & Wine From France, 46 Piccadilly, W.1.

17

Auvergne and the Massif Central

Although very beautiful, this region is not particularly famous gastronomically. Agriculturally it is poor, except for the flocks from whose milk the regional cheeses are made. Good simple fare is available and, of course, improved communications have brought the branded products of the supermarket even to villages, but the toughness of life in the mountains and the poor soil do not encourage a tradition of delicate dishes.

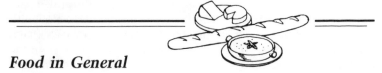

Food in General

The two predominating vegetables are potatoes and cabbage and there are also vast quantities of different mushrooms to be found. Le Puy is famous for green lentils and, in the Liagne, north-east of Clermont-Ferrand, fruit is abundant, especially apples — as may be imagined, the area is lovely in blossom-time. From the mountain streams eels and various fish are caught, including salmon, but these days trout are more likely to come from a fish farm. Pork, mutton and veal are the main meats and there is some small game, as the high pastures encourage little birds; the thrushes of Brioude are written about. *Coq au vin* is often seen on menus and, although it is traditional in many regions, it is certainly useful here, the recipe giving tenderness to a stringy old hen.

There are many sweet dishes, cherry tarts being somewhat of a speciality — the cherry-trees also give grace to the barren landscape in the spring — and one version of these tarts is *milliards*; *clafoutis* another, although this last is also a Limousin speciality. *Fouasse* is a type of brioche in the Cantal region, the *picoussel* of Mur-de-Barrez is a version of a wholemeal loaf. Royat is a town specializing in chocolate, and many candied fruits and jams are made here, some from the mountain berries and wild fruits.

Coffee is still sometimes served in a *mazagran*, which is a vessel rather like a small flower-vase or elongated eggcup.

Specialities and Dishes

Soupe aux choux is the substantial cabbage-soup of the region; another version is *la potée*, which is cooked in a covered dish and can include meat as well as vegetables. *Jambon d'Auvergne* and other pig products, including a variety of sausages, are seen in many *charcuteries*. You may find them more strongly flavoured than the hams of milder regions. *Tripaux* are stuffed sheeps' feet. *Fricandeau* is a type of pork *pâté* in a pastry case. *Tourte à la viande* is a mixture of pork and veal in pastry. *Friands de Saint-Flour* is a type of sausage-meat wrapped in leaves — often those of the ubiquitous cabbage. *Oeufs à l'Auvergnate* are poached eggs with cabbage and potatoes.

La truffado is a dish rather like a potato pie, which may contain cheese and also be flavoured with garlic, but it is so much a peasant recipe that most households will evolve their own versions. *L'aligot* or *alicot* is another potato dish, for which the potatoes are first cooked and mashed, sometimes cabbage being added to them. *Pommes de terre au lard* is a recipe incorporating diced bacon or ham and onions, plus herbs. It will be understood that these are all thrifty dishes, aimed at providing substantial fare at low cost in what can be gleaned from the garden. You are not likely to find this kind of thing on the menu of an hotel or restaurant, but, especially if you are doing your own catering, it is often possible to ask a willing neighbour to show you her version of this type of local fare.

Bourrioles d'Aurillac are sweet pancakes, made with buckwheat flour. *Cornets de Murat* are cream horns. *Tarte à la crème* is a cream tart, a speciality of Vic-sur-Cère.

Drinks

Until recent years the wines of this region were definitely little and local, but today some pleasant ones are made and even find their way on to export markets. The best-known is probably the white Saint Pourçain from the Allier, but versions of this that are *rosé* and red may also be found. Chanturgue, from near Clermont-Ferrand, and the wines of Châteaugay and Corent are light-bodied reds that are worth trying.

Things to See and Do

There are interesting displays of local costumes, furniture and exhibits of regional life in the Musée J.B. Rames at Aurillac; the *donjon* of the Château at Châteaugay has a Musée de la Vieille Auvergne. The Musée du Ranquet, in the former Hôtel Fontfreyde at Clermont-Ferrand, also has local exhibits and some souvenirs of Louis Pasteur (*see p.271*).

Moulins is still able to show several buildings delectably *Belle Époque* in style, including shops, a *chocolatier* and the big central café.

Thiers is a centre for cutlery and the Musée de la Coutellerie et d'Art Locale, at 8 rue de Barante has important exhibits. The Société Générale de Coutellerie et d'Orfèvrerie, at 45, Avenue Pierre-Guéron, will, on application, arrange to show round visitors interested in seeing how the local cutlery is made. Château de Tournoël has a large kitchen, a pressroom and old wine press, with a huge stone container for 13,000 litres of wine.

Vichy has a folklore and local history museum at the Maison du Baillage. The mineral-water establishment of Vichy-État is open to visitors and for a delightful account of this thermal establishment, try to read Tom Vernon's *Fat Man on a Bicycle* (Michael Joseph, 1981).

Bordeaux and the Landes

Bordeaux is in many ways not at all typically French. The city stands at an intersection of rivers and roads, the harbour, sheltered by the Gironde estuary, having easy access to the sea. Phoenicians, Romans, Norsemen and Scandinavian pirates, pilgrims *en route* for Santiago by sea or land, scholars coming to the university, refugees from political and religous persecutions in Spain, Portugal, Germany and the Low Countries and, certainly, the English who, for 299 years, owned the entire region, have all left their traces. It is a wine city, not merely a wine town, and the majority of its inhabitants are at least interested in wine if not actively concerned with it. It has also been called *'la cuisine de la France'*, the cooking incorporating many varied traditions, most recently that of the *pieds noirs*, the settlers from the former French Algeria; yet, in general, dishes are not particularly rich, although some are definitely succulent, and are usually highly acceptable to the Anglo-Saxon.

The Landes are the great stretches of pine forests south of Bordeaux. They were virtual deserts of sand, in danger of literally being blown away, until engineer Nicolas Brémoutier, in the eighteenth century, had the idea of planting the trees to hold the sand in place; these plantations now provide both resin and wood. Otherwise, although the wooded areas are a source of certain forms of game, pastures are rather poor. There is no particular Bordeaux cheese, although the red-rinded 'Hollande' is widely served, apparently as the result of a deal in cheese for wine made with the Low countries centuries ago. Many of the richer ingredients of traditional dishes come in from the north-west and east, as they would have done in the past, when the rivers were used for transporting goods.

First-time visitors who expect Bordeaux to be somehow picturesque may be initially disappointed, though St Émilion is certainly that. Bordeaux itself is impressive and even a short tour will show a jumble of medieval buildings almost overwhelmed by those of more recent times, especially the grandeur of the eighteenth century, when the prosperity of the place and the taste of the ruling powers who employed architects of the greatest ability, gave it monuments of lasting importance. *(see p.219)*. The presence of water cannot be overlooked: Aquitania, the Roman name for the province, means 'land of waters' and the 'Deux Mers' of the 'Entre-Deux-Mers' are the Rivers Dordogne and the Caronne; the huge 'Bassin' of Arcachon bites into the flat land to the east of the city and little lakes provide water at intervals throughout the long tongue of the Médoc, which licks up into the Atlantic.

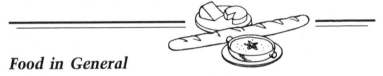

Food in General

One of the delicacies of the region is — or used to be — the caviar of the Gironde. Into this estuary comes the sturgeon, and its roe is a treasure. The late Emile Prunier, father of Madame Simone Prunier, began to develop the local caviar when, in 1917, he was unable to get supplies for his Paris restaurant from Russia. However, the sturgeon is currently protected, so as to revive the caviar business, so that officially Gironde caviar is unobtainable. Of course, if a fish just happens to be washed up on the Gironde banks where somebody is fishing . . . but the traveller must not count on finding any.

Another odd creature found in the estuary is the lamprey, about which there are many misconceptions. It is eel-like, but without a backbone; it does, however, have a poisonous vein running the length of it and this has to be removed before cooking. A type of sucker enables it to fasten itself to things. The lamprey is found in many estuaries, including even the Bristol Channel, although the method of boiling it and serving it with white sauce, which I have heard has been tried, would not produce anything worthy of gastronomic note. The 'died of a surfeit of lampreys' tag is attached to Henry I of England, but, as this monarch in fact departed this life in Normandy, near Rouen, it may very well have been the inefficiency of some scullion in not removing the poisonous vein or, simply, a lamprey that had 'gone off' that was responsible for the fatal dish.

At Arcachon the local oysters are *gravettes* (a type of *'plate'* or flat oyster), and *Portugaises;* the latter began to thrive in the region when in 1868 the *Morlaisien*, bound for England with a cargo of *Portugaises*, had to shelter near Pauillac in the Gironde during a storm; the cargo began to smell and the captain threw overboard what he thought must be the dead oysters. However, many survived and began to thrive, although these days they are found more at Point de Grave and on the west coast. It is sometimes customary to serve them accompanied by slices of cold sausage or salami or small, hot garlicky sausages.

Petits Royans are sardines, which are especially succulent at vintage time. The tiny river fish, *trogues*, are somewhat like whitebait, often served as *friture. Piballes* are elvers or tiny eels, in season during the late winter and up to March — it is a special treat to serve them at Christmas. They look like silver-grey threads, are usually deep-fried in the Spanish manner (there is a substantial Spanish colony in the Gironde) and served with garlic, sizzling hot, so that one is given a wooden fork to eat them. As mentioned earlier, anything metal would burn the mouth. The great river fish is the *alose* (shad), which has many bones, in spite of its delicate flavour; it may be served hot, often deliciously grilled *sur les sarments* (over vine prunings) or else cold, when a vinaigrette accompanies it.

There is a certain amount of small game, including *ortolans* (wheatears, *see p.62*), *palombes* (wood pigeon) and *becfigues* (figpeckers) from the Landes; *cailles* (quails), *bécasse* (woodcock), *perdreaux* (partridge), *alouettes* (larks), and *canard sauvage* (wild duck) may feature on menus. Certain gastronomes eat *ortolans* rather like people inhaling Friar's Balsam — they put a napkin right over their head and, while enjoying the aroma of the cooked bird, gobble it up, head and all.

Agneau de Pauillac is famous, the sheep fed on the salty *prés salés*, or shore pastures washed by the tide. But lamb is in general frequently served — it is particularly suited to accompanying claret, although beef is also featured, often being grilled *'aux sarments'* (over the vine prunings) or even sometimes *'au feu de bois'* which, in a shipper's establishment, may mean that the wood of the fire is fuelled by chunks of wine-soaked casks. *Gratons de Lormont* are somewhat similar to Touraine's *rillettes. Foie gras* is also often served at rather important meals — it may astonish visitors in the Sauternes district to find that it may be partnered by a glass of the sweet golden wine of the region. Shallots often feature in recipes here, as the dominant flavouring vegetable. Truffles come from the Dordogne and *jambon cru* or raw ham is sent up from Bayonne (*see p.102*). The market gardens are very productive and the artichokes of Macau are famous. Try, if possible, to walk round the 'Marché aux Grands Hommes' in the centre of Bordeaux, where the superb produce is wonderful to see.

The *rhums* of the French Antilles are included in many sweet recipes, as is the anisette of Marie Brizard. *Pruneaux fourrés d'Agen* are stuffed Agen prunes, St Émilion's macaroons are lighter and more succulent than the ordinary macaroon. Fruits are as might be expected in season, although the *fraises des bois* grow in the woods at Pessac until well into the autumn.

Specialities and Dishes

The great speciality is the *cèpe*, a large mushroom, which may be cooked in various ways, all of them invariably contributing to a richness whose aroma is marked; if you order one portion, bear in mind it may well serve two.

Lamproie à la Bordelaise is cooked in a red wine sauce, with leeks. It is rich but not in the least 'fishy'. Although it is not in season all the year round, the advent of the can and the freezer may make it available. The flavour is somewhat between that of turbot and rabbit.

Grillé aux sarments means, as explained earlier, that the meat, fish, poultry, or whatever, has been grilled over a fire of vine prunings, which impart a delicious flavour.

Entrecôte à la Bordelaise is a steak with a Bordelaise sauce — wine, butter, shallots, beef marrow and seasonings, sometimes plus tomato. But, as Waverly Root has pointed out in *The Food of France* (Cassell), it can mean that the sauce is a *mirepoix*, a rendering down of vegetables (carrots, onions, celery) with ham, thyme and bay, or else that the vegetable accompaniment to a dish so described will be potatoes and artichokes. *Entrecôte marchand de vin* will be an *entrecôte* with a red wine sauce. *Foie de canard aux raisins* is duck's liver, cooked in a wine sauce with various vegetables and flavourings and served on *croûtons*. It is very rich — and expensive.

Oie farcie aux pruneaux is a dish from Agen — where the plums come from — in which the goose is stuffed with plums which themselves have been stuffed with ham, olives and onions. It is often served with chestnuts.

Tourin is onion soup, or onion and garlic soup. *Soupe des vendangeurs* is what is usually served in vintage kitchens to the pickers in the vineyards during the harvest. (They get plenty to eat as well as the soup.) Different estates pride themselves on their reputation for good food at this season of the year and the *soupe des vendangeurs* usually contains lots of vegetables, plus meat or chicken in generous portions, before the lunchers get down to the subsequent meat or poultry (often a grill), followed by cheese, fruit and sometimes a fruit tart or cake, washed down with the property's own wine. If you are lucky enough to be invited to share in this meal, be prepared for husky fare — which is usually first-rate.

Faire chabrot is a country custom which involves a little wine being poured into the last of the soup in a plate, which is then drunk.

Drinks

A number of drinks other than the great wines are made in Bordeaux, including *rhum*, the herb-flavoured Lillet, Vieille Cure and the wide range of liqueurs produced by Marie Brizard and other establishments (*see p.172*). Cordial Médoc is based on claret, deep red and slightly sweet, plus herb flavouring. But the region's glory is its wines. The Gironde is the largest fine wine area in France. Anyone trying to understand Bordeaux wines seriously should really have an additional reference book — there have been plenty written about them! There are dry and medium dry whites, luscious sweet whites, some *rosé* and even a little sparkling white wine; but the reds are the wines for which the area is best known these days. In Britain and some English-speaking countries these red wines are called 'claret', a name that I find needs a little explanation, because the rest of the world says 'Red Bordeaux'.

In medieval times, the port of Bordeaux received vast quantities of wine from the hinterland, including many, such as the 'black wine' of Cahors, that were darker in colour and usually fuller in flavour than the lighter (*plus clair*) red wines of the Bordeaux region itself, which, in those days, was of course smaller. The high country wines were often used to deepen the tone and improve the taste of the Bordeaux reds in indifferent years; indeed, the wine-makers of Rioja and Penedés will tell how their wines 'helped' out many of Bordeaux's, and nineteenth-century wine lists show how certain Bordeaux wines were sold 'Hermitagé' or not, in other words, pepped up with the dark red Rhône wines to pander to public taste. The Bordelais did try to maintain the style and standard of their wines, which they began to call '*clairet*', and this word became claret; recently there was a great argument in the E.E.C. about the use of this term (for '*clairet*' today is a rather different sort of Bordeaux wine, subject, though, to controls) and for once the British won the right to keep on using their word claret.

In fact, it was the attempts at keeping the Bordeaux wines apart that resulted in the expansion of the wine trade and the building of the picturesque quaysides; the local authorities insisted that only true Bordeaux wines could be kept in the city precincts (where there were vineyards until quite recent times), so merchants dealing in other wines had to establish themselves outside the walls — and began to extend their premises along the river. This gave them a great advantage, because of course in the days when new wine was better than old, the casks could be rolled across from the shippers' premises to the ships tied up opposite and then the wine fleet would race to the export ports — London, Bristol, Plymouth and the North Sea. The capacity of a ship was measured in how many of the huge 'tonnes' or mighty casks could be loaded into the hold — hence 'tonnage' is the term used for capacity today, although the tonne has long since been obsolete. Because of the pirates who preyed on the ships from the coastal harbours, the wine fleet began to carry arms and have escort vessels — which was the beginning of the Royal Navy. To show that a ship sailing up from Bordeaux to the sea had paid the requisite port dues, a branch of cypress would be hoisted on the mast; as the vessel passed the Château de Beychevelle, at one time the property of the Grand Admiral of France, the sails would be dipped — which is the origin of its name — *baisse voile*.

Bordeaux became the property of the last heiress of Aquitaine, Duchess Eleanor, and the area stretched from the Loire to the Pyrenees and across to the borders of Burgundy; when Eleanor married the Count of Anjou, Henry Plantagenet, after getting a divorce from the King of France, she began to produce an unruly and fierce family but, when Henry became King of England in 1154, it was the English crown that dominated a large area of France and continued to do so for 299 years, until Dunois drove out the English in 1453. So naturally the English court drank claret and went on doing so even after the Battle of Castillon when the Gironde became French once more. The French court drank Burgundy — that duchy was a powerful ally. In the eighteenth century, however, the satyr-like Duc de Richelieu became Governor of Bordeaux and persuaded Louis XV to drink red Bordeaux; it was Richelieu's Parisian architect, Victor Louis (who designed the Paris Opéra), who influenced his pupil, Combes, who built Château Margaux and many of the beautiful buildings in and around the city. This was the time when many families from the British Isles settled in Bordeaux and founded great wine dynasties: the Johnsons and Lawtons are French now, but their family portraits show faces that might have come out of the shires; the Anglo-Irish Bartons have never become French or married into France in three hundred years. There are also many other non-French names — Eschenauer, Casteja, Schÿler, Mahler being only a few, and anyone walking about in the centre of the city will note many place-names that certainly do not seem French. The *'noblesse de bouchon'* (the bottle aristocracy) has far-flung origins. One of the most famous estates in the Médoc is that of Palmer, named for the general in Wellington's army who bought it after 1815, when it was the Château de Gasq. These days several other great properties are wholly or partly in the hands of the British too.

Although among the hundreds of the Gironde estates there are properties of both large and small size, each one is owned either by an individual or a company; the land itself can be in plots that are

not always all in one piece, but many are. Although the various different vine varieties are naturally planted and harvested separately, there is not the complexity of the Burgundy vineyards, where a number of people may own strips in one section and each make and handle the wine slightly differently. These days most of the finer wines are bottled at the château where they are made, although some may be bottled in Bordeaux.

It is sometimes easy to become confused by the term 'classification' as used in the Bordeaux region. With the exception of Pomerol, the wines of each of the main regions have now been sorted into growths, the top category sometimes being 'Premier cru', sometimes 'Grand cru'. 'Classed growths' therefore may come from one of several regions, although, when the term is loosely used, they are probably the 'crus classés' of the Médoc, the categories of which were last established in 1855 and have remained like this ever since, in spite of various attempts to rearrange the wines — causing tremendous arguments and quite violent disputes, as may be imagined. What have been more recently established are the categories of the bourgeois growths — which are divided often into the ordinary and the exceptional — and the artisan growths a little lower down the scale. The important thing to remember, however — and the subject really is complex — is that the 1855 classfication was not the first to be made and that when the brokers of Bordeaux decided to re-categorize the wines in 1855 they were doing so for the Paris Exhibition, primarily to establish the sort of prices that certain wines might be expected to achieve. At this time some estates did not submit their wines (the great red Graves, Haut Brion, is the only wine outside the Médoc to appear because it did), some had been split up and were therefore not considered, some were going through a bad patch and got low down in the list. Since 1855 the quality of certain properties has gone up — and down; some have virtually disappeared. It may be said in very general terms that, whereas the classed growths are certainly the aristocracy of their areas, it is not always correct to suppose that those in the first or top categories are invariably far superior to those in the second, third, fourth or fifth. Usually, the first growths of the Médoc are very fine wines — and the prices they attract when they offer their vintages (later than the other growths) are invariably high. But, depending on individuals and particular circumstances, other growths can give equal or, sometimes, more enjoyment and should not be ignored; exactly the same applies to the *crus bourgeois* and *crus artisans*, because, these days, improved knowledge of wine-making has made many of these very good indeed. In general, they tend to mature somewhat faster than the majority of the more important classed growths, so that sampling them can provide an opportunity of seeing how certain vintages are progressing and getting an idea of the overall character.

My advice to the traveller — and I suppose I know the Gironde better than any other area of France — would be to explore the wines of each main region: drink as expensively as you can (one never regrets this!) and do not forget that the French will list wines when, according to the notions of many British, they are still very young. If you wish to drink the finest wines, do not order them just anywhere — either enjoy them in the sort of restaurant where someone knows how to handle and/or decant them, or simply try something young, little-known and small-scale and perhaps reserve the top wines for enjoyment when you get home and can serve them yourself.

White Wines

These are made from the Sauvignon, Sémillon and Muscadelle grapes. The Sauvignon is increasing in popularity now, although thirty years ago it was not a wine that was thought would be much liked. The Sauvignons of this region tend to be a little softer — which does not mean sweet — than those of more northern vineyards. The white wines come from Blaye, also Bourg, the Premières Côtes de Bordeaux, Entre-Deux-Mers; some of the regions make red wines as well and this is true of the Graves, where some properties make both red and white wines.

The Sauternes region — within which is the area of Barsac — produces the famous sweet white wines. Until just over a century ago, these were not very sweet; their evolution is said to be due to the instruction to the bailiff at Yquem not to start picking the grapes until his master got back — and, as this was delayed by illness, the grapes began to shrivel on the vines. Instead of being a disaster, as it would have been if the fruit had simply rotted, it was a triumph — due to the action of *pourriture noble* (noble rot) which, by acting on the juice inside each grape, produces a luscious wine. Vintagers here cannot just be the ordinary pickers, engaged to get the grapes in bunch by bunch when the person in charge thinks fit: pickers must go many times through a vineyard, snipping off the 'nobly rotten' grapes with special scissors, only occasionally being able to harvest whole bunches. The region here is odd — even the brokers tend to get lost when they drive around — and there is one signpost that directs you to the same place but via two different directions! Essentially, the conditions favourable to the formation of 'noble rot' involve a long warm autumn — not inevitably a year that is a good vintage for the wines elsewhere in the Gironde — with a mist rising from the river in the form of a type of fog. The great Sauternes are sweet and develop a crescendo of sweetness as they are drunk; the Barsacs have a curious flick of dryness as they leave the palate. The white wines of Cérons, between Graves and Sauternes, have something of the fresh dryness of the former and the sweetness of the latter; across the Garonne, the Sainte Croix du Mont wines are slightly like small-scale versions of Barsacs and the Loupiac wines of Sauternes.

Red Wines

The grapes making them are the Cabernet Sauvignon, Cabernet Franc, Merlot, Petit Verdot, with a few others still permitted but less used. Each region uses different proportions of grapes, so does each estate — whether or not those in charge actually reveal the proportions to those who write books about the wines. Claret can, in certain years, have the life of a man — or even more. But it is relevant to know that these days it is not economic to have huge stocks of wines that require maturation for thirty-forty-fifty years either in the cellars of a shipper or merchant; the wines must be ready to drink while they are younger — and able to earn their keep. This does not, it should be stressed, mean that wines that are at their peak even in great vintages today are somehow less good than in the past. Then the exceptions survived, today many can and do, even of lesser growths. The contemporary clarets are able to provide the sort of pleasure that even their long-lived predecessors did.

Generalizations about wines are dangerous, but some may guide the visitor to enjoyment. From Bourg, rather earthy reds are made (more reds than white wine), and from Blaye (where more white is made) the wines are usually somewhat thinner in body. The Premieres Côtes de Bordeaux, where *clairet*, a light pink wine, is still made, produce both red and white but the reds are rather light in body, very pleasant when fresh and young. St Émilion produces what are sometimes rather misleadingly termed the 'Burgundies of Bordeaux', fullish wines, that have a very attractive robust style, sometimes a little earthy, often mouth-filling and full of fragrance. The Pomerol wines tend to be a little lighter in body and sometimes more elegant and reminiscent of the red Graves — because there is a streak of gravel in the Pomerol vineyard. The wines of the different St Émilion regions, plus those of Néac, Lalande de Pomerol, Fronsac and Côtes de Canon Fronsac, are rewarding to those who can sample them on the spot, as they are seldom featured on export lists. The red Graves are not, perhaps 'beginners' wines', because they have a complexity that does not always immediately appeal, but they can be delicious, subtle, spicy and fruity. The gravel implied in their name gives them finesse.

North of Bordeaux, the Médoc produces mostly red wines, some of the most famous in the world. Each commune or parish has its own individuality — do not ignore any chance to try the wines that you may not know on export lists. Some of those with apparently modest A.O.C.s may be wonderful.

The whole town has an air of almost depressing opulence. . . One feels it to be a monument to the virtue of the well-selected bottle. . . . I should venture to insist on this and . . . travel an analogy between good claret and the best qualities of the French mind . . . and that, correspondingly, there is a touch of French reason, French completeness, in a glass of Pontet-Canet. The danger of such an excursion would lie mainly in its being so open to the reader to take the ground from under my feet by saying that good claret doesn't exist. To this I should have no reply whatever. I should be unable to tell him where to find it. I certainly didn't find it at Bordeaux, where I drank a most vulgar fluid; and it is of course notorious that a large part of mankind is occupied in vainly looking for it. There was a great pretence of putting it forward at the Exhibition, which was going on at Bordeaux at the time of my visit. . . . Here were pyramids of bottles, mountains of bottles, to say nothing of cases and cabinets of bottles. The contemplation of these glittering tiers was of course not very convincing; and indeed the whole arrangement struck me as a high impertinence. Good wine is not an optical pleasure, it is an inward emotion; and if there was a chamber of degustation on the premises, I failed to discover it.

HENRY JAMES, *A Little Tour in France*, 1882

The wines of Moulis, Listrac, Macau, Ludon are all graceful, usually elegant in style. Those of Margaux tend to have a ripe fruit quality, with much bouquet; the St Julien wines have a fine-drawn velvety character, silky and close-knit. The Pauillacs, which have the aroma of cedarwood or evoke the inside of a cigar-box, are bigger in stature, very complex and intense, wines that compel attention and that, according to what they are, demonstrate fruit, firmness of constitution and a fascinatingly cerebral style. St Estèphe wines are, when young, somewhat tannic and astringent, but they can mature to great power and even charm. At the northern reaches of the Médoc these days many properties make wines that are very finely constituted and display all the attributes of good claret — do not hesitate to try even an unknown name, which may be a wine you will long remember.

Things to See and Do

If you wish to tour the whole of the main wine region, allow at least three or four days. Otherwise, some Graves estates, virtually at the gates of Bordeaux, can be seen in two to three hours. The Sauternes circuit (where one inevitably gets lost) is further south and one should allow a morning or afternoon. To see the Médoc, allow a day if possible and longer if any visits are to be made. To see St Émilion and Pomerol, allow a day or a long afternoon or a morning plus the lunch-hour. A very attractive route is through the Bourg and Blaye regions, the time depending on the point from which you start, although two or three hours are a comfortable time on the somewhat winding roads. The Premières Côtes are really beautiful, and although there are not so many great wine estates, there are plenty of works of art and historic things to see, as also in the extreme south of the area, on the road to Spain.

Visits are usually indicated by signs and, even though there may not be a reception-room, someone will usually be around (though not at lunch-time) to guide you. Visitors will be shown the *chais* — above-ground stores of wine, with the young wine in the first-year *chai*, the wine of the vintage before that in the second-year *chai*, in which the bungs will have been driven tight and the *barriques* turned on their sides. As has been mentioned, tasting — always of the young wine — may not be invariably offered, as stocks get depleted by numbers of people trying the wine which, at this stage, is really only of interest to the serious and must be spat out anyway.

In the Médoc you can see many of the great estates from the *'route du châteaux'*. There is a small Maison du Vin at Margaux, another on the quayside at Pauillac, where leaflets and some information can usually be obtained. At Château Mouton-Rothschild the magnificent wine museum, which is usually able to be seen by those taking the guided tour of the premises, is definitely not to be missed. At Château Loudenne, with its many associations with the British, there is another wine museum and a beautiful restored vintage kitchen. In St Émilion there are many impressive historic monuments and no one should miss walking through the cobbled streets and imagining the various ceremonies that take place at the *Ban des Vendages* (vintage proclamation). The wine estates here are rather more hidden, but some are only walking distance from where cars may be parked; otherwise, circulate with a detailed map — in the lanes it is easy to take the wrong turning.

Bordeaux itself is well worth exploring (*see also p.208*): note the quaysides, with the old houses, cellars below ground, offices on the ground floor and former dwellings above, where casks could be rolled across the road to be loaded onto ships. The wealth of the city is evident in the superb Place de la Bourse, Grand Théâtre, and many other fine buildings, but there are hidden historic treasures too and a good guide book is really essential if you are to profit by even a short visit. The Maison du Vin (C.I.V.C.) at 1 Cours du 30 Juillet can provide information and the Syndicat d'Initiative, on the corner of the Cours du 30 Juillet and the Allées de Tourny, have particulars of any tours organized to see the region. The rue Xavier Arnozan is particularly fine and indicates something of the style in which the well-to-do wine traders lived — and still do. The Musée des Arts Décoratifs, in which was formerly the Hôtel de Lalande, has numerous exhibits relating to the history of Bordeaux and many objects associated with wine. The liqueur establishment of Marie Brizard, in modern style, is also often open to visitors.

Other museums of interest to the wine-lover and gastronome include that in the Aquarium at Arcachon, where one section is devoted to oysters and there are exhibits of many types of fish. In the Citadelle at Blaye there is a small museum in the Maison du Commandant d'Armes devoted to local history and art. At Pauillac there is a small Musée du Vin in the former Château du Grand Puy Ducasse, on the quayside; at Villandraut there is the great castle, former home of the man who became Pope Clément V. Cadillac has the tasting-room and information-centre of the local wine growers in the Château des Ducs d'Épernon. Le Prieuré Lichine, in Margaux, has a kitchen with the complete equipment of former times. Buildings open to the public include the Châteaux de Malle, Roquetaillade, Mongenan at Portets; the stables at Lanessan; the numerous historic monuments in the centre of St Émilion and Chateau de la Brède, home of Montesquieu.

Bordeaux is unquestionably the most beautiful city in France. . . . I have an astonishing appetite. Two and a half hours after eating an excellent dinner at the Café de Paris (2 francs 16, plus 4 sous for the tip; total 3 francs), I felt a great desire to consume the second rice pudding of the day.

STENDHAL, *Travels in the South of France*, 1838, trans. Elisabeth Abbott

---

19

Brittany

Ars Mor or *Armorica* is the old name for Brittany, meaning 'the country of the sea'. Many of the foodstuffs are affected by the sea's proximity: for example, the slightly salty butter and the lamb from tide-washed pastures which becomes the prized *pré salé,* and of course fish and crustacea of many kinds. The style of cookery is not elaborate, but the basic ingredients are first-rate.

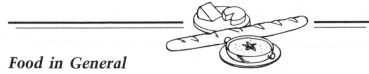

Food in General

As well as salt-water fish there are river fish, such as carp and salmon. Lamb, as has been mentioned, is famous, so is the ham of Morlaix and there are many pork products, sausages of various kinds, *pâtés* and versions of salame. The market gardens are also well-known: new potatoes, artichokes, carrots and cauliflowers are grown in abundance, and of course the famous onions, which are mostly grown around Roscoff and St Brieuc. They are pinkish-skinned when ripe and remain firm for many months when stored. The travelling salesmen, who go all over Europe with them, are known in the UK as 'Roscoff Johnnies'. The strawberries of Daoulas and Plougastel are also famous and there is a strawberry feast in the last-named place on the third Sunday in June. Walnuts, pears, grapes for the table and melons are also grown and, as mentioned earlier, it was Claude of Brittany — married to François I — who gave her name to the *reine claude* or greengage.

The first cannery was started at Nantes in 1824 and Brittany is the biggest source of canned fish in France: sardines, mackerel and tunny are the most important lines, but other fish are canned too. Meats, *pâtés*, peas and French beans are also canned in quantity.

Sweet things include various biscuits and wafers from Nantes, where biscuit-making is big business; a type of *bon-bon* called a *berlingot* (similar to what the British would call a satin cushion) is also made there. Rennes specializes in caramels, Châteaubriand in angelica and the sugared burnt almonds called *Pralines Duchesse Anne* (the 'Duchess in sabots' of the nursery song). Most famous of all are the twists of fragile wafers called *crêpes dentelles*, which come mainly from Quimper and are frequently served with ice-cream and *compôtes*.

Specialities and Dishes

Cotriade is described by some as a northern version of *bouillabaisse* — it is subject to variations, but may be a fish stew, with potatoes served on a separate plate. Various fish or crustacea may be included, although not lobster, and there is one cotriade recipe made only from mackerel. *Brochettes de coquilles Saint Jacques* is a *brochette* of scallops — like a scallop kebab.

Palourdes farcies are clams stuffed with shallots and herbs and put under the grill. *Homard à l'Armoricaine* is a controversial dish. As has been mentioned (p.48), it means 'in Brittany style' but the recipe, usually involving tomatoes, herbs and garlic, is more suggestive of the south of France. Some authorities think that it was a dish created in Paris and became '*a l'Américaine*' by someone not reading the original name correctly — or wishing to pay a compliment to American visitors.

Courraye is cabbage stuffed with a mixture that may be composed of rabbit or hare. It sometimes accompanies quails or other small game birds.

Bouillie is very much a peasant dish — a type of porridge made with the buckwheat flour that, as far as I know, seldom features in the dishes of other regions (buckwheat is *sarrasin* or *blé noir*). It can be served *à la crème* or with cider. I suppose it is a Breton cousin of the Italian polenta.

Beurre blanc, described on p.290, is also very much a speciality of Nantes.

Une andouille, a type of tripe sausage, is described elsewhere (p.242) but it is quite common in Brittany.

Sauce bretonne or *à la bretonne* can have various implications. The original sauce bretonne is a relation of Sauce Espagnole, a game sauce base, plus butter, browned onions and chicken essence, but the simpler version that is often found is made from onions, carrots, leeks, butter and either cream or white wine, depending on what the sauce is to accompany. If a dish is described as *à la bretonne* it probably means that the meat, usually lamb, is accompanied by white haricot beans.

Gâteau bretonne is a flattish fruit-cake and *Galette bretonne* is a flat, round cake, rather like gingerbread without the ginger or — as Britons may understand it — a maid-of-honour cake without the almonds.

Far is a very odd thing. The great Raymond Oliver (*p.19*) describes it as one of the most ancient forms of food — it could certainly have existed from very early times indeed. There are apparently two types, the savoury and the sweet. As I have come across it, *Far breton* is a batter mixture with raisins in it and, when the recipe was first described to me, I rather astonished my kind Breton hosts by remarking that in fact it is a sweet Yorkshire pudding — but actually this is just what it is: a batter that can be augmented with fruit or meats. It is usually made at the bakery and, if it gets home in time, is served hot, otherwise cold.

Farsac'h is claimed as being the ancestor of the traditional English plum or Christmas pudding — which, in medieval times certainly, was a savoury dish, made with minced meat. *Farsac'h* now contains raisins, plums and, maybe, apple brandy or *rhum*. The Breton use of much dried fruit is interesting — the sailors could of course carry such items, valuable sources of sugar and other nutrients in the winter, very much in the same way that some northern countries make fruit concentrates to use in winter soups.

Bigoudens are biscuit-like cakes, made of almond-paste.

Beignets de Mam-Goz are rather neatly translated by one gourmet guide as 'Granny's fritters'. They are potato-cakes, made sweet with chunks of peel, are fried crisp and served with jam.

Maingaux Rennais is a combination of both thick and fresh cream, whipped together and served with strawberries or raspberries. As the name suggests, it is a speciality of Rennes.

Crêpes are certainly the best-known Breton speciality. It may surprise some travellers, however, to find that they are not often included in the menus of hotels and ordinary restaurants. To eat them, you go to a crêperie, which sells nothing else. Crêperies may be small and chic, or of the capacious snack-bar type of eating-place, or they may even be just a travelling barrow-cum-stall. The crêpes are always freshly made — none of the leathery pseudo-pancakes piled up hours in advance for the Breton! There are several sorts of crêpe, but all are made on a special griddle, or large flat *galettière*, on which the batter is spread out very thinly with a *raclette*, a device rather like a small rake but without prongs. (Those who know the Swiss country dish, raclet, will realize that this, made by scraping layers of cheese onto bread while the cheese is held in front of a hot fire, makes use of the same method to utilize food economically, although the result is quite different.) Crêpes made of *froment* or wheat flour are used for the sweet fillings — jam, jelly, honey, with sugar; they are more like what the Briton understands as a pancake. The crêpes of *sarrasin* or *blé noir* are from buckwheat, something like wholemeal flour and darker than *froment* crêpes; they may be served with ham, cheese, tomatoes, rather like a savoury omelette, as required. Crêpes are usually good value and a cheap meal of one savoury and one sweet can easily be made. The accompaniment is usually Breton cider, served in a *bol* or *bollée*, which looks somewhat like a teacup minus a handle. Do not assume that this is a low alcohol drink.

Drinks
Cider is the 'beer' of Brittany. It will not always be available in restaurants, but bars and crêperies will serve it, often by the *bol* or pottery cup. Although some local cider is only a version of faintly alcoholized apple-juice, other ciders are definitely strong — it is wise to ask before you order more *bols*, because the little cup seems to hold only a modest measure, which slips down easily. The cider can be sparkling or still, and be either the sweet cider, which many travellers will know in its British version, or else the 'hard' or dry cider. *Cidre bouché* or corked cider undergoes its fermentation in bottle, with the cork held down by a metal clamp — somewhat similar to the Champagne *agrafe* (*see p.244*).

There are no vineyards within the Breton peninsular, but the wine associated with Brittany is Muscadet. Wine has been made in the region of Rhuys, but I have never come across it and it cannot be a commercial product these days. It is said that, to drink it, four men and a wall are necessary — one man to hold the glass, another to do the drinking and two more to hold him up against the wall.

Muscadet is often proudly tagged as 'the wine of Abelard', who was a Breton. Rabelais mentioned it in 1530 — as he did many wines. But the wines they drank would have been totally dissimilar to anything we know today, because in 1709 the Muscadet vineyards were destroyed by severe weather and the despairing *vignerons* went to Burgundy to get fresh vines, which were named

Melon de Bourgogne or Muscadet. The wine remained very much a local drink until in 1929 the *sommeliers* of Paris were conducted on a trip through the vineyards and were sufficiently impressed to begin recommending Muscadet, especially in restaurants and bars where fish was a speciality. As, over the years, the price of white Burgundy rose steadily, Muscadet began to be more widely consumed and when, in 1956, terrible frost virtually destroyed the Chablis vineyard, Muscadet began to be very chic and was drunk in quantity.

Muscadet is made only from the single grape — which, it must be noted, is nothing to do with Muscat or Muscadelle. Indeed, some authorities think that as the Muscadet is also the Weisser Burgunder and, as this grape is sometimes called the Pinot Blanc Chardonnay, the Muscadet vine may actually be a type of Chardonnay! But the very different climate and soils — the Muscadet is very hardy — and centuries of acclimatization have certainly made the Muscadet an individual as a vine. However, chauvinists in Brittany may well inform the traveller that Muscadet is the only French wine to be named after one single grape; mention Alsace, and the retort may well be '*Oh — l'Alsace, ce n'est pas la France!*' with a fine disregard for the proximity of Lorraine and Jeanne d'Arc, who most people would think of as France's patron saint (whereas it is St Denis).

There are three main A.O.C.s of Muscadet: Muscadet, Muscadet des Coteaux de la Loire, and Muscadet de Sèvre et Maine, the last category generally being considered the best. The wine is thought to be at its peak when quite young; I have drunk a very elderly Muscadet, which was quite sound as a wine but had turned into something very different from its younger self. Muscadet '*sur lie*' is wine that has been bottled directly off the lees in the cask or vat, so that it may still go on, slightly, 'working' or fermenting. The mini-prickle this gives to the wine can be very refreshing and Muscadet *sur lie* is esteemed and considered rather a smart drink. The other wine of the region is the Gros Plant. Until fairly recently it was mostly drunk in the region, but now some is exported. In fact, the vine is the Folle Blanche, one of the vines of the Cognac area, and also the Picpoul, grown in parts of the south of France. The grapes make very hard, thin, acid wines and people who have enjoyed Gros Plant with a big platter of *fruits de mer* and mayonnaise when sitting out in the sun, may get a surprise of a not entirely agreeable kind when they drink the wine again in a chilly climate. Gros Plant has now got an A.O.C. If you intend to try both of these wines at a meal, drink the Gros Plant first.

Things to See and Do

The Gulf of Morbihan and the oyster-beds are where the majority of flat oysters (*ostrea edulis*) begin their lives, especially around Locmariaquer. The oyster requires a certain type of water in which to live and thrive, both tides and the amount of salt affecting its development, and very seldom does it grow satisfactorily to maturity in the same place where it has been born.

Severe winters, that have destroyed many oyster-beds in recent years, have caused a decline in traditional methods of rearing oysters and the increase of industrial waste has presented a real hazard. So oysters today are reared by attaching the spat or tiny oysters to whitened tiles, which look somewhat like the curved roof tiles of the south; these tiles are held together in bunches by wire and, at various stages in the spat's growth, the tiles are put into deeper and deeper water — of the kind likely to be favourable to the oyster — and then brought to be 'finished', as it were, at certain areas already famous for oysters, such as Cancale in Brittany. The tiny oyster is almost invisible, like a minute crumb, when it is first attached to the tile; at six months it is taken off its first tile and, now looking rather like a cornflake, is attached to another tile ready to go into deep water in the oyster park in the spring. Ridges on the oyster's shell indicate its age, although an oyster that grows up naturally, not attached to a tile but possibly attached to a huge bank of oyster shells, sometimes grows two coats to its shell in one year. Oyster buyers can rear their oysters elsewhere until they are five years old, but, by this time, the oysters will be quite large — fried-egg size — and, in Europe, customers do not want them any larger. The older oysters mature in shallow trays in the oyster parks; it is a skilled business to care for them because, especially when the workers handle the little ones, any error with the knife detaching them will kill the oyster.

There is nothing else spectacular to see at Locmariaquer, but the interested visitor should certainly ask to see the oyster parks. Anyone seriously concerned with marine biology, especially shell-fish, should write to the Institut Scientifique et Technique des Pêches Maritimes, at Auray, as this is the great centre for studies of this kind.

Audierne's lobster pens are open to view — and it goes without saying that, both here and at Locmariaquer, as well as all around the coast, there will be plenty of opportunities for buying the oysters and crustacea. Roscoff, at the Charles Pérez Aquarium, can show most of the Channel fish in natural surroundings; it is one of the foremost establishments of its kind in Europe and a highly important French marine laboratory.

Morlaix has been a tobacco trading centre since the eighteenth century, when the Compagnie des Indes founded a farm and a factory there. It was, as might be expected, very convenient for smugglers running tobacco over to England to avoid paying duty, and local tobacco producers were said to have kept bands of smugglers actually on their payrolls. There is still a large tobacco factory, specializing in cigars, at Morlaix, although this is not generally open to visitors.

Nantes is the seat of the Comité Interprofessionel des Vins d'Origine du Pay Nantais, which is at 17 rue des Etats. Here you can obtain information about the wines and details of the circuit of the Muscadet country, with places where you can visit and taste along the way. There is also a fine collection of shells in the Natural History Museum in the Place de la Monnaie. In the Musée Salorges there is a room devoted to the various food industries of the region, including canning and preserving.

Rennes has its Palais de Justice literally built on cider and wine and staffed by spices, because funds for the construction were raised by levying taxes on wine and cider, and the judges were paid by their clients in the precious spices that were imported from the east.

Vitré is known for the Château des Rochers, nearby, which was the home of the Marquise de Sévigné, where she stayed when she was trying to economize after the extravagances of her husband and her son. Of the official banquets held at Vitré, the Marquise commented, 'As much wine passes through the body of a Breton as water under the bridges.'

Museums of Breton Art and Interiors
The Château de Dinan has exhibits of interesting kitchen equipment of past times, including a *plat à galette*, cider cups and huge salt and tobacco jars, which are in the room with the collection of Breton coifs.

In the Château de Nantes there is a comprehensive collection of popular art, with reconstructions of Breton interiors, also the *cellier* of the Chevaliers Bretvins, with an old wine press.

In the Tour de l'Oratoire in the Château de Vitré there is a reconstruction of a Vitré house, with a fine collection of china and pottery, perforated dish covers, a cider press and all the utensils associated with the hearth.

20

Burgundy, the Beaujolais and the Lyonnais

For centuries Burgundy has been a rich and powerful region. As an independent duchy, its dukes reigned in state often superior to that of the King; its merchants prospered; its religious establishments were without parallel — Cluny in its prime was the most important foundation in Christendom. The network of monasteries and abbeys linked throughout Europe to Cluny exerted enormous influence on many aspects of life. Politics, scholarship, teaching, running hospitals, encouraging artists, arranging pilgrimages and many aspects of local rural economy all came within the scope of the monks of Cluny, whom Sir Stephen Runciman has neatly described as 'the American Express of the Middle Ages'.

The natural resources of Burgundy are great: lush pastures, streams full of fish, forests abounding in game, even the scrubbier wild region of the Morvan is famous for raw ham and, of course, the vine, which will grow where other crops might fail, and has made Burgundy one of the most famous wine areas of the world. The Beaujolais, to the south, is a jovial and also well-endowed region and the people of the Lyonnais are convinced that their city is the centre of French gastronomy. The visitor should be warned to go easily until accustomed to the copious, often rich fare.

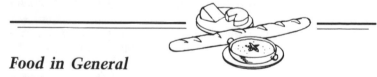

Food in General

The culinary traditions have developed in accordance with the needs of people who work hard physically and have a robust, often sensuous appreciation of the good things in life. Their diet is high in protein — lots of meat, and fine cheeses — and many of the regional recipes incorporate wine and cream. Some writers describe Burgundy as famous for beef, mustard and wine. The great white Charollais cattle produce meat that gets them a mention on menus. Dijon mustard, in many variations, is famous everywhere; it is made from *verjus*, the juice of unripe grapes, plus mustard-seed; not only does it go well with many of the beef-based dishes (and is seldom too strong for the accompanying wine), but it may be directly involved with recipes, such as *lapin à la moutarde* (rabbit with mustard).

The pig provides many specialities, notably the *jambon persillé* (ham in parsley-flavoured jelly), sausages of many kinds, including *cervelas* (saveloy) and *andouilles* (chitterlings), and pork and poultry are used in the fillings of the numerous *pâtés, ballotines, galantines* and *brioches* that make a *charcuterie* fascinating to study, especially at the time of any of the traditional festivals. The fat Burgundian snails, the decorated joints of meat and poultry, shimmering with aspic and enhanced with truffles, and the *gougères* (cheese puffs) and *feuilletés* (cases of flaky pastry ready for filling), are endless temptations for anyone buying a picnic.

Brillat-Savarin did not have a particularly high opinion of Burgundian truffles, but they are used in some local dishes, notably the *poulet demi-deuil* (chicken in half-mourning), a Lyonnaise speciality, in which the white breast of the chicken is threaded with the black truffles. The creative elaboration of the local dishes — which does not necessarily mean excessive garnishes — is typified by the *saulpiquet*, a ham dish, difficult to make (impossible in small quantities) and, with its spiced cream sauce, very delicate in flavour. The name has its origin in *'sau'*, an old word of Latin derivation, meaning salt, and referring to the seasoning and spicing of the meat and the sauce. In addition to the *quenelles de brochet* (pike sausages in a rich sauce), there are *quenelles de volaille* (chicken, pounded and poached, with a sauce). A *pouchouse* or *pochuse* is a stew of freshwater fish plus white wine, and a *meurette* is the same sort of thing, but made with red wine. *Coq au vin* is of course the traditional chicken dish, the particular wine often being specified — sometimes it is difficult to believe it is what it is, but it tends to be true that the better the wine, the better the dish. There are plenty of vegetables: *gâteau de courges* is a pumpkin tart, and *artichauts* are abundant.

There are many orchards in this region — beautiful in the spring — and the pastrycook shops are full of fruit-tarts; *groseilles* (redcurrants) are much in evidence. *Bugnes* are a type of doughnut; a *rabotte* is an apple-dumpling.

Pain d'épice (a type of honey cake) is a Dijon speciality and it is presented in fantastic shapes for the various public holidays: bells, snails, toy animals and, for April 1st, the *'poisson d'avril'* or April fish, in all sizes. The shops are full of such fantasy presentations at holiday times and the *chocolaitiers* (chocolate shops) are also adept at making chocolate snails, bunches of grapes, bells, often put in the miniature baskets copied in shape from the traditional *'paniers Beaunois'*, the double-bellied baskets used by the vintagers, which are now rapidly being replaced by lighter — and easier to clean — plastic. Cassis liqueur is used as a filling and flavouring for all kinds of sweets, cakes and chocolates, as well as for ices and sorbets.

The Côte d'Or, its heights within sight of Mont Blanc, gets icy winds from the mountain in winter, but the summer makes up for everything. No wonder that a certain nonchalance, even mental laziness, is imputed to the Burgundian character. Nowhere in the world is there more jollity and open-heartedness; yet as the famous wine of Bourgogne is none the less rich and mellow on account of its sparkle, so the character of the people, with all its effervescing gaiety, lacks neither depth nor solidity.

Hospitable of the hospitable, is the old-fashioned gentilhomme of Vendée. In my honour an elaborate déjeuner — this meal not as yet called lunch — was given by my hosts, an old Vendean gentleman and his niece. . . . The repast of many choice dishes, accompanied by equally choice wines and liqueurs, began on the stroke of mid-day and we did not rise from table till the clock was well on its way to le tantôt, as our neighbours call the afternoon; that is to say, near four o'clock. The extraordinary part of the banquet, after all, consisted neither in its luxuriousness nor its length, but in the fact that we all rose from the table every whit as alert and fresh as when we sat down!

MATILDA BETHAM-EDWARDS, *Unfrequented France — by river and mead and town*, Chapman and Hall, 1910

Specialities and Dishes

Oeufs à la bourguignonne are eggs poached in red wine and, sometimes, a rich meat stock, served on *croûtons*. If you are looking for a light dish, eschew this, although it is very good. *Gras double Lyonnais* is tripe with onions and parsley. *Tabliers de sapeur* is a colloquial name for grilled tripe with a Sauce Béarnaise. *Jouée* is a type of pastry, with bacon. *Oreillons de veau farcis* are calves' ears, stuffed with pounded pike meat and cooked with white wine. *Fressure de porc* or *ferchus* is pigs' fry, cooked with red wine, onions and herbs. *Oyonnade* is a type of stew made with goose. *Boeuf à la bourguignonne* is beef cooked in red wine with onions, mushrooms and diced bacon — a very traditional dish. *Selle de lièvre* is saddle of hare, cooked in wine with onions and mushrooms. *Jambon à la lie du vin* is ham braised in the lees of red wine. *Haricots au vin rouge* are beans cooked in red wine. *Hommes à la lyonnaise* are potatoes cooked with onions; the term 'Lyonnais' usually means that onions are in the recipe. *Gounerre* is a type of potato *pâté*.

The sweet dishes include *Tourte Charollaise*, which is an open tart, filled with cooked pears and covered with cream. *Rigon* is a type of fruit-and-walnut custard.

Drinks

Cassis (blackcurrant) is the great spirit of the region, as the fruit grows well. It should be stressed that *cassis* varies according to its quality (*see p.173*) and also according to the style of the establishment making it. At its best, it is a delicious drink, taken in small quantities, and also enhances many sweet dishes and ices. It is, of course, the liqueur that makes *vin blanc cassis* or '*Un kir*' (the drink named after the late Canon Félix Kir, Mayor of Dijon and Résistance hero), but visitors may find that, on the spot, the Burgundians make this drink rather stronger than may be expected — deep pinky-red. In the Beaujolais a similar mix is made using the red wine, and the result is called a '*rince cochon*' (hogwash), although when the late Nikita Krushchev visited the area it was thought rather impolite to use the term so, for the time being, the drink officially became '*Un Nikita*'.

Marc de Bourgogne is the local brandy, distilled from the final pressings of the wine. It has its devotees, but can be somewhat forceful and fiery. *Fine Bourgogne* is the distillation of Burgundy wine, not quite the same thing as *marc*. It should certainly be tried.

The wines are both complex and complicated. It has been said, with some truth, that, whereas the wine-lover endowed with adequate funds can manage to drink a fine or great claret at least once a month, the Burgundy devotee will be fortunate to enjoy a great Burgundy once a year. The area is not really very big and demand has kept prices high. At the same time, it must be stressed that true red Burgundy is an elegant, delicate wine, with infinite shades of fragrance and flavour, in no way resembling the coarse, treacly stuff that sometimes appears bearing a famous vineyard name — and the label of an unknown shipper. Fine Burgundy, both red and white, is truly '*fin*' and people who want what they may describe as a 'big strapping wine' would probably be better pleased with some wines from further south (though even fine red Rhône should never be an obvious or overwhelming wine). What may be said with more truth is that, in contrast to red Bordeaux, red Burgundy is a sensual rather than a cerebral wine and it is a perfect accompaniment to typical Burgundy food; the white wines can mostly be enjoyed by themselves, but in general Burgundy needs food to go with it.

To my friend Graham Chidgey, an eminent Burgundy shipper and author of a book, *Guide to the Wines of Burgundy* (Century), that explained many things to me that previously had not been clear, I owe the explanation as to why the Burgundians do not decant their wines. They will, if you insist, but in general they do not. True, the deposit is not often as heavy as that thrown by certain clarets. But, as Graham remarks, the Burgundian wine-grower is usually a peasant or farmer; he lives 'above the shop' and when he wants another bottle of wine he goes down into the cellar and fetches it. His meal is often magnificent — and not accompanied by much formality. Nor, in the past, did Burgundy benefit by the establishment of any of the great glassworks, such as were in production in other regions — Bordeaux had a large number, especially at the time when English glass was highly esteemed throughout Europe.

Quite a lot of sparkling wine is made, including some red. This can be a clean, pleasant drink and is sometimes used to make a luxury version of *vin blanc cassis*. Much Bourgogne Mousseux will also have the proud description '*Méthode Champenoise*' on its label. Centres of the sparkling wine production are Rully, in the Côte Chalonnaise, and also Nuits St Georges.

The Aligoté grape makes the 'everyday' white Burgundy and it is this that is the traditional wine for *vin blanc cassis*. These days it can be an agreeable dry wine, sometimes a bit hard, but refreshing. Otherwise, the fine white Burgundies are made from

232

the Chardonnay grape, the fine red burgundies from the Pinot Noir, red Beaujolais from the Gamay. A combination of Pinot Noir and Gamay, of which one-third must be Pinot Noir, is called *Passe-Tout-Grains*, literally 'process all the grapes (together)', from the time when small wine-makers could not separate grape varieties to make the wines individually; this wine can be deliciously refreshing — Michelin often indicates it as a speciality of local restaurants and it is very much the sort of drink that commercial travellers, those connoisseurs of value for money in eating-places, détour to enjoy.

Chablis is somewhat outside the main Burgundy area, a dumpy-towered grey little town on the banks of the River Serein. The wines are some of the most famous in the world, but it is fair to say that, although a good and, certainly, a great Chablis is a wonderful thing, many people may find it difficult to enjoy these wines at first: they are big, assertive, very dry indeed. Do not be disappointed if your first experience of a great growth of Chablis does not please — try a more modest Chablis or Petit Chablis, to get the concept of the wine's style. There are several odd things about Chablis: the 'real thing' has a curious greenish glint to it which no pseudo-Chablis is ever able to imitate. Nor does the wine darken much in tone as it ages — I once read about some supposed connoisseur of wine sipping the 'rich golden wine of a

233

matured Chablis' and wondered what on earth he was actually drinking! Chablis of the finer growths is well partnered by one of the richer fish dishes, where its dryness is able to cut any unctuousness.

Beaujolais is now made in white as well as red versions, but the red will always be the more important. In very general terms, it is usually at its best, both white and red, when fairly young, so that the delectable fruit makes the wine irresistibly 'moreish'. *'Vuidons les tonneaux!'* is the motto of the Compagnons du Beaujolais and certainly the temptation to pour it down the throat is strong. Each commune (parish) produces vines of individual character and, today, there are some estate wines too. Remember that the French will always drink these younger than many British — who still cherish the illusion that an old wine is invariably 'better'. The fruit is delightfully accentuated if the wine is served cool, and the 'Mousseux' and young wines should be.

The Côte Chalonnaise, making white and red wines, is assuming increasing importance, because these are Burgundies that can still — just — be afforded by people who want to drink Burgundy frequently. Rully, Mercurey, Givry and Montagny are names worth noting: Montagny makes only white wine, Rully also. Mercurey makes a little white and so does Givry, but their reds are the important wines. Try them on the spot and remember them when you get home.

The Côte d'Or is the truly 'Golden Slope' of Burgundy, divided into the Côte de Beaune, where the very greatest wines are the whites, and the Côte de Nuits where the reds are the glories. Not much white is made in the Côte de Nuits, but a fair amount of red in the Côte de Beaune. However, the visitor should not always aim at the most expensive wine on a restaurant list — and go hungry for the following day; it is sometimes wise to concentrate on wines that may be more modest in price but will provide greater enjoyment and, certainly, if you are on the spot, it is sensible to concentrate also on the wines of the growers. This is not to scorn the wines of the great shippers, but these can often be sampled from export lists. Remember, though, that sometimes a shipper will put out a wine under his label bearing quite a modest A.O.C., which in fact is a declassified wine of much higher quality.

The whole matter of Burgundy names really should be studied, because the vineyard scene is intricately arranged: each vineyard may have a number of strips or allotment-sized plots, each separately owned; this means that each owner will cultivate his vines and, eventually, make his wine (if he makes it, instead of selling the grapes to a shipper), in an individual way. If the big shipper buys the wines, he can blend them — to the advantage of the consumer in many instances, because the customer wants continuity of style and may have already formed a liking for the wines of a particular establishment. The small grower may not be able always to make his own wines — equipment costs money — but, if he does, he is faced with the problem of having only a very limited stock of wine to sell; whether he sells this to the buyer from an export market, who descends on him, hoping to find some treasure for discriminating customers, or to a chic Paris restaurant, or in the form of 'cellar-door' sales, this is his decision. It is the decision of the customer as to whether he relies on — in an export market — the advice of his merchant (essential here as, perhaps, with no other wine), or whether he takes a chance, according to what he can pay. It is always worth remembering, though, that fine wine is never produced in sufficient quantity, so that the apparent 'bargain' may be of doubtful value. In order to understand the wines in Burgundy, then, some knowledge of the way the wines are named is important. Try to do a little homework before you go.

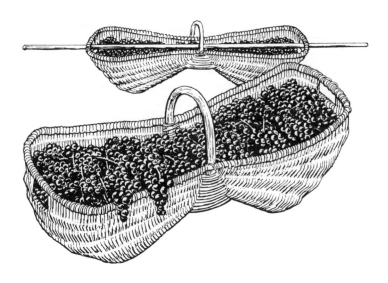

Tasting-cups. In front, the Burgundy *tastevin* with irregular interior indentations, so that the colour of the wine as it runs over these will show up in an ill-lit cellar. There is a thumb-rest and loop to facilitate hanging round the neck while travelling. In former times such cups were used in many regions. The Bordeaux *tasse à vin* is quite plain with a single convex bulge — it was formerly used in tasting-rooms and the above-ground *chais*.

In general, the appellations fit inside each other: a wine that bears just the name of a vineyard, such as Corton or Chambertin, is a category up from a wine that carries only the name of the village made famous because of the wines from these vineyards — Aloxe-Corton, Gevrey-Chambertin. But sometimes the name of another vineyard is attached to that of the great one, such as Charmes-Chambertin; this means — usually — that the wine will rank just below that of the great Chambertin vineyard, but above that bearing the name of the village of Gevrey. So the Burgundy visitor ought to try to accustom himself or herself to the names of the main villages of the Côte d'Or. However, the rule is not absolute. At Corton, the white Corton-Charlemagne is a finer wine (by implication) than the white Corton. This is easy to remember, as most Corton is red wine. But try to understand the ways in which the label can guide you — because the information is there if you can interpret the significance of the terms. And never forget that, although an A.O.C. that is superior in standing to another *should* provide a finer wine, no piece of paper can guarantee this, any more than it can ensure that you will enjoy the wine; only the maker can endow the wine with quality, only you, by discovering what you like and remembering names — and not being unwilling to take a chance with others — can find pleasure.

Tasting is often done in Burgundy by means of a *tastevin*, the shallow, irregularly indented cup (glass, pottery, silver plate or silver) that in former times was carried by those dealing in wine, who could not count on being offered a glass. The indentations serve to show up the colour of the wine when this is tasted in a cellar, where illumination may be very limited, even today. In addition, the *tastevin* — there were similar tasting-cups used in the past in other wine regions — projects the wine to the mouth in a way that is not quite similar to what happens when one tastes from a glass: the wine from the *tastevin* hits the different parts of the mouth more broadly — try and you will see. A different impression may be gained and it is worthwhile trying to use a *tastevin*, even if only to link yourself with the wine trade of the past and, still, of the present.

Note, when examining labels, that the word '*domaine*' is not quite the same thing as 'estate', in the Bordeaux sense. A *domaine* label will state whether the wine has been bottled at that *domaine*, but remember that a *domaine* may be the owner of a fairly large patch of vineyard, or even a company, managed for the shareholders by someone who actually does the work.

Glasses in Burgundy do, unfortunately, often pander to the taste of people who prefer '*le grand chi-chi*' and pay for it. You may be given a gigantic glass — some of those in which the Romanée-Conti wines are sometimes served will hold a bottle or more. The balance and bouquet of the wine are, to me — and to many Burgundy specialists — completely distorted by this excessive aeration, in addition to which the vulgarity of the giant vessels is gross. Anyone who knows anything about wine will ask for an ordinary glass of suitable proportions.

Things to See and Do

Visiting wine firms can, ideally, be arranged by whoever your wine merchant is at home. But the Office du Tourisme and Syndicat d'Initiative in Beaune can provide information about cellar tours of the big establishments, which are well worth visiting. The firms out in the country are less organized about visits, but there are a number of places with local tasting-rooms where one can sample the local wines. You need a guidebook for these and if I again recommend Graham Chidgey's book, it is because I insisted, as editor, that he put in all the places where the traveller could stop, taste and perhaps have a snack meal in various different circuits aimed at showing as much as possible of the countryside.

In the Beaujolais there are a series of regional tasting-rooms in the centre of the various communes, where several wines are always available to taste. The tasting-room at Juliénas is in a deconsecrated church and perhaps it is worth bearing in mind that the murals with which it is now decorated are extremely uninhibited. There is a tasting-room at Beaujeu, which is the village from which the entire region got its name, and it has a good Musée Folklorique et des Traditions Populaires. Vaux-en-Beaujolais, the original of Clochemerle, although the television filming was done in nearby Saint-Lager, has the Cave de Clochemerle, illustrated by scenes from the Clochemerle books, and is the headquarters of a 'Bacchic brotherhood', Les Compagnons du Gosier Sec. On the main road, N6, the Maison du Beaujolais at Saint Jean d'Ardières offers not only tastings — in 33 cl. bottles — but some of the local sausages and *andouillettes* to act as 'blotting-paper'. Also in the Beaujolais — at Romanèche-Thorins — is the house of Bernard Raclet, which is now a museum. Raclet discovered how to combat the praylis grub, afflicting the vines in 1829, and at the end of each October his work is commemorated in the *Fête Raclet*. At the Château de la Chaise in Brouilly, outside Odénas, are what are said to be the longest cellars in Europe — 340 feet; application must be made to see them. There is a tasting-room at Saint Amour, where a little white wine may also be tried, another at Deschamps, on the edge of Chénas and Moulin-à-Vent, yet another one at Villié-Morgon and a tasting-room with light food available at Moulin-à-Vent as well.

In Beaune itself, the Hôtel Dieu is a 'must' — impressive and beautiful, with many great works of art. Although there are other great establishments supported by wine, this is probably the most famous, and at least an hour should be devoted to seeing it. The Musée du Vin de Bourgogne is the former Hôtel des Ducs de Bourgogne, containing a most interesting collection of objects both past and present to do with wine, including the Lurçat tapestry of the wine triumphing over death. Beaune has a number of the cellars of the big *négociants* (shippers) that are open to the public, so visiting here is not a problem. The establishments in the walls and bastions are especially impressive and picturesque.

Out in the country, there are several estates that can be visited, although inquire about opening times beforehand; Burgundy is not like Bordeaux and there are only a few properties where people can be shown around, although the Burgundians are usually willing to advise where this can be arranged. What must be seen, however, is the great Cistercian building at Clos de Vougeot, now the property of the Chevaliers du Tastevin, where the annual banquets are held; the sloping roof served to catch every drop of rain. The gigantic beam press is only one of the things to see inside. There are other huge presses, dating from the fifteenth century, at the Cuverie des Ducs de Bourgogne at Chenôve.

Dijon is full of great works of art — in Burgundy, almost more than anywhere else, the religious associations of the vine have resulted in wonderful carvings and statuary. Growers, merchants, buyers and all aspects of vineyard routine are portrayed in many places. In the Musée de Beaux Arts, in the Ancien Palais des Ducs de Bourgogne, there are, in addition to the art treasures, the enormous ducal kitchens, that date from 1435. The Musée Perrin de Puycousin has many exhibits relating to past life in Dijon and Tournus. The Cellier de Clairvaux (the monks made wine but were not allowed to drink it) is now a regional tasting-room. The Hospice de Meursault, at Meursault, capital of the white wines of the Côte de Beaune, includes the ruined ancient hospital, Le Manoir Murisaltien, a tasting-room open to the public, and the Château de Meursault, now owned by Patriarche, which can be shown to visitors. At Nuits St Georges the Hospices, which are supported, like the Hospices de Beaune, by the sale of their wines, are not usually open to visitors, although — for the seriously interested — application to see the cellars can usually be made.

Fontenay was founded by St Bernard in 1118. It is well worth seeing and the monks' bakehouse and dovecote are on view.

I must mention a special cheese called Minstère, like Camembert, only better, which they gave us here (Hôtel de la Post, Beaune), and which we could get nowhere else. . . . As for the fine de la maison 1858, which, in a breathless hush, was slowly poured into glasses so overwhelmingly huge that any of them could have been used as a rose-bowl in the centre of a mayoral banquet, that brandy was almost anaesthetic in bouquet. I believe in glasses of this size, for brandy.

G.B. STERN, *Bouquet*, 1927
[No comment! P.V.P]

Montréal's church has remarkable carvings, showing scenes from Burgundian life — including, among other things, wine merchants enjoying a drink. Montbard is the town of the great eighteenth-century naturalist, Buffon (*Truite farcie caprice de Buffon* is a stuffed trout, accompanied by a banana). Vincelottes has a fine twelfth-century cellar, formerly used by the monks of the Abbey of Reigny who not only kept their wine there but were able to move it easily to market, as Vincelottes is near to the Yonne, a river formerly much used for heavy traffic.

Tournus' Hôtel Dieu is staffed by the Soeurs Hospitalières de Sainte Marthe, like the Hôtel Dieu at Beaune. There is a fine pharmacy and kitchen and, in the Musée Bourguignon, rue Perrin de Puycousin, important collections showing aspects of Burgundian everyday life in the past, also a reconstructed cellar. At Montargis, the chef of the Duc de Plessis-Praslin invented a sweetmeat — roasted almonds covered with sugar; they were such a success with the court ladies in Paris in the time of Louis XIII that the Duc allowed them to bear his name — which is the origin of pralines. The Ursulines of the convent at Flavigny invented an aniseed sweet in the seventeenth century. Autun is important for the house of Chancellor Nicolas Rolin, now the Musée Rolin, which has many exhibits of Burgundian art; also in the Musée Verger-Tarin there is the reconstruction of a nineteenth-century interior, with additional objects such as would have been accumulated from an earlier time.

21

Champagne and the Ardennes

'La Champagne' is the region, 'le Champagne' the wine. As mentioned earlier, the word 'Champagne' means open country-side, as opposed to wooded regions. Strictly, the area includes Sainte Ménéhould, which, in this book, is in Lorraine (*p.194*); it is also much influenced by being fairly near to Paris, therefore the cookery is based on butter and involves many of the pork and game products of the Ardennes and the Franco-Belgian border. Tourists travelling along the ruler-straight roads, built first in Roman times, may think the area is dull — and, seeing the appalling perspectives of the great war cemeteries, depressing. But away from the main roads there are beautiful forests and stretches of peaceful landscape, elegant country houses, picturesque sleepy little towns and many superb churches and cathedrals. In many works of art the activities of *vignerons* and *tonneliers* (coopers) are depicted and, in the daytime, most grey villages look quite deserted, because everyone is out in the vineyards.

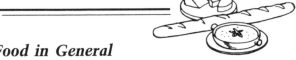

Food in General

River fish are plentiful and *brochet* (pike) is a speciality, its pounded flesh being made into a type of fish sausage or fishball, served with a rich sauce. *Quenelles de brochet* are also a Burgundy speciality, but those of Champagne are famous. The pig contributes the Ardennes smoked ham and many *pâtés*, *petits pieds* (stuffed trotters) and *andouillettes* (tripe sausages); Reims ham in

241

pastry will also be seen in the shops and is useful for picnics.

Cabbages are grown in vast quantities and some go into *chouc-route* — which, of course, contains pork products. Beets are served with many pork dishes and *pissenlits* (dandelions) are made into a salad with diced bacon. The Ardennes are a region for wild boar and there is at least one hotel where there is an enclosure for a family of boars as part of the 'unusual attractions', although I do not know that the head of a patriarchal beast, tusks dripping blood, on the wall of the dining-room is a particular enhancement.

Reims and Provence are famous for a particular variety of pear called the *rousselet*; it is so rich and juicy that it cannot be packed and sent to any market. This pear was the traditional gift that Reims would present to any visiting celebrity or monarch — 'Kings of France are made at Reims', Jeanne d'Arc told the Dauphin — and the pears are known as *poires tapées*. Walnuts (*noix*) come from Saint Gilles and an apple called the *croquet des Ardennes* from the region. In the summer there are plenty of strawberries and cherries.

Specialities and Dishes

Menus will often make mention of Champagne being in a recipe. It is usually the still wine that is involved, though occasionally specific mention of one still red wine from the villages making it may be referred to.

Andouillettes are the tripe sausage supposed to have been first made by the pork butchers of Arras, somewhat outside the Champagne region. This type became famous and sought-after, so that the makers coloured the outside of the sausage red — and earned themselves the name of 'Redguts' as a result. *Andouillettes de mouton* are a speciality of Troyes, and might be translated as chitterlings made with mutton. Troyes produces vast amounts of tripe sausages and in fact they once actually saved the town: in the religious wars of the sixteenth century the troops besieging Troyes managed to breach the defences and entered a part of the town where the *andouillettes* were made. Being hungry, they fell on the sausages — which are rich and satisfying — and spent so much time enjoying them that the defenders were able to bring up reserves and drive out the enemy.

Cervelas de brochet is a type of pike sausage made with the addition of potatoes. *Pain à la reine* is a fish mousse, pike being a main ingredient.

Cailles sous la cendre are stuffed quails, wrapped in vine leaves before being roasted. *Gougère de l'Aube* is a type of cheese *brioche* or cheese puff.

Pieds de porc à la Sainte Ménéhould are poached, grilled pigs' feet, often featured on regional menus, especially near the border with Lorraine.

Potée champenoise is a substantial soup, which includes meat (usually pork), possibly chicken, sausages and/or chunks of ham, plus vegetables and potatoes.

Biscuits de Reims are small, oblong macaroons, the traditional accompaniment to a glass of Champagne.

Massepains de Reims are marzipan sweets. *Pain d'épice*, a type of spiced honeycake, is another Reims speciality.

Reims mustard, often put up in pots shaped like big Champagne corks, is of course made with the local wine.

Wines

The traveller driving along the autoroutes and *routes nationales* may well wonder where the vineyards are — vines are not obvious, unless you know where to look. The great chalky undulations, pale and reflecting light upwards, with miles of galleries excavated underneath Reims, Épernay and Ay, are conducive to the production of vivaceous dry wine. The region has been under vines since Roman times, but the wines have not always been mainly white and fully sparkling. Kings, including our own King Henry VIII, and Charles II, 'the merry monarch', have delighted in the wines and it was during the exile of the Marquis de St Evremond by Louis XIV that the wines of the Marquis's friend, the Marquis de Sillery, came to England in quantity in the seventeenth century. Later in the same century the cellarmaster at Hautvillers Abbey, Dom Pierre Pérignon, evolved a method of blending the different wines of various plots and grapes to make the *'cuvée'*, so that his wines became famous, and he also reintroduced the use of cork as a stopper for the lively wines. Prior to this, bottles had been used more as carafes are and the stopper, usually of wood, was more in the nature of a bung. It is thought that Dom Pérignon may have worked in the Benedictine establishments of the Iberian Peninsula and seen the use of the bark of the cork oak, or maybe Benedictines from this region came through Champagne, carrying the little barrels that are still often used as travelling wine containers, so that the brothers of the Hautvillers house were shown the cork stoppers.

Most of the great Champagne establishments have their own 'house style' and will make several types of wine. The bulk of Champagne is non-vintage and made of wine from both the black Pinot Noir grape and the white Chardonnay, together with other permitted varieties; nowadays, *'blanc de blancs'* — white wine from white grapes — is often made and indeed the tag is applied to other wines rather foolishly, because obviously a wine made wholly of the juice of a white grape, such as the Sauvignon, could not be anything else but 'white from white'. In general, the white grapes contribute finesse and delicacy to the wine, the black grapes body and fruit.

Many of the Champagne houses own some vineyards, but their properties would not be sufficient to provide the wine they require, so it is bought, either as wine or grapes, from the numerous small growers in the region — each patch of vines must be within an approved site and every detail of production is very strictly controlled; for example, mechanical pickers are still not used in the Champagne vineyards at all. In very general terms, the method whereby the wines are subjected to the special Champagne process is as follows: the wine is made, subject to controls, and begins life as a still wine. Then, in the spring after its vintage, the wines from various sections of vineyard will be blended to compose the *'cuvée'* or vatting required and the wine will go into bottle, to await the *prise de mousse*, a type of secondary fermentation which essentially is the sparkle captured within the bottle — the carbon dioxide that would be given off in an open vat or cask being retained in the bottle, which is secured, these days, usually with a crown cork but, sometimes for the very finest wines, with a cork held onto the lip of the bottle by a metal clip called an *agrafe*. You can tell by looking at the bottle which has been used — the crown cork will go over a curved lip, the *agrafe* requires a squared-off lip on which it is fastened.

During the next stage of the process, any sediment in the wine must be brought down to rest on the first cork. This is done by allowing the bottles, resting in slots in racks called *pupitres* — the original is supposed to have been cut from an upended kitchen table in Madame Clicquot's cellars — to be turned and shaken, so that the deposit slides down to rest on the first cork. Today, there are all the Champagne houses and, indeed, others making sparkling wine according to this method. The process, called *remuage*, is now often carried out by mechanically, the bottles being slotted into huge frames, which are turned by electricity and, once programmed, will work day and night, so that the *remuage*, which could, with stubborn deposit, take as long as three months, may be completed in a much shorter time. However, anyone seeing round a Champagne cellar will certainly be shown how *remuage* is done — the skilled worker makes a noise like giants playing castanets and gets through an amazing number of bottles daily.

When the bottles have been inclined so that they are almost upside down, they undergo a further period of maturation, resting '*sur les pointes*', the neck of one bottle being inside the punt in the base of the bottle underneath. Positioned like this, with the first cork still in, Champagne can remain in good condition in its home cellar for many years. When the wine is needed, the disgorging process takes place; nowadays this, too, is usually done by freezing the necks of the bottles, so that the first cork can be taken off, the pellet of ice containing the deposit removed and the bottle topped up, then the second cork being inserted. The original method, *à la volée*, was to whip out the cork by hand, top up the foaming bottle and force in the second cork — sometimes visitors may also be shown this procedure, which requires great strength as well as skill.

The 'dosage' or sweetening with which the bottle is topped up varies according to the type of wine required; the dosage is sugar dissolved in wine. There is a vogue for absolutely dry wine — although the UK was the first market to require this and some Champagne makers refused to produce anything but a slightly dosed wine for the local market at one time. *Brut zéro* means no sweetening at all; *brut* may imply a very slight dosage; *très sec*, means extra dry; extra *sec* mean a little sweetening has been added; *sec* is slightly sweet; *demi-sec* is truly sweet, and *doux* or rich — beloved of the Imperial Russian Court — is a sweet but sometimes charmingly luscious sweet wine, admirable at the end of a meal, when the bone-dry Champagnes can seem rather hard.

Rosé or pink Champagne is made by allowing the skins of the black grapes to remain with the '*must*' or grape-juice long enough for it to tint it, or by blending in red wine. Vintage Champagne is the wine of a single year, although — for this is a northern vineyard — a percentage of wine from other years can be added if the maker thinks fit. The *de luxe* Champagnes are the very finest a house can make, often giving the names of past makers to them: Dom Pérignon, Dom Ruinart, La Grande Dame, and many others. These are, of course, never cheap. A B.O.B. Champagne is a wine made for a customer such as a particular merchant, retail chain or hotel or restaurant group; some will probably be the product of a wholly reputable establishment and is slightly lower in price than the well-known names, simply because it will not have to bear the costs of advertising and publicity. As each Champagne must have a code number on its label, it is always possible to trace each wine back to its source.

It should always be remembered, when old Champagnes are being served, that the wine generally begins to age fairly rapidly after the stage at which the second cork goes in. Up to that time, in the cellar where it has been made, its progress can be slow, but, once disgorged, it does not have an indefinite life: in very general terms, a vintage Champagne is inclined to reach its peak seven to twelve years afer its vintage date, although it may be perfectly drinkable and, indeed, enjoyable long after that. An old Champagne, served in a Champagne establishment, may in fact have been disgorged only hours or even minutes before being poured.

In recent years a type of Champagne known as 'crémant' has been made. This is very slightly less fizzy than the full sparkling wine, the difference, expressed in atmospheres, which represent the pressure behind the cork, is that a fully *mousseux* wine will be of about 5.6 atmospheres, a *crémant* wine 3.5 – 4.5. This type of wine can please those who do not like a very lively wine, but unless you compare two glasses side by side the difference is not usually noticeable.

Because all the great Champagnes are blends of wines, some growers nowadays are trying to make wines from single vineyards. It is always interesting to taste these, especially, perhaps, the *'Blanc de noirs'* — white wine from black grapes — but, as it is the real art of the blender that makes some of the great Champagnes as great as they are, it would be wrong to assume that single growths Champagnes are in any way 'better' — they are different.

The Still Wines

In former times these were often known as 'Champagne nature', but the official term now is *Coteaux Champenois*. They may be white or red — the red wines come from various villages where the wines are those of the black grapes; there are several of these, but Bouzy, for obvious reasons, is the best-known; others include Cumières and Ambonnay.

Ratafia is made from Champagne grape-juice and brandy. The Champagne region is apparently the only place where it is now produced, although in former times there were many different sorts. The term comes from the Latin phrase *'Ut rata fiat'* with which legal documents would conclude, and the drink would then be shared by the lawyers and the parties to the proceedings.

Things to See and Do

The three great centres of Champagne are Reims, Épernay and Ay, but there is another area of production in the south of the region, around Sézanne, where a lot of wine is produced and which, in itself, is interesting as regards many museums and works of art.

Detailed information about establishments open to visitors, hours and the availability of multi-lingual guided tours (some houses even take visitors around in little trains, useful for people who cannot walk a lot), may be obtained from the Bureau de Tourisme, 1 Rue Henri Jardart, Reims or, in London, from The Champagne Bureau, Crusader House, 14 Pall Mall, London SW1Y 5LO. It is worth knowing that some of the houses are open almost all the year round. Do not forget that quite a lot of walking will be involved and that it will be cold, also that the cellars are really deep and tourists will remain quite a long time underground, although anyone hesitating about such a guided tour can usually remain in the reception room — where there may be souvenirs and things to look at, also cloakrooms.

Ideally, try to see at least one establishment in Reims that has *crayères*, the odd, flask-shaped openings deep into the chalk that were excavated by the Romans, who probably used them for storage. Pommery has a large number of these and it is an impressive sight to visit them, also to remember how the entire population of the city lived in these underground cellars for over a thousand days in the First World War, while a few dedicated vineyard workers crept out to tend the vines even at the worst times of the battles. Along the Marne Valley, the 1917 vintage was actually picked under fire — by women, children and old men, some of whom were killed at the time. Épernay is quite different from Reims, and Ay is different again, each of them contributing wines of individual character: Épernay is at the foot of the Côte des Blancs, the white wine vineyards, Reims amid many of the black grape plantations, such as those on the Montagne de Reims.

The leaflets available from the C.I.V.C. tourist offices indicate certain routes that enable you to see the main vineyards and that are easy to follow. The *Route Bleue* covers the Montagne de Reims and Ay; the *Route Rouge* follows the Marne from Épernay to Dormans via Hautvillers and Châtillon; the *Route Verte*, south of Épernay, shows the Côte des Blancs. In the southern region,

Sézanne, Troyes and Bar-sur-Aube are the main centres and a Chalet de Dégustation is on Route National 19, just outside Bar-sur-Aube. But local producers will provide information about what may be seen in this charming region.

The Abbey of Hautvillers, where Dom Pérignon lived and worked, belongs now to Moët et Chandon, but, even if you cannot apply to them to see round, it is possible to see the adjoining church, which is on the road and contains Dom Pérignon's grave. Adjacent to the church, within what was formerly the enclosure of the Benedictine Abbey, there is a most interesting reconstruction of part of the establishment from the earliest times to the period when Dom Pierre Pérignon was working there, with all the different departments within which the monks would have been engaged. In part of the winery, one sees how the bottles were formerly upended in a section of sand. Alongside this fascinating museum — although it is a living rather than a static arrangement — there is a vineyard, laid out with varieties that Dom Pérignon would have known, all ungrafted vinestocks. To see the Moët et Chandon establishment is impressive — as it is to see the many other Champagne houses open to visitors — but Hautvillers is unique and a wonderful evocation of the earlier times of Champagne. (In Reims, the establishment of Clicquot-Ponsardin also have admirably produced films and audio-visual displays for visitors and, for the very privileged, a type of theatrical-cum-shadow play in the cellars, where the personalities of former times show the bottling of Champagne — tying the corks down with looped twine — and, even, the occasional appearance of the shade of Madame Clicquot herself, still working among the millions of bottles. But this really is for the honoured guest — so it cannot be arranged for everybody.) Ask about seeing Hautvillers and allow a good hour to appreciate the experience.

Épernay is these days a bustling town, but until fairly recently it was quite small. However, the great Avenue du Vin de Champagne, with many impressive houses, leads off the square and should be seen. This is where the Musée de Vin de Champagne is situated, in a former private house. It has displays of the equipment involved with making the wine and a model of the Abbey of Hautvillers.

Ay is a small place, but has an interesting little museum and merely a walk about in this 'village that made the reputation of Champagne' is a pleasant experience.

Reims is a huge city, rich in works of art — and, obviously, wealthy. The Maison Vergeur contains a number of exhibits of old

Reims; in the Musée des Beaux Arts the tapestries of the life of St Rémy show the saint blessing an empty cask — which miraculously became full of wine. Windows in the Cathedral show wine-making and various related activities. Although, as you may know, St Vincent is the patron of all *vignerons*, at Reims, St John is the patron of cellar staff and of all those engaged in work making Champagne.

Troyes has a fine recreation of a medieval pharmacy in the Hôtel Dieu le Comte. The Hôtel de Vauluisant contains a fine museum showing the local folklore and the Champagne region in general. The Church of St Urbain, where Princess Catherine of France married Henry V of England, has a particularly beautiful statue of the Virgin and Child, the Madonna with the curly smile, more famous, perhaps, as shown on the smiling angel on Reims Cathedral, but said to be typical of the Champagne woman. The Baby is wholly preoccupied by a huge bunch of grapes. Soissons' great Abbey of St Jean des Vignes is now a ruin, but visitors can see the refectory and, sometimes, the great cellar. Bar-sur-Aube has the Chapelle des Vignerons in St Peter's church, where the walls and roof are decorated with vine branches and pruning knives.

22

Cognac and the Surrounding Regions

This section covers the Charentes area plus the regions that lie between the Loire, the Auvergne, Périgord and the beginning of the Bordeaux or Gironde districts. It is quiet countryside, but with plenty of attractions, especially for those who like informal holidays: the coast is sometimes referred to as *'opale'* (opalescent), for its skyscapes are beautiful and sailors enjoy its beaches and seas. Inland, there are many treasures of art and architecture, for this was one of the areas traversed by the pilgrims going south to Santiago del Compostella, and the wonderful churches merit many détours.

The food can be good, even very good. It is said with justification that the two French words known throughout the world are 'Paris' and 'Cognac' — the latter, in various debased spellings, being used for various types of brandy that, while possibly paying tribute to 'the real thing', are only very remotely like it.

Regions within the area that may have their names attached to dishes and which are not always familiar to travellers, include: the Angoumois, Aunis, Saintonge, which together make 'les Charentes'. The province of the Vendéc is on the coast, south of the Loire; a section of Poitou, together with the Gatine region, is to the east; the Limousin and its northern area, the Marche; then there are the Corrèze in the Bas Limousin, and the Deux Sèvres, which are approximately in the area bordered by Niort, Poitiers, Parthenay and Fontenay-le-Comte. The Vienne (a confusing word to find on a menu if its immediate associations are with schnitzels and Austrian dishes) and the Haute Vienne are the regions that extend around Poitiers and Limoges.

Food in General

The cooking medium is butter. *'Beurre des Charentes'* is famous. Onions and shallots appear in many dishes, but garlic is used sparingly. Various types of casserole recipes are typical of the area — Curnonsky *(p.33)* said that this was a region of true country cooking. The *coup du milieu* is something occasionally noticed at feasts in the country — a glass of Cognac served as a digestive in the middle of a big meal. The salty marshes of Poitou and the coastal pastures feed the *pré salé* (lamb), very much a speciality, and there are many small game birds found here, also inland in the forests, together with freshwater fish of many kinds, also eels. The snails that feed voraciously on the vines are known as *cagouilles* and, in the Deux Sèvres region, there is a stew made from them known as a *lumas*; the Charentais people are sometimes scornfully referred to as *'cagouillards'* on account of their supposed sluggishness.

Along the coast, first-rate fish and crustacea are available: sardines, tunny, shrimps, plaice, skate, also oysters, mussels, lobsters and a clam-like shellfish called *lavignon*.

There is a great deal of market gardening, so vegetables are plentiful and diverse. Cabbage is the great vegetable of the Vendee and there are a lot of white beans, called *mojettes*, also the rich mushroom known as a *cèpe (see p.56)*. The Charentais melons are of course famous.

Many towns and villages produce special sweets: macaroons at Thouars and Dorat, meringues at Uzerche, angelica at Niort. *Massepain* (marzipan) and a type of pancake called a *flognard* are general regional specialities. *Tertus* are flattish cakes made with buckwheat flour; *tourteaux fromagers* are open tarts filled with cream cheese. Poitiers and Nevers specialize in nougatines and chocolates called *marguerites*, and *duchesses* are sweets made at Angoulême.

Tobacco is grown here and one often sees the huge leaves hung up to dry outside houses in the country.

Specialities and Dishes
Many of these are found in adjoining regions as well as some that obviously have their origin in Spain. Being on the great pilgrim route, the towns have acquired all sorts of relics of former times.

Andouilles limousines are tripe sausages, usually served grilled. *Bréjauda* is a soup, made with cabbage and bacon. *Broccana* is finely ground pork and veal, served in pastry.

La chaudrée is a soup made from very small sea fish and is something of a speciality of La Rochelle. The word *'chaudrée'* is an archaic one, meaning cauldron, and it can be found in the other regions where soups and stews are made. Specialists in *chaudrée* like to stipulate that the fire beneath the cauldron should be of *sarments* (vine prunings), preferably from the islands off the coast, which are said to have acquired a slight flavour of *varech* or seaweed.

Farcidure is a type of dumpling, usually made of stuffing the leaves of a cabbage with sorrel, beets and buckwheat flour, possibly with the addition of bacon. Dumplings of this sort are sometimes put in soup or accompany meat dishes. *Farcidure de pommes de terre* are dumplings made from potatoes and other vegetables, usually served with *andouilles*. A colloquial country name for *farcidure* is *poule sans os* (boneless chicken).

Lièvre en chabessard, or *en cabessa* or *chabessal* is a recipe for hare, the *cabessal* or *chabessard* being a round pan, carried on the heads of the sturdy country women when transporting a load. The hare is stuffed with spices, pork, ham, veal, plus shallots and garlic, and then cooked in wine and tied up into a round shape, so as to fit into the traditional pan.

Lièvre à la royale is another hare dish, cited by many as a local recipe. However, Mrs Elizabeth David quotes an article in *Le Temps* of 29th November, 1898, in which a Monsieur Couteaux writes to the effect that he invented the dish, having spent a week hunting the special type of hare he required 'with red fur, killed if possible in mountainous country, of fine French descent (characterized by the light nervous elegance of head and limbs)'. M. Couteaux's recipe takes from midday until seven in the evening to prepare and cook and it involves the hare being stuffed with *foie gras*, shallots, its own liver, lights, parsley, truffles, several bottles of wine and glasses of brandy. Not the sort of thing many people make these days, so if you see it on a menu, it is worth trying. Certainly hare recipes are something of a regional speciality.

À la limousine is a description that usually means the dish is accompanied by cabbage with chestnuts.

Pâté de fromage is a sweetish ewe-milk cheese tart.

Clafoutis are custard tarts made with black cherries.

Drinks

There are a number of local wines made in this region and, these days, many are interesting *vins de pays*. In the Vienne region *vin gris* is said to be made, although I have not noted it, and the Co-operative of Haut Poitou, just outside the town, is a source of many first-rate V.D.Q.S. wines that have proved popular in the UK: Sauvignon, Chardonnay, Cabernet Franc (and a *rosé* of the same) and sparkling Chardonnay, a rare sparkler. The regional aperitif is Pineau des Charentes, consisting of grape-juice and Cognac, and possessing an A.O.C. — unusual for an aperitif. Pineau is slightly sweet but, well-chilled, is a pleasant any-time tipple. A number of liqueurs, including one based on angelica, are made at Niort and nearby.

Cognac, the world's supreme brandy, (*see p.167*) is made in a strictly delimited area of the Charentes: in ascending order of quality, the Cognac regions fit inside one another — *bois communs, bois ordinaries, bons bois, fins bois, borderies, petite champagne* and *grande champagne*, all names vaguely descriptive of the type of countryside from which they come. As already mentioned, 'Champagne' refers to open country, as in Shakespeare's 'Daylight and Champaign discover not more.' Although brandy can be, and is, made in other regions where wine is available for distilling, in Cognac country the spirit must be made in a pot still, according to the strict local regulations. It has been made here since at least the seventeenth century and there are many fascinating details involved with its history; the Cognac wine-makers are thought to have turned to distilling when they had a glut of wine and were trying to appeal to the trade of the Low Countries. Obviously, a spirit was not only popular in regions

Several English ships were taking in their cargoes as I passed by Tonnay Charente and long lines of nice-looking trim new casks, smart with innumerable hoops, were occupying the whole length of the quay. All the Cognac brandy comes down river to this little port; and it would require but the wreck of one or two of those richly-freighted barges . . . to make the Charente run with most admirable punch.

T. ALDOLPHUS TROLLOPE, *A Summer in Western France*, Vol.II, 1841 where strong, warming drinks were already made and liked, but brandy took less space to transport than wine.

The wine from which Cognac is distilled is thin, harsh and not very pleasant to drink. Some vineyards are owned by the great Cognac houses, whose huge installations dominate Cognac and Jarnac, but many plots belong to peasant owners from whom the big establishments buy in the wine for distilling. The distilling process is carried out twice and, although nowadays instruments and scientific controls look after the different stages whereby Cognac comes into being, it is still not unknown for a distiller, at the time of making the brandy, to have a bed alongside the still, to supervise every movement of the carefully directed running of the still.

The Cognac is then put into casks of Limousin or Tronçais wood — nowadays very expensive — and there it matures. A considerable amount evaporates — 'The sun is our best customer', comment the Cognac makers, or ruefully admit that a high percentage is 'the share of the angels'. A black deposit forms on the roofs of the warehouses where the Cognac is lying — easy, say the makers, for the customs officers to know where it is! This deposit is caused by a fungus which feeds on the alcohol in the air as evaporation takes place.

Cognac matures only in wood, but not indefinitely and, once it goes into bottle, it will not undergo further marked changes or improvement. The notion of 'old Napoleon brandy' is erroneous — Cognac does not mature in bottle. Some very old brandies are put into *tierçons* (puncheons) of glass, each holding 120 gallons. The spirit is drawn from the cask by means of a device called *une preuve*, which is like a metal test-tube suspended from a wire. The area in the huge installations where the finest brandies will be stored is referred to as a *paradis*, for obvious reasons.

The blender, who is the kingpin of a Cognac house, will make up his 'marks' of the different categories of brandy from a *bibliothèque* or library of samples from different areas, different distillations and of different ages. It is the blending that enables the great Cognacs to maintain their special styles. It is not permitted by French law to sell vintage Cognac these days, but the privileged visitor may be allowed to taste the Cognac of a single year. But great age is not necessarily an advantage in a Cognac blend — after a certain time, the spirit will decline and deteriorate, although it is fair to say that in any fine Cognac there will certainly be some old brandy of the region.

If you should be offered 'something special' that purports to be old Cognac, the thing to note is the date when the spirit went into bottle; if it was a mere ten years old when this bottling was done, then it will still be a ten-year-old brandy when the bottle is opened. So do not waste money or pander to the cobwebbed bottles (probably topped up from quite ordinary ones) that may be wheeled to the table of *chi-chi* restaurants. And never allow the use of the goldfish-bowl type of brandy glass or the performance involved with heating this — no one knowing anything about good brandy and, certainly, good Cognac, can approve such practices. A glass able to be cupped in the hand and warmed gently in this way is all that the discriminating require — the account of the parvenue Rex, in Evelyn Waugh's *Brideshead Revisited*, is both accurate and damning in the scene where he orders a syrupy brandy, in a huge glass, to the embarrassment of his companion and, indeed, the good restaurant.

Things to See and Do

Angoulême: There is a fine collection of Charentais china in the Musée Municipal. The Chapelle des Cordeliers was the church belonging to the monastery where Jean Thevet was a member of the brotherhood; it was he who, in 1556, brought from Brazil what he called *'L'herbe angousmoisine'*, which in fact was the tobacco plant, before its more famous importer, Nicot — who gave his name to nicotine.

Aubusson: The Maison du Vieux Tapissier has the reconstruction of the interior of an old house.

Bassac: The Abbaye de Bassac, 6 km. east of Jarnac, can show the abbey kitchen, which dates from the seventeenth century, although the abbey itself was founded in the eleventh.

Celles-sur-Belle: Seven km. north of Melle, the seventeenth-century kitchen and refectory of the abbey church are open to visitors.

Cognac: The main brandy houses are open to visitors, the largest being those of Martell and Hennessy; Otard is installed in the Château de Cognac. There are plenty of facilities for visiting most of the establishments, although for the smaller concerns and some of those at Jarnac an introduction may have to be arranged.

Fontenay-le-Comte, Guéret, Saint Martin de Ré and Saintes have exhibitions relating to the past history and folklore of the region

— consult the guidebooks for up-to-date information.

Limoges: The Musée Adrien Dubouché has one of the finest collections of china in France, showing the evolution of this fragile work of art since the earliest times. Interested visitors should also see the enamels in the former Palace of the Archbishop and, if possible, a porcelain and enamelling works — inquire about these. Note also the seventeenth-century butchers' shops in the rue de la Boucherie: the butchers' church, St Aurélien, is also in the same street.

Maillezais: The salt store, cellars, refectory and octagonal kitchen of the fourteenth-century monastery are open to visitors.

Montmorillon: There is a Romanesque kitchen attached to the Church of Saint Laurent.

Nieul-sur-l'Autise: The refectory and cellars of the abbey — seventeenth century — may be seen.

Poitiers: The Grande Salle or Salle des Pas Perdus (waiting-room) of the Palais de Justice is one of the most beautiful rooms ever to have been built for the purpose of giving parties — it was here that the Courts of Love, presided over by Eleanor of Aquitaine and her daughter, were held in the twelfth century. The great fireplaces on the dais were added later, but the room gives a wonderful impression of what a great medieval hall was like — it is as if the original users had only just gone out of the door.

Pons: At the Hospice des Pelerins, on the road to Bordeaux, the pilgrims' seats, some of their graffiti, and the horseshoes they hung up on the wall are still to be seen.

Riochecorbon: In the château there is a typical Saintonge room and a seventeenth-century kitchen.

La Rochelle: The Musée Lafaille can show the Cabinet Lafaille, just as it was in the eighteenth century. In the Musée d'Orbigny there is an important display of china and a pharmacy from the local hospital.

Saint Michel en l'Herm: Here the huge *buttes huîtrières* or banks of oysters may be inspected. Were they formed naturally or as the result of some shipwreck?

23

Corsica

This, the 'scented isle', is a poor country as regards pasture or crops. The gastronomic specialities are therefore those of the mountains and the forest, plus whatever comes from the surrounding sea.

Herbs are used a great deal and they achieve much in seasonings, especially for what might otherwise be somewhat indifferent meat. Olives, too, are often ingredients in recipes. Meat is often roasted and *cabri* (kid) appears on menus, so do all types of small game birds — including *merles* (thrushes) — as well as hare and boar, in addition to a wide range of pork dishes; poultry is also much featured, although *coq rôti à la maman* is a joke name — it is actually roast veal! The pig contributes also to the different sorts of *charcuterie*, the various local sausages and hams making self-catering and picnic meals interesting for the shopper. *Lonzu* is a type of salt pork in sausage form — something found on other Mediterranean islands — and *prisuttu* is a type of ham.

Corsica goes along with Portugal in making use of salt cod recipes and there are a number of fish soups. Molluscs, including *encornes, calmars* (*see p.49*), and *poulpe* (octopus) may feature on menus, in addition to the more usual fish, shellfish and crustacea. Snails are also a Corsican dish.

There are various pleasant cakes and pastry dishes as the sweet course and local fruits often form part of the ingredients. Anise is much used in the Corsican kitchen too. *Marrons* (sweetchestnuts) are here often called *châtaignes* and are abundant in the local forests; they often form part of sweet dishes.

Drinks

The aperitif Cap Corse (*see p.188*) is world famous and the local anise liqueur is widely consumed, Cazanis being a well-known brand. It is not quite the same as the anise drinks in the south of France, although akin. One day I saw an eminent Monsignor sitting under a tree with parishioners, apparently enjoying a tomato-juice — but, as a true Corsican, he was actually drinking a *tomate*, which is grenadine plus *pastis* or anise. There are several different brands of *pastis* made here too, most worth sampling; they, too, are unlike the south-of-France versions of this drink and, sometimes, seem less liquorous.

Corsican wines are beginning to be known on export lists now. The best usually come from the north of the island, the Patrimonio region being specially reputed for quality. The whites can be typical of hot country vineyards but, with modern resources, can be pleasant, aromatic and firm; the *rosé* wines are dark in tone, as are many Mediterranean *rosés* and can be agreeable, clean drinks, of immediate appeal and quite robust. The red wines, however, are usually full-bodied and decidedly gutsy — as the Corsicans like them. Today, enormous improvements have been made in their production and they can be good with the typical dishes — including the local goat cheeses. Some of them are now respected and enjoyed among the *vins de pays* and it is a happy chance that one of the categories here is '*Île de Beauté*'. Each winery usually produces a range of different wines, most of them well worth sampling.

24

The Dordogne, Lot, Quercy and the Limousin

This is a region beloved by many Britons — and inhabitants of other countries. It is a smiling land, with a wonderful climate and the charm of country life that the French too now appreciate. The influence of such affection has, sometimes unfortunately, affected the gastronomy, but there is plenty of true country cooking, away from the well-known haunts of the wealthy. You will have to pay up if you eat in the publicized restaurants but away from them it is still possible to eat well and cheaply. The area I have taken as representing a gastronomic region is extensive: it includes part of the Limousin in the north, Périgord, the troubadour country in the centre, Quercy between the Rivers Dordogne and Lot, the Agenais (after Agen, the plum town) to the south-west, and the Rouergue to the south-west. People travelling south will, if they wish, be able to détour through part of this region; those making an excursion from the east can easily reach it; from the north a route directed at its centre will provide unusual and rewarding scenery and art treasures as well as culinary delights.

Food in General

The description *'Périgourdine'* applied to a dish usually means that it contains truffles — the 'black diamonds' of the area — and even *foie gras* as well. The Périgord truffle is black; attempts are made to encourage its growth, but it tends to manifest itself capriciously, in wild surroundings, often beneath or near oak trees. Young female pigs — known as *chercheuses* — are taught to sniff out the *chêne truffiers*, oaks where the truffle may be found; they root out the precious item and the person in charge of the piglets snatches it up before it can be eaten — although the finder animal is usually rewarded by a few slivers of the delicacy. Miss Joy Law, who has had a house in the Dordogne for many years, writes most interestingly about truffles and the way they are sought[1]; she tells how trials for truffle-hunting dogs are held each year — the 1976 champion found six truffles in fifteen minutes. She categorizes the different sorts of truffles: '*Truffes 1er ebullition*' seems the best, for the truffle will have been cooked only once; other truffles may have been washed several times. '*Truffes brossées*' are equally good — whole cleaned truffles. The time to shop for the curious things is in the local markets before Christmas and early in the New Year. Even a few shreds of truffle can add delectably to the flavour of many foods.

Goose fat is the cooking medium in this region. The geese are usually a special kind, fattened specifically for making *foie gras*; the method, stuffing them with grain by a funnel held in the beak, horrifies many people, but if anyone cannot bear the idea of thus enlarging the livers of the birds, then the only thing to do is to avoid eating *foie gras* and avert the eyes from such postcards as depict the fattening of the geese. Authorities say that the Périgord *foie gras* is more unctuous than that of Strasbourg, but I have never been able to make a side-by-side comparison. Both here and in Alsace *foie gras*, plus a little of its jelly, may be served at the beginning of the meal, or sometimes it comes in the middle, replacing a salad, although many who should know are against this. Indeed, it is rather rich to enjoy after a main course.

Walnuts are grown in huge amounts in this region. The two chief varieties are the Corne and the Grandjean, the latter coming mainly from the Sarlat area, where it contributes to *huile de noix* (walnut oil). The use of even a proportion of this in a salad — for it is both rich and of a very definite flavour — will usually be marked as special on the menu.

Vegetables are plentiful and many go into the thick soups typical of the area. *Cèpes, asperges, salsifis* are grown as well as the more ordinary vegetables; haricot beans are locally known as *mounzettas*.

The streams yield plenty of fish, including the *barbeau* (barbel) and game comes from the forests, even the humbler kind, such as

1 *Dordogne*, (MacDonald, 1981).

hare and rabbit, being more than mere country fare when truffles go into the recipe. Goose is seldom served roasted, as it might be elsewhere, but is much used for *confit d'oie*, the method whereby it is cooked and preserved in its own fat and juices, to provide a delicacy for winter. *Confit de canard, confit de dinde* and *confit de porc* are other forms of this type of preserve. *Confit d'oie à la sarladaise* is accompanied by potatoes and truffles fried in the goose fat. Chicken may often be served with truffles, and *boudin blanc* (*see p.102*) may also contain them. *Pintade* (guinea-fowl) may be stuffed with truffles, so may partridges, quails, and *cochon de lait* (sucking pig); vegetables accompanying a meat or poultry dish may also contain truffles, cooked with potatoes, onions and tomatoes in goose dripping.

There is plenty of fruit and the local markets are picturesque with a variety of cherries, greengages, peaches, pears, plums and strawberries in season. Table grapes, especially the Chasselas Doré, are prized and in September there is a *Semaine du Chasselas*, or fair, celebrating the crop.

Sweet dishes tend to be cakes and buns: the *fougasse* is a large, light, rich bun; *jacques* are apple pancakes; *pascades* are Rouergue pancakes that may be made with walnut oil; *milleflasses* are flaky pastry cakes made with corn meal; *mique* is a type of dumpling of corn meal and wheat flour, sometimes served with a stew, but also

---

At about ten o'clock the big bell that hangs outside the château is rung, and the mowers, dropping their scythes, leave the field and troop into the great kitchen, which has changed so little for centuries. . . . Richard Coeur-de-Lion, when campaigning in Guyenne, may have sat down many a time to such a table as this . . . with the exception of the coffee and rum. Let us take a look into the great caldrons. . . . One contains two full-sized turkeys and several fouls, another a leg of pork, and a third a considerable portion of a calf. Then there is a caldron of soup, made very 'thick and slab'. Home-baked loaves, round like trenchers, and weighing 10 lb. each, are on the side table, together with an immense bowl of salad and a regiment of bottles filled with the wine newly drawn from the cask.

EDWARD HARRISON BARKER, *Two Summers in Guyenne*, 1894

---

being a sweet cake when made with sugar. There are candied walnuts and sweets made of chestnut flour, as there are many sweet-chestnut trees in the region and chestnut flour is sometimes referred to as *pain des paysans*.

Specialities and Dishes

Truffles can be incorporated in salads, stuffings and scrambled eggs, when they give the dish the name *brouillade Périgourdine*. The most famous presentation is when they are served whole, lightly seasoned and sprinkled with brandy, then being wrapped in a layer of dough or salt pork and cooked *sous la cendre* (in the ashes of the fire — like baked potatoes). Sometimes *foie gras* is put in as well. The dish is very rich indeed and those who are making its acquaintance may find it advisable to share one truffle and, certainly, to choose a plain menu otherwise. *Tourte de truffes* is a hot tart of truffles and *foie gras*; *truffes en pâté* are truffles enveloped in *foie gras* and baked in a crust, a small-scale version of the *sous la cendre* dish.

Anguilles au verjus are eels, grilled and sprinkled with the *verjus* — the juice of unripe grapes — but I have never sampled this dish.

Cou farci is goose-neck, stuffed with pork, truffles and *foie gras*.

Pommes sarladaise is a potato pie, baked with truffles.

Crispés de Montignac are egg croquettes with tomato sauce.

Enchaud Périgourdin is roast rolled pork fillet.

Purée aux marrons is a combination of sweet-chestnuts, potatoes and herbs, served on a *croûton*.

Sabronade is a soup made with vegetables, pork, ham and so thick that it is really more like a stew.

Tripou Rouergat is lambs' tripe, baked in a caul.

Gougeas de Quercy are small baked pumpkin puddings.

Friands de Bergerac are sweetened potato-cakes.

Tourteaux are pancakes made with maize flour.

Drinks

Various nut liqueurs are made and the home-made versions may be offered in small country restaurants. *Eau de noix* is a type of walnut brandy, *crème de noix* is a sweet liqueur. *Mesclou* is *eau-de-vie-de-prune* and *liqueur de noix* combined.

There are a number of wines, some of them now becoming widely known, thanks to improved methods of making and keeping. The Bergerac region, touching that of Bordeaux, has long been famous for Monbazillac, wine traditionally made subject to the action of *'pourriture noble'* (*see p.140*). The wines of the regions of Castillon, the Côtes de Duras, the Bazadais and the Marmandais also come into lists, because they, too, are near at hand and even get exported. The same applies to Montravel and Pécharmant, which makes both white and red wines and sometimes sparkling wines. Bergerac wines are now exported and the dry whites are very pleasant, some red also being made; the wines of Gaillac are mostly white and range between dry to sweetish, with some *pétillant* wine being made.

The wine of Cahors, however, is even more interesting. The red wine — past writers refer to the white, but I have never found any of quality — used to be known as 'black wine' because its deep colour and full character made it very useful for blending with the lighter wines of Bordeaux in unsatisfactory years when the wines of the 'high country' or hinterland of Bordeaux were sent down to the port. Many have praised the black wine, including Rabelais (though one suspects he would have praised anything drinkable that someone else had paid for), and the eighteenth-century English writer, Arthur Young.

Only a small proportion of the formerly extensive vineyard is producing today. The Malbec vines, often extremely old, make a profound, firm but almost gentle wine; when made according to traditional methods, the wine stays in cask until it is thought to be ready for bottling and this, astonishing though it may seem, does not result in it becoming oxidised or even weakened. If I had not been able to sample such wines, thanks to a grower whose family have made wine here for over a thousand years, it would have been difficult to believe this, but I shared the experience with several qualified members of the wine trade. Unfortunately, Cahors has of late years become somewhat chic — well-known politicians and 'personalities' having country houses in the area, so that the true 'black wine' is rare these days. Do not be misled by very fancy labels, which sometimes are put on to very ordinary, albeit adequate, red wines made according to contemporary methods. The 'real thing' is worth paying for — if it can be found.

Things to See and Do

Museums the gastronomic tourist may find of interest include the one at Agen, where there are fine examples of Palissy ware and other china; the regional museum and the Musée du Tabac (the only one of its kind) in the Hôtel de Ville at Bergerac; the Musée Ernest Rupin at Brive-la-Gaillarde, where the folklore and industry of the region are the themes, and the Musée Municipal at Cahors which has rooms devoted to local history and personalities. Regional china and furniture and a reconstruction of a Bas Quercy kitchen are in the Musée Moissagais at Moissac; at Toulouse, the Musée Saint Raymond has collections of china and bronze ware and the Musée Paul Dupuy has examples of Languedoc popular art.

The kitchens and dining-rooms may be seen at the Manoir d'Autoire, at Autoire, a small house furnished entirely as it was in the eighteenth and nineteenth centuries; also at Azay-le-Ferron, where the château has collections of china and a fine dining-room. At Brantôme, the Abbaye de Brantôme is open to visitors, who can see the refectory, bakehouses and the cellar of the ancient foundation. The Château de Lanquais has a good dining-room and old kitchen; the large dining-room in the Château de Meillant is worth seeing; at the Abbaye de Noirlac visitors can see the twelfth-century refectory and cellar; the Château de Biron, dating from the sixteenth century, has what is supposed to be the largest castle kitchen in France.

Montaigne preserves the tower of the great essayist, although the castle itself is a reconstruction made in the last century after the buildings were destroyed by fire. Visitors should apply to the owners for permission to see the apartments, which are of great interest. Montaigne was quite gastronomically inclined, preferring bread made without salt in the dough, being greedy about fish and liking melons more than other fruit.

Franche Comté and the Jura

Some writers describe Franche Comté as 'the lowlands of the Jura', but even the peaks of rock that rise about the numerous winding streams seem quite high. In general, this is a varied, unspoiled and — for many — an unknown mountainous region. The forests are extremely beautiful, notably the Forêt de Joux, and the area is ideal for a quiet holiday. The food is good and, unless you stay in a luxury hotel, not elaborate; the cheeses and the wines are particularly interesting. The ingredients are generally first-rate.

At one time Franche Comté belonged to the Duchy of Burgundy, then to the Holy Roman Empire. It was briefly Spanish from 1556 – 1598 and subsequently became the property of Austria, only finally becoming French after numerous campaigns and pockets of resistance in 1674. Spanish influence seems to have made some gastronomic impact and this, the 'Free county' — as its name asserts — may rightly claim to have introduced sweet-corn to the US, by Comtois settlers who went there, plus their traditions, two and a half centuries ago. The region enjoyed a certain special prosperity because of its salt deposits; before salt became plentiful and cheap, it was of great importance as a preservative as well as a seasoning and the tax imposed on it — the *gabelle* — was both oppressive and, to those benefiting, a large source of revenue.

Food in General

The high pastures are good grazing and both the dairy products and meat are of fine quality. As in other mountain regions, pork is plentiful, ranging from the *cochonnailles* (assorted cold cuts) of an *hors d'oeuvre*, to the *jambon droz*, a type of smoked ham, cured and prepared in a local way, and the *Jésu de Morteau*, a large smoked sausage, flavoured with aniseed. *Brési* is smoked beef, which is sometimes added to a stew, and *langues fourrées* (stuffed tongues) are a Besançon speciality. Soups can also be unusual: frogs are used in some, although I have never tried these, and cherries are also utilized in this way — it is a great cherry district and, in the springtime, the blossom is breathtakingly beautiful. There are many different types of mushrooms incorporated in the local dishes of both fish and meat: *cèpes, mousserons, oranges, morilles, bolets, craterelles, lépiotes, russules, chanterelles* and *jaunottes (see p.56)*.

This is a popular fishing area and the streams and rivers provide an abundance of fish for the table: trout, carp, salmon and *brochet* (pike), which is often served with the Sauce Nantua named for the town on the edge of the lake of the same name. A *gratin de queues d'écrevisses* (gratin of crayfish tails) is another speciality.

Chevreau (kid) and even *écureuil* (squirrel) are also local foods, but although some gastronomic guides mention bear, I have never seen this on menus — probably, as in the Pyrenees, it has not existed for many years.

Cheese is an ingredient in many recipes and there is a local type of fondue or melted cheese 'dip'.

Sweet dishes are numerous, many of them originating in the religious establishments of the area. Two houses, each requiring an impressive number of 'quarterings' on the coats of arms of the inmates, were at Baume-les-Dames and Baume-les-Messieurs — the names indicating the nobility of those forming the community; royalty and the nobility tended to use these establishments rather like luxury hotels, putting up there with their suites for a refreshing break. Some of the sweetmeats invented by the cooks to please noble ladies in retirement include: *Craquelins des Chanoinesses de Baume-les-Dames; gaufres* (wafers, somewhat akin to today's waffles); *pets de nonne* (literally 'nun's farts', little doughnuts, like fritters), all of them from Baume-les-Dames. *Pain d'oeuf au caramel*, a superlative version of *crème caramel*, came from the Abbey of Château Chalon. *Galette de goumeau* is an open tart filled with a mixture of cream and egg; *flan au fromage* is a shortcrust case filled with cheese and eggs, similar to a quiche; *unchères* are little tartlets flavoured with lemon and vanilla; *sèches* are small, biscuity cakes; *ronçon aux cérises*, a speciality of Montbéliard, is a moulded baked pudding, composed of eggs, crumbs soaked in milk, with sugar and cherries. Various *beignets* (fritters) are found, including one made with acacia flowers, also quince and apple jelly and a variety of jams and biscuits.

Specialities and Dishes

Les gaudes: A type of cornmeal porridge or thick soup, which is a real country recipe, unlikely to feature on the menus of smart hotels.

La Craiche: This is the melted butter which rises and is skimmed off *Les gaudes* — often served on toast. Another very homely dish.

Croustade, Croûte Comtois, Croûte Jurassienne: This is toasted cheese, plus onion and chopped bacon.

Féchum, Féchun: This is cabbage, stuffed with bacon, vegetables and, sometimes, eggs, either served by itself or with boiled beef. The name recalls the Provençal 'Fassum'. It is a speciality of Montbéliard.

Les rôts: Grilled maize (sweetcorn).

La panade: A type of bread broth.

Matefaim: A thick pancake, supposed to be of Spanish origin.

La flamusse: A maize dough.

The next day . . . they were to pass the boundaries of the Côte d'Or, and to enter the Department of the Jura. . . . A most superb breakfast, consisting of mutton cutlets, an excellent ham, French beans, and an extraordinary woodcock, hung to an hour, roasted to a minute, and served on toast in the most approved manner, was the only circumstance connected with the village at Genlis which left any impression on the minds of our Englishmen.

CHARLES ALSTON COLLINS, *A Cruise upon Wheels, the chronicle of some autumn wanderings along the deserted post-roads of France*, 1862

La meurette: A stew of freshwater fish. Red instead of the more usual white wine is used for a *meurette*. The dish is also found in Burgundy.

Quenelles de brochet: Fishballs made with pounded pike (*brochet*) and often served with a Sauce Nantua. These, too, are often featured as a speciality of Burgundy and of the Champagne region and are regarded as the test of a chef — they should be very light and delicate. They are, however, very rich.

Drinks

Many fruit brandies — *alcools blancs* and liqueurs — are made, as in Alsace. *Kirsch* (cherry), *mirabelle* (from the *mirabelle* plum), *prunelle* (sloe), *gentiane* (gentian), the bitter liqueur of which the bright yellow Suze is a well-known brand, are all made in the region; also a curious drink made from fir-tree shoots, called Sapindor; this is rather strongly piney and is often put in a bottle looking like a chunk of pine-tree (*see p.178*). Macvin or Macquevin is a curious concoction, very much a family-made beverage, although there are commercial versions. It is white wine boiled up with brandy, sugar and spices. Hypocras, an old-fashioned red wine mixture, often served at christening parties in the country, is said to have been first made by Taillevent (q.v.) in the fourteenth century and it was certainly drunk throughout the Middle Ages, either as a type of aperitif (it was a version of aromatised wine, or even of vermouth) or at the end of a meal. Obviously, both these drinks are survivals of the time when old wine in cask might have become undrinkable without various additions to make it palatable, so that it was not wasted.

The wines of the Jura seem to have been famous since Roman times and certainly the vineyards were cultivated by the religious houses. Henri IV used Jura wines as presents to friends — even by way of making up quarrels. The Emperor Maximilian admired them to the extent of granting them tax free entry to all his lands in 1493. Celebrities such as Rousseau, Voltaire and Alexandre Dumas all enjoyed them. Prince Metternich, that wily statesman, ingratiating himself with Napoleon I, remarked, when the Emperor complimented him on his estate of Schloss Johannisberg, that there was a finer wine in France — Château Chalon; he was not being insincere, because his family had been buying quantities of it since 1780.

The proudest part of the history of Jura wines, however, is the work of Louis Pasteur (1822 –1895), who was born at Dôle and grew up in Arbois. Although he does not seem to have been especially interested in food and drink (his usual lunch consisted of a lamb cutlet or chop with chips, or, occasionally, a sausage with red beans), he would have been familiar with the curious phenomenon 'the veil', forming on the surface of certain Jura wines; this, unique in France to the region certainly contributed to his discovery of the action of bacteria, for this is what it is. (*See p.27.*)

Red, white and *rosé* wines are made, the latter sometimes being referred to as *vins gris* (grey wines), because of their pale, almost lilac tone. Some sparkling wine is made by the Champagne method, but the much publicized *'vin fou'* or mad wine is made by bottling either the white or *rosé* wine at the peak of its first fermentation, thereby conserving the fizziness in the bottle. The Henri Maire establishment owns the largest single vineyard in the Jura, that of Françoise de Montfort, which makes a *rosé* wine; but visitors should also try to sample the wines of other makers, notably those of Jean Boordy.

Some of the grapes used for Jura wines are unfamiliar: the red wines are made from the Poulsard and Trousseau, also the Pinot Noir, the whites from the Melon, a type of Chardonnay. The Poulsard is sometimes referred to as the *'Plante d'Arbois'* and makes wines described as being *pelure d'oignon* (onion-skin) in colour, because they are pinkish-tawny-brown. (This term is also often used for the south of France *rosés*.)

Two extraordinary wines are the *vins jaune* and *vins de paille*. It has been suggested that, during the occupation of Franche Comté by Spain, the abbess of one of the convents brought in and planted vines from the sherry region to make these 'straw' and 'yellow' wines. Certainly they do have certain traits in common with sherry.

Vins jaunes are made solely from the Sauvignon grape. Like sherry, they are left in cask, in cool cellars, for at least six years, during which time they cannot be topped up. During this time a covering of a fuzzy whitish stuff forms on the wine's surface — this is *'le voile'* or the veil, similar to the bacteria that forms on the surface of a fine sherry (*Mycoderma vini*). The yellow wines that result after this lengthy maturation in cask do in fact taste a little like sherry, although they are 'light' wines, as they are not fortified in any way. Those coming from the Château Chalon region are considered the finest (this is an area, not a single vineyard or estate). To be granted the A.C. Château Chalon the *vins jaunes* must attain a minimum strength of 12 per cent; the other yellow wines are required to reach 11 per cent. Château Chalon wines are put into a dumpy bottle, known as a *clavelin*. Neither they nor any *vins jaunes* are ever cheap. They can be drunk by way of aperitif or with certain first courses and, in the region, will be served throughout a meal, though their rather assertive flavour may not be to the taste of everyone.

Vins de paille (straw wines) are made from the Poulsard and Trousseau grapes and get their name because the grapes are dried after being picked, sometimes being laid out on straw mats (again like sherry) or, occasionally, hung up on racks. The grapes shrivel to raisin-like blobs, containing a little very sweet juice. They are not pressed until the February after the vintage in the autumn of the previous year and the fermentation process takes a long time, because of the high sugar content of the *must* (the unfermented grape-juice). They too remain in cask for many years, sometimes for as long as ten, prior to being bottled. The A.O.C. regulations require them to attain 15 per cent of alcohol by volume, which is why they are not often seen in export markets, as wines of this strength pay higher duty. As a certain amount of sugar remains in the wine, it is not usual to drink a *vin de paille* throughout a meal, though it is agreeable with fruit or postprandially. Although, like the *vins jaunes*, *vins de paille* are white wines, some suppose their name to derive from their colour. Their fragrance is marked. L'Étoile is the name of another region, where white wines, *vins de paille* and *vins jaunes* are made. The white wines are pleasant accompaniments to fish.

It is said of the Arbois wines that '*Plus on en bois, plus on se tient droit*' — the more you drink, the more you stand up straight, implying that they do not affect the drinker much. However, there is another saying:

> '*Le bon vin d'Arbois*
> *Dont on ne boit*
> *Qu'un verre à la fois.*'

(The good wine of Arbois — of which one takes only one glass at a time.)

Wines of the Côtes du Jura include the following: Pupillon, Montigny-les-Arsures, Ménétru-le-Vignoble, Quintigny, Césancy, Saint-Laurent-la-Roche and Château d'Arlay. They are not often seen on export lists nor, indeed, in other regions of France, so that they should certainly be tried by anyone visiting the region. The *vin de pays* of the area is 'Franche-Comté (Jura)'.

On the first Sunday of September the *Fête de Biou* is held in

270

Arbois at the time of the vintage. A huge bunch of grapes — the *biou* — is carried in procession to the church and, after the service, hung up as an offering to St Just, the patron of Arbois. On the last Sunday of July there is usually a sale and exhibition of Jura wines in Arbois, plus a procession and general merrymaking.

Things to See and Do

Arbois: the house where Pasteur grew up, furnished as it then was, may be seen, also his laboratory. Pasteur's vineyard, still making wine, is 4 km. outside Arbois; he bought the property in 1874 and it was here that his great work on fermentation was begun in 1878. The Musée Sarret de Grozon contains furniture, china and the reconstruction of a nineteenth-century room — all background to Pasteur. In the centre of Arbois, the Henri Maire establishment is open to visitors.

> Narrow, noisy, shabby, belittered and encumbered, fulled with chatter and clatter the Hôtel de France.... The landlord sat at supper with sundry friends in a kind of glass cage ... the waiters tumbled over the loose luggage in the hall; the travellers who had been turned away leaned gloomily against door-posts; and the landlady ... bandied high-voiced compliments with voyageurs de commerce. At ten in the morning there was a table d'hôte for breakfast — a wonderful repast, which overflowed into every room and pervaded the whole establishment.... It was very hot and there were swarms of flies; the viands had the strongest odour; there was in particular a horrible mixture known as gras-double, a light grey, glutinous, nauseating mess, which my companions devoured in large quantities.
>
> HENRY JAMES, *A Little Tour in France*, 1882

Arc-et-Senans: The Saline Royale de Chaux, the royal salt works, where a whole town was planned around the salt production in the eighteenth century, may be seen.

Baume-les-Messieurs: The eleventh-century cellar of the abbey is open to visitors.

Dole: The house where Pasteur was born, in the Rue des Tanneurs, has been made into a museum.

Lons-le-Saunier: The eighteenth-century Hôpital, with pharmacy and kitchen fully equipped, is open to visitors.

Montbenoît: The kitchen in the fifteenth-century abbey is open to visitors.

Pérouges: The entire town (named for Perugia in Italy) has been carefully restored to give an impression of what it was like in the sixteenth century. Innumerable historical films have been shot here. The shops of various tradesmen and craftsmen are on show, a wine press of the type known as à l'écureuil (squirrel press), like a treadmill, operated by men walking round a wheel to turn it, is on view. The village inn is now a restaurant, with a luxury hotel attached.

Poligny: The seventeenth-century Hôtel Dieu is not usually open to visitors, but if application is made to the nuns, the pharmacy, vaulted kitchen, and the refectory may be seen.

Salins-les-Bains: The saltworks are open to visitors. In the seventeenth-century Hôtel Dieu there is a fine collection of jars and equipment in the pharmacy.

26

The Île de France

Many books have been devoted to eating in Paris, but a capital city must inevitably be a mixture of gastronomy from many regions. Here, then, are some regional specialities and things to see, with a little gastronomic background. For shopping and dining, there are many other guides available.

Food in General

The great markets, Les Halles, have now been moved to Rungis where, although they are perhaps not as picturesque, they are certainly more convenient for those dealing with them. The most spectacular displays are probably those of vegetables, which are rushed to the markets from outside the city to supply the *primeurs* or first crop of things as they come into season and are eagerly featured on menus. Asparagus comes from Argenteuil, Laon and Lauris; peas from Clamart; beans from Arpajon; carrots from Crécy; lettuce from Versailles. There are plenty of mushroom caves around Paris, producing *champignons de Paris* (the white, button type) and in the surrounding woods there are *morilles* as well as field mushrooms. Potatoes are plentiful and the term 'Parisienne' applied to a dish may mean that potatoes are included, not necessarily that they will be cooked in the tiny ball shapes with which the adjective is also associated. The surrounding countryside is able to supply fish of various kinds from the rivers, the Loing being known for its *brochet* (pike); the *matelote*, a type of fish stew, is said to have been first made in Paris. Game comes from the various forests that were once the hunting grounds of royalty and the nobility.

In the middle of the sixteenth century François I sent for a grower from Cahors to start a royal vineyard at Fontainebleau. It is possible, too, that this was an early instance of grapes being grown specifically for the table, not merely for wine. The *Treille du Roi* (King's trellis) in the park of Fontainebleau is a huge Chasselas vine, supposed to have been established in 1730; the grapes are sold off annually by auction. There were certainly vineyards on the Left Bank in the Middle Ages, the Montagne Sainte-Geneviève apparently being covered with them, although they were progressively built over to accommodate lodgings for the students in the twelfth century. Vintage celebrations are depicted in various works of art. The wines best k nown were Argenteuil, Auteuil, Nanterre, Bagneux, La Courtille and Montmartre. Some traces of certain of these survived until this century and one writer affirms that the Bagneux was vintaged until 1957 and that some Suresnes and Montmartre exist still. But they must be more in the nature of ornamental vines rather than significant producers of wine. There is a centre of grape cultivation at Thomery, with an estimated extent of over a hundred miles of trellises for growing the fruit. Table grapes are kept by putting the stems in water after the bunches have been cut; this was an invention of a vine grower called Lapenteur who, in 1848, gathered such magnificent Chasselas grapes from his vines that he vowed to offer them to St Vincent, patron of vine growers, whose feast is celebrated on 22 January. By putting the cut stems in water, Lapenteur was able to fulfil his vow.

Some Dishes

Potage St Germain is a thickish pea soup — although it was actually first supposed to have been made at St Cloud. But a gastronomic dictionary says that it is the invention of a Comte de Saint-Germain, who was struck by the delicious taste of *petits pois* during a visit he paid to Copenhagen; dissatisfied with his life in France, he went to live in Sweden, where he concentrated on making his cooking famous.

Sauce béarnaise seems to have been invented at the Pavillon Henri IV at Saint Germain; as it is made with egg-yolks, tarragon, vinegar, white wine and shallots, it may well be somehow related to Bayonnaise or, even, mayonnaise (*see p.27*). Sauce Robert is an onion and mustard sauce. Sauce gribiche is a vinaigrette with chopped hard-boiled egg in it, although some books give it as a type of tarragon mayonnaise. Sauce ravigote is another type of vinaigrette, plus chopped herbs, anchovies, and pickled cucumbers or gherkins. These sauces are supposed to have been perfected in Paris, even if they were first made elsewhere.

Sauce Bercy is a sauce made with white wine, meat gravy and shallots. It is named after the huge *entrepôt* in Paris Bercy, where all the wine comes in and is held in bond or kept until it is bottled. Anything described as 'Bercy' will relate to this and the dishes are usually substantial, suited to the workers of the area. Sauce marchand de vin is another Bercy speciality, but with the white wine in the sauce replaced by red wine. The term '*marchand de vin*' as applied to a steak, however, means usually that the meat is grilled with shallots and served with a bit of beef marrow on top — a way of cooking that might be done in a cellar or the *tonnellerie* (cooperage) for a worker's lunch, and there is no formal sauce except for a little red wine added to the meat juices.

Oeufs Bercy are eggs with pork sausages. *Entrecôte Bercy* is steak with watercress and Bercy sauce. *Foie de veau Bercy* is grilled calves' liver with Bercy sauce. *Merlans Bercy* is whiting with white wine, shallots and butter.

Haricot de mouton is a stew of mutton, turnips, potatoes and onions. There are not *haricots* (beans) in the dish, because this word derives from '*halicot*', an archaic term meaning a stew. *Miroton de boeuf* is boiled beef with onion sauce.

Crème Chantilly is sweetened whipped cream.

Gâteau Saint Honoré is a rich, elaborate creamy dessert cake.

Various dishes either first made by or becoming the speciality of great chefs or famous restaurants of the past also bear their names, such as Marguéry, Dugléré and so on.

Things to See and Do

To see Paris Bercy it is necessary to have an introduction to one of the huge wholesale wine establishments, who blend and market *vins de consommation courants* as well as handling bottles of fine wines.

Museums with special displays for the gastronomically minded include the Musée des Arts et Traditions Populaires, in the Palais de Chaillot. The Musée Carnavalet, 23 rue de Sévigné, is the Marquise de Sévigné's house, now housing a collection relating to the history of Paris and Paris life over four centuries; the Musée de Cluny, 5 rue Paul Painlevé, has a showing of medieval arts and crafts; the Musée des Archives Nationales, Hotel de Soubise, 60 rue des Francs Bourgeois, is the museum of the history of France. Among other treasures, it has a letter from Parmentier, suggesting the possibilities and advantages of potato cultivation. In the Musée de la Conciergerie, 19 quai de l'Horloge, there are the kitchens of Saint Louis. At Coulommiers in the Musée Municipal there is a folklore section.

Chantilly was the place where the unfortunate Vatel, supervising the reception of Louis XIV and his court, who were guests of Condé, found, after twelve sleepless nights involved with preparing the feast, that, on the first evening, the roast had ran out. (There were sixty tables, with eighty people at each.) The next morning news came that the fish had not arrived, at which Vatel rushed up to his room and fell on his sword — and almost immediately afterwards the fish was delivered. Culinary historians have been somewhat harsh to Vatel, describing him as more of a caterer than a cook; a true chef, they say, would have invented something marvellous and novel in such a crisis, turning disaster into triumph. However, it was while he was chef at the great Fouquet's house that Vatel evolved Crème Chantilly.

Rosny-sur-Seine is where the Duc de Sully ordered the great horticulturalist Olivier de Serres to lay out the nursery garden, including 8,000 mulberry canes. Serres (whose name appropriately means 'Olive tree of greenhouses' — he gave his name to the word *serre*, which is greenhouse), was born in 1539, in Pradel in the Vivarais and, rather unusually for a nobleman, devoted himself to agriculture. It was Serres who pronounced the famous phrase: 'Tilling and pasturing are the two nipples of France'. His book on agriculture, dedicated to Henri IV, was reprinted six times and included numerous recipes for all sorts of dishes, sweets and preserves; he concerned himself with the growing of rice, then newly imported from Italy, hops, from the north, experimented with silkworms, the process of incubating eggs as practised by the Chinese and advocated growing beet and potatoes — although it was only in Alsace that the tuber became a staple, the French finding it lacking in chic when the King was said not to care for it.

At Saint Germain-en-Laye *pommes soufflés* were created by accident when the first rail service from Paris was being inaugurated. The train was late and the chef had to take the potatoes he was frying out of the fat, later flinging them back to be finished, at which they all puffed up and a new dish was born.

Villers Cotterets is where Alexandre Dumas was born and spent his youth and the museum there that bears his name is naturally of interest. As mentioned earlier, he hoped to be remembered more for his *Dictionnaire de Cuisine* than for all his other bestsellers.

At Rambouillet, Marie Antoinette's dairy is open to visitors.

The thirteenth-century refectory and kitchens of the Abbaye de Royaumont are on view.

There are various fairs devoted to certain foods: at Arpajon, a market gardening centre, a *Foire aux Haricots* is held in September. The special type of bean grown there is called *chevrier*, after the man who evolved it in 1878. A *Foire au Pain d'Épice* is held after Easter in the Avenue de Trône, Place de la Nation, Cours de Vincennes. A *Foire aux Jambons* is held from the evening of Palm Sunday until Easter Day in the Boulevard Richard Lenoir (home of Simenon's Inspector Maigret), rather oddly, as the period includes Holy Week, but the fair has been held since 1222.

The cold is almost insupportable! Parisians are so accustomed to their horrible climate, that Madame Barraud cannot understand my feeling it, and I have great difficulty in getting even the one little fire we have, and am occupied all day in shutting the doors, which every one else makes a point of leaving open. . . . Though she will give me fifty times more food than I wish, nothing on earth would induce her to light the fire in my bedroom. . . . She hangs up the chicken or goose for the next day's dinner in the little passage leading to my room, and in the middle of the night I hear stealthy footsteps, and a murmur of 'Oh, qu'il est gras! Oh qu'il sera délicieux!' as she pats it and feels it all over.

AUGUSTUS HARE, *The Years with Mother*, George Allen, 1896

27

Languedoc and the Tarn

The food of this very varied region is robust rather than delicate —
life has been hard here and the locals have needed sustaining fare.
In the Mediterranean hinterland of the area the food is supposed to
show the influences of both the Romans and the Arabs: the
various bean recipes may be due to the former, the many sweet
things and pastries to the latter. A considerable spice trade passed
through Montpellier from quite early times, influencing various
recipes; the large Spanish colony in Toulouse makes the cooking
of many restaurants here and in the surrounding country unlike
that of other French towns — and, here again, the influence of the
former Kingdom of Catalunya, which straddled the French-
Spanish eastern border, is strong — the beans and sausages have
spread from the area around Barcelona up the coast. Clive of India
(1725–1774) gave at least one recipe to the region, and another
Englishman, Harmsworth, was responsible for the development of
one of the best-known French mineral waters (*see p.192*). Now that
the salty pastures of the Camargue (which is, strictly, in Provence)
are being developed for crops (and even vines), the large-scale
growing of rice is causing many dishes to be made using this
cereal, sometimes in recipes that have obviously been brought in
from Italy.

Food in General

The cooking medium is oil, pork fat is also used in the mountains. Garlic features in many dishes. In the mountain streams trout, eels, shad (*alose*) and many freshwater fish, including crayfish (*écrevisses*) are found, and one local recipe I have not noted anywhere else is a chicken cooked with these small crayfish (*poulet aux écrevisses*). On the coast there are the little octopus (*poulpes*) and cuttlefish (*seiches*), as well as the usual Mediterranean fish. Snails are abundant (*see p.280*).

On the *causses*, the high, barren pastures of the Tarn, thrushes (*grives*) are plentiful, also small game birds, including quails (*cailles*). The flavour that the juniper and thyme of the stony moorland (*garrigue*) gives to their flesh makes them especially succulent, likewise any dishes with hare (*lièvre*).

The forests yield *pignons* (pine nuts), which are sometimes served with trout instead of the more usual almonds, but they can also form part of a sweet dish, such as an omelette. Chestnuts (*châtaignes*) are sometimes served in the Cévennes as a vegetable, in a purée. Artichokes and truffles are among other vegetables found locally. Nîmes olives are highly esteemed, likewise their oil, and there is plenty of fruit.

Pork dishes are common: *fritton d'Albi* is a type of pork brawn; *salaisens de Corbières* are a variety of sausage; there is the *saucisse d'Arduze*, which may be grilled or put into a stew, and the raw ham of Saint Gaudens is famous.

Among the sweet dishes are the *gratin de Vivarais* (although this area is more truly in the Rhône Valley), a dish that may be described as a type of pumpkin meringue pie. Carcassonne is known for *marrons glacés* (candied sweet-chestnuts), Toulouse for *violettes pralinées* (candied violets), and Narbonne for honey. Jams include *confiture de figues* (figs), also of *pastèque* (water melon). *Touron Languedocien* is a type of soft nougat, a speciality of both Limoux and Carcassonne. *Biscotins*, small hard biscuits, are a speciality of Montpellier; *réglisse* (liquorice) is made in Uzès and Bragnols-sur-Cèze; bonbons called *minervas* (after Goddess Minerva) are special to Nîmes; *flaunes de Lodève* are light-textured buns, made with ewe's milk cheese (those are very much a Mediterranean recipe, often made particularly at Easter), and the *fouasses* of Millau are sweet pastries.

Specialities and Dishes

Cassoulet: This is one of the famous dishes of the south-east. It is named for the *cassole*, the archaic term for the local cooking-pot (such as you can still sometimes buy in the markets). Ideally, the *cassoulet* should go on cooking for ever — Anatole France (1844–1924) once wrote that the *cassoulet* in his favourite Paris restaurant had been on the stove for twenty years, refreshed from time to time — that was when fuel was cheap. Prosper Montagné commented irreverently that *cassoulet* was the god of the west, God the Father was the *cassoulet* of Castelnaudary, God the Son of Carcassonne, God the Holy Spirit that of Toulouse. Locals fiercely debate the qualities of their specific recipes, but essentially the dish consists of white beans and pork, plus sausage, the 'crust' being broken up and, according to tradition, stirred in seven times. The Toulouse *cassoulet* usually contains bacon, sausage, *confit d'oie* (preserved goose in fat); the *cassoulet* of Carcassonne contains mutton and partridges if available; the *cassoulet* of Castelnaudary — supposedly the most ancient recipe — only makes use of pork. *Cassoulet*, however it is made, is a very substantial dish.

Sometimes snails are featured on menus as '*rapides*' in a facetious way. Usually they are poached in a *court-bouillon*, but the accompanying butter or sauce is capable of many variations: *Li cagaraulo à l'ailloli* (in Provençal) makes use of the garlic mayonnaise — *aioli* — of Provence. *Escargots au beurre de Montpellier* means that they are served with butter, plus lettuce, herbs and pounded anchovies and gherkins. *Escargots à la Languedocienne* means that the sauce is based on goose dripping, flavoured with ham, garlic, saffron and herbs. *Escargots à la Lodévoise* has a sauce made with onions, garlic, herbs, egg-yolks and walnuts. *Escargots à la Narbonnaise* are served with a mayonnaise mixed with milk and pounded almonds. *Escargots à la Nîmoise* has a sauce of ham, herbs, garlic, some vegetables and pounded anchovies. *Escargots à la Gayouparde* are served with a sauce containing diced ham, which has been browned in walnut or olive oil, plus garlic, pounded green walnuts and parsley. *Escargots à la Sommièroise* — Sommières is near to Nîmes — are served with a *court-bouillon* that has been cooked with orange peel, to which chopped bacon, pounded anchovies, walnuts and garlic are added, the whole accompanied by spinach.

Other Dishes

Grives à la Cévenole are roasted thrushes, served on *croûtons*, plus a sauce made with the wine of Frontignan (*see p.282*).

Ouillade or *oulade* is a soup, made with beans and cabbage, first cooked separately, mixed only before serving. The name *oulade* is used in the Cévennes, where the soup will contain potatoes and, possibly, sausage. The *Aigo bouillado* soup of the Basses Cévennes also contains garlic.

Montairel is a recipe from the Rouergue and is a chicken boiled with a *saffron bouillon*. *Alicot* or *Alicuit* is another Rouergue dish, consisting of the leftovers of either duck or goose, served with *cèpes* and chestnuts. Do not confuse it with the local cheese, Aligot (*see p.67*). *Sauce aux briques* is a stew, made with sausages, *boudin noir* and a *confit* (preserve) of either goose or poultry, cooked with garlic, tomatoes, peppers and herbs. *Les manouils* is a ham dish, the meat being mixed with garlic and herbs, then rolled up in tripe and cooked in a *pot-au-feu*. *Le gras double* is a speciality of Albi — a soup made with tripe, ham, vegetables, garlic and herbs. *Anchoïade* is the sort of cocktail snack now often served in smart restaurants — fresh anchovies fried after being soaked in milk, together with onions, garlic and bay, served hot with diced onion.

Brandade is a dish which you either love or cannot like: dried salt cod is made into a creamy mixture with milk, oil, garlic and lemon-juice. If well done it is delicious — if not, atrocious! It is a Nîmes speciality.

Fèche sec is pig's liver, lightly pickled, served hot or cold. I cannot tell what it is like, as I have never had it, but it could be slightly piquant and agreeably rich.

Fouace de gratillons salés are little hot tartlets, made with *gratons* or *grantillons*, scraps of fried bacon or smoked ham. They are usually served as an *hors d'oeuvre* or part of one.

Tripes de thon is another recipe I have never had — and nor will the ordinary travellers, unless they are either sailors or go on a boat-trip, for it is tunny, cooked in white wine with vegetables and herbs, plus a good dollop of seawater and sometimes *rhum* as well. It is a speciality of Palavas-les-Flots and of Agde.

Wines

The Hérault district is the biggest wine-producing region of France and, these days, many wines that would formerly have been sent to the great establishments making vermouth, or else be bought for incorporation into the various *vins de marques* (branded wines), are beginning to be sold as V.D.Q.S. or *vins de pays*, well worth trying when you are on the spot and many of them now becoming popular in export markets.

In the valley of the River Aude, the white wines of Limoux are made, the most famous being the Blanquette de Limoux, so called because the Mauzac grape, which is used for the finer wines, has a whitish underside to its leaves and therefore is known as 'Blanquette'. The sparkling wines are made by the Champagne method, but the locals are proud of the tradition that — in registered terms — enables them to call this *'le plus vieux brut du monde'*, as they are definite that the fizz was harnessed in the bottle by the use of cork from the nearby Catalan cork oak forests, before Dom Pérignon rediscovered its use for the vivacious wines of Champagne; there is also a suggestion that, as a young man, Pierre Pérignon may have worked in one of the Benedictine houses in this part of France or Spain. The Cave Co-operative at Limoux is open to visitors and there are various other establishments whose wines should certainly be sampled.

Several *vins doux naturels* (*see p.186*) are made in Languedoc-Roussillon and are other local drinks that should be tried; their slightly higher-than-table-wine strength makes them liable to 'heavy wine' duty in the UK, but they are well worth drinking on the spot and their slight sweetness can be most enjoyable. It is significant that the French have never believed in the foolish snobbery that somehow it is 'better' to 'drink dry', as witness the lines of the poet Géraldy:

> *Aujourd'hui, les Messieurs austères*
> *Boivent des vins secs en grognant;*
> *C'est un goût vient d'Angleterre . . .*
> *Le vin qui réchauffait Voltaire*
> *C'est le Muscat de Frontignan*

[These days, people of austere tastes drink dry wines — though under pressure. This is an English-founded fashion . . . The wine that cheered the heart of Voltaire was the Muscat of Frontignan.]

The best-known wines of this type include Muscat de Frontignan and Muscat de Minervois and, in the Roussillon, the Muscats of Rivesaltes, Maury and Banyuls. The Cave Co-operative at Maury is open to visitors.

Among other wines of the region are dry whites, Clairette de Languedoc, Clairette de Bellegarde, and the V.D.Q.S. Picpoul de Pinet, each named for the grapes that make them. The reds include the A.C.s Fitou, Collioure, Côtes du Rousillon and the V.D.Q.S. Corbières, Minvervois (now getting known abroad), Coteaux du Languedoc, St Chinian, St Georges d'Orques, Costières du Gard, La Clape and Quartourze and Pic St Loup. There are a great number of *vins de pays* and the Vin de Pays d'Oc — the old French 'oc' sound, meaning 'Yes' was used in the south, whereas the 'oil' sound, also meaning 'Yes', was the northern version — which became '*Oui*'; hence — Languedoc means 'the region of the "oc" tongue'. My personal taste tags on some of these wines are: a minerally dryness for those of the Tarn, an open-textured style for the Hérault, and a slightly 'buttery' fat flavour for the Aude.

Around Sète, and indeed in much of the huge wine region of the Hérault, the wines used to be bought up by the great vermouth firms, notably that of Noilly Prat, and sent to these establishments to be '*vermouté*'. Today, these wines are, thanks to modern know-how and improved methods of making, getting on to the market under their own names; the many kiosks along the road offer opportunities to try some. For vermouth, the Clairette, Picpoul and Muscat grapes are often used. At Marseillan the casks of wine are stored out of doors so as to be exposed to the sea air — about 10 per cent of each cask will evaporate during the two years or so of this maturation; then they go to Sète for blending and, eventually, to Marseille where, in the big installations, herbs and other spices, barks and peels are added and the vermouth is finally ready to go on sale. Many of the vermouth establishments are open to visitors, but it is wise to arrange in advance — through an introduction by a wine merchant if possible — should you wish to see the details of the production.

Things to See and Do

Albi: The Verrerie Ouvrière, founded in 1896, is one of the first factories to be managed by the employees. Visits to the glassworks may be made by appointment.
Alès: The Station Séricole concentrates on mulberry cultivation and the silk-worm — consequently it is closely connected with the work of Pasteur, whose researches saved the silk industry in the nineteenth century when pests attacked the mulberry plants.
Béziers: The Musée du Vieux Bitorrois et du Vin contains exhibits dealing with local history, the reconstruction of a room in a nineteenth-century inn and special exhibits relating to wine.
Frontignan: Many establishments offer tastings — but you may be expected to buy wine.

Mas Soubeyran: In the Musée du Désert the section in the Maison de Roland is exactly as it was in the seventeenth and eighteenth centuries, with a kitchen and all its equipment.

Montpellier: To refer to 'Montpellier' in a wine context signifies the great École d'Oenologie, not usually open to casual visitors, although if applications are made by serious students of wine they can generally be shown round; also view the École de Viticulture and the École National Supérieur Agronique. The old name for Montpellier was Monspistillarius — Mount of the Spice Merchants, and the medical properties of spices resulted in the foundation of a medical school (where Rabelais took his doctor's degree), which is now the university.

Pézenas: The speciality of this delightful old town are the *petits pâtés* and locals will say that they were invented by the chef of Lord Clive (Clive of India) who stayed nearby at the Château de Larsac in 1753, convalescing from his Indian campaigns. The Indian chef, visitors may be informed, used an Indian recipe — but in fact the *petits pâtés* are composed of mincemeat, made as it would have been in England at that time, from fresh meat, spices and peel, in a pastry crust, something like a variation on the traditional Banbury cake.

Roquefort-sur-Soulzon: The Société des Caves, where the world-famous cheese are matured, arrange visits but, for obvious reasons, these depend somewhat on the time of year, so inquiries should be made in advance.

Saint Guilhem-le-Desert: On the Thursday of Holy Week, pilgrims go in procession to the church where there is a relic of the True Cross. Each carries a snail-shell, tranformed into a minute oil-lamp, hence the name of the event *'La Procession des Escargots'* (The Snail Procession).

Sète: This odd, canal-divided town is one of the centres of the vermouth makers, many of whose establishments can be visited.

Vergèze: Fifteen miles from Nîmes, this is the site of the Perrier spring *(see p.192)*.

28

The Loire

The Loire is the longest river in France. Its tributaries — the Loir, the Vienne, the Creuse, the Indre, the Clain, the Cher and the Allier being only some of these, with the Maine and the Sèvre flowing into it in the Muscadet country — make up a varied landscape, with the foods and wines preserving their local style and traditions even today.

It is rather curious gastronomically. Anjou gave England the Plantagenet kings ('The Devil's brood' as St Bernard commented with some justification), Jeanne d'Arc came to Chinon to recognize the Dauphin and, from the time of the unification of France, the region was regularly visited by the various kings and queens, the royal mistresses and their surrounding courts. The royal households moved around from time to time and, as far as the Loire was concerned, the fact of the area being superb hunting country was a great attraction. Not only did the enormous households bring their cooks along with them, building gigantic kitchens in many of the places where they habitually stopped, but the influx of Italian artists and craftsmen, employed by the court and also hoping for the patronage of the nobility, further influenced gastronomy. There are many Loire dishes that seem to bear the stamp of feminine influence: Catherine de Medici, who brought her cooks with her when she came as a bride to marry Henry II, compounded lotions and comfits, possibly far more than the poisons with which her name is associated, in her secret cabinet at Chaumont; the great Duc de Guise was picking out sweetmeats from a comfit box when he was assassinated at Blois; Rousseau, tutor to the children of Madam Dupin, then owner of Chenonceaux in the eighteenth century, admitted to getting 'as fat as a monk, the cooking was so good'. Madame de Staël, able to go no nearer to Paris than Chaumont, under Napoleon's decree, entertained there. There are the writers — Rabelais with his almost non-stop feasts and *fouaces*; Proust with his famous madeleine, and many poets. . . .

The refinement of what may have started as ordinarily regional dishes was at least in part due to the frequent visits of extremely worldly people: the rich but not heavy pork and game dishes, the fish with their subtle sauces, the sweet things, the cakes, fruits and sweetmeats are, if one thinks about it, the sort of things that well-to-do and, usually, well-fed people enjoy eating when on holiday. The wines, in this sometimes chilly region, are sometimes a little shivery likewise, but light, charming, seemingly made to be drunk from elegant glasses or, for the more luscious, sipped from precious metal.

Anyone visiting the châteaux for which the region is so famous, may be able to picture a court lady or gentleman, stretching out a hand for a cake or some fruit, with a tall glass of a fragrant local wine at their elbow, in the embrasure of a window, overlooking a courtyard planned for displays of horsemanship, or in a gallery with a view of the river.

Much of this region is known as 'the garden of France' and indeed one of the *vins de pays* bears the title Jardin de la France. There are extensive nursery gardens, orchards and spectacular displays of flowers, especially roses. The religious establishments all have gardens, fish-ponds, as well as facilities for fishing in the rivers, and vineyard cultivation started early. Saint Martin of Tours, the Roman soldier who, accosted by a beggar, divided his military cloak with the man and, later, was told in a dream that it was Christ, became a Christian convert and, later, Bishop of Tours in the fourth century. He was not only active as a missionary, he instructed his monks in wine-growing and it is alleged that when the asses used by the brothers had nibbled the young vine shoots of a vineyard which, later, yielded superlatively, this was the origin of pruning. (But this cannot be true as Romans had known about it many centuries before.)

Saint Martin died at Candes, near Tours, in 397 and the locals wished to keep his body to attract pilgrims. But his disciples, knowing his wish to lie in the Abbey of Tours, passed Martin's corpse by night out of the window of the Candes church, so that it could be taken off by boat — the river flowed nearer the little church at this period. This was on 11 November and, as the little boat moved along the river, the trees on the banks are said to have

Regional glasses for sparkling Vouvray – the Vouvray motto is *'Je réjouis les cuers'* (I make hearts glad).

bowed down their branches and put forth foliage and the flowers to have broken into blossom — hence the origin of the expression 'Saint Martin's summer' for the period of fine sunny weather in autumn that can greatly assist the formation of the 'noble rot' on the sweeter wines. It is perhaps worth knowing also that, in some later pictorial representations of this saint, a goose is shown — because November is the time of year when the geese may migrate.

The pilgrim route to St James of Compostella (Santiago) brought many travellers to cross the Loire at different points and the great churches provided accommodation, as may be noted in some of the surviving buildings at Chartres, Orléans, Tours, Vendôme and Châtellerault. Royalty and the nobility had to be entertained there as well as in the castles and their comments have been treasured — possibly even improved on — ever since: Henri IV, *'le vert galant'*, is reported as praising the wine of Chavignol as the best he had ever drunk. Louis XIII, that rather sad king, is supposed to have enjoyed doing his own cooking when staying at Amboise, his speciality being an onion omelette. One would give much to know of any culinary quirks associated with Leonardo da Vinci, another of the Italians brought to the region to adorn it with works of art.

The way in which the French love royalty — especially the British — is indicated by the pride with which the people of Sancerre will tell you that it was their local 'crottin' cheeses that were included in the Coronation Banquet of Queen Elizabeth II.

Dishes of the region often bear names of specific localities, but these may not be obvious to the visitor as, for example, are 'Sancerrois' or 'Orléanais'. So here are some terms that may be seen on menus: La Beauce is the great plain around Chartres — from far away you can see the twin spires of the cathedral sticking up like horns. The Gâtinais is the region to the west of Montargis; the Sarthe is the area around La Flèche, along the river of the same name. The Perche-Gouët is between the Rivers Loire and Huisne; it is famous for apple-trees and, therefore, cider, but is perhaps best known for the huge dappled horses known as *percherons*. The Blésois is the region of Blois; Les Mauges the area south of the Loire, between Nantes and Anjou; the Véron is north of Chinon; the Vendée is south of Cholet. Poitou is the old province of pre-Revolution France, south of Thouars and Châtellerault; Maine is the old province around Laval and Le Mans, and Berry or Berri the former province south of Bourges; the nobles dominating all these were of impressive power.

Food in General

Fish, from the rivers and streams, are plentiful, varied and good. They include *carpe* (carp), *brochet* (pike), *alose* (shad), *saumon* (salmon) and *anguille* (eel), but there are many others and sea-fish will come in from the Atlantic. At Vierzon there are even lampreys (*see p.208*), although I have never been offered them. Frequently the fish are made into some form of *matelote* or stew, or they may be little mixed fish, which are fried and served as *friture*.

Pork dominates many dishes. There are all kinds of sausages and potted meats, and sometimes the pork is combined with fruit of the regions, such as *noisettes de porc aux pruneaux* (pork with prunes). It has made me wonder whether the English tradition of pork with apple-sauce might have come over with the Angevins who accompanied Henry II when he succeeded to the English crown. There are also many chicken dishes, some of which feature the *géline de Touraine*, a smallish black fowl, very succulent.

Among the game dishes, there are recipes for *lapereau* (young rabbit) and *lièvre* (hare), even *chevreau* (kid). A great deal of pastry features in main dishes, including vol-au-vent and puff pastry cases filled with various things, and *pâtés* in different types of *croûte* (crust).

Asparagus is plentiful in season — the fat white kind, served either with an Hollandaise sauce, or *beurre fondu* (melted butter), or, cold, with a vinaigrette. *Cardons* (cardoons) are also grown; they occasionally appear in British greengrocers', and are something like large-scale celery; more plentiful in the south of France, their presence here indicates how mild certain patches of the country may be. Various sorts of beans are frequently offered and there are numerous caves for the cultivation of mushrooms in the limestone banks of the rivers, some of which may be visited.

Anyway, raw mushroom salad is a delight of the Loire, so do not hesitate if you see it on a menu — the mushrooms will be thinly sliced with a light dressing.

The regional fruits are a source of great pride. There are plenty of peaches, pears, including a fat type called Bon Chrétien, and apples, of which local sorts are Reinette de Mans and Crat Vert. *Petits damas* are St Catherine plums and *coings* (quinces) and melons are all available in season, also an odd fruit that I have never eaten, called the *alberge de Tours*, which seems to be an apricot-peach cross. Around Angers a variety of cherry is called a *guigne*, hence the liqueur called *guignolet* (*p.291*). Dessert grapes are hung with their stems in water in special temperature controlled storerooms, so that they stay fresh for months.

Fouaces and *cassemusses* are sweet buns; a *sablé biquette* is a goat-cheese biscuit; a *Vouvraysien* is an almond cake — good to nibble with the local wine. The macaroons of Cormery are associated with a legend that relates how the local Abbot prayed for guidance as to how he might make the local macaroons special and famous — to increase the funds of the establishment. He was told that he should go to the kitchen and decorate the macaroons with the very first thing he saw when he opened the kitchen door. This happened to be immediately after Frère Jean, the cook, had dropped a live coal on his stomach, where it burnt through the habit, so that the Abbot's eyes were fastened on the worthy brother's navel — and so the Cormery macaroons have a hole in the centre.

Specialities and Dishes
Cerneaux au verjus are green walnuts in tart grape-juice ('green'

i.e. sharp), which, with salt and pepper, are sometimes served as a first course.

Jambon de volaille is a dish from Richelieu — stuffed chicken legs.

Beurre blanc is a sauce that can be the accompaniment to fish all along the river. It is made from fresh butter, shallots and vinegar and is rich and creamy.

Rillettes is a great Tours recipe — potted pork. But *rillettes* made with rabbit may have the suffix either *'de lapin'* or *Solognote* — from the Sologne, an area famed for rough shooting. *Rillauds* are a speciality of Angers, pieces of pork breast cooked and served hot.

Poulet en barbouille is another Berri dish — the blood of the chicken is added to the sauce, making it rich.

Carpe, or sometimes, *saumon, à la Chambord*, is a recipe in which the fish is cooked in red wine — those who are conservative about 'white wine with fish' will receive a pleasant surprise.

Pâté de Chartres is a dumpling of stuffed partridge.

Pâté de Pithiviers is a lark pastry, made at the shop Gringoire for the past two hundred years. It is supposed to have been first concocted as an impromptu snack offered to Charles IX when out hunting, the king being so pleased that he created the inventor a royal pastry-cook, a title the family kept for three centuries. Do not confuse this *pâté* with the *Gâteau de Pithiviers*, which is an almond-paste tart.

Quiche Tourangelle is an open tart, made with *rillettes*.

La chouée is a cabbage dish, rich with butter.

Truffiat is a potato-cake.

Honey from the Gâtinais is considered very good. *Cotignac*, a stiff jelly of quince and apple, also *pâté de coings*, a thick quince jelly, similar to the 'membrillo' of the Iberian Peninsular, are also specialities. A Berri dish is *citrouillat*, a type of pumpkin tart.

Poire belle angevine is a pear in syrup, with added liqueur (often Williamine) and sometimes stuffed with ice-cream.

Tarte des Demoiselles Tatin is a flat tart of apple or peach slices, caramelized and covered with pastry.

Orléans vinegar is famous — the local wine can be sharp and high in acid — so salads are plentiful and vinegar is used in some recipes. Mustards, too, are a speciality of Orléans and can be featured in dishes.

Drinks

Cider is made in the Perche. There are an enormous number of fruit liqueurs made throughout the region; travellers may see some that will never be exported, so it is a chance to try the unusual — although you may well then decide that the better-known ones thoroughly deserve their reputation! One, *guignolet*, made from a special cherry, is associated with Angers, where, outside the town in the industrial centre, there is the vast Cointreau establishment; they make a huge range, in addition to their famous bitter-orange flavoured drink to which the family — it is still a family concern — gave its name. (*See p.175*).

The wines of the Loire have been praised for centuries. Charles d'Orléans, Ronsard, Joachim du Bellay, Rabelais, Jules Lemaître all wrote enthusiastically about them. The great scholar, Alcuin of York (735–804), who ended his days as Abbot of St Martin of Tours and who is probably the very first English wine writer, was a discriminating drinker and, in a letter he wrote from England to a French friend, he ordered some Loire wines that he liked to be sent over to him. It may surprise the visitor to find such a great variety — red, white, pink, dry through to lusciously sweet, still, *pétillant*, fully sparkling — and, as some of these may be truly 'local' and not exported because the production of some growers is small, advantage of being on the spot should always be taken to try them. Many have local names. For example, the Cabernet Franc, from which the quality reds are made, is called '*le Breton*', because Cardinal Richelieu — whose town is a wonderful example of planning — sent his intendant, Abbé Breton, down to Bordeaux to get vine cuttings and it was the Cabernet Franc that yielded most satisfactorily in the Loire. A great deal of Gamay is also planted and, before controls became strict, it is said that much of the wine from this grape went elsewhere to augment Beaujolais. Muscadet and Gros Plant are the wines of the sea end of the Loire. At the top of the river, the Sauvignon is used for the finer wines — all Sancerre, the best of Pouilly-sur-Loire and Quincy. In the Pouilly region the local name for the Sauvignon Blanc is 'Blanc fumé', which is why the name Pouilly Fumé came into use. The grape used for the more ordinary white wines here is the Chasselas. It is not generally realized, however, that, until the Second World War, more red Sancerre was produced than white and that this was made from the Pinot Noir. A little of this and the Sancerre *rosé*, from the same grape, is now reaching export markets, but travellers should certainly try it on the spot.

In the central area of the Loire, the Chenin Blanc is the grape used for most white wines. Its nickname is Pineau de la Loire — do not confuse 'Pineau' with 'Pinard', the latter being the name of the wine ration in the Army. Although there are many huge concerns, especially those around Saumur, it is worthwhile sampling the wines of small growers — ask your hotel or restaurant for recommendations as to what they drink themselves. The red wines of the central area, too, are delightful, if you enjoy crisp, zippy wines, although some Britons find them lightweight. The *rosé* wines are famous, especially those made in Anjou; different categories are now available, varying in quality and price, but the majority are pleasant drinks, usually best when young and fresh. The best are usually made from the Cabernet Franc, but the Gamay contributes to others.

The Chenin Blanc also makes the sparkling wines. The best of these are produced by the Champagne method and can be first-rate; conditions — and the deep cellars in the limestone — are ideal and technical skills are far advanced. Highly mechanized installations will impress any visitor. The *vignerons* of Vouvray tell with pride how, after the *phylloxera* disaster in the late nineteenth century, it was from Vouvray that the labour and skills came to rehabilitate the vineyards of Champagne.

The wines of Vouvray — a charming village — are very varied; the finer examples must mature for years, so that the more 'commercial' establishments of here and Moncontour will make either straightforward dryish wines or lightly agreeable sparkling wines. The most esteemed producers will make wines that require time and some that, many years after their vintage, are categorized as *'moelleux'* or luscious — wines that in fact are not merely sweet, but complex, meriting sampling on their own, either as an aperitif or between times, rather than competing with some sweet course. They can be great and should not escape the attention of the discriminating traveller.

In fact, the existence of the sparkling wines of Saumur is due to a romance: the son of one of the Champagne establishments had been ill and went down to the milder region of Saumur to convalesce. While there, he fell in love with one of the local girls who, conveniently, was the daughter of a banker. The two families set up the young people in business — and the great house of Ackermann Laurence was founded.

The Chenin also makes the sweet wines. The region south of the Loire near Angers makes these delectable, lightly luscious wines in the Coteaux du Layon, Coteaux d'Aubance, Bonnezeaux and Quart de Chaume areas; they are from grapes subject to the *'pourriture noble'* and lovely drinks with fresh fruit, never as assertively sweet as those made in more southern vineyards. But the dry white wines from this area, too, are very fine.

Perhaps the best red wines come from around Chinon, Bourgueil and St Nicolas de Bourgueil. Nowadays they are made to be drunk young, but in former times they could have long lives and be most impressive. The reds of Saumur and Saumur-Champigny are lighter, but extremely pleasant. Around Sancerre and Pouilly, try to sample the wines of individual growers, Quincy, Reuilly and, if you venture almost into the Burgundy area, any wines made there from the Sauvignon, such as that of St Bris. Do not forget the red and *rosé* Sancerres.

Other dry or dryish whites, from the Chenin, include the wines of Reuilly, Jasnières, Cheverny, Azay-le-Rideau, Chaumont, Beaugency and Orléans and, of course, all the still whites of Saumur, Montlouis (unfairly called 'the poor man's Vouvray' at one time, but capable of being very good). Nearer the sea, Parnay, Tigné, Turquant, Montsoreau, Souzay and Dampierre and the Coteaux de l'Aubance and Coteaux de la Loire wines, such as those of La Roche aux Moines, Coulée de Serrant and Savennières, in addition to the sweeter wines, should be tried. Less important wines include those made from the Gamay, such as those of Touraine, red and *rosé* Coteaux d'Ancenis, as well as the better-known white, Menetou Salon, the white and red wines of Thouars and the red Gris Meunier of Orléans — this region also makes white wines from the Auvernat grape, which is the local name for the Chardonnay. This whole area is so much 'wine country' that the visitor should never hesitate to try the carafe wines of any restaurant and, if possible, ask advice about anything somewhat special and likely to be in short supply anyway. Do not forget, as mentioned earlier, that the French tend to like to drink many wines while these are younger than most Britons prefer them, but, if you find any stocks of older wines in some eating-place where the owners may have taken over past stock or simply have not bothered much about vintages, you may enjoy a delicious surprise — though such wines are seldom made these days.

Things to See and Do

There are collections of things to do with food and drink in many local museums, including: La Porte Royale at Loches; Maison de la Reine Bérengère at Le Mans — here you can see *'simarts'*, metal goblets in which the city used to offer a welcoming drink to important visitors; Musée de Sologne, Hotel de Ville, Romorantin; Musée de Berry, Hôtel Cujas, Bourges; Musée Folklorique de l'Orléanais, in the Château de Dunois, Beaugency, where there is a poem to wine by Jules Lemaître; Musée du Vieux Chinon, Chinon. The Château de Plessis-les-Tours has a museum devoted to the silk industry and the reconstruction of the interior of an old house; the Château de Gien, at Gien, has a display of the local ware in a department of the Musée de la Chasse à Tir et de la Fauconnerie; at Cours Cheverny the hunting museum, even if not strictly gastronomic, is certainly impressive.

Château de Montgeoffroy, east of Angers, and visible from the main road on the north bank of the river, is not only beautiful, but of great interest. It belongs to the Contades family, the eighteenth-century Maréchal de Contades built it — and it was his chef, Jean Close, who, when the Maréchal was Governor of Alsace, evolved *pâté de foie gras en croûte* (*see p.195*). Not only is the building superb architecturally but, unlike many of the Loire properties that were sacked in the French Revolution, all the furniture that was originally designed for this great house is still there — except one piece, the table in the oval dining-room. This is because, when the house was built, the family used small tables (*see p.25*) — such as royalty used when dining — and, when a large-scale meal was planned for some public function, the caterer (*traiteur*) would put up trestle tables. This is why there are no big tables for dining dating from the eighteenth century in France — and this cutting off the 'haves' from the 'have nots' may well have been one of the forces contributing to the French Revolution.

Villandry has a reconstruction of a Renaissance kitchen garden, as well as a flower garden.

Dovecots: In former times the number of pigeons allowed to be kept depended on who you were and how much land you owned. The nobility were allowed two pigeons per half hectare. At the Château de Villesavin, near Bracieux, there is a most interesting old kitchen, with a separate pastry oven and many antique utensils, plus an enormous *colombier* (dovecot), with a revolving ladder inside so that the eggs could be gathered — it can take 5,000 pigeons. At the Château de Talcy there is a large sixteenth-century dovecot, also a four-hundred-year-old wine press that can still be used.

Kitchens: The most important of these — which merits a détour — is the Romanesque kitchen of Fontevrault l'Abbaye; British visitors should go here anyway, to see the tombs of the Plantagenets and some of their wives. The kitchen is unique, planned to provide food for the five different sections of the enormous religious establishment; it has twenty chimneys and five separate cooking areas. The local wine order recently made use of these — and they work. At Brissac the local Cave Co-operative have taken over the kitchen alongside the Château and made it into a tasting-room, where their wines may be sampled. Visitors should note the kitchen's well, an alcove for washing-up — rather like the sink in an old-fashioned butler's pantry. At Châteaudun, Dunois's castle, visitors can see both the kitchens and cellars, which date from the fifteenth century. At Montreuil-Bellay there is a Gothic kitchen in the château, modelled on that of Fontevrault. There is also a seventeenth-century kitchen in the Château de Ménars, the property that belonged to the brother of Madame de Pompadour. There is a Renaissance kitchen in the Château of Azay-le-Rideau and a seventeenth-century kitchen in the abbey buildings at Pontlevoy.

Wine Museums, Tasting-rooms, Cellars
Angers: The Conseil Interprofessional des Vins d'Anjou et Saumur, 72 rue Plantagenet, can provide information about the

---

We sat at a round table . . . the maid, a young girl with a twinkling eye, bright cheeks, and rather straggling hair, came in and plonked the soup-pot down on the stand in the middle of the table (when) both the fonctionnaire and M. Reynard threw crusts of bread at her. This was evidently a recognised custom, like the tiny embraces which she administered to the company when she brought the écrevisses. These dainties from the river, small fresh-water lobsters, appreciated by those clever enough to know how to eat them, were apparently forbidden by law. The widow came in from the kitchen . . . with the solemn injunction to us that we were not to sneak to the inspectors who were in the neighbourhood. Not even the added charm of their being forbidden fruit, however, enabled me to get very much satisfaction out of their unbreakable 'nippers'.

DOUGLAS GOLDRING, *The Loire: The Record of a Pilgrimage from Gerbier de Joncs to St.Nazaire*, Constable, 1913

---

wines of the region. Also in Angers, the Hôpital Saint-Jean has a museum of glasses and bottles, drinking-vessels and the moulds for *gauffres*, holy wafers — which look rather like waffle irons — and there is a small wine museum in the twelfth-century cellar. Also near Angers, in the industrial centre, the Cointreau establishment is well organized to receive visitors.

Beaulieu-sur-Layon: There is a small Caveau du Vin installed in a house on the D55 road, where old bottles and glasses may be seen.

Bourgueil: The Cave Touristique is outside the little town and has a collection of ancient presses and objects to do with wine.

Montrichard: Wine cellars in the hollowed-out caves in the rock are open to visitors.

Saumur: There are many tasting-rooms to the east of Saumur on the south bank, with cellars cut into the cliffs, most of them belonging to small wine-dealers, restaurants or bars. In the suburb of St Hilaire St Florent many of the main wine firms have their establishments: Rémy Pannier is the largest and here and at Ackermann Laurence next door, visitors may be shown round to see the region's table wines and sparkling wines. East of Saumur, with a fine view above the river, the Gratien Meyer establishment, makers of sparkling wines, can also receive visitors. Out in the country, the Cave Co-operative of St Cyr en Bourg has impressive underground cellars and a very modern installation.

Tours: The cellars of the Église Saint-Julien date from the twelfth century and sometimes there is a performance there of Son et Lumière about the wines of Touraine. Just outside Tours, the Musée d'Espelosin or Musée Tourangeau de la Vigne et du Vin in the Château de Basses-Rivières has a collection of objects to do with wine, including the regional *'dames jeannes'*, a large bottle from which the word 'demi-john' is derived.

Other Things to See

Illiers, in the Loir Valley, was the birthplace of Dr Proust, father of the novelist Marcel. It is the original of *Combray*, and the Maison de Tante Léonie, furnished as it was in Proust's time and where the famous episode of the madeleine dunked in lime-tea took place, may be visited.

At Vernou-en-Sologne the installations devoted to fruit research may be seen if an application is made in advance. The same applies to the rose gardens and nursery garden establishment at Orléans.

29

Marseille and the Riviera

This part of France will be familiar to many holiday-makers. But, more than ever these days, the gastronomy of resorts tends to consist largely of what is far too often the anaemic and unsatisfactory 'international cuisine' of medium-grade hotels, or else the folksy versions of traditional dishes, rendered acceptable to the unadventurous — which often means leaving out ingredients such as garlic and many seasonings. (Money saved on the dishes may go into the deceptively simple-seeming peasanty tableware and décor.) There are some superb restaurants — which are also extremely expensive — and some admirable hôtels, where true *haute cuisine* is presented. But few people wish to eat like this every day, even if they are able to do so.

Away from the Côte d'Azur, however, many thoroughly enjoyable dishes may be found. The raw materials of the countryside and the Mediterranean can be very good, although the region is not rich. The influence of Italy can be noted in many recipes. The inventiveness of local cooks has been well described by Stephen Lister in *Fit for a Bishop* and *More for a Bishop* (Peter Davies); he lived in the south both before and after the Second World War and stressed the quality of dishes made with very little money. This is the place where many artists have loved to work and to live: the simplest *hors d'oeuvre*, salads, stews and bowls of fruit and platters of cheese are arranged with great taste, making even a humble table, possibly covered with oilcloth or even being a bare scrubbed board, become a still-life satisfying to the eye. Anyone attracted to tableware will find endless temptations in the various local potteries, even if funds do not extend to the remarkable creations of Vallauris, where Picasso's influence has been marked, or Biot, where Fernand Léger has also been important.

The use of the Provençal language, revived as an appreciated and beautiful literary medium in the nineteenth century, notably by Frédéric Mistral (1830–1914) and his colleagues, was never forgotten by the country folk; many dishes and foodstuffs, therefore, may seem to have strange names on menus. The ordinary dictionary may not give any clue as to what something is. It should also be borne in mind that the sort of food eaten in the great city of Marseille, where so many sea-going peoples, in addition to ordinary travellers, visit and create specialized demands among the true 'locals', cannot be typical of Provence, unless one is fortunate enough to be invited to a private house and a family who are true Provençaux, any more than the food of one of the luxury hôtel-restaurants out in the country is typical of the fare of a family in some remote 'mas' or farmhouse. But the local specialities are well worth exploring.

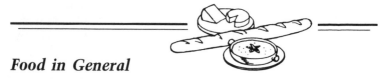

Food in General

Olive oil is the supreme cooking medium and although good Provençal oil does undeniably taste of olives, it has none of the rancidity or over-fatty flavour that some people are too ready to associate with it.

Fish in great variety is naturally plentiful along the coast. There are fresh sardines, *poulpes* (small octopus) and *supions* (another name for squid); small fry, often on menus as *petite friture de la rad*; a curious but excellent thing called *poutina et nounat*, which is a combination of very young fish and their roe. Anyone who has struggled with the fish vocabulary in the Marius-Fanny-César trilogy of plays by Marcel Pagnol, will remember the *violets* (a type of shellfish tasting of iodine and named as 'sea-anemones' in some dictionaries), *clovisses* (a large clam) and *praires* (a small clam) sold by Fanny at her fish-stall; there are also *oursins* (sea-urchins), which look just like prickly chestnuts and taste rather like a snail that has been taken to the sea, and a number of fish regarded highly by the makers of *bouillabaisse* (*see p.300*) which appear to have no exact English language names — *rascasse, galinette, chapon, grondin* (rather like a red mullet, but uglier), *congre* (conger eel), *fiélas, sarran, orade*, and *pagel*. The *loup de mer* (sea bass) is usually served grilled over sprigs of fennel which may have been sprinkled with brandy. *Estocaficada* is dried salted stockfish, which is usually imported from Norway, transformed by southern magic into something delicious, and most restaurants make a *soupe aux poissons*, incorporating a variety of fish, though this, it is worth remembering, is not like *bouillabaisse* in which the fish are whole or at least solid, but one in which they have been either reduced to pulp or else pounded — a definite soup and not a fish-stew. Shellfish such as crabs, lobsters, and mussels are also plentiful. Anchovies feature in many dishes, and there is an eel-stew called *la raïto* which is a Christmas dish. Grey snails, called *cantarèu*, are also found.

Because of the rather poor pasturage, meat is not always of very high quality in this region, although one may find *menon* (roast kid) on a special menu, but the vegetables and fruits certainly are. The Cavaillon melons, asparagus, peaches, figs, artichokes, are sent to the Paris markets and abroad; pumpkins, aubergines, water-melons, peppers and tomatoes, spinach and every kind of salad vegetable and herb make the menu varied and colourful. *Polente*, similar to Italian *polenta* (maize flour), and other pasta

are featured. Garlic, of course, comes into many dishes, especially *aioli*, the Provençal version of mayonnaise, served with raw vegetables and shellfish, and *rouille*, a red pepper and garlic sauce sometimes stirred into soups and stews to give spice and flavour. *Pissala*, another cooking essence, containing anchovies, is also often used in this way.

Blète is a vegetable rather like Swiss chard, the stems being slightly similar to asparagus and the leaves to spinach. A type of vegetable tart called a *tian* is made and so, of course, is *ratatouille*, for which the local name is *ratatouia*. Black olives are inseparable from the southern table, and radishes and *fèves* (small beans) are also usual among *hors d'oeuvre*. *Basilic* (sweet basil) is frequently used for flavouring. Table grapes appear regularly at the ends of meals, and nuts are also abundant — Olivier de Serres planted his own Asian almond-trees in his estate at Pradel. A *pâté* of *coings* (quinces) similar to the *cotignac* of the Orléanais, is often made.

Among sweet things, the little almond biscuits called *calissons d'Aix* are especially famous. Grasse makes *fleurs pralinées* (candied flowers) and Nice candied flowers and fruits of various kinds. *Chaudèus* are orange-flavoured biscuits.

Specialities and Dishes

Bouillabaisse: This is certainly the great dish of the south of France. It must immediately be admitted that, however good it is, I do not like it, just as I do not like any of the great fish-stews *pochouse, cotriade, ttoro* and so on. But *bouillabaisse* has been a favourite even before Thackeray wrote a ballade to it, though ideally it should be made specially for you (which disposes of the restaurants who keep a large pot simmering) as each fish must be cooked just to edibility and no longer; the whole operation should not take hours anyway. It is often served in two plates, liquid in one, fishes in the other. There are endless arguments as to which combination of fishes make the best *bouillabaisse*. The dish is said to have been of Greek origin and even a favourite of the gods, for Venus is said to have given Vulcan a dish of fish and saffron (a supposed soporific) when she wanted to meet Mars. Each town has its own recipe for *bouillabaisse*, the only point on which everyone seems to be agreed being that it should contain garlic, olive oil, tomatoes, saffron and a hideous looking fish called the *rascasse*. Various other fishes are included, according to what recipe is followed, together with herbs, and a slice of bread over which the *bouillon* is poured. Sometimes grated cheese is served too. There are, however, seldom shellfish in *bouillabaisse* (useful for people with allergies to remember), although it is possible to find it made with lobster and mussels. *Bouillabaisse borgne* (literally 'one-eyed) is a vegetable soup made in the same way as the fish variety, with poached eggs in the *bouillon; bouillabaisse de sardines* contains only fresh sardines; *bouillabaisse d'epinards* is a *bouillon* of the same olive oil, saffron, garlic, plus potatoes, poached eggs and spinach.

Bourride: Also a fish soup, but generally consisting solely of white fish, and, according to some authorities, made without saffron — though saffron is often included, and possibly *aioli* and egg-yolks too.

Soupe au pistou: A type of *minestrone*, a speciality of the Nice region, which derives from the Genoese *pesto*, a sauce consisting of pounded basil, cheese, pine nuts, oil and garlic. This concentrated sauce is put into the vegetable soup, which usually includes tomatoes, beans, onions, and a little vermicelli, as well as other vegetables.

Aïgo saou: A fish and vegetable soup, with *la rouille* added to it.

Aïgo boulido is a Provençal vegetable soup into which egg has been beaten.

Sou fassum: Stuffed cabbage. A Grasse speciality.

La socca: A huge, thin, flat pancake, made of chickpea flour, oil, water, salt and pepper.

Pissaladière: A Nice speciality, and a version of Italian pizza — an open tart with onions, anchovies and black olives, sometimes with tomatoes.

Pan bagna: Another Nice speciality and a type of giant sandwich. A roll or *baguette* is sliced and filled with tomatoes, peppers, black olives, anchovies, and possibly hard-boiled eggs, radishes and onions, the bread being well sprinkled with oil.

Anchoïade: Anchovies pounded with garlic and oil.

Poutargue: Grey mullet roe, with onions, hard-boiled eggs and oil. A Martigues speciality.

Tautènes farcies: Squid stuffed with onions and tomatoes, usually served *au gratin* with spinach.

Salade Niçoise: An *hors d'oeuvre* which varies but should contain black olives, anchovies, green peppers, tomatoes, olive oil and possibly hard-boiled eggs. Additional vegetables and tunny fish are sometimes added.

Pieds et pacquets: A Marseille speciality of tripe and sheep's trotters in rolls, cooked in a *bouillon* with vegetables.

Bléa tourte: A vegetable tart of beet leaves, pine-nuts and currants.

Esquinado Toulanais: A type of *gratin* of crabmeat and mussels.

Wines
Vines abound in this part of France. Nowadays many of what were previously merely pleasant holiday drinks can be first-rate, for all but the most important occasions. The Côte de Provence wines, white, pink and red, are often presented in the curvy, waisted bottle to which they are entitled. Many growers have begun to plant grapes such as the Cabernet Sauvignon and other classics associated with finer wine regions, and it is interesting to try these. Cassis, Bandol and Bellet are interesting wine areas and the seriously interested should make notes of names, as increasingly areas of vines are being planted. It is a comment, not a criticism, to say that, in this area, wines intended to accompany the fairly gutsy recipes, redolent of spices and herbs and often with quite rich sauces, are mouth-filling and substantial, rather than subtle — they cannot be anything else. If you are catering for yourself, give such local wines the chance to show their quality by treating them well, as you would something finer from another area. Ratafias of orange flowers, jasmine and other flowers are also found locally.

Things to See and Do

Aix-en-Provence: The Musée du Vieil Aix contains a collection of local objects relating to the region, including *santons*, the small figures carved for putting round Christmas cribs — which feature local crafts and trades. The Pavillion de Vendôme is a seventeenth-century house furnished in Provençal style.
Bandol: On the nearby Island of Bendor, M. Paul Ricard (formerly of the *pastis* firm, see p178) has installed a museum of the world's wines and spirits.
Near Brignoles: The Abbey of Thoronet, built in the twelfth century, is open to visitors, who can see the refectory, cellar and an oil press.
Cagnes: The Musée in the Château contains exhibits to do with history and a complete display dealing with the cultivation of olive trees and the production of the oil.
Grasse: The Musée Fragonard contains exhibits relating to the life of Lower Provence, including furniture and ceramics.

Marseille: The establishment of Noilly Prat, the largest of French vermouth houses, is open to visitors. Those who wish to visit Sète and the region where many vermouths begin their life, should inquire at local tourist offices to find which houses can receive visitors, but there are plenty, also those who make the Muscats much appreciated in this area.

Menton: The Musée contains exhibits of local folklore and history. There is a Lemon Festival and fruit show, together with a 'Race of the Golden Fruits' held each February.

Moustiers: The Musée des Faïences has an important collection of pottery, including exhibits showing how it was made.

Nice: The Musée Masséna, as well as containing collections specially relating to the history of Nice and of the work of artists who worked in the region, also has exhibits of pottery and porcelain.

Roquebrune-Cap-Martin: In the *donjon* of the castle of this village, visitors can see the dining-room, kitchen with bread oven and furnished rooms of what is thought to be the oldest feudal castle in France — end of the tenth century.

Vallauris: The Hall du Nérolium is open in summer with an exhibition of the local pottery.

Vence: There are two oil presses which are still working, and the baronial mill of Boursac is open to the public.

Anchovies, besides their making a considerable article in the commerce of Nice, are a great resource in all families. The noblesse and bourgeois sup on salad and anchovies, which are eaten on all their meagre days. The fishermen and mariners all along the coast have scarcely any other food but dry bread, with a few pickled anchovies; and when the fish is eaten, they rub their crusts with the brine. Nothing can be more delicious than fresh anchovies fried in oil: I prefer them to the smelts of the Thames.

TOBIAS SMOLLETT, *Travels Through France and Italy*, 1766
[The 'meagre days' signify fast days. P.V.P.]

30

Normandy, Picardy, Artois and Flanders

Normandy is the supreme butter and cheese country and the whole of its northern coastline abounds in good fish and shellfish. The well-known restaurants are serious eating-places and the richness of some of the superlative 'farmhouse fare' featured by many is sometimes responsible for travellers who land in France and let themselves go, then feeling somewhat stuffed or queasy in the early stages of a trip. The people are all hearty eaters and often tend to prefer first-rate ingredients made into substantial, satisfying dishes to versions of *haute cuisine*; this tradition of solidly good food may well be the result of the sometimes severe weather and, also, the long history of invasions, occupations, battles across this sometimes rather bleak countryside — when a table can be well provided, it is at least something to enjoy immediately. Vegetables do not always feature specially. Towards the north, there are many different pork products, blood-sausages and other sausages. Cream and butter go into many Norman dishes, plus the local spirits. The account of the wedding feast in Flaubert's *Madame Bovary* (1857) is worth quoting — one is told of somewhat similar celebrations in Normandy to this day:
'they sat down forty-three to table and remained there sixteen hours; it was resumed next day and in a lesser degree on the following days ... On the table were four sirloins, six dishes of hashed chicken, some stewed veal, three legs of mutton, and in the middle a pretty little roast sucking pig, flanked by four pork sausages flavoured with sorrel. Flasks of brandy stood at the corners. A rich foam had frothed out round the corks of the cider bottles. Every glass had already been filled to the brim with wine. Yellow custard stood in big dishes ... For the tarts and sweets they had hired a pastrycook from Yvetot.'

Food in General

Among the fish and shellfish, there are *demoiselles de Cherbourg*, which may be either of two things — a small lobster or an enormous shrimp. There are different types of herrings from Flanders, either *harengs salés* (salted) or *harengs fumés* (smoked), which may, colloquially, be referred to as '*gendarmes*' (policemen), and also the '*franglais*' *harengs* — which are, as one would suppose, kippers.

Pâtés are numerous and varied; the shops in Amiens will tempt picnickers. Small game birds, such as *bécasse* (woodcock) and *bécassine* (snipe) are also often featured — in the shooting season, the open meadows and woodland are busy with those who enjoy *la chasse* (hunting and, in this instance, rough shooting).

Vegetables that may certainly be cultivated here include *endive* (chicory) and salsifis. Otherwise, of course, there are potatoes and root vegetables. The cooking medium is usually butter, plus, as has been mentioned, cream, but there is also the *graisse normande*, which is a mixture of pork fat and the fat from around a calf kidney; it may be flavoured with vegetables and does, as may be imagined, enrich the food.

Other popular ingredients are apples — and both cider and calvados. The *trou normande* is the portion of calvados drunk in the middle of a very copious and rich meal, to act as a digestive and enable the diner to continue the long repast.

Sweet things include *les chiques de Caen*, which are rather like the British bulls'-eyes, striped mint-flavoured sweets; biscuits from Abbeville; aniseed biscuits from Honfleur; candied fruits from Beauvais; *sablés* (rather dry biscuity cakes) from St Quentin; *tuiles d'Amiens* (chocolate and orange biscuits); *Duchesses de Rouen*, which are macaroons, and *mirlitons de Rouen*, a type of cream puff. *Citron confit* (candied lemon-peel) and *falnes normandes* (flat cinnamon cakes) are other specialities. *Le gâteau de Trouville* is a cake filled with apples and cream; *le pain de pommes des Picards* is a *compôte* of fried apples; *la bissade* is a type of round *brioche*; *la rabote* or *le bourdelot* is a confection of apples baked in pastry, like dumplings, and *douillons* are pears similarly prepared.

Specialities and Dishes of Normandy

Andouille fumé de Viré: Smoked chitterlings, served hot or cold.
Andouillettes grillées: Small tripe sausages, special to Caen (although *andouillettes* may be found in many regions), also Viré, Rouen and Pont-Audémer.
Sanguette: This is an Orne speciality, which I have never been able to try, but it is a type of *boudin* (black pudding) made with rabbit.
Matelots are stews of freshwater fish of various kinds. The *matelot normande*, however, is made with sea-fish.
Omelettes: Mont St Michel is very famous for these, especially the type evolved by the Mère Poulard. Her version is a fluffy omelette, the whites and yolks of the eggs being separately beaten. The result is large, light and spongy.
Soles: Naturally, there are many ways in which this superb fish may be cooked and presented. The *sole normande* often found on menus is the fish accompanied by a sauce normande, made from butter, flour and cream; this is the smart restaurant version, but the *vraie sole à la normande* that may be featured in the country of its origin is much simpler — the fish simmered in cream in a covered dish. *Sole Dieppoise* is sole cooked in a white wine sauce, plus shrimps and mussels; *sole Fécampoise* is the same, with the addition of soft roes.
Tripes à la mode du Caen are tripes cooked slowly with onions, carrots, apples and herbs, with cider and Calvados.
Caneton Rouennaise is a duckling special to the region, which is mostly reared around Yvetot. The bird is lightly roasted and cooked with wine and brandy — a rich but delicious dish.
Salade cauchoise is a type of potato salad.
Poulet Vallée d'Auge is a chicken recipe, involved with cream, mushrooms and wine, named for one of the most picturesque and gastronomically rich regions.

Specialities and Dishes of Picardy, Artois, Flanders

Le caqhuse is cold leg of pork, with onions.
Le hoche pot is, as you might guess, a type of 'hotpot', or northern French version of *pot-au-feu*, a substantial meat stew.
Flamiche au poireaux is a leek tart — a substantial type of quiche.
Flamiche à la citrouille is pumpkin tart; one sees the huge pumpkins lolling about in many fields.
L'étouffée is a version of potato-and-onion pie.
Daussade à la crème is a mixture of onions, lettuce, cream, served on bread.

Le pain daussé is onions mashed in cider, served on bread.
Le dius is a dish of sliced potatoes, cooked in the oven.
Les bêtises de Cambrai are mint sweets, evolved years ago by an apprentice who made a mistake — *une bêtise* — that turned out a success.
Un faluche is a round, flattish loaf that you may sometimes find in bakers.

Drinks

No wine is made in this northern region, but there are many types of cider; these range from a very pale, almost greenish version to a dark orange type and cider here may be dry or sweet, sparkling or still. The best is supposed to be that of the Vallée d'Auge. Normans are proud of their cider, which, thanks to the enormous revival of interest in and consumption of this drink, is now sometimes exported to the UK. Do not imagine, though, that any cider of this sort is light in alcohol — it may be quite strong.

Calvados or apple brandy is the great *eau-de-vie* of Normandy. That of the Vallée d'Auge is entitled to an *appellation contrôlée*. Calvados is mostly distilled by small-scale individual producers and, ideally, is supposed to undergo maturation in oak for at least ten years. There are a few names that may be known in export markets, but a glance along the shelves of a Norman supermarket will indicate that a fairly large number of concerns are making this spirit.

Bénédictine liqueur (*see p.173*) is made at the distillery at Fécamp. Around Mont Saint Michel Michelaine is made, a herb-based liqueur from an ancient recipe; it is usually available in its yellow version but, as with some other liqueurs, the green version is stronger.

Many types of beer are available — nowadays one even sees many signs up in the Pas de Calais indicating that an eating-place or bar stocks a British beer.

Things to See and Do

Conches: The Church of Sainte Foy has a particularly fine window, showing the 'mystic wine press'.
Fécamp: Although Fécamp is not an obviously attractive town, the Bénédictine distillery — well indicated by signs — is impress-

ive and well worth a visit. As the guided tour is quite extensive, including the museums of the fantastic building, as well as the distillery, allow some time. The organization provides multi-lingual translations of the guide's commentary — even making the fine distinction between 'English' and 'American'. The Musée Municipal at Fécamp has collections relating to domestic local life in past times.

Jumièges: Visitors to the ruins of the twelfth-century abbey can see the cellars.

Mont Saint Michel: This is an astonishing building, where the guest reception-rooms and mighty kitchen fireplaces of the original foundation may still be seen.

Villedieu-les-Poêles: This is a picturesque little town — and the suffix indicates that it is a place to buy copper kitchenware, the local speciality.

There are collections illustrating the local life of the past in Granville and the Abbaye de la Lucerne and of local Bray art at Neufchâtel-en-Bray. If you are in the Pays de Caux, you may still see the old-fashioned method of grazing the animals, by attaching them to stakes so that they crop the grass around in a circle. The meat of beasts pastured in this way is said to have a slight flavour of parsley — but I have never noticed it.

Anyone who, as a cheese devotee (see p.71) goes to Camembert, may note a memorial to a lady who was particularly fond of Calvados. Her husband wrote:

> 'Ci-gît qui, dans son agonie,
> N'imagina rien de plus beau
> Que d'être mise en un tombeau
> Comme une prune à l'eau-de-vie.'

[A rough translation might be: 'Here she lies, who, ending her days, thought it would be marvellous to be entombed just like a plum in brandy.']

31

The Pyrenees

This mountain range includes some of the most beautiful and varied countryside in the whole of France and preserves many individual traditions of several ancient kingdoms. As in most mountain regions, the districts have firmly clung to many old ways of food and drink and, as many Allied escapers have reason to know, frontiers are not barriers to those who live in such places.

There are many influences affecting gastronomy — the proximity of Spain, the Atlantic and Mediterranean, the circumstances of the great medieval pilgrim routes. The names of the main regions are often applied to dishes. Going across the Pyrenees and their foothills from the Atlantic to the Mediterranean, these areas are: the Pays Basque. There are seven Basque provinces, three of them in France, including the old Kingdom of Navarre. Then comes Le Béarn (associated with Henri IV, often known as 'le Béarnais'); La Bigorre; Le Comminges; the Pays de Foix; the Pays de Sault; La Cerdagne; Les Corbières and Le Roussillon; this last is really Catalan France — Catalan is still spoken by many there — and in former times the Kingdom of Majorca was a part of this. Catalyuna was an independent kingdom until as recently as 1714 and not only have Catalan artists and musicians enriched the world, but it was a Catalan, Arnaud de Vilanova, who introduced distilling to Europe.

In very general terms, goose fat is the cooking medium of the west of the region. There is a saying about Béarn cooking that you 'plunge up to the elbows in fat' — in mountain regions, for obvious reasons, fat does tend to be of importance in everyday fare. In the central region of the Pyrenees much of the cooking is based on butter and, on the Mediterranean side, as might be expected, oil is the fat. Food tends to be husky: there are a huge selection of recipes — which, remember, may not be on the menus of hotels and ordinary restaurants — all very varied, in accordance with the independent spirit of the people, many of whom feel strongly that the former kingdoms should be returned to them. Local cooks ring infinite changes on dishes based on rice, pulses and involving both meat or poultry and fish — rather as in Spain. If you can get the genuine local cooking, it will be satisfying, substantial rather than delicate, but the sort of homely fare I admit to finding extremely acceptable.

Food in General

Trout are still found in some mountain streams. *Chipirones* (small squid or inkfish), sardines (the same word) and *thon* (tunny) or *bonites* (small tunny fish) may be on menus anywhere near the Atlantic coast. Sardines can sometimes be eaten on the quayside — it is chic to go into Spain and do this at San Sebastian — when one holds them up by the tail and nibbles, minus knives and forks. Mediterranean fish are found on the eastern end of the Pyrenees, especially *anchois* (anchovies). Snails, grilled, are called *cargolade* and are a Catalan speciality: the local saying is '*En juillet, ni femme, ni escargot*', though I have never been able to understand why.

There is plenty of game in the region. The *becfins* or *becfigues* (garden warblers) are plump little lark-like birds, a speciality also of the Landes. *Ramereaux* (ringdoves), *ortolans* (wheatears, another Landes bird, *see p.62*), and, in the Roussillon, *étourneaux* (starlings) and *perdreau* (partridge) are other local birds that may be mentioned on menus. The *izard* is the Pyrenean chamois which, on very special occasions, may be featured in a *civet* ('jug' might be the equivalent cooking term). Some books still mention *ours* (bear) as being a local dish, but, although there certainly were bears in the Pyrenees until the last century, I doubt that any exist today.

Chickens are plentiful — as they were when Henri IV expressed his wish to obtain a weekly *poule au pot* for everyone — so are geese and the various *confits* (*see p.53*), some made of pork too and many other pork products are featured. Beans of various sorts, sweet peppers and cabbage are found in many dishes.

Fruit is plentiful, especially in the Roussillon. Wild fruits, such as *myrtilles* (bilberries) are often mentioned and *châtaignes* (sweet chestnuts) can accompany meat dishes, as well as being used in dessert dishes.

There are many kinds of cakes. The flat gâteau Basque is like a large maid of honour (the English almond tart), but of softer consistency and with a dollop of jam inside. *Rosquillas* are almond cakes, *bunyetes* a type of fritter, *croquets* are almond biscuits, and there are various forms of *pastis*, which are nothing to do with the anise drink (*see p.172*), but are types of cake-cum-bun, flavoured with liqueur. *Pâte de cédrat* is citron (lemon) jelly, a Bayonne speciality; there is a *confiture de myrtilles et de raisins* (bilberry and grape jelly) and macaroons, which are made in Saint Jean de Luz, Orthez and Bayonne. It was to Bayonne that the Jews who had been driven out of Spain and Portugal brought the tradition of chocolate drinking, which was subsequently made fashionable because of the two Spanish queens of France, Anne of Austria, wife of Louis XIII, and Marie-Thérèse, wife of Louis XIV, who enjoyed it. Chocolate was considered to be an exotic beverage; maybe because it was popular with the Moors and was often spiced with cloves and cinnamon; it was thought to have aphrodisiac properties, and, like many gastronomic innovations, received denunciations from moralists, although the fashionable ladies became so addicted that they would even sip chocolate in the confessional (*see p.24*). Madame de Sévigné mentions a friend who craved for it during a pregnancy and produced a chocolate-coloured baby!

Specialities and Dishes

Jambon de Bayonne is raw ham, cured by being rubbed with Bayonne salt and then buried in the earth. It has a succulent, delicate taste and is often served as a first course.

Cousinette is a vegetable soup, containing spinach and *cousine*, which is a type of marrow, plus sorrel and lettuce with shin of veal. It is a Béarn dish.

Bouillinade des pêcheurs is a fish soup from the Roussillon — therefore with Mediterranean fish.

Elzekaria is a Basque soup of onions, carrots, beans, cabbage and garlic.

Ttoro is a Basque fish soup, which will usually also contain peppers, garlic and tomatoes.

Garbure is a very substantial regional soup — indeed, one is told that the ladle should be able to stand upright in a properly made *garbure*. It varies from place to place and according to what is available, but generally contains potatoes, beans, vegetables in season, occasionally garlic, also peppers and some kind of meat — which is generally referred to as *le trebuc* — which may be bacon, ham, goose, pork or sausage. *Garbure* is made in an earthenware pot with a glazed inside; this is called a *toupi*. When the helping is nearly finished, the eater may pour a little wine into the soup plate and eat the combined remainder. This is known as *'faire goudale'*.

Ouillade or *ouliat* is another soup, but although it is found in various places, the first form of the name is Catalan. It is made in two dishes, called *ouilles*, and these must never be washed or allowed to get cold — one imagines them being stored alongside the stove. In one of these are cooked the vegetables (except for beans), the cabbage and anything else that is going into the soup; in the other *ouille* are put the beans, garlic, salt and pepper. The two mixtures are only combined when the *ouillade* is about to be served. In the Roussillon eggs are sometimes added. If tomatoes are an ingredient, the soup may be referred to as *tourin*; if leeks, cheese and tomatoes are part of the recipe, it is sometimes called *soupe du berger* (shepherd's soup); an onion soup made in Bigorre in the same sort of way is a *toulia*. In the Cerdagne, *braou bouffat* is a vegetable soup, similar to the *potée* that is found in many regions.

Pâté aux anchois de Collioure is a type of savoury doughnut, containing anchovies. Bread plus cheese and salt fish is often found around the Mediterranean — a convenient portable form of nourishment.

Poule au pot dou nouste Henric is the famous 'chicken in the pot' of Henri IV. The bird is stuffed with a mixture of Bayonne ham, herbs, garlic, moistened with Armagnac; some of this stuffing is rolled up separately in cabbage leaves. Then all is poached, in a *bouillon* of vegetables and the giblets. The traditional way of extracting it from the pot is to pull it out by a string attached to one of its legs, hence the name *poulet à la ficelle*. *Poulet farci à l'ariégeoise* is the version made in the Ariège region.

Estoufat or *daube de boeuf à la béarnaise* is a stew of beef, vegetables and red wine, which is often served with *broye*, a type of cornmeal mush, which may also be referred to as *paste, pastet,* or *yerbilhou* (I suppose according to whichever language — French, Basque, Catalan or local dialect — is being spoken).

Poitrine de mouton farcie à l'ariégeoise is breast of mutton, stuffed with ham, eggs, garlic and other seasonings, cooked with vegetables and served with potatoes and stuffed cabbage. *Pétéran* is another mutton dish, but a stew, with veal and potatoes, a speciality of Luchon.

Loukinka is a Basque garlic sausage, of small size; *tripotchka* is a type of blood-pudding made with veal, also Basque.

Pipérade is a Basque omelette, with the addition of sweet peppers and tomatoes, made so that its consistency is that of scrambled eggs. This is perhaps the best-known Basque recipe and the one likely to be found by the majority of tourists.

Poulet béarnais is chicken, cooked over mounds of whole heads of garlic. Henri IV is supposed to have had his baby lips rubbed with garlic, hence the frequent association with him in the region and with garlic dishes. This recipe, however, although it certainly is redolent of garlic, is not fierce in flavour and anyone nervous about taking large quantities of garlic should read the quotation from Ford Madox Ford in Elizabeth David's *French Country Cooking* and be reassured. (In brief, it relates how a beautiful model, threatened with dismissal from her job in a couture house because she would eat garlic, cooked herself a *poulet basquaise* in a last defiance and went to give in her notice — and was congratulated on her appearance and her self-denial — because her breath did not smell!) It seems as if the damage is done when only a *little* garlic is used — as on the *chapon,* or piece of bread that is rubbed with it to flavour a salad. When large quantities of garlic are eaten, the system appears to resign itself — and deals with the stuff so that there are no after-effects. But, if you are still hesitant, remember that chewing a spring of parsley or a coffee-bean will take away any garlic on your breath.

Magret is duck, cooked in its blood plus peppers, served with an hollandaise sauce.

Merguez is a strong-flavoured pink sausage — although it is now associated with the *pieds noirs* or French Algerians from North Africa, it may well have been a version of a Moorish or Spanish dish. *Saucisse à la catalane* is a long, coiled-up sausage, cooked with plenty of garlic, herbs and a little orange-peel. *Perdreau à la catalane* is partridge cooked with — preferably — bitter oranges, and a rich sauce.

The term *à la catalane* implies the use of a lot of garlic, so does the term *'en pistaches'* — do not confuse this with *'aux pistaches'*, which means with pistachio nuts.

The term *basquaise* usually means that sweet peppers are involved. The little ones, which are *piments,* are not usually either as hot or as coarse in flavour as the large, bulbous, red and green ones, which are *poivrons.* This may seem an unlikely way

313

round, but, as I cannot digest *poivrons* at all, I can speak from experience that a modest amount of *piments*, the small type, does not affect me. But the term *'piment doux'* may be misleading — if you share my disability, ask about whether the vegetable is *'très fort'* or *'véritablement doux'* before you order.

The term *bayonnaise* usually signifies that *cèpes* are included in a fried dish. But travellers should be warned that locals will claim that the sauce bayonnaise is in fact a mayonnaise — which is said to get its name from the siege of Fort Mahon. It seems to this irreverent writer that there may well have been sauces made from eggs and oil for centuries and that the association with Mahon or Bayonne is fortuitous or, maybe, due to those writing about the delicious thing, due to a 'cold in the nose'.

Drinks

There is a Basque cider, known as *pittara*, which is rather sharp. The Basque liqueur Izarra (which means 'star') in the language is made from Pyrenean herbs and flowers, plus Armagnac *(see p.169)*. The green version is slightly stronger than the yellow. If you ask for *'Un episcopal'* you will get both green and yellow poured over crushed ice and drunk through a straw — a delicious anytime drink as well as a digestive.

Armagnac is 'the brandy of the Gascons'. It is not, as some believe, 'weaker' than Cognac — it is different, very aromatic and the method of production is slightly different *(see p.169)*. A *Pousse Rapière* is a fairly recently evolved aperitif: a measure of Armagnac is topped up with the local dry (very dry) white sparkling wine of the Gers region, garnished with a twist of orange-peel. It is now available in ready-prepared packs, although a good restaurant should make up the individual drink. The name comes from the *Three Musketeers* era (when heroes had 'thews of iron, wrists of steel'). It is supposed to be the drink that gave just that additional bit of strength to someone who had spitted his opponent in a duel and wanted to withdraw his blade, though one feels the unfortunate recipient of the coup would have been in greater need. However, it is a delectable drink — with a very definite, albeit unsuspected, strength!

There are a number of wines made in the western area of the Pyrenees, although until recently these were seldom found outside the region — and, truly, were neither of a character nor a quality to warrant being exported. Now things are different. There is Jurançon, which is now available in both dry and sweet versions, very agreeable; it is supposed to have been — like garlic

— one of the things that moistened the lips of Henri IV (a sweetish wine could have soothed any teething infant). The red, *rosé* and white wines of this end of the Pyrenees include those of Béarn, Irouléguy and Tursan; the tendency is to make red wines these days in Béarn. Writers record a curious white, called Tursan, made after the grapes had virtually dried on the vines. I have never succeeded in finding it and, maybe, these days it is either not made at all, or else only in tiny amounts. Possibly someone will revive a version of it. Madiran is a red wine, traditionally allowed to stay for some years in cask before being bottled — like the true old Cahors. It is fair to say that not all Madiran today is made like that, but it can be a pleasant drink. *Pacherence du Vic Bilh* is a local white.

The Roussillon, however, makes many different wines, of which the *vins doux naturels* are certainly the best-known locally (*see p.186*). For *vins doux* here, the Grenache, Macabeo, Malvoisie

---

All the dishes were very delicate, and a vast change from the simple English system, with its joints, shoulders, beefsteaks and chops; but I doubt whether English cookery, for the very reason that it is so simple, is not better for men's moral and spiritual nature than the French. In the former case, you know that you are gratifying your animal needs and propensities, and are duly ashamed of it; but, in dealing with these French delicacies, you delude yourself into the idea that you are cultivating your taste while satisfying your appetite. . . . It is certainly throwing away the bounties of Providence to treat them as the English do, producing from better materials than the French have to work on nothing but sirloins, joints, steaks, steaks, steaks, chops, chops, chops, chops! We had a soup today, in which twenty kinds of vegetables were represented, and manifested each its aroma; a fillet of stewed beef, and a fowl, in some sort of delicate fricassee. We had a bottle of Chablis, and renewed ourselves, at the close of the banquet, with a plate of Châteaubriand ice. It was all very good, and we respected ourselves far more than if we had eaten a quantity of roast beef; but I am not quite sure that we are right.

NATHANIEL HAWTHORNE, *French Note Books*, 1858

grapes are used, plus some of the Muscat variety, and the place-names to note are: Banyuls, Maury, Muscat de Rivesaltes and Rivesaltes. The producers have a dilemma — in export markets, the strength of their wines, slightly higher than that of table wines, is against them as regards duty, and the competition by the established aperitif firms and those of the sherry houses is daunting. *Vins doux naturels* are delicious between-times drinks — and should certainly be tried by anyone in the region.

The Roussillon table-wines are becoming well-known. Thanks to the improved technology in wine-making and the use of discreet amounts of *macération carbonique* wines (*see p.152*), some of the previous hard, tough, barely palatable southern wines of the region can now be mouth-filling, fresh, fruity drinks. They will never be wines to put away for long-term maturation, but they give great pleasure as everyday drinks. Although the white wines can be somewhat 'southern' — a little full, fat and lacking in crispness and bouquet — the reds, made from the Carignan, Grenache, Cinsaut, Mourvèdre and Syrah grapes, can be thoroughly enjoyable. The Côtes du Roussillon wines provide good value today and, if you are on the spot, try to find some of those that are truly 'local'.

Things to See and Do

Bayonne has, in the Musée Basque, a complete record of Basque history and life; it is one of the finest museums of its kind. You are able to visit the Distillerie de la Côte Basque, which produces Izarra and the Armagnac Clès des Ducs. If possible, explore the chocolate shops *'sous les arceaux'* (under the arches) in the rue du Port Neuf, where the shops sell cakes and pastry as well as sweets and superb chocolates — they will post foodstuffs, but remember, preservatives may not be in the chocolates. You can also see good displays of Basque table linen in this street.

Banyuls has an aquarium where most Mediterranean fish may be seen.

Biarritz has a well appointed aquarium, with a seal pool and aviary.

Oloron Sainte Marie is where the church, formerly the cathedral, has a remarkable doorway to the porch of the belfry: part of this represents various local activities, which include work in vineyards, cheese-making, curing hams, hunting the boar and salmon fishing.

Thuir is famous for the Byrrh establishment, which is open to visitors — the enormous cask is displayed with pride and the aperitif may be sampled.

Museums

At Lourdes, the Musée Pyrénéan in the Château Fort has a collection of objects portraying Pyrenean life in past times. At Pau, the Musée Regional Béarnaise in the château shows objects involved with Béarn life in the past, including cooking utensils. The small Musée du Pays de Bigorre at Tarbes has a collection of objects concerned with local life. In the cloisters of the cathedral at Condom there is the Musée de l'Armagnac, showing the equipment and stages of production of the spirit; Nogaro, the establishment of Dartigalongue et Fils, which was founded in 1838, has a museum that shows that firm's history, together with bottles and *bonbonnes* of old Armagnacs of vintage years.

32

The Rhône Valley and Provence

This region is really several. Provence begins, strictly speaking, south of Orange; the Lyonnais extends throughout the upper reaches of the Rhône Valley and the foothills to the east, the uplands to the west each have their own, often very ancient, culinary traditions. These days wine regions that were hardly known even ten years ago are making excellent wines of many types — the Ardèche, Tricastin, Vivarais, Gard, Ventoux, Vaucluse are only a few of the names now to be seen on export lists.

From before records were kept, traders came in from the Mediterranean, bringing produce and recipes. Peter Hallgarten, in his *Guide to the Wines of the Rhône* (Century), says that some of the traditional Provençal soups can be traced to the Greeks who first came to the south; Italians from over the border have of course influenced many dishes. The Romans, who used the river itself as a highway — as did subsequent traders and travellers — have left traces everywhere; merchants from the Middle East landed at Marseille and ventured north with their wares. The mountains were not insuperable barriers to hardy mountain folk and from Switzerland and northern Italy people came in to work, to study, to take a ship or pursue a pilgrim route. As early as around 600 B.C. the Phoenicians, Greeks from Asia Minor, are supposed to have introduced the culture of the grape, although it seems as if it was the Romans, requiring wine for the armies, who established the region as a source of wine. Lyon was the capital of Gaul in 27 B.C.. But it was in the truly dark ages, when pirates from northern Europe, Saracens, and other marauding bands ventured to this obviously rich territory, that the great religious houses began to be established, providing places to stay for travellers in addition to acting as hospitals, schools and makers of wine. Many of the great vineyards of today were first cultivated by monks. When, in the fourteenth century, the Pope came to Avignon, the region enjoyed enormous prosperity — the popes accumulated huge stocks of wine and the banquets of some of those who were known more for their hospitality than their saintliness were impressive: Clément VI, known as 'the Magnificent', gave a banquet at which a wine fountain was brought in to the hall after the fifth course, and from which flowed the wines of the Rhine, Burgundy, St Pourçain, La Rochelle and Provence. The local 'Courts of Love', which, presided over by great ladies and attended by poets and troubadours, were where the young sons and daughters of the nobility went to be 'finished' — and enjoy civilized eating and drinking. In more recent times, the Rhône was the route for many making the 'grand tour' — often with their servants and cooks — and, doubtless, leaving traces of their eating habits behind them, just as one of the most famous of 'milords' left his name on the numerous 'Hôtels Bristol' after his luxurious touring. Then there were the artists and writers, the former profiting by the wonderful light and subjects that often included food and drink; the latter often going down to the south because it was cheap. Writers George Sand and Alfred de Musset stopped at Pont St Esprit with Stendhal while *en route* for Italy and Stendhal got tipsy and danced wildly with the waitress. A sketch of this incident, by de Musset, still exists. Poet Frédéric Mistral (1830 – 1914) revived the use of Provençal as a language and the local fairs and fêtes began to attract many visitors, who revelled in the picturesque costumes, the wealth of folklore and traditions, not forgetting the food and the wines.

The countryside is very varied, often dramatic and wild, the climate likewise. A river-bed may be dried up one day and barely contain a raging torrent the next. The Mistral — the drying wind that scorches down the Valley — the sun that bakes all but the stones to splitting point, the beautiful but barren stretches of land, over which the wind brings wafts of the fragrance of herbs, are all examples of extremes — and there is nothing indeterminate about a Rhône Valley or Provençal market or table, either. Even the simplest dishes of olives, radishes, *pâté*, and the most straightforward soup or salad are usually colourful and invariably arranged with unconscious artistry.

Food in General

There are three supreme elements in Provençal cooking: olive oil — a fish 'lives in water and dies in oil' is the saying; garlic — 'the truffle of Provence', although real truffles are also found there — which is associated with many health-giving properties and longevity; and tomatoes, which, irregular in shape and often huge, glow in every market. But garlic as used here is not necessarily aggressive, nor is oil so 'oily' that the Anglo-Saxon need be intimidated into ordering omelettes day after day. Oil is often used for making pastry as well. The herbs are varied and wonderful — one can smell them from miles away: *romarin* (rosemary) is used with lamb, *basilic* (basil) and *fenouil* (fennel) with fish, and *frigolet*, the Provençal wild thyme, is also much used. Because of the poor pasture, the animals tend to develop muscles rather than fat, but, as many of the recipes involve long slow cooking, this does not mean that meat is tough.

Artichauts, courgettes, aubergines, cardons (chard), *poivrons* (peppers) are only some of the vegetables, and there are plenty of mushrooms of various kinds. *Pois chiches* (chickpeas) may be found in salads. Truffles are a speciality of Carpentras and Tricastin. In season, there is asparagus, but *'asperges Vauclusienne'* is a joke-name for artichokes. In recent years the plantations of rice in the Camargue have resulted in the use of this in a number of ways as well. There is plenty of fruit, including the famous Cavaillon melons, *pastèque* (watermelon), figs, pomegranates and *kaki* (persimmon) and every kind of soft fruit.

Brochet (pike) and other river fish are found in the streams and trout in the foothills of the Vaucluse. Tiny fish are presented in a *friture* or *matelote*. Around Valence there is a very odd fish, called the *pogne suisse*, which, as far as I can make out, is a relation of the pike. On the coast there are the usual crabs, lobsters and langoustes. Toulon *moules* (mussels) are famous and there are also *palourdes* (clams), *patelles* or *arapèdes* (limpets), *poulpes* (octopus), *seiches* or *supions* (cuttlefish), *tautènes* (tiny inkfish or squid), *oursins* (sea-urchins), *favouilles* (little crabs), sardines and, of course, the *loup de mer* (sea bass), sometimes grilled over herbs. Snails, often called *limaces*, may feature on menus or, as a joke, be referred to as *'les rapides de Provence'*.

There are many variations on the *daube*, or stew, flavoured with herbs and onions, plus wine and, usually, garlic. The *pré salé* lamb of the Camargue is considered very good and many different regional dishes for lamb as well as beef are to be found. An *estouffade* is another type of stew. *Poulets de Bresse* (Bresse chickens) actually have their own *appellation contrôlée* and they too are the base of many chicken recipes. Hare and rabbit, which have fed on the herb-rich pastures, are of excellent flavour and so are small game birds, including *grives* (thrushes), which are often presented *en brochette*, spitted and roasted. The pig contributes various sausages and hams — that of Mont Ventoux is well-known — and wild boar are also found here, as well as the more usual types of game.

The abundance of fruit means that this is invariable at the end of a meal, but jams, preserves and whole preserved or candied fruits are also made; shops can usually show a tempting range. Montélimar is the nougat capital — in the sixteenth-century almond-trees were planted there, having been brought from Asia, and it was discovered that the nuts and local honey — also fragrant with the herbs of the *garrigue* or upland pastures — made a specially delicious sweetmeat. Carpentras is famous for *berling-ots*, a hard sweet that might be described as a type of 'satin cushion', and there are many biscuits made with honey and almonds, as well as sweet dishes.

Specialities and Dishes

Aioli is virtually garlic mayonnaise — often served with raw or cooked vegetables, as an *hors d'oeuvre*. Anything described as 'Provençal' on a menu will generally include garlic and, possibly, tomatoes. *Aïgo bouïdo* is garlic soup; *aïgo sau* is a fish stew, with potatoes, onions, mushrooms, artichokes, olive oil and garlic; *raïto* is a sauce of herbs, pounded walnuts, onions, tomatoes, red wine and garlic; *pesto* or *pistou* is the great sauce of garlic and basil, plus Parmesan or other hard grated cheese, often used with soup or pasta; *rouille* is another sauce with garlic, yolks of eggs, oil and tomato-paste, plus chilli — it is added to various fish soups and stews — and it is really hot. Because garlic, even in the mild variety of Provence, does crop up in so many dishes, this may be a place to remind travellers that, unless they are accustomed to it, initially a garlicky dish can be a trifle 'loosening' but not harmful; also, that a coffee-bean or sprig of parsley chewed after eating anything containing garlic removes the smell from the breath. *Anchoïade* is pounded anchovies, served on toast. The Provençal tradition favours little 'nibbles' of this kind by way of accompaniment to drinks before a meal or, in more substantial form, as an *hors d'oeuvre*.

Tapenade is pounded black olives, served in the same way, plus capers, anchovy, tuna, lemon-juice and olive oil — or whatever variations the locality finds acceptable.

Poutargue is the roe of grey mullet, sometimes served in salads or as an *hors d'oeuvre*. *Bourride* is an *aioli*, to which the stock of a hot fish-soup has been added, the fish being served separately. *Catigau d'anguilles* is a type of eel stew, plus onions, tomatoes, oil and garlic. *Brandade de morue* is a purée of smoked cod, incorporating cream, oil — and garlic. It should not remind you of the worst type of boarding-school fish pie — in fact, if your mouth gets clogged with bones, you can be sure the *brandade* is not a good one (so write to whichever restaurant guide recommended it). *Rastegais* is a type of fishcake.

Panisso/panisse is a mush or purée of chickpeas or maize, cooked until solid, then fried. It is one of the 'fillers' that appear in most styles of cookery where basic and expensive ingredients have to be eked out. *Pieds et paquets* is a Marseille speciality but can appear in other regions — tripe and trotters in little bundles, poached with vegetables. It is far more delicious than it probably sounds. *Cayettes de sanglier* is something that might be translated as 'a Provençal version of haggis': liver of wild boar, compounded with bacon, boar's flesh, herbs and wine, chopped vegetables, put into a caul and cooked. It is usually served cold, but I have no experience of it.

Soupe d'épautre is a stew of beef or beef and veal, plus herbs, vegetables and garlic. *Fassum* is stuffed cabbage, flavoured with herbs and poached.

A *tian* is a dish in which certain things are cooked — a baking or soufflé dish — but the term sometimes refers to the recipe. This mades use of a variety of different vegetables, herbs and eggs, plus rice; everything is baked together in the *tian* and served, like a *gratin*, from the dish.

Ratatouille must be familiar to many. It is a mixture of aubergines, courgettes, onions, peppers, herbs and seasonings, sliced and fried in oil.

Pastèque à la Provençale is watermelon, scooped out and filled with red wine.

Gâteaux soufflés aux pignons are pastry puffs, made with pine-nuts.

A pertinent comment made by cookery writer Anne Willan is to the effect that many of the vegetable and some other dishes of this part of France are and should be served tepid — to chill them is to deprive the diner of much of the delicate flavour.

Drinks

The famous aperitif of the south is *pastis* (*see p.177*), but if anyone does not like the flavour of anise, there are plenty of others. The *vins doux naturels* are particularly pleasant between-times drinks: they are (*see p.186*) wines that are slightly higher in strength than table-wines, made with the addition of alcohol — as has been mentioned, the French do not like or, indeed, understand the term 'fortified wine', so be careful about using it casually. The additional 'strengthening' may be achieved either by the blending in of some spirit or else with the addition of *mistelle*, a type of concentrate of grape-juice and spirit. Most famous in this part of France is the Muscat de Beaumes de Venise, which can attain delicious style and true quality — each establishment making it will produce a slightly different version, but it is a perfect drink for the conclusion of a good meal or by way of an anytime refresher. Another sweetish aperitif wine is Rasteau, of similar style, though Rasteau makes table-wines as well. As these wines are seldom able to be exported — their alcoholic strength means that the duty penalizes them — anyone on the spot should certainly try them.

The vines of this extensive area are of great interest — and increasingly so. Our ancestors loved them and it is fair to say that many who spend large sums on 'Burgundy' of possibly dubious quality and definitely doubtful provenance would be better pleased with a Rhône wine. Those of the south and Provence are much more interesting these days than mere 'holiday' wines and, as has been mentioned, there are many areas that are now making good wines that are reaching export markets. The majority have a direct appeal and are not difficult to understand; some of the finest merit keeping and if you are fortunate enough to find some older wines on the list of a restaurant, they may be treasures. A big range is made: leaving aside the *vins doux naturels*, there are sparkling wines, still whites and still reds, involving a great number of different grapes and, usually, several are used — there are, for example, thirteen permitted for Châteauneuf-du-Pape, although these days only about nine are of importance. There are a few single grape varieties being made, however, so that it can help to register such important and influential grapes as the Syrah. This region deserves study, especially as the wine-makers, although many of them are only small-scale growers, are overall well-organized about visits and there are many tasting-rooms for the general public. It is only possible here to give brief notes on some of the main wines of the different areas. Do not overlook the fact that many first-rate wines are, according to regulations, quite meekly labelled and the A.O.C.s may only be Côtes du Rhône, or Côtes du Rhône Villages; there are a few single estates, in the sense that the Anglo-Saxon will understand the term that '*Domaine*' implies, there are many larger firms who buy in from small producers and who may also own vineyards themselves.

Red and white still wines are made, the sweet wines have already been mentioned — especially Muscat de Beaumes de Venise — and there are sparkling wines made at Die, from a blend of Muscat and Clairette, with a very long history, and at St Péray, a wine that also is mentioned by writers of ancient times, and was liked by both Napoleon and Richard Wagner (when he was composing 'Parsifal'). Personally, I do not accept either of these eminent persons as authorities on wine, but the Rhône white sparkling wines are of interest — clean, light, dry.

In the north of the Rhône Valley there are the Côte Rôtie vineyards, across the river from Vienne, tottering down the slopes above Ampuis. They consist of the Côte Blonde and the Côte Brune, the picturesque tag being that the owner had two daughters, one blonde, the other brunette, but in fact the soil of one section of the vineyard is darker than the other. The Viognier vine, used in these, is utilized alone to make the white wine of Condrieu, the 'house white' of the great Restaurant de la Pyramide at Vienne and of Château Grillet, the tiny property that fortunately can be seen, on a shelf of the hillside, from the main road; it makes about 11,000 bottles annually and it is the one vineyard to have its own individual A.O.C. Personally, although the fame of this wine has spread far and wide, I am inclined to think that the scarcity is what has endowed it with most of its reputation — it can be very good, but although one should certainly try it when possible, it may not impress the wine lover, who has enjoyed experience of many fine wines from throughout the world, as truly 'great'.

Côte du Rhône whites are full, dry and somewhat aromatic — not wines to drink casually and perhaps at their best with food. The reds are full, rounded, fruity, usually excellent value. At the point where the Rhône twists sharply, the twin towns of Tain l'Hermitage and Tournon provide opportunities to view the vineyards, which are quite spectacular as they are terraced above the Rhône, and register the wines of St Joseph and Cornas as well as those of Crozes-Hermitage and Hermitage. It should be borne in mind that Hermitage is a wine that, from a fine maker, needs time to mature and is usually imposing — not, it should be noted, 'strapping', in any vulgar sense — and that the Crozes wines are usually ready and at their peak somewhat earlier than the Hermitage wines.

Châteauneuf-du-Pape has been famous, even outside France, for a very long time. The vineyards of this district are extraordinary: some consist of sand, others of enormous orange stones, many the size of a human head, making it extremely difficult to walk on them; these act as 'night storage heaters' and, during the night, reflect the heat they hold up onto the vines. They look exactly like baked potatoes. The various different makers all follow individual styles and there are some estates, which naturally are distinctive in character; there is some white wine made as well. If you get the opportunity to try either the white or red wine of Château Rayas, they will make a lasting impression. Nearby, Gigondas is another area well worth getting to know — mostly red wine is produced here — which used, until fairly recently, to be put into blends for Châteauneuf-du-Pape. But there are many: Lirac, Cairanne, Laudun, Vacqueyras, Côtes du Ventoux, Coteaux du Tricastin. Tavel is certainly the most famous *rosé* wine in the world, but it is never cheap, even in the region. There are even a few estates, but most is made by co-operatives. Other good *rosé* is made at Chusclan and several of the regions previously mentioned.

One of the most important contributions made by this vineyard area to modern wine-making is the process known as '*macération carbonique*' (*see p.316*), which was pioneered by the late Baron le Roy, a dynamic personality in the Rhône Valley wine world. Indeed, everywhere visitors will see new vineyards being created, usually by means of the most modern machinery, and most installations, make use of wholly up-to-date methods.

Since 1979 certain Côtes du Rhône wines may be bottled in a 'Rhodanienne' bottle which has a defined but sloping shoulder.

Things to See and Do

Wine visits can be arranged to many establishments — consult the well-organized Maison du Tourisme, 41 cours Jean Jaurès, Avignon. But you may simply see notices drawing attention to the de Dégustation, which may be quite small and modest, or built on a large scale, with exhibits relating to wine as well as samples available for tasting. Theoretically, says the admirable book on the Rhône wines by John Livingstone-Learmonth and Melvyn Master (Faber)[1], these *caveaux* are open seven days a week, but this is something that cannot be guaranteed, especially outside the summer season. As far as growers are concerned, an appointment must be made in advance and kept to, as there is seldom a large staff employed at individual premises.

Among some tasting-rooms and cellars that may provide useful information are the Père Anselme establishment, at Châteauneuf-du-Pape, which has a large wine museum and is generally open. There is a small but attractive tasting-room at Sainte Cécile des Vignes. The Abbaye du Bouchet, near Tulette, now belongs to the Celliers du Dauphin, who have converted the Cistercian abbey into an impressive cellar, well worth seeing. There is a section devoted to wine in the museum at Cairanne. The famous establishments at Tain-Tournon of Paul Jaboulet Aîné and Chapoutier can receive visitors if prior notice is given, and this applies also at Ampuis and Condrieu, where the house of Vidal-Fleury is of importance, although there are other smaller concerns that enjoy great prestige. Château Grillet is too small to receive visitors, but a very good view of it may be had if you stop on the main road.

At Suze-la-Rousse the fifteenth-century château has been converted into the Université du Vin. This is a magnificent project and students from many countries attend the courses. Specialists give lectures and there are sessions in languages other than French, dealing with all aspects of wine for the different types of people engaged in the trade — *sommeliers*, caterers, oenologists, ampelographers and many more. It is well worth the while of any serious lover of wine to arrange a visit; the tasting-rooms are unique and the place itself is beautiful as well as practical — alongside is a Jeu de Paume, which is said to be the oldest in existence.

Arles has a very fine museum in the form of the Muséum Arlaten, which was founded by Frédéric Mistral with the money he received for the Nobel Prize. There are many exhibits relating to local life, including the various different loaves baked for special festivities, utensils involved with the various crafts, and so on.

1 *Guide to the Wines of the Rhône*, 1984.

The Abbaye de Silvacane has a fine large refectory, which was rebuilt in the fifteenth century.

Montélimar's nougat factories may be seen — apply to the Chambre Syndicale des Fabricants de Nougat de Montélimar.

Kitchens, often of great historic interest, may be seen in the Palais des Papes in Avignon, plus the larder, butler's storeroom and pantry; there is a typical Provençal kitchen in the château at Ansouis, which is open to visitors; at Salon-de-Provence there is a Musée du Vieux Salon, of regional exhibits; at Cavaillon the Musée du Vieux Cavaillon has many exhibits of local arts and crafts; at the Musée du Vieux Beaucaire there are exhibits relating to the famous fair, plus local furniture and domestic equipment.

Just opposite Tournon rises the world-famous hill of the Hermitage, where the noble wine is grown. As every inch of the ground is of almost fabulous value, the hill-side, which is very steep, has long been artificially cut into terraces supported by walls, which spoil its beauty entirely. Behind Tournon, the road leads up a hill . . . and . . . a magnificent view. . . . That was a sight to compensate for the ugliness of the vineyards by the river. . . . A vine-land is very splendid in autumn . . . but in summer the dull green is sadly wanting in variety and in the dreary blaze of unchanging sunshine the low vines offer no shade. Besides, one has no sense of liberty when looking on a French vine country, for it is not a pleasant land to walk over, in the narrow paths between the sticks. The vines may be an agreeable sight for those whom they make rich . . . but a landscape painter, who likes to surround himself with an abundance of natural beauty, does better to avoid them.

PHILIP GILBERT HAMERTON, *Round my House, notes of rural life in France in peace and war*, 1876

33

Savoie and Dauphiné

This is a beautiful and unspoiled part of France, still compara-tively unknown to visitors from abroad. For the purposes of this chapter, I have made the boundaries limited by the Rhône on the west, the Swiss and Italian borders on the east, have arbitrarily drawn a line from Geneva to Bourg in the north and from Montélimar to the border in the south. Savoie (or Savoy), formerly an independent duchy, was only united with France in 1860; the Dauphiné, which gave its name (rather as a sop) to the heir to the French throne, henceforth known as the Dauphin, has been French since the fourteenth century. Italian and French influences are both evident in the gastronomy, though the people are as independent in temperament as one expects those who live in mountain country to be.

The food is usually delicious, both because of the high quality of such ingredients as the butter (the best butter I have ever had in my life was in the Vercors), the cream, cheeses, fish from the mountain lakes and meat from the high pastures. The region, a little apart but not remote from the richness of Burgundian and Lyonnais cooking and the spicy dishes of the south, has produced remarkable numbers of great chefs and thousands of first-rate cooks: the number of starred restaurants in the region is consider-able. If it is possible at all to generalize, perhaps it might be said that the *haute cuisine* of the area combines the comforting quality of everyday, simple dishes with the lightness and inspired indi-viduality of great cooking; it is the sort of French food that is immediately easy to like, even for people who are hesitant about strange things or who have delicate digestions as far as most elaborate recipes are concerned. It can be no mere chance that

Brillat-Savarin, author of one of the most sensible and practical books on gastronomy and one of history's most considerate hosts, was born and lived here (*see p.333*). Even the ultra-aesthetic John Ruskin brought back a recipe for soup from Chamonix. Elizabeth Ayrton's novel *The Cook's Tale* (Chatto and Windus) describes the life (and gives some recipes) of a restaurant in that part of France.

Food in General

Excellent dairy produce comes from the pastures. *Fondue*, the appetizing cheese 'dip', appears on menus, though sometimes it is more like a cheese pudding than the Swiss version of the recipe. The mountain lakes and streams yield fine fish, of which three anyway are unlikely to be found elsewhere — the *féra, lavaret* and *omble chevalier*; all are types of salmon, but the last looks more like a trout. Carp, eel, pike, perch, crayfish and burbot (*lotte*) are also plentiful. As in many mountainous and rather wild regions, the smoked pork products and sausages are abundant — husky fare for climbers and those engaged in ski-ing and outdoor sports; *cochonnailles* (assorted pork meats) feature as *hors d'oeuvre*, smoked raw ham and smoked sausages, sausages called *longeoles* which are flavoured with anise. Other variations on the pig include *le caïon* (loin of pork in a marinade). Slightly exotic game, such as hedgehog (*hérisson*), squirrel (*écureuil*) and marmot (*marmotte*) are mentioned in books about the regional foods before the 1939 war, but they have not come my way. The *chamois* (same word) gets featured, so do thrushes (*grives*) from which a variety of *pâtés* are made, and the *civet*, a term best translated by our culinary word 'jug', can include hare or pork in a rich sauce.

The chickens of Bourg-en-Bresse (this is just on the edge of the region and Franche-Comté) are famous throughout France, and in fact they have an *appellation contrôlée* guaranteeing their quality and are to be identified by a ring on the bird's foot. They are fed on corn and wander about the roads in the Bresse plain, plumpening visibly; when killed, they are bathed in milk and the flesh is very white. If you see them alive in the market, you will note their blue legs, wattles and combs. The flavour is delicate and therefore such a bird will usually be offered plainly roasted, when the skin turns a beautiful crisp golden-brown; the *poulet de Bresse* (*poularde* is the hen-bird, should a menu be that precise) will cost more than the ordinary *poulet de grain* (grain or maize fed yellowish-looking chicken), but it should be worth the extra. However, the A.C. can be given to birds actually not of the original Bresse breed, which are either reared in the region or else brought in to be finally fattened in it, so you may be in for a slight disappointment, though it is fair to say that I have on occasion had a chicken that was as good as all but the finest of the Bresse type and only found it to be an outsider by inquiring.

Noodles (*nouilles*) are often featured in dishes as well as being served as vegetables, showing the influence of Italy's pasta, and there is the vegetable called the *cardon*, which is an 'edible thistle' known elsewhere sometimes as Swiss chard. The potatoes are usually excellent, and feature in the numerous *gratins* (see below). There are plenty of mushrooms of different kinds, including one called a *mousseron*, in addition to *cèpes, morilles, truffés,* and there is even *épis de maïs* (sweetcorn), which elsewhere is considered as mainly only a cattle food. Pumpkin (*courge*) is another vegetable not often seen much elsewhere. The nuts, both walnuts (*noix*) and chestnuts (*châtaignes*), from around Grenoble are famous and *huile de noix* (walnut oil) is often used for salads and seasoning as in the Dordogne.

A curious sweet dish is made with potatoes, which is called *le farçon* or *le farcement*; it involves the potatoes being beaten up with eggs, sugar and butter, sometimes even with fruit and a liqueur, as well as salt, pepper and possibly chervil, then being grilled. *Talmouses* are like small sweetened potato fritters. There are many other sweet things, the *nougat* of Montélimar being very well-known (the town is virtually one long nougat shop, see p.321); *sucre d'orge* (sticks of barley-sugar) from Evian; honey from Queyras; *pets de nonne* (small potato and sugar yeast buns) from Chamonix; *noix confits* (candied walnuts), from Grenoble; and all kinds of chocolates from Grenoble, including a type called *délices à la Chartreuse*, which are filled with the liqueur. *Biscuits de Savoie* are also well-known.

Specialities and Dishes

Le gratin: This in various forms, is *the* local dish. The word actually means crust, hence the French slang term '*le gratin*' means 'the upper crust' of society. In cooking, *gratin* means anything on which a crust has been made to form after the application of heat; thus it applies not only to things with a crisped surface of cheese, but dishes with crumbs on top, or even just milk or cream. Of the *gratin Dauphinois* the following rhyme has been written:

Non, tu n'es point un mets vulgaire,
Savoureux gratin dauphinois,
Blond chef d'oeuvre d'art culinaire
Qu'on mange en se léchant les doigts.

(Though why one should need to lick one's fingers after eating any *gratin*, except the famous one with crayfish tails, I cannot imagine.) There are a whole range of *gratins*, including those made with millet, pumpkin, different fruits, thrushes and *bolets* (*boletus* mushrooms), but the two most famous are undoubtedly the *gratin de queues d'écrevisses* (crayfish tails), referred to above, which are poached and served in a rich creamy sauce, and the two sorts of potato *gratin*. These last are really like the nursery-dish, potato pie, but can achieve such delicacy of quality that I have known local gourmets argue for a considerable time as to the precise texture of the potatoes and the proportions of the particular cheeses possibly involved in a *gratin*. The *gratin Dauphinois*, in addition to thinly sliced potatoes, contains milk, eggs, butter and grated cheese; the *gratin Savoyard* is made with *bouillon* instead of milk. Potatoes served as accompaniments to dishes are sometimes described as *à la savoyarde*, or *dauphinois* and will be cooked in these respective ways. Omelettes containing potatoes and cheese are also made with the same description applying to them.

Angurre de Belley: Pickled water-melon.

Caillettes: Pig's liver chopped with spinach, herbs, rolled in a caul and baked and served hot or cold. *Caillettes triscabines*, a speciality of Pierrelate, also contain chopped white truffles.

Pain de lapin dauphinois: A type of *quenelle or meat-ball of pounded rabbit and cream, in a cream sauce.*

The Savoyard nobility here keep as good tables, without money, as those in London who spend in a week what would be here a considerable yearly revenue. Wine, which is equal to the best burgundy, is sold for a penny a quart.

LADY MARY WORTLEY MONTAGUE TO LADY POMFRET, Chambéry, 3 December, 1741

Défarde Crestoise: A curious stew of tripe and lambs' feet, boiled with vegetables and herbs, and served in a sauce of white wine, tomatoes and stock. A speciality of Crest.

Pogne: This is a great sweet dish, but can vary considerably according to where you are. In north Dauphiné it is usually a deep, open fruit-pie, with pumpkin filling or fruit, but towards the south it may be a sweet *brioche* or bun.

Drinks

Ciders and beers are made in this region, as well as wine, but the drink that, in my opinion, best deserves wider knowledge is the vermouth of Chambéry, in which the herbs of the mountains are incorporated. Chambéry is very delicate, usually dry and rather fragrant and is mostly drunk by itself as an aperitif, chilled and sometimes with a twist of lemon. It is unlike other French vermouths (*see p.187*).

If you ask the *sommelier* for a fine red wine, he will probably recommend one from the Beaujolais or Côte Rôtie, in adjacent regions, but the red Savoy Montmélian, Saint Jean de la Porte, Côte Hyot should be tried when one is on the spot. The remainder of the wines are white. Seyssel is possibly the best known wine of Savoy, white, dry and pleasantly fresh. In addition, there is Chablais from the north of Savoie, Crépy from the borders of France and Switzerland, Frangy, Egignin, Aise and Roussette. In and around Chambéry a white wine called Apremont is to be had, also dry, and there is another called Marétel which is rather sweeter. All these wines go well with the region's fish and creamy dishes, such as the *gratins*. Seyssel is sometimes made into a good sparkling wine, but perhaps the best-known sparkling wine of the Dauphiné in export markets is Clairette de Die, made according to the local regulations, in various styles, some of them sweet, but usually very pleasant.

Fruit liqueurs are made, as they are in most mountain regions, and the slightly bitter *gentiane*, an excellent digestive, appears in various branded preparations. China, an odd name, is a liqueur made from wild cherries and is a speciality of Grenoble, which is also responsible for the violet coloured and scented Parfait Amour; camomile liqueur, different kinds of cherry brandy and *kirsch*, and fruit brandies made from *plosses* or *airelles*, berries variously translated as bilberries or barberries, are also found. Genopy des Alpes is a digestive from Grenoble and Voiron and Vespétro a sweetish digestive, also from Grenoble. *Marc* is made, as it is in most wine regions, but there is also a strange and very fierce liqueur called *la lie* which is distilled from all the residue of the grapes after the final pressings. (I have not come across it.)

The great liqueur of the area is, of course, Chartreuse (*see pp.174–5*), named for the Carthusian order founded by Saint Bruno at Chartreuse near Grenoble in 1084. It was a group of French army officers, billeted in the abbey at Voiron in 1848, who spread the fame of the different liqueurs made — green, yellow and something known as elixir de Chartreuse, pure white. A distillery was built at Fourvoirie in 1860 and did good business until the Carthusians were expelled from France in 1903, when they took the secret of their liqueurs to Tarragona. They returned to France in 1931 and, after the Fourvoirie distillery was destroyed in 1935, another one was built at Voiron.

Things to See and Do

Albertville: The Musée de la Maison Rouge contains exhibits and furniture of Savoyard life.

Annecy: The Palais de l'Isle contains the Musée du Vieil Annecy, with the reconstruction of an old kitchen and equipment. The Hôtel de Ville contains local china and glassware in its museum.

Bauges: In this region *'argenterie des Bauges'* means wooden tableware, a craft now on the decline, but of interest to anyone interested in handwork.

Belley: The birthplace of Brillat-Savarin (1755–1826), author of *La Physiologie du Goût*, and containing a statue of him.

Bourg-en-Bresse: Visitors to the church at Brou, a masterpiece of French art, should see the Cloître de Cuisines in which there is a reconstruction of a Bresse house with furniture and equipment.

Chambéry: The Grande Distillerie Chambérienne is open to visitors and is of special interest because two quite different types of vermouth are made there — Gaudin and Dolin. The two other big vermouth establishments, Richard and Chambéry-Moulin, are also well worth seeing.

The Musée Savoisien contains exhibits of popular life. It was in the part of the Château destroyed in 1798 that the famous feast was given by which a cake created a duchy. This was when Count Amédée of Savoy was entertaining the Emperor Sigismond in the huge Imperial salon in 1416; no expense was spared, each course was presented by the local lords, each on horseback and magnificently caparisoned, prancing into the salon. A gigantic cake was finally brought in, made in the shape of the Comté (County) of Savoy and Amédée, proudly displaying it to the imperial guest, casually remarked 'It would make a nice duchy, wouldn't it?' The Emperor took the hint and Savoy did in fact become a duchy and Amédée a duke.

Die: There are some local exhibits in the Musée.

Evian-les-Bains: Visitors may see the Source Cachat and bottling of the mineral waters.

Gap: In the Musée Départemental there are exhibits of local furniture and furnishings and china.

Château de Ripaille: As well as the Château, the gardens and kitchens of the Carthusians, who inherited the property from the last Duke of Savoy, are open to visitors. The curious expression *'faire ripaille'* originally implied that a life of abstinence was lived, like that of Amédée VIII, who renounced his dukedom to live a monastic existence in 1439. Later on, however, the expression acquired the completely opposite meaning and, due chiefly to Voltaire, *'faire ripaille'* came to mean 'to live a luxurious and self-indulgent life of feasts and parties'.

Thonon-les-Bains: In the Château de Sonnaz a museum of the region has been set up. At the Établissement Domanial de Pisci-culture there is an important series of exhibits of fishes and material to enable visitors to study their development, including the regional *omble chevalier*.

Voiron: The distillery where Chartreuse liqueur is now made, under supervision of the monks, may be visited. The monastic buildings of La Grande Chartreuse are not open to visitors. The former distillery built at Fourvoirie in 1860 was destroyed by a landslide in 1935, but the ruins may still be seen.

Festivals and Fairs

Throughout the year there are numerous exhibitions, wine and food fairs and festivals of various kinds in most regions. As the dates can vary, it is advisable to get information on these from either the local tourist office or from any of the syndicates whose addresses are given here. The big wine fairs are likely to be of more interest to people seriously concerned with wine than the more casual tourist, so professional or trade credentials are sometimes necessary if you wish to be allowed to buy a ticket.

What is also worth bearing in mind is that any major event of this kind will attract crowds of visitors and, in consequence, hotel and restaurant accommodation may be difficult to find and otherwise quiet villages and towns will be thronged and noisy.

If you are unable to make direct contact with any branch of the French Government Tourist Office, or the organization known as S.O.P.E.X.A. or Food & Wine from France, which has a number of offices in different countries, then any good travel agent, especially those featuring 'special interest' holidays and tours (many nowadays include wine, cookery courses and vineyard visits), should be able to obtain information. Offices of French Railways, Air France and, of course, the local representatives of the major wine concerns can also often give useful information and advice.

335

Sources of information in France

Alsace
Comité Interprofessionnel des Vins d'Alsace (C.I.V.A.)
12 Avenue de la Foire aux Vins
68003 Colmar CEDEX   *Tel.*(89) 41 06 21

Beaujolais — Bourgogne — Mâconnais
Union Interprofessionnelle des Vins du Beaujolais (U.I.V.B.)
210 Boulevard Vermorel
69400 Villefranche-sur-Saone   *Tel.* (74) 65 45 55

Comité Interprofessionnel des vins de Bourgogne et Mâcon
   (C.I.B.M.)
Maison du Tourisme
Avenue du Marechal de Lattre de Tassigny
71000 Mâcon   *Tel.* (85) 38 20 15

Comité Interprofessionnel de la Côte d'Or et de l'Yonne pour les
Vins A.O.C. de Bourgogne (C.I.B.)
Rue Henri Dunant
21200 Beaune   *Tel.* (80) 22 21 35

Bordeaux
Conseil Interprofessionnel de Vin de Bordeaux (C.I.V.B.)
1 Cours du 30 Juillet
33000 Bordeaux   *Tel.* (56) 52 82 82

Champagne
Comité Interprofessionnel du Vin de Champagne (C.I.V.C.)
BP 135
51204 Épernay   *Tel.* (26) 54 47 20

Côtes du Rhône
Comité Interprofessionnel des Vins des Côtes du Rhône
Maison du Tourisme
41 cours Jean Jaurès
84000 Avignon   *Tel.* (90) 86 47 09

Jura
Société de Viticulture du Jura
Avenue du 4ème. R.I.
BP 396
39016 Lons-le-Saunier CEDEX
Tel. (84) 24 21 07

Languedoc-Roussillon
Conseil Interprofessionnel des Vins du Fitou, Corbières
et Minervois
R.N. 113
11200 Lezignan Corbières   *Tel.* (68) 27 03 64

Confédération Générale des Vignerons du Midi
1 Rue Marcelin Coural
11100 Narbonne   Tel. (68) 32 03 50

Syndicat du Cru Minervois
10 Boulevard Louis Blazin
34210 Olonzac   *Tel.* (68) 91 21 66

Syndicat des Costières du Gard
Domaine de la Bastide
Route de Générac
30000 Nîmes   Tel. (66) 38 02 23

Groupement Interprofessionnel de Promotion des Côtes
  de Roussillon
19 Avenue de Grande Bretagne
66000 Perpignan   *Tel.* (68) 51 31 81

Syndicat des Coteaux du Languedoc
Domaine de Maurin
BP No 9
34970 Lattes CEDEX   *Tel.* (67) 27 84 11

Comité Interprofessionnel des Vins doux Naturels
19 Avenue de Grande Bretagne
66000 Perpignan   *Tel.* (68) 34 42 32

Loire Valley
Comité Interprofessionnel des Vins de Touraine
19 Square Prosper Merimée
37000 Tours   *Tel.* (47) 05 40 01

Comité Interprofessionnel des Vins d'Origine du Pays Nantais
Maison des vins — Bellevue
44690 La Haye — Fouassière   *Tel.* (40) 36 90 10

Conseil Interprofessionnel des Vins d'Anjou et Saumur
Hotel Godeline,
73 rue Plantagenêt
49000 Angers   *Tel.* (41) 87 62 57

Union Viticole Sancerroise
Fontenay
18300 St. Satur   *Tel.* (48) 54 03 51

Poitou — Charentes
Bureau National Interprofessionnel du Cognac (B.N.I.C.)
3 Allée de la Corderie
16100 Cognac   *Tel.* (45) 82 66 70

Comité National de Pineau des Charentes (C.N.P.C.)
112 Avenue Victor Hugo
16100 Cognac   *Tel.* (45) 32 09 27

Provence
Comité Interprofessionnel des Vins de Côtes de Provence
Maison des Vins
RN. 7
83460 Les Arcs sur Argens   *Tel.* (94) 73 33 38

Savoie
Syndicat Régional des Vins de Savoie
3 rue du Château
73000 Chambéry   *Tel.* (79) 33 44 16

South-West
Comité Interprofessionnel des Vins de Gaillac
Abbaye St Michel
81600 Gaillac   *Tel.* (63) 57 15 40

Union Interprofessionnel des Vins de Jurançon-Madiran-
  Béarn-Irouléguy
33 Avenue Henri IV
64290 Gan   *Tel.* 68 70 03

Conseil Interprofessionnel des Vins de la Région de Bergerac
2 place du Docteur Cayla
24100 Bergerac   *Tel.* (53) 57 12 57

Syndicat de défense et de contrôle des Vins de Madiran et du
  Pacherenc du Vic-Bilh
Madiran
65700 Maubourguet   *Tel.* (62) 96 88 09

Syndicat Interprofessionnel du Vin de Cahors
Avenue Jean Jaurès
BP 199
46004 Cahors   *Tel.* (65) 22 55 30

Bureau National Interprofessionnel de l'Armagnac
Place de la Liberté
BP 3
32800 Eauze   *Tel.* (62) 09 82 33

Annual wine occasions (in addition to general vintage parties)

Exact dates for these vary, but local tourist offices should have
particulars and also provisional programmes. Otherwise, the
French Government Tourist Office (178 Piccadilly, London, W1)
or their branches in other countries may have details of the
regional events.

35

Books, Guides, Maps

There are literally hundreds of books about France and French food and wines. Because of the impossibility of recommending a very few — and being faced with the writer's problem of what to do about his or her own books — I can only suggest that the prospective traveller spends some time browsing in a good bookshop, comparing volumes and choosing what seems to be most appealing. There are plenty of good paperbacks on wine and on French recipes but, with the wine books, I do urge that, for practical purposes, a fairly up-to-date text is chosen; changes in the wine world can make the most authoritative book out of date and, perhaps, misleading after only a few years; what you now see in the vineyards and wineries may be totally different. Volumes in the wine series published by Faber, also some of the Mitchell Beazley pocket books may be of use. Books by Elizabeth David, Jane Grigson, Anne Willan are invaluable about wine as well as recipes. Don Philpott's recent book *The Vineyards of France* (Moorland) lists vineyards open to visitors.

The same applies to guidebooks. Again, examine several and see which you find most sympathetic; books that merely list hotels, restaurants and garages are not always adequate if you want to find out something of the history of a place or which works of art or museums may prove interesting, and a little 'homework' done along the way can save you from wasting time, and often result in delightful détours. The current red Michelin guide is virtually essential and, as its contents are expressed in symbols and figures, there is no problem about language, because you have a key to the contents anyway. The Michelin *Green Guides* are also excellent for the various different regions. Otherwise, remember that some guidebooks also get out-of-date.

What always surprises me is the way in which many travellers in France omit to provide themselves with a good map or set of maps; even if you get one of the motoring organizations to plan a route for you, this will certainly not be detailed enough to be helpful if you miss the way or want to go off the main road. The sort of maps that show the whole of France on one sheet will get you from place to place, but, especially if you are exploring villages in wine country, you must have a map that shows the country lanes. Fortunately, many garages do stock maps of this kind and again, those that are up-to-date will show autoroutes, new roads and one-way systems.

Finally, if possible, do keep some sort of record of any trip you make. Whether this is in the form of a diary, scrapbook, notes on meals and wines, it will be the best souvenir of all. Hotel and motoring organizations will be grateful for your views on places where you have had good — or not so good — experiences; friends will thank you for comments on out-of-the-way recommendations of shops, restaurants and how long certain journeys took — something not always easy to work out just by looking at a map. Your wine merchant will certainly be interested in what you tasted and where — jot down full details, both of the wines and personalities you met *en route*. The odd comment, scribbled down at the time, no matter where, can be far more valuable, whether you then rewrite it or not, than such recollections as remain to you at the end of a tour or, even, at the end of a day.

Bonne route et bonne chance!

Why do the wrong people travel, travel, travel, when the right people stay back home?

NOEL COWARD, *A Taste for Travel*, ed. J.J. Norwich, Macmillan, 1985

Index

352